12/12

Please return/renew this item by the last
date shown. Books may also be renewed
by phone or Internet.

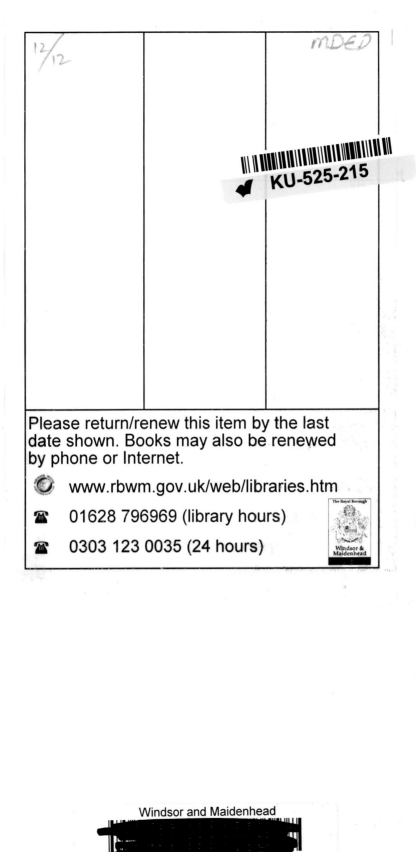 www.rbwm.gov.uk/web/libraries.htm

☎ 01628 796969 (library hours)

☎ 0303 123 0035 (24 hours)

The Royal Borough
Windsor &
Maidenhead

The Genealogist's Internet

The Essential Guide to Researching Your Family History Online

5TH EDITION

Peter Christian

The National Archives

B L O O M S B U R Y

First published in 2012 by

Bloomsbury Publishing Plc
50 Bedford Square
London WC1B 3DP
www.bloomsbury.com

A CIP record for this book is available from the British Library.

ISBN: 978-1-4081-5957-6
10 9 8 7 6 5 4 3 2

Cover photographs author's collection. Top left: Winifred Marshall, c. 1910;
Top right: Alexander McCurry and Charlotte King, 1919; Middle: Frederick Marshall,
commissionaire, c. 1890; Spine: Sgt Frederick Marshall, The Queen's (Royal West
Surrey Regiment), c. 1915.
Back cover author photograph © Alessandro Purghicetti

This book is produced using paper that is made from wood grown in managed, sustainable
forests. It is natural, renewable and recyclable. The logging and manufacturing processes
conform to the environmental regulations of the country of origin.

Design by Goldust Design
Typeset by Saxon Graphics Ltd, Derby
Printed and bound by CPI Group (UK) Ltd, Croydon CR0 4YY

Dedicated to the memory of
Douglas Godfrey Christian
1923–1974

CONTENTS

PREFACE

The statistics tell us that a large and increasing majority of the UK population have internet access at home,[1] and many others no doubt have access from work or a local library, so this book assumes a reader who has at least basic familiarity with the internet, using email and a web browser. However, I have not assumed any experience of other internet facilities, nor any technical knowledge, so even the absolute internet novice should not be unduly baffled. The book is about what you can do online rather than on the technology behind it. All the same, there are one or two areas where it's useful to have some understanding of how things work (and why they sometimes don't), so there is detailed discussion of search engines, mailing lists, and web publishing in the later chapters. The professional internet user will probably want to skip some of this, but the queries and problems which are raised in online discussion forums suggest that even quite seasoned internet users do not always exploit these resources as fully as they could.

This book also does not assume you are already an expert in genealogy, but it can't pretend to be a general introduction to researching your family tree, nor provide guidance in how to organize your research. The basics of family history are covered briefly in Chapter 2, 'First Steps', along with some recommended internet resources for the beginner, and the chapters relating to records explain briefly why you might want to look at those records. But if you are completely, or fairly, new to family history you'll need a good book on offline genealogy as well (see p. 6 for recommendations).

Web addresses

Web addresses were never designed for print, and the longer they are, the more of a challenge they present to the typographer. Many of the longer URLs in this text have necessarily been broken over two lines, but the URL

---

1 At the beginning of 2011, according to research from Ofcom, 77 per cent of UK adults had internet access at home, and 74 per cent a broadband connection (see <stakeholders. ofcom.org.uk/market-data-research/market-data/communications-market-reports/ cmr11/uk/> – these statistics are taken from Figure 4.14 in the full report).

should be read as an unbroken sequence of characters – there are *never* spaces or line breaks in internet addresses. (Some sites don't seem to know this: where you see *%20* in a web address, it's a replacement for an improper space.)

Addresses for web pages are *partially* case sensitive. Anything up to the first / is not case sensitive; anything after that usually *must* be in the correct case.

In general, I have indicated titles of websites solely by initial capitals, while individual pages are between inverted commas. However, the distinction between a site and page is not always easy to make, and I wouldn't claim to have been thoroughly consistent in this respect.

Occasionally, a URL has been so long that I have given instructions on how to get to the page rather than give the full URL. Unfortunately, this tendency for long URLs seems to be increasing, as more and more sites deliver their pages from a database or content management system. Another increasingly popular practice is what might be termed the 'we-are-giving-this-document-an-incredibly-long-web-address-so-you-are-in-no-doubt-what-it-is-about-and-if-you-have-to-type-160-characters-it-is-not-our-problem' approach. County record offices and government websites seem to have a particular propensity for unwieldy URLs, and the longest URL for a resource mentioned in the book is a 187-character address for a page on the Customs and Excise site:

<customs.hmrc.gov.uk/channelsPortalWebApp/channelsPortalWebApp. portal?_nfpb=true&_pageLabel=pageLibrary_PublicNoticesAndInfo Sheets&propertyType=document&columns=1&id=HMCE_CL_000157>

In such cases the direct link is available on the website for this book at <**www.spub.co.uk/tgi5/**>.

Wikipedia

Wikipedia consistently bases the web address of each article on the exact wording of its title, so the article on the 'History of the English fiscal system', referred to on p. 119, is located at <**en.wikipedia.org/wiki/History_of_the_ English_fiscal_system**>, with underscores standing in for spaces. Citing both title and URL in the text is therefore redundant, and I have quoted only the page title for Wikipedia articles. The easiest thing, assuming you're not just following the link from the website for this book, is to go to any page in the English-language Wikipedia at <**en.wikipedia.org/wiki/**> and start typing the title in the search box at the top right. That will soon bring up a link to the page in question. Wikipedia URLs, incidentally, are not case sensitive.

Disappearing resources

Internet resources are in a constant state of flux. Each revision of this book finds around 20 per cent of the links in the previous edition no longer work or, even worse, take you to quite different material. All of the URLs will have been checked just before the book goes for printing, and if you're reading this as a newly published book, you will find, with any luck, that none of the URLs have gone out of date while it was at the printers. After that, you're certain to find *some* dead links; at some point one of the major sites will undergo a complete overhaul and a dozen links will expire overnight.

Of course, we should be grateful when out-of-date material is removed from public view, and it is only to be expected that personal sites will move or vanish without warning. In a number of cases, valuable material is preserved only in web archives (see below).

Official and commercial sites are less likely to disappear as a whole, but are regularly being improved by redesign and reorganization, as one would wish. Unfortunately, their consideration for users does not always extend to redirecting you from the old pages to the new. Too often they simply tell you the old page is not there – actually not even that, they simply say there is no such page and don't indicate whether they've moved the page or you've mistyped the URL. They then expect you to use their search engine to see if the material is still anywhere on the site. To those responsible for such sites: sorry folks, I know that maintaining a large website is hard work, but this is bad practice, and doesn't do much for your image either!

For print, this instability raises insurmountable problems, and it is something all internet books have to live with. But one of the advantages of the web is that links can be kept up to date, so on the website for this book at <www.spub.co.uk/tgi5/> there are links to all the resources mentioned in the text, and the aim to is to keep those links current or, if necessary, to flag the material as no longer available.

Web archives

A website or page that is no longer present at its original home may nonetheless have been archived online and still be accessible. This is perhaps most useful for sites run by individual volunteers, where valuable material may disappear simply because the person concerned no longer has either the time or the funds to keep it going. For sites that are still up and running, it might seem there is no virtue in accessing an old version with, presumably, outdated information, and in general this is true — an old version of Cyndi's List or a Genuki page may have curiosity value but is not of practical use for family historians. But major sites that undergo a redesign often abandon useful material not because it is out of date but simply because it does not fit in with the way the site has been reorganized.

The URLs for material in these archives are often unwieldy, since they include both the original web address and the location in the archive. The last version of the old FamilyRecords site, for example, is at <collections.europarchive.org/tna/20090804161046/http://www.familyrecords.gov.uk>. For that reason, I have cited these by naming the archive, giving the original URL and the date of the latest usable version of the site (that date is necessary because the archive will often also hold a later post-closure notice). Once you are at the archive site, you can type the original URL in the search box and then select the date from the listing offered.

There are two web archives relevant to the material in this book:

- **The Wayback Machine**
  at <www.archive.org> has an archive of over 150 billion pages dating from the last 15 years. It covers all sorts of sites, though it does not necessarily include every page. In addition to its own archiving activity the Wayback Machine provides web archiving facilities for individual institutions.
- **The UK Government Web Archive**
  managed by The National Archives, is at <**www.nationalarchives.gov.uk/webarchive/**> and aims to preserve the content of UK government websites. To locate an archived site, go to the 'Quick search' at <**collections.europarchive.org/tna/quick_search/**>, enter the URL in the search box and select 'the URLs' from the drop-down list to the right of the search box.

The British Library, incidentally, also has a Web Archiving Programme which is described at <**www.bl.uk/aboutus/stratpolprog/digi/webarch/**>. However, it archives only selected significant UK websites and at present has very limited value for family historians.

What's new in this edition

The many resources that have moved or disappeared since the previous edition of this book at the start of 2009 are one good reason for revision. Some of the most important sites have undergone major reorganizations: both the UK National Archives and the National Archives of Ireland have a completely new look, as does the Royal Navy's site. The General Register Office no longer has a distinct site at all but its material is now split between three different sites. Closures include the Family Records site in September 2009 (a poor decision, leaving no single official starting point for new family historians) and Geocities, which was widely used by individuals for putting genealogical material online, only some of which has reappeared in a new location.

But there are also some more positive reasons. Probably the most important is the launch of a brand new FamilySearch site, replacing the old site originally launched in 1998, and bringing a significant expansion in the UK records available online, not to mention at least some Irish civil registration indexes. The launch of the British Newspaper Archive in November 2011 (p. 198) is a major advance in making historical newspapers more accessible.

Digitization of the 1911 census is now complete for the whole of the British Isles, and we are at last in a position where there are several different indexes available for almost all the censuses of England and Wales, and Scotland. The Irish census material has been completed, too, with the 1901 household schedules joining those for 1911.

With the censuses done and dusted, the commercial data services have been turning their attention to other records for digitization, and all of them are now offering a much wider range of material. There have been some very welcome developments for those with Irish ancestors, with the Irish government's launch of an official site for church records (p. 107), the Irish Family History Foundation's RootsIreland site (p. 57), and Findmypast's dedicated Irish data service (p. 54). But alas, at the start of 2012, we are still waiting for the General Register Office to make up its mind about the digitization of civil registration records for England and Wales, whose future seems no clearer than it did in 2009.

In the commercial sector, the pace of takeovers and mergers has slowed. The only significant change is that in 2010 Genes Reunited was purchased from ITV by Brightsolid, the company behind ScotlandsPeople and Findmypast, and most of its data collections replaced by the equivalents from Findmypast.

This edition again has some extra pages to cope, in part, with this expansion – there are now over 1,700 web resources mentioned. However, as before, there are an increasing number of useful websites that simply could not be fitted in. This applies particularly to the material in Chapters 8 to 11 and to resources that are of purely local interest. The text will alert you to the *sort* of things that are available and highlight some of the best examples, but you will need to see for yourself whether there is equivalent material for a particular village, regiment, church, etc., that is relevant to your own family's history. Nonetheless, you will find further recommendations and some new post-publication discoveries among my public bookmarks at <**delicious.com/petex**>.

One other relatively recent development is that many organizations and online projects now have not just a website and an email address, but pages on social networking sites (Facebook is the most popular) and a Twitter account, which allow them to disseminate announcements and interact in real time with their clientele. Some of the more generally useful Twitter feeds are discussed on p. 386, but I have generally not seen any reason to mention that a site has a presence on Facebook or Twitter, since this is usually indicated by the appropriate icons on the home page.

Changes, of course, are ongoing. In particular, The National Archives will be launching its new Discovery service (p. 210) while this book is being printed, and the new FamilySearch site is still constantly being tweaked. New datasets are being added to the range of online genealogical records all the time. The best way to keep up with such changes is to follow some of the blogs mentioned below.

Acknowledgments

Since this is the first edition of the book under a new imprint, it is perhaps a good place to record my thanks to the publishing team at The National Archives (alas, disbanded in the reorganizations of 2009) and to my editor Sheila Knight for seeing the first four editions through the press.

Many of the new sites covered in this edition are here because someone drew them to my attention. While I can't thank everyone who has ever made me aware of a new site, there are some regular sources of new material to which I am particularly indebted: Dick Eastman's online newsletter (p. 382), Chris Paton's British GENES blog (p. 384) and the Cyndi's List mailing list (p. 24), have all been invaluable. Peter Calver's LostCousins newsletter (p. 236) and the GeneaNet newsletter (p. 383) are notable for carrying useful news about a lot more than their own companies' activities.

Again, I have to thank John Dawson for suggesting a number of improvements over the previous edition. Thanks are also due to Guy Grannum of The National Archives for help with the changes to TNA's site, which will be rolled out while this book is at the printers. Linda Clare offered some helpful suggestions on Chapter 18.

Finally, I am grateful to Nigel Bayley of The Genealogist, Debra Chatfield of Findmypast, Ian Galbraith of Origins, and Robert Woods of Familyrelatives for giving me advance notice of planned new developments on their sites. Some of these will undoubtedly already be live by the time you read this.

1

INTRODUCTION

Genealogy and the internet

The steady growth in the number of people interested in family history in recent decades no doubt has several causes. Certainly, television series like *Who Do You Think You Are?* and *Heir Hunters* have exposed a larger audience to the fascination of family history and to some of its sources and techniques. The availability of DNA testing to establish family relationships or trace migration patterns has also contributed to a surge of interest. But neither of these could have had as much impact without the growth of the internet and the inexpensive and increasingly widespread access to it among the entire population. While the internet has not changed the fundamental principles of genealogical research, it has changed the way in which much of that research is done and made a huge difference in what the individual genealogist can do with ease.

Indexes to primary records, in many cases linked to a digitized image of the original document, are now widely available online. Even where records themselves are not online, the ability to check the holdings of record offices and libraries via the web means that a visit can be better prepared and more productive. Those who have previously made little progress with their family tree for lack of time or mobility to visit archives can pursue their researches much more conveniently, with access to many records from their desktop. Likewise, those who live on the other side of the world from the repositories which hold records of their ancestors' lives can make progress without having to employ a researcher. Online data is a boon, too, for anyone who has difficulty reading from microfilm or original records.

Archives have realized that the internet is also a remedy for some of their pressing concerns: lack of space on their premises, the need to make their collections available while preserving them from damage, not to mention the pressure from government to provide wider access. In addition, there is the obvious commercial potential: online record transcriptions can attract distant and, particularly, overseas users in large numbers, while even those living less far away will use a charged service which saves them time and travel costs.

Genealogists also benefit from the ease with which messages and electronic documents can be exchanged around the world at effectively no cost. It is easier than ever to contact people with similar research interests, and even to find distant cousins. It is easier than ever, away from a good genealogy library or bookshop, to find expertise or help with some genealogical problem. And if you need to refer to a book, there are genealogy bookshops with online catalogues and secure ordering, while for older books you may even find the whole text online.

Any information stored digitally, whether text or image, can be published on the web easily and at relatively low cost to publisher and user alike. This has revolutionized the publishing of pedigrees and other family history information. It has allowed individuals to publish small transcriptions from individual records, material which it would otherwise be difficult to make widely available. Individual family historians can publicise their interests and publish the fruits of their researches to millions of others.

The internet has enhanced co-operation by making it possible for widely separated people to communicate easily as a group. While collaborative genealogy projects did not start with the internet, email and the web make the co-ordination of vast numbers of geographically distributed volunteers, such as the 11,000 or so involved in FreeBMD (see p. 70), much easier.

Offline genealogy

Over the last few years the internet has matured as a resource for family historians. There is now hardly any aspect of the subject which is not catered for online. In some cases, such as census records, the online facilities have made their offline predecessors more or less redundant. I'm sure it is now the case that anyone starting out on their family history assumes that most of their research will be carried out online. Inevitably, however, this has given rise to unrealistic expectations in some quarters. Stories of messages posted to mailing lists asking, 'Where will I find my family tree online?' are not apocryphal.[1]

The fact is that if you are only beginning your family tree, you will have plenty to do offline before you can take full advantage of what is online. For a start, because of privacy concerns, you won't find much online information about any ancestors born less than a century ago. Scotland has some more recent records online for marriages and deaths (see p. 77), but for England and Wales there are so far only *indexes* to twentieth-century birth, marriage and death records online. This means that in

1 See 'Internet Genealogy » Cyndi's Soapbox' at <**www.cyndislist.com/internet-genealogy/cyndis-soapbox/**> for a look at some of the common misconceptions about what the internet can do for the genealogist.

tracing the most recent generations most of the work must be done offline, though for living people you may well be able to find addresses, phone numbers and perhaps Facebook pages. But even if recent primary records are not online, you can still expect to make contact with other genealogists who share your interests. To do this effectively, however, you will need to have established a family tree for the last three or more generations. The reason for this is as follows: you presumably know or knew your grandparents and their siblings (your great aunts and uncles), so you know or are at least aware of your first and second cousins. On the whole, then, any new relatives discovered via the internet will be no closer to you than third cousins, descended from your great-great-grandparents, who were born perhaps 100 or so years before you. Unless you know the names of your great-great-grandparents and where they came from, you will probably not be in a position to establish that you are in fact related to someone who has posted their pedigree online.

Of course, if your surname is unusual, or particularly if your family has not been geographically mobile in recent generations, you may be able to make contact with someone researching your surname and be reasonably certain that you are related. Or you may be lucky enough to find that someone is doing a one-name study of your surname. In this case, they may already have extracted some or all of the relevant entries in the civil registration records, and indeed may have already been able to link up many of the individuals recorded.

But, in general, you will need to do work offline before you can expect to find primary source material online and before you have enough information to start establishing contact with distant relatives.

However, one thing that is useful to every family historian is the wealth of general genealogical information and the huge range of expertise embodied in the online community. For the absolute beginner, the internet is useful not so much because there is lots of data online, but because there are many places to turn to for help and advice. And this is particularly important for those who live a long way away from their family's ancestral home.

All the same, it is important to remember that, whatever and whoever you discover online, there are many other sources for family history which aren't on the web. If you restrict yourself to online sources you may be able to construct a basic pedigree back to the nineteenth century, but you won't be able, reliably, to get much further, and you will be seeing only the outline of your family's history. On the other hand, if you are one of those who refuses on principle to use the internet (and who is presumably reading this by accident, or to confirm their worst fears), you are just making your research into your family history much harder than it need be.

History

We now take the ready availability of genealogical records and information on the World Wide Web for granted. But most of the sites we rely on are of relatively recent origin. Before 2002, there were *no* UK censuses online, for example; before 2003, no civil registration indexes. Indeed, only a handful of genealogy sites can trace their history back to the twentieth century: FamilySearch was launched in 1999, Cyndi's List in 1996, Genuki in 1995. But in fact the web is only the latest electronic medium for genealogy resources, and 'online genealogy' has a longer history that those facts suggest.

On the internet itself, before the web had been invented, online genealogy started in 1983 with the newsgroup net.roots and with the ROOTS-L mailing list. Net.roots became soc.roots, and eventually spawned all the genealogy discussion forums covered in Chapter 18. ROOTS-L gave rise to RootsWeb <**www.rootsweb.ancestry.com**>, the oldest online genealogy co-operative, now hosted by Ancestry.[2]

But in the 1980s internet access was still largely confined to academia and the computer industry, so for many people online genealogy meant bulletin boards run by volunteers from their home computers and accessible via a modem and phone line. A system called FidoNet allowed messages and files to be transferred around the world, albeit slowly, as each bulletin board called up its neighbour to pass messages on. The only commercial forums were the growing online services which originally targeted computer professionals and those in business, but which gradually attracted a more disparate membership. Of these, CompuServe, with its Roots forum, was the most important. One significant feature of these commercial services was the ability to access them from all over the world, in many cases with only a local call. Even so, to keep costs down, people would make sure they kept their time online to a minimum.

These systems had the basis of what genealogists now use the internet for: conversing with other genealogists and accessing centrally stored files. But the amount of data available was tiny and discussion was the main motivation. Part of this was down to technical limitations: with modem speeds something like five hundred times slower than a modern broadband connection, transferring large amounts of data was unrealistic or at best painfully slow, except for the few with deep pockets or an internet connection at work. No government agencies or family history societies had even

---

2 For a history of the newsgroups, see Margaret J. Olson, 'Historical Reflections of the Genealogy Newsgroups' at <**homepages.rootsweb.ancestry.com/~socgen/Newshist.htm**>. For the history of ROOTS- L and RootsWeb, see <**www.rootsweb.ancestry.com/roots-l/**>.

contemplated an online presence, though genealogical computer groups were starting to spring up by the end of the 1980s.

What changed this was the World Wide Web, created in 1991 (though it was 1995 before it started to dominate the internet), and the growth of commercial internet services. The innovation of the web made it possible for a large collection of material to remain navigable, even for the technologically illiterate, while at the same time the explosion in public use of the internet was providing the impetus for it to become more user-friendly.

The result of these developments is that the internet is now driving developments in access to genealogical information – just as computers had done in the 1980s, and microfilm before that. This in turn is drawing more people to start researching their family tree, which increases the chance of encountering distant cousins online, and motivates record holders to make their material available on the web.

We are also seeing a change in online culture brought about by a new wave of changes, often referred to as 'Web 2.0'. Until recently, the internet was treated by most people as a combination of library and postal service – you used the web to retrieve information and email to correspond with friends and family. A relatively small proportion of family historians actually used the web to publish their own family trees. But the last few years have seen the development of a much greater level of interactivity, whether it is in social networking sites like Facebook and YouTube, in the ability to run a blog which people can comment on, or in the move towards 'cloud computing' where the software you use is hosted on a website and not on your own computer. The combination of these developments and the rise of the always-on broadband connection means that the internet is less a special place to go and get information, more just part of the research environment of anyone tracing their family tree.

The role of computers and the internet in the history of UK genealogy is discussed in more detail in chapter 8 of Michael Sharpe's *Family Matters* (Pen & Sword, 2011). The Genuki Timeline at <**homepages.gold.ac.uk/ genuki/timeline/**> offers an overview of some of the more significant online developments for family historians in the British Isles and gives starting dates for many key websites and online facilities.

2

FIRST STEPS

Your first online steps in genealogy will depend on how much research you have already done on your family tree, and what your aim is. If you are just beginning your family history, you will be able to use the internet to help you get started, but you shouldn't expect to find much primary source material online, i.e. original records, until you get back to the early twentieth century.

The box on the next page shows a simplified outline of the process of constructing a family tree, which is the foundation on which your family history will be built. For the first two steps, you will find indexes to certificates online (see Chapter 5), but not the certificates themselves, and online materials won't help you work out which is going to be the certificate you need. This stage is mostly about interpreting information from family members and trying to verify it. It's only once you get to step 4 that you will find a significant amount of source material online. In the initial stages, the internet will probably be more important as a source of information, help and advice. The material in the 'Tutorials' and 'Getting help' sections below should help you get going.

If you are not new to family history, but have just started to use the internet, your needs will be rather different. You will already be familiar with civil registration and census records, and know what is involved in researching your family tree, so your initial questions will not be about constructing a family tree but: what's online and how do I find it? Who else is working on my family?

Beginners' guides

One area where internet resources still have a great deal of catching up to do is in tutorial material for the new family historian. It will be some time before you can start your family tree without a good reference book. If you are a relative beginner, you might start with Simon Fowler's *Tracing Your Ancestors*, or Nick Barrett's *Who Do You Think You Are? Encyclopedia of Genealogy*. If you have already made some progress, Mark Herber's *Ancestral Trails* should be on your bookshelf.

1. Interview your elderly relatives and collect as much first- or second-hand information as you can (and continue doing so, as you find out more in subsequent steps).
2. Get marriage and birth certificates for the most recently deceased ancestors.
3. From these, work back to the marriages and then births of the parents of those ancestors.
4. Keep repeating this process until you get back to the beginning of General Registration (1837 for England and Wales, later for Scotland and Ireland).
5. Once you have names and either places or actual addresses for a date in the nineteenth or early twentieth century, refer to the censuses to see
   (a) whole family groups;
   (b) birth places;
   (c) ages, from which you can calculate approximate birth years.
6. Once you have found a census entry for an adult ancestor who was born before the start of General Registration, use the birth place and age information in the census to locate a baptism in parish registers.
7. From this, work back to the marriages, and then baptisms, of the parents of that ancestor in the parish registers.
8. Repeat for each line of your ancestry until you hit a brick wall (at which point you will need to consider other approaches and other sources).

Nonetheless, while individual web resources cannot compare in scope to these printed works, there is a great deal of helpful material online covering the essentials of genealogical research in the British Isles.

British Isles

The Society of Genealogists (SoG) has a number of introductory leaflets online at <**www.sog.org.uk/leaflets/leaflets.shtml**>. Though they are not designed as a coherent introduction to family history, they include 'Starting genealogy' and cover the queries most often raised by newcomers to genealogy. The Federation of Family History Societies (FFHS) has 'Research Tips. First Steps in Family History' at <**www.ffhs.org.uk/tips/first.php**>. GenDocs has a substantial page for those 'New To Family History' at <**homepage.ntlworld.com/hitch/gendocs/newbie.html**>.

The BBC has long had an excellent family history site, part of its extensive coverage of history, at <**www.bbc.co.uk/history/familyhistory/**> (Figure 2-1). There are two main tutorial sections linked from the current home page, 'The Basics' and 'Next Steps', both of which have very comprehensive

Figure 2-1 The BBC's Family History site

coverage of all the main aspects of family history research. The 'Timeline' pages, which you might be tempted to ignore, have sections devoted to occupations, the military, migration and 'family secrets'. BBC Wales has its own family history site at <**www.bbc.co.uk/wales/history/sites/themes/family.shtml**> with some material specifically relating to Welsh family history. One important source for such materials is Genuki (described more fully in Chapter 3, p. 18f.), which has a page devoted to 'Getting Started in Genealogy and Family History' at <**www.genuki.org.uk/gs/**>. There are individual pages on major topics, such as that for 'Civil Registration in England and Wales' at <**www.genuki.org.uk/big/eng/civreg/**>. Roy Stockdill's concise but comprehensive 'Newbies' Guide to Genealogy and Family History' is available on Genuki at <**www.genuki.org.uk/gs/Newbie.html**>.

The National Archives (TNA) has extensive family history material on its website. Most of it will be found by following the link for 'Looking for a person?' on the 'Records' menu on the home page at <**www.nationalarchives.gov.uk**>, which will take you to <**www.nationalarchives.gov.uk/records/looking-for-person**>. The problem with this material for the absolute novice is that the articles tell you about what records there are and where they can be found, but not how you actually use the information they hold or how to plan your research around them. However, a previous incarnation of TNA's site had a 'Pathways to the Past' section with much more guidance for the beginner, and this is still available in the UK Government Web Archive: <**www.nationalarchives.gov.uk/pathways/familyhistory/**> (15 February 2006).

Probably the most comprehensive set of guides to British and Irish family history are the materials on the FamilySearch website of the Church of Jesus Christ of Latter-day Saints (LDS) at <**www.familysearch.org**>. The 'Learning Resources' page at <**www.familysearch.org/learn**> (or follow the 'Learn' link on the home page) offers two main resources: a wiki, with reference material for genealogical sources and research in a wide range of individual countries; and around 300 video tutorials on general research techniques and research in particular countries. The videos are discussed below, with other online lectures.

The Research Wiki, like all wikis, is a work in progress, so there is some unevenness in coverage, but there is a considerable amount of material for each of the nations of the British Isles, with less detailed pages for individual counties. There is no list of articles, and you can find relevant material either by searching for a subject or browsing the list of countries. Each main country page has a list of topics for which there are separate articles. These cover all the main types of genealogical record as well as a few more general subjects such as history or place-names. Particularly useful if you are just starting are the 'Featured resources'. In the case of Scotland, for example, there are links to articles on 'Getting started with your Scottish Research', 'Researching Your Scottish Ancestry Before 1855' and the ScotlandsPeople data service (see p. 50). The wiki includes guides on research strategies, i.e. how to approach finding a particular type of information for a particular country in a particular period. These articles are not linked from the country pages in a consistent way, so if you cannot see a 'research strategies' link, just do a search.

Other introductory material specific to Scottish research includes the 'Getting Started' section of ScotlandsPeople – go to <**www.scotlandspeople.gov.uk**>, select 'Help & Other Resources', then 'Getting Started' – and the Scottish Archive Network's family history pages at <**www.scan.org.uk/familyhistory/**>. Genuki has an 'Introduction to Scottish Family History' at <**www.genuki.org.uk/big/sct/intro.html**>.

For Ireland, the Irish Ancestors site has an excellent range of introductory material at <**www.irishtimes.com/ancestor/browse/**>, including information on the counties and emigration (see Chapter 11) and good pages on the various Irish genealogical records. This is based largely on John Grenham's book *Tracing your Irish Ancestors*. Also by John Grenham is the

Figure 2-2 The Scotland article in the FamilySearch wiki.

'Irish Roots' section of Moving Here (see p. 165) at <**www.movinghere.org.uk/ galleries/roots/irish/irish.htm**>. The Irish Genealogy Toolkit at <**www.irish-genealogy-toolkit.com**> offers guidance on getting started in Irish family history.

On Cyndi's List (see p. 24) you will find a comprehensive 'Beginners' page at <**www.cyndislist.com/beginners/**>, and a collection of links on 'Researching: Localities & Ethnic Groups' which will be useful if you need to start looking for ancestors outside the UK and Ireland. Cyndi's 'How to: tutorials and guides' section at <**www.cyndislist.com/how-to-tutorials**> provides an outline of all the introductory materials on seven major genealogy sites. These sites are US-based, so much of the material on specific records will not be of use unless you are tracing American ancestors. However, Cyndi's links are a good way to find some of the more general information buried in these sites.

About.com has a large collection of introductory articles at <**genealogy. about.com**>. The best way to find material on particular topics is to go to the list of articles by category at <**genealogy.about.com/od/internet/u/search_ online.htm**>. Although, again, many of the articles on specific records are intended for those researching American ancestry, there is useful material on general topics, such as 'Top Ten Genealogy Mistakes to Avoid' at <**genealogy. about.com/od/basics/ss/mistakes.htm**>, and links to articles on the British Isles will be found at <**genealogy.about.com/od/british_isles/**>.

Wikipedia's 'Genealogy' article has links to articles on the major types of record used in genealogy and a number of other introductory topics. The material is not specific to any one country.

Researching from overseas

If you are trying to research British or Irish ancestry from overseas, Genuki's 'Researching From Abroad' page at <**www.genuki.org.uk/ab/**> will be useful. The SoG has a leaflet 'Notes for Americans on tracing their British ancestry' online at <**www.sog.org.uk/leaflets/americans.pdf**>.

Among its useful video resources, FamilySearch's Learning Center (see below) has two video/slide presentations by Audrey Collins of The National Archives which are particularly useful for those from outside the British Isles: 'What is Britain?' will explain exactly the differences between terms such as Britain, Great Britain, England, and the United Kingdom, while 'The English Parish' explains the nature and significance of this geographical unit for genealogical research.

If you are unfamiliar with the administrative subdivision of Britain into counties and parishes, you should consult Jim Fisher's page 'British Counties, Parishes, etc. for Genealogists' at <**www.jimella.me.uk/counties.cfm**>. This also explains the meaning of names for regions such as the Peak District or the Wirral, which are not those of administrative divisions and are not necessarily well defined. Genuki's pages on 'Administrative Regions of the British Isles' at <**www.genuki.org.uk/big/Regions/index.html**> is also worth consulting. See also the section on 'Counties and towns' on p. 259.

Research methods

Most of the material on these sites relates to genealogical research specifically in the British Isles, but the principles of genealogy are universal and there are a number of resources online for advice on how to manage your genealogical research, wherever your ancestors came from. The key issues are how to draw reliable conclusions from genealogical records, how to organize and record your research and how to cite your sources so that your conclusions can be verified by others.

The Society of Genealogists has a set of 'Standards and Good Practice in Genealogy' at <**www.sog.org.uk/education/standards.shtml**>. The US National Genealogical Society has a set of six standards relating to various aspects of genealogical research, all linked from <**www.ngsgenealogy.org/ cs/ngs_standards_and_guidelines**>.

Good advice on note-taking is provided by the SoG's leaflet on 'Note taking and keeping for genealogists' at <**www.sog.org.uk/leaflets/notes.pdf**> and in Genealogy.com's 'Taking Notes' page at <**www.genealogy.com/ 00000001.html**> (that's seven zeros).

About.com has a concise guide by Kimberley Powell 'Cite Your Genealogy Sources. A Guide to Documenting Your Genealogy Research' at <**genealogy.about.com/od/citing/a/sources.htm**> and ProGenealogists have an 'Internet Citation Guide for Genealogists' specifically dealing with the issue of how to cite online resources at <**www.progenealogists.com/ citationguide.htm**>.

If you are using a genealogy database to store your family tree, the online help will almost certainly have pages devoted to showing how to use the software's source citation facilities and offer guidance on how to document particular types of source.

Cyndi's List has around 80 links to relevant material on the 'Citing Sources' page at <**www.cyndislist.com/citing/**>.

Online lectures

The widespread availability of broadband has meant that making audio and video available over the web has become straightforward and commonplace. Apart from the general improvement in the availability of material that is already being broadcast in other media, it allows lectures by family history experts to reach an audience far beyond the lecture hall or conference.

Originally, internet broadcasting meant downloadable audio and was called 'podcasting', but now streaming is the norm (i.e. playing live on your computer without downloading a file first) and includes video, so strictly this is 'webcasting'. However, the BBC and many other services treat 'podcast' as a term for 'audio only', however it is delivered.

All the main UK broadcasters have a selection of past programmes available on the web, though these tend to be only those that have been broadcast fairly recently and they are generally not accessible outside the British Isles. Among the radio programmes available on the BBC podcast site at <**www.bbc.co.uk/podcasts/**> are eight programmes from Radio 4's 'Tracing Your Roots' at <**www.bbc.co.uk/podcasts/series/tyr**>. The BBC provides video by means of the iPlayer at <**www.bbc.co.uk/iplayer/**>. This will usually have the programmes of the most recent series of *Who Do You Think You Are?* and *Heir Hunters.*

The most significant collection of podcasts relating to British genealogy and history, by far, is that of The National Archives, with over 200 audio lectures, going back to 2006. All audio and video material is available from TNA's Archives Media Player at <**media.nationalarchives.gov.uk**> (Figure 2-3). The material is split into broad categories, including 'Family history', but within each category items are simply listed in reverse order of date, so you will need to use the search facility to find recordings on a particular topic.

Figure 2-3: The National Archives' Archives Media Player

As mentioned above, FamilySearch has a growing range of online lectures and courses at <**www.familysearch.org/learningcenter/**>. At the time of writing, there are around 80 covering UK and Ireland topics, though perhaps 50 of these are audio lectures sourced from TNA. The lectures tend to be video only, but items described as 'online lessons' typically comprise video of the speaker synchronized with presentation slides and accompanied by a hand-out.

YouTube at <www.youtube.com> is *the* site for amateur video publishing, but it is also used by professionals, and a number of organizations and groups are using it as a way of broadcasting online. FamilySearch in fact has a channel on YouTube at <www.youtube.com/user/familysearch/>, though so far the material is mostly about FamilySearch's own projects and material aimed at US beginners.

The Family History Show at <www.youtube.com/user/familyhistoryshow> is presented by Nick Barrett and Laura Berry as a genealogy magazine programme, with several separate brief items making up a single 'show'.

In 2011, the Public Record Office of Northern Ireland (see p. 214) launched its own channel on YouTube at <www.youtube.com/user/PRONIonline> with a series of lectures on 'Exploring Local History'.

Among individual contributions on YouTube are Robert Raglan's range of five-minute genealogy lessons available at <www.youtube.com/user/5minutegenealogy> and Mike O'Laughlin's 15 videos relating to Irish genealogy at <www.youtube.com/user/Mickthebridge>. The Genealogy Guys use podcasts as a way of broadcasting monthly programmes of genealogy news. The home page at <genealogyguys.com> gives a detailed synopsis of each bulletin.

There is a brief listing of relevant sites on the 'Podcasts for Genealogy' page on Cyndi's List at <www.cyndislist.com/podcasts/>, while webcasting comes under the heading 'Internet video' at <www.cyndislist.com/video/internet-video/>.

Getting help

Even with these materials, you may still have a question you can't find an answer to (though the sites discussed in Chapters 5 to 7 should answer most questions you are likely to have about the first documents you encounter – civil registration certificates and census records). One solution is to use a search engine to find pages devoted to a particular topic (see Chapter 19). However, this can be a time-consuming task, since you may end up following quite a few links that turn out to be useless before you find what you are looking for. Also, if you are new to family history, it may not at first be obvious how authoritative or comprehensive the material on any site is.

The various discussion forums described in Chapter 18 are ideal places for getting help and advice. Before posting a query to one of these, though, look for a FAQ (Frequently Asked Questions) – see p. 328. This will give the answers to the most common questions.

A useful mailing list for beginners is GEN-NEWBIE-L 'where people who are new to computers and genealogy may interact'. Information on how to join this list will be found at <**www.rootsweb.ancestry.com/~newbie/**>, and past messages are archived at <**archiver.rootsweb.ancestry.com/th/index/ GEN-NEWBIE**>. A list with a similar purpose but a UK focus is UK-GENEALOGY-NEWBIES at <**lists.rootsweb.ancestry.com/index/intl/ UK/UK-GENEALOGY-NEWBIES.html**>, but it seems to be moribund and is unlikely to be very helpful. More useful is the 'Genealogy Beginners' forum on British-Genealogy (see p. 324) at <**www.british-genealogy.com/ forums/forumdisplay.php/40-Genealogy-Beginners**>.

If you are already a member of a family history society, it may have a mailing list where you can turn to other members for assistance.

Genealogical terms and abbreviations

Whatever your level of experience in family history, you're very likely at some point to come across unfamiliar terms and, especially, abbreviations. Internet resources for legal terms are covered in Chapter 16 (p. 294) while words for obsolete occupations are covered in Chapter 9 (p. 129). But genealogy as a discipline has its own specialist terms, which may baffle at first.

GenealogyPro has a Glossary of Genealogy Terms at <**genealogypro.com/ details/glossary.html**> with around 130 entries, while Sam Behling has a page of about 400 terms at <**homepages.rootsweb.ancestry.com/~sam/ terms.html**>. Gareth Hicks's page on Technical Words/Expressions at <**www.rootsweb.ancestry.com/~ukwales2/hicks3.html**> is arranged under a number of key topic headings, which is useful if you're not sure of the distinction between a vicar, rector and parson, for example. This provides quite detailed explanations of historical terms, and is more or less an encyclopedia. Dr Ashton Emery's 'A-Z Of British Genealogical Research' at <**www.genuki.org.uk/big/EmeryPaper.html**> covers about 100 important terms presented as a dictionary rather than a connected account. As this has not been updated in the last 10 years, references to organizations will often be out of date, but the other material remains useful.

In the long run, the most comprehensive online reference work of this type will probably be the collaborative online Encyclopedia of Genealogy at <**www.eogen.com**>, started by Dick Eastman in 2004, which has articles on a wide range of topics, entries for abbreviations and acronyms for genealogy organizations. The advantage of this project is that it allows users to comment on and correct the entries, as well as submitting new entries of their own.

If you have to read documents written in a language other than English then the FamilySearch Research Wiki at <**www.familysearch.org/learn/**

wiki/> has wordlists of key genealogical words for 20 European languages. These lists are split into two main parts: key words, i.e. words like 'husband', 'parish' and 'baptism', which are essential to understanding genealogical records, and a more general wordlist, which generally includes numbers and dates as well as a selection of the general vocabulary. You can get a list of all these articles by entering 'word list' in the search box on the wiki home page. Web resources for Latin, Scots, Welsh and Irish are discussed in Chapter 16 (p. 291ff.)

One frequent question from those getting started is about the meaning of phrases like 'second cousin once removed'. To help you with this, About.com has a Genealogy Relationship Chart at <**genealogy.about.com/ library/nrelationshipchart.htm**>. Genealogy.com's article 'What is a First Cousin, Twice Removed?' at <**www.genealogy.com/genealogy/ 16_cousn.html**> explains all. Irritatingly, if you try and access this page via a UK ISP you will get an intervening page which asks whether you want to remain on Genealogy.com or go to the Ancestry UK site – select Genealogy. com, otherwise you will end up at the Ancestry UK home page.

For making sense of abbreviations and acronyms, there are a number of sites to help you. Most of the glossaries mentioned earlier include many abbreviations. Mark Howells has a page devoted to 'Common Acronyms & Jargon' found in UK genealogy at <**www.oz.net/~markhow/ acronym-uk.htm**>, and N2genealogy has around 600 entries on its 'Terminology, Meanings and Descriptions of Genealogical Abbreviations' page at <**www.terms.n2genealogy.com/abbreviation.html**>. But by far the most comprehensive is GenDocs' 'Genealogical Abbreviations and Acronyms' page at <**homepage.ntlworld.com/hitch/gendocs/abbr.html**> with over 2,000 entries.

For links to other online dictionaries and lists of abbreviations, look at the page on Cyndi's List devoted to 'Dictionaries & Glossaries' at <**www.cyndislist.com/dictionaries**>. The *Oxford English Dictionary* is discussed on p. 186, and can be helpful for establishing the meaning of terms at particular historical periods – it is well worth looking at the various definitions of 'cousin', for example. Dictionaries for other languages are discussed on p. 291ff.

3

ONLINE STARTING POINTS

Subsequent chapters in this book are devoted to particular types of genealogical resource or internet tools. This one looks at some of the online starting points for genealogy on the web, sites which provide information about and links to other resources. These go under various names: directory, gateway or portal. Although these terms are often used interchangeably, there are in principle distinctions to be made:

- An internet directory is the electronic equivalent of the Yellow Pages, a list of resources categorized under a number of subject headings.
- A gateway is a directory devoted to a single subject area, and may also offer knowledgeable annotation of the links provided as well as additional background information. A gateway is not just a directory; it can be more like a handbook.
- A portal is a site which aims to provide a single jumping-off point on the internet for a particular audience, bringing together all the resources they might be interested in. Like a gateway, a portal may provide information as well as links.

In genealogy, since the audience is defined by its interest in a particular subject, it is not always possible to maintain a clear distinction between gateways and portals. 'Portal' tends to be the preferred term in the case of a site which has some official status or which aims to be definitive. Both gateways and portals are selective and only include links to recommended resources, whereas directories tend to be less scrupulous.

Directories, gateways and portals are not the only way to find information on the internet: general-purpose search engines such as Google <**www.google.com**>, discussed in Chapter 19, can also be used to find genealogical material online. The differences between directories, gateways and portals on the one hand and search engines on the other are summarized in Table 19-1 on p. 332. The most important is that directories, etc. provide lists of web*sites* while search engines locate individual web *pages*, so the former are better for locating significant resources on a particular topic rather than mere mentions of a subject. This makes them preferable for initial exploration. The fact that the entries are selected, and perhaps helpfully annotated, makes them even more useful. However, there are certain things they are poor for, notably information published on the personal websites of individual family historians, and material relating to individual surnames.

In addition to the genealogy gateways discussed below, the general directories of the web – the best known are Yahoo at <**dir.yahoo.com**> and the Open Directory Project at <**dmoz.org**> – also provide a small selection genealogical links. On the whole, anyone who is sufficiently interested in genealogy to be reading this book will probably find these directories much less useful than the dedicated sites mentioned in this chapter, not least since they do not seem to be edited and maintained by people with expertise in the subject, and cannot aim to be comprehensive.

The British Isles

Official sites

Since the closure of the FamilyRecords site in September 2009, there is now no official gateway for UK family history, a site which collects together links to the websites of all the relevant official bodies.

There is a general-purpose government gateway called Directgov at <**www.direct.gov.uk**>. This site provides access to *all* official information online, with links to all branches of local and national government. It therefore covers local authorities, who are responsible for county record offices and public libraries. For local government websites, from the home page, select 'Home and community', then 'Your local council – services and information'. This page even links to a brief 'Research your local, family or house history' page. Library and record office websites are covered in Chapter 13.

Any body that holds archival records will be listed in the ARCHON directory (see p. 205) which has links to each repository's website.

The official website of the Irish government will be found at <**www.irlgov.ie**>, and this has links to sites of government departments and state organizations. The National Archives of Ireland at <**www.national archives.ie**> has a genealogy page at <**www.nationalarchives.ie/genealogy/**> with links to information on Irish sources and other useful websites.

Genuki

The most comprehensive collection of online information about family history for the British Isles, with an unrivalled collection of links, is Genuki, the 'UK & Ireland Genealogical Service' at <**www.genuki.org.uk**>. Genuki describes itself as 'a virtual reference library of genealogical information that is of particular relevance to the UK & Ireland'. As a reference source, the material it contains 'relates to primary historical material, rather than material resulting from genealogists' ongoing research'. This means it is effectively a handbook of British and Irish genealogy online. But Genuki also functions as a gateway, simply because it has links to an enormous number of online resources for the UK and Ireland, including every genealogical organization with a website.

Genuki has its origins in the efforts of a group of volunteers, centred on Brian Randell at the University of Newcastle and Phil Stringer at the University of Manchester, to set up a website for genealogical information in 1995, when the World Wide Web was still very young. Genuki has always been an entirely non-commercial and volunteer-run organization. All the pages are maintained by a group of about 50 volunteers on many different websites, mostly at UK universities or on the personal sites of the volunteers. Many other individuals have provided information and transcripts of primary data. Genuki started as an entirely informal group, but is now a charitable trust.

There are two distinct parts to Genuki. First, there are a number of pages devoted to general information about family history in the British Isles:

- 'Frequently Asked Questions' (FAQs) – typical queries asked by Genuki users;
- getting started – a range of beginners' guides (or links to them). See 'Introductions and tutorials' on p. 6;
- pages devoted to individual general topics, such as 'Military Records' or 'Immigration and Emigration', all linked from <**www.genuki.org.uk/ big/**> (many of these are mentioned in later chapters);
- researching from abroad – useful information for those who dwell outside the UK, especially in North America;
- genealogical events relating to UK and Ireland ancestry (see p. 378);
- information on Genuki itself – how it is run, the principles on which it is structured.

Second, it provides geographically based information and links to online resources for all the constituent parts of the British Isles, with pages for:

- England, Wales, Scotland, Ireland, the Isle of Man and the Channel Islands;
- every individual county in these areas;
- many individual towns and parishes.

The county pages in turn provide links to the websites of:

- county record offices and other repositories of interest to family historians (see Chapter 9);
- local family history societies (see Chapter 18);
- county and other local mailing lists (see Chapter 15);
- county surname lists (see Chapter 10);
- any online data collections for the county;
- other online resources relating to genealogy in the county.

Each county page (the top of the Sussex page is shown in Figure 3-1) has a link to a list of individual towns and parishes, and many of these have their own pages with local information and links.

Most material on Genuki will be found on these geographical pages, which are organized hierarchically. Figure 3-2 shows a diagram of the hierarchy.

Genuki also has central listings of:

- national genealogical organizations and local family history societies at <**www.genuki.org.uk/Societies/**>

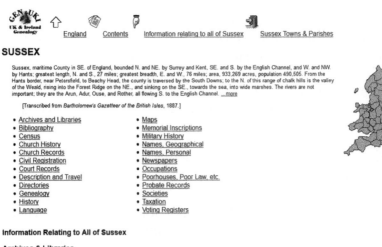

Figure 3-1 A Genuki county page

- all discussion groups relevant to British and Irish genealogy at <**www.genuki.org.uk/indexes/MailingLists.html**>
- all county and other surname lists at <**www.genuki.org.uk/indexes/SurnamesLists.html**>

It also has two important databases: a gazetteer and a church database, both described on p. 256. Its event calendar GENEVA is discussed on p. 378.

Because of the enormous amount of material on Genuki – there are around 60,000 pages in all – it is well worth taking the time to look at the 'Guidance for First-Time Users' at <**www.genuki.org.uk/org/**>, which gives an outline of what Genuki is. There is a more detailed online user guide 'How the information on this server is presented to the user' at <**www.genuki.org.uk/org/user.html**>.

A particular virtue of Genuki is that it uses well-defined subject categories, which are based on those used in the LDS Church's library catalogue and have therefore been designed by genealogically literate librarians. Its coherent coverage of every county, with a long-term aim of covering every parish, is the other feature which makes it useful. The list of categories used on Genuki is shown in Table 3-1.

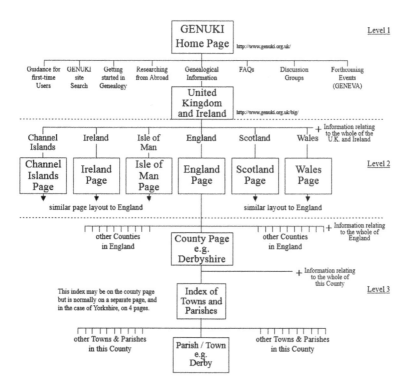

Figure 3-2 How Genuki is organized

Table 3-1 Genuki subject headings

Almanacs	Medical Records
Archives and Libraries	Merchant Marine
Bibliography	Migration, Internal
Biography	Military History
Business and Commerce Records	Military Records
Cemeteries	Minorities
Census	(Monumental Inscriptions – see
Chronology	Cemeteries)
Church Directories	Names, Geographical
Church History	Names, Personal
Church Records	Naturalization and Citizenship
Civil Registration	Newspapers
Colonization	Nobility
Correctional Institutions	Obituaries
Court Records	Occupations
Description and Travel	Officials and Employees
Directories	Orphans and Orphanages
Dwellings	(Parish Registers – see Church Records)
Emigration and Immigration	Pensions
Encyclopedias and Dictionaries	Periodicals
Ethnology	Politics and Government
Folklore	Poorhouses, Poor Law, etc.
Gazetteers	Population
Genealogy	Postal and Shipping Guides
Guardianship	Probate Records
Handwriting	Public Records
Heraldry	Religion and Religious Life
Historical Geography	Schools
History	Social Life and Customs
Inventories, Registers, Catalogues	Societies
Jewish History	Statistics
Jewish Records	Taxation
Land and Property	Town Records
Language and Languages	Visitations, Heraldic
Law and Legislation	(Vital Records – see Civil Registration)
Manors	Voting Registers
Maps	Yearbooks

Some of these categories – Handwriting, or Politics and Government, for example – will be relevant only at the top, national levels, but topics such as church records, local records and maps should be represented on every county page. Since the list of subject headings predates the internet, there are no specific categories for internet-related subjects such as surname lists and mailing lists, so Genuki places these under the Genealogy heading.

Genuki also has a search facility at <**www.genuki.org.uk/search/**>, discussed on p. 352.

Because Genuki is very comprehensive, it can be easy to overlook the fact that there are things it does not do. First, it has deliberate restrictions in its linking policy: it does not link to sites which provide information only on an individual family, pedigree or surname; its links are strictly confined to sites which are relevant to UK and Ireland genealogy. However, as long as what you are looking for is available online and falls within Genuki's scope, you should expect to find it listed.

Another service Genuki does not provide is answering genealogical queries from individuals. There is a Genuki email address, but this is intended only for reporting errors on the site or drawing attention to new resources not listed on Genuki. See 'Getting help' on p. 14 and Chapter 18 for places to post genealogical queries.

Local

While the Genuki country and county pages are the main starting points for links to local web resources, there are other resources which give links just for a particular region, of which the following are a selection.

The Irish Ancestors site has links to the major Irish bodies with genealogical material at <**www.irishtimes.com/ancestor/browse/links/**>, with sub-pages devoted to libraries, societies and individual counties, as well as to passenger lists and emigration resources.

Chris Paton's Walking in Eternity blog has a posting with 'Resources for Western Isles research' at <**walkingineternity.blogspot.com/2011/07/ resources-for-western-isles-research.html**> which has around 60 links for the various islands.

Figure 3-3 The M&LFHS Toolbar

A useful browser tool is the M&LFHS Toolbar developed by the Manchester & Lancashire Family History Society. The toolbar provides links for all the Lancashire record offices and sites with records for the county, but in fact there are dozens of links of broader interest organized under 10 main headings – see Figure 3-3. Versions are available for all the main browsers and can be downloaded from <**www.mlfhs.org.uk/toolbar/toolbar.php**>.

General genealogy gateways

If you have ancestors who were born or lived outside the British Isles you will need to look at some of the general genealogy directories and gateways. Indeed, even if all your ancestors were British or Irish, there are good reasons to use other gateways and directories. Since Genuki takes a strictly geographical approach, you need to look elsewhere for genealogical resources, such as computer software, which are not tied to a particular country or region.

Cyndi's List

By far the most comprehensive genealogy gateway is Cyndi's List at <**www.cyndislist.com**>, maintained by Cyndi Howells, along with Genuki one of the oldest genealogy sites on the web. You can get an idea of the scope of the list, which has over 300,000 links, from the 180 or so main categories listed at <**www.cyndislist.com/categories/**> (or click on the 'Categories' button on the home page). The categories fall into three main groups:

- around one third are for individual countries, geographical regions or particular ethnic groups;
- a large number cover aspects of ancestors' lives and the relevant records;
- the remainder are a miscellaneous collection, which might broadly be described as the tools and techniques of genealogy – anything from scanners to DNA to 'Writing Your Family's History'.

The geographical coverage is very considerable, both in terms of the countries covered and in the number of links – there are even over 40 links for Antarctica. Coverage for the United States is particularly strong, accounting for around half the links on the site. The main UK & Ireland page at <**www.cyndislist.com/uk/**> links to sub-pages for the various parts of the British Isles, to general UK sites and to British military sites. Within each of those are further categories relating to the various types of record.

Beyond the geographical coverage, a number of the other categories and topics on Cyndi's List are worth noting. The pages devoted to individual religious groups will be useful if you have Catholic, nonconformist or Jewish ancestors (covered in Chapter 11). The 'Software & Computers' page <**www.cyndislist.com/software/**> has a very useful collection of links for genealogy software. The 'Personal Home Pages' section at <www.cyndislist.com/personal/> lists over 10,000 websites of individuals, while the 'Surnames' pages linked from <www.cyndislist.com/ surnames/> has thousands of sites for individual surnames.

While Genuki relies on a body of volunteers, Cyndi's List is maintained more or less single-handedly by Cyndi Howells. For this reason, it is not surprising that there are some dead links, and some links to sites that are now moribund.

The site has a very comprehensive page of 'Handy Online Starting Points' at <www.cyndislist.com/handy>, with over 150 sites which provide general genealogy links.

GenWeb

For ancestors from outside the British Isles, you will find a wide coverage of countries and regions on Cyndi's List. But there is also a purely geographical gateway with worldwide coverage in the GenWeb projects. In GenWeb, the world is split into a number of regional projects, each of which has its own website, and a separate volunteer is responsible for each individual country or island in the region. Apart from USGenWeb at <www.usgenweb.org> and CanadaGenWeb at <www.rootsweb.ancestry.com/~canwgw/>, which are independent, the remainder are co-ordinated under the WorldGenWeb project at <worldgenweb.org>.

In all, there are around 100 countries, islands or island groups for which there are actively maintained websites, grouped as follows:

- Africa
- Asia
- Canada
- Caribbean
- Central Europe (actually Northern Europe would be a more accurate description)
- Eastern Europe
- Ireland and United Kingdom (whole of British Isles plus British Overseas Territories)
- Mediterranean (more like Southern Europe, since it excludes African and Middle Eastern states, though it includes Turkey)
- Middle East
- North America (actually Central America, since it excludes Canada and the US)
- Pacific, including Australasia
- South America
- United States

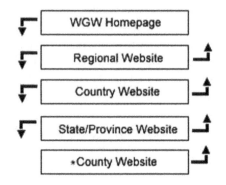

* Not all countries have counties.
The term county is used here in the general sense and
refers to the most common political or administrative district
in a country. Other names include shires, parish, townlands,
states, prefects, rajones, etc.

Figure 3-4 How WorldGenWeb is organized

Most of the links to UK and Irish material at <**www.iukgenweb.org**> will in fact be found on Genuki, whose county pages are generally more comprehensive. So the real strength of the GenWeb sites, from the point of view of British and Irish family historians, lies in the material relating to former British colonies and those countries from which immigrants came to the UK (see Chapter 11). The Caribbean GenWeb at <**www.rootsweb. ancestry.com/~caribgw/**>, for example, is an essential starting point for West Indian ancestry.

There is huge variation in the amount of material available: for some countries there is a single page, while for others there are individual pages for administrative subdivisions, for example French *départements*. In general, the level of detail does not go down to the equivalent of individual parishes, though for each US state there are pages for the constituent counties. The structure of GenWeb, taken from <**worldgenweb.org/index.php/ policies-and-procedures**>, is shown in Figure 3-4.

While most of the pages are in English, quite a few are maintained by natives of the countries concerned and are in the local language. Some, notably the Caribbean and South American pages, are available in more than one language.

On the WorldGenWeb projects, the topics on each page are sorted under the following headings:

- History
- Resource Addresses (libraries, archives)

- Society Addresses
- Maps
- Geography
- Culture and Religious History
- Query Board
- Mail List
- Reference Materials (census, deeds, biographies)

Beyond this, the pages do not necessarily have the same layout or look. A useful feature to note is that every GenWeb page has a Query Board where readers can post queries. Such a board is often available for countries which have no maintained web page.

Other gateways

While Cyndi's List may be the most widely used general genealogy directory, and Genuki is certainly the pre-eminent gateway for UK material, there are many others. Each has its own particular strengths, though many are US-based and are therefore naturally stronger in US resources. There is not enough space here to list them all, let alone describe them in detail, but good examples are:

- Genealogy Links at <**www.genealogylinks.net**>
- Genealogy Gateway at <**www.gengateway.com**>

Many others are listed on the 'Handy Online Starting Points' on Cyndi's List at <**www.cyndislist.com/handy/**>.

Gateways for particular subject-areas within family history are mentioned in the appropriate chapter.

4

USING ONLINE SOURCES

The core of any family history research in the British Isles is the information drawn from the registrations of births, marriages and deaths over the last 170 years, and from the records of christenings, marriages and burials in parish registers starting in the sixteenth century. Linking these two sources are the census records, which enable an address from the period of civil registration to lead to a place and approximate year of birth in the time before registration.

The three following chapters examine online sources for each of these sets of records in turn, and subsequent chapters look at other types of record on the web. The aim of this chapter is to look at some of the general issues of using the internet for genealogical data and the major data services which provide access to these records online.

Approaches to digitization

While the internet is the ideal way of making genealogical records widely available, particularly to those who are distant from the relevant repositories and major genealogical libraries, the fact is that a huge amount of work is involved in publishing such material on the web. For example, there may have been as many as 100 million births, marriages and deaths registered between 1837 and 1900; between them, the censuses of England and Wales from 1841 to 1911 include details of around 200 million individuals. Nonetheless, there has been enormous progress over the past few years in putting genealogical data online.

There are a number of ways in which genealogical data projects can be funded. Volunteer-run projects tend to rely entirely on goodwill and occasional sponsorship, while a number of projects have public funding, usually from the Heritage Lottery Fund or from academic funding sources. In such cases, access to the data is normally free.

Other record and data holders have taken four main routes to making their records available online commercially:

- setting up an in-house data service;
- setting up a joint data service with a commercial partner;

- licensing a commercial firm to digitize records;
- licensing of existing digital data records to third parties.

The first of these was the route taken by The National Archives (TNA) for its online document service (see p. 58). It is also something that is done on a smaller scale at local level, such as Essex Record Office's Essex Ancestors service (see p. 104).

The second was the initial approach taken both by the General Register Office for Scotland (GROS) and TNA and in the first two big projects to put national record sets online: the digitization of Scottish records and the 1901 census for England and Wales. However, this monopoly approach, which was probably the only option at a time when there were no established genealogy data services in the British Isles, has not been without problems. Some of these are discussed among the 'Issues for Online Genealogists' in Chapter 22.

The National Archives has moved to the third type of system, which solves the issue of how to fund the initial digitization (which is *very* expensive) but subsequently frees up records for wider commercial exploitation. Although the 1901 census digitization started out as an exclusive arrangement between TNA and QinetiQ, the digitized images were ultimately made available for wider licensing. The result was that Ancestry launched its own 1901 census index in April 2004, with other companies following, so that the original index now has three competitors. For the 1911 census, even though the initial digitization contract involved an exclusive deal with Brightsolid/Findmypast, once the entire census had been online for six months, the images were available for other companies to license and by the time you read this, the 1911 census should be available in its entirety on three distinct different sites, with the same images but independent indexes.

The Scots have been slower to come over to this model. In spite of a public statement from GROS in 2007–08 about opening up the licensing of records, Ancestry had to go ahead with its Scottish census indexes without the agreement of GROS and unable to license the images. At the start of 2012, there are certainly more Scottish records coming online on commercial services, but still no images of those records except on ScotlandsPeople.

Record holders and data services are not the only ones involved in creating digital records – family history societies (FHSs) and individual genealogists have been creating computerized indexes for around 25 years. But generally they have neither the funding nor the technical infrastructure to mount their own commercial data service and have licensed their data to commercial services. British Origins was in fact launched in 2001 with a number of indexes which had been created by the Society of Genealogists, and in 2003 the Federation of Family History Societies launched FamilyHistoryOnline to draw on the vast body of FHS indexes. Since the closure of FamilyHistoryOnline, FHSs have been increasingly licensing their data to the commercial services, which have also been drawing on the work of individual transcribers. The obvious merits of this are that records are indexed by people knowledgeable about the records and the locality, while the technical infrastructure is high quality and resilient. However, these indexes tend not to be accompanied by images of the original records.

Indexes, transcriptions and images

There are three main ways in which any historical textual source can be represented digitally:

- as an image – the original document is scanned;
- in a transcription – the full text of a document is held in a file;
- as an index – a list of names, with or without other details, directs you to
  - a transcription;
  - the relevant scanned image;
  - the location of an original document.

Ideally, an online index would lead to a full transcription of the relevant document, which could then be compared to an image of the original. But for material of any size this represents a very substantial investment in time and resources, and very little of the primary genealogical data is so well served, nor is it likely to be in the foreseeable future.

The reason for this is the very great disparity between the amount of data involved in making text and images available online. In spite of advances in information technology, images require significantly more resources from the website which hosts them, both in terms of disk space for storage and the bandwidth to download them to the user. Even disregarding the labour and other costs for creating the digital images of source documents, for a large project this can mean enormous differences in financial practicability between a text-only data collection and one which includes digitized documents.

Images can be supplied economically for census records because they are central to family history and are universally needed, which means that costs can be covered. This has also been done in a number of lottery-funded projects for less widely used material, such as the Old Bailey Proceedings (see p. 124), where costs do not have to be recouped at all. It has been done for wills, where a transcription of the entire text would be commercially impracticable, but where a higher charge can be made for a complete digitized document. Generally for non-commercial projects, images of records are the exception – the only large-scale examples that spring to mind are FreeBMD (p. 70) and the new FamilySearch (p. 41), though there are quite a few smaller, local projects.

However, there are many more images than transcriptions. For a document containing running text, a transcription takes much more time to prepare than an index, and except for particularly difficult documents (e.g. a seventeenth-century will) is not really necessary, as long as there is good indexing. A project like the Old Bailey Proceedings, which has document images with an indexed transcription, is in fact exceptional. On the other hand, it is certainly true that with some sources, such as the censuses, comprehensive indexing can sometimes approach a full transcription.

Most online data, then, comes in the form of indexes linked to images, or, more often, just plain indexes. And this has important implications for how you use the internet for your research: you simply cannot do it all online. Except where you have access to scans of the original documents, all information derived from indexes or transcriptions will have to be checked against the original source. This might not be apparent to you if you are just starting out, since the first online sources you use, the GRO indexes and census records, are available as images, but you will find a very different story once you get back beyond 1837. Older printed sources will have been scanned, but there are as yet very few earlier manuscript sources which have been digitized.

▍ Quality issues

The perfect index would be made by trained palaeographers, familiar with the names and places referred to and thoroughly at home with the handwriting of the period, working with original documents. Their work would be independently checked against the original, and where there was uncertainty as to the correct reading, this would be clearly indicated.

Needless to day, very little of the genealogical material on the web has been transcribed to this sort of standard. The material online has been created either in large-scale projects or by individual genealogists, and often working from microfilms, or digitized images of them, not original records. In academic projects high levels of accuracy and quality control are a fundamental part of the process, but for other large-scale projects the data are input at best by knowledgeable amateurs such as family history society members, and more often by non-specialist clerical workers. In the latter case, there will always be a question about the quality of data entry. It is self-evident that adequate levels of accuracy can only be achieved where there are good palaeographical skills, and knowledge of local place-names and surnames.

Even so, one must recognize that our manuscript historical records are sometimes very hard to read, never mind transcribe with absolute certainty. Although I am quite critical of the quality of some of the online indexes, one cannot escape the fact some of the errors are completely understandable, and one cannot really expect a commercial index to a census of, say, 20 million individuals to allow transcribers five minutes to stare at every difficult surname. When compiling some census error statistics for *Census: The Expert* Guide (see p. 36), I spent many hours poring over the pages for a single small enumeration district and was still left with an average of perhaps one surname every other page I could not be absolutely sure of. It would be unfair to expect non-expert clerks working to commercial targets to do better. To see the sort of thing a transcriber has to cope with, look at the scans for a servant in the household of Sarah Maskell in the 1871 census for Peckham (RG 10/734, fol. 64, p. 54) shown in Figure 4-1. At the top is the greyscale image from Ancestry, below it the black and white scan from Origins. The latter seems slightly easier to read, but I would be surprised at anyone claiming to identify the surname with 100 per cent confidence from either of them.

The only area where one can expect a lower error rate is in the transcription of printed sources such as trade directories, where problems of identifying names or individual letters are less great. On the other hand, printed sources lend themselves to optical character recognition (OCR), but this is a mixed blessing. Although OCR is much less labour-intensive than manual transcription, it can produce spectacularly inaccurate results where the original documents are poorly printed, and therefore requires laborious proof-reading to guarantee accuracy, something that is simply not practicable in a large project. You can get a good idea of the limits of OCR from the recently launched British Newspaper Archive, discussed on p. 198. Figure 4-2 shows two identical reports on the loss of a naval ship, one almost perfectly captured, the other quite seriously garbled.

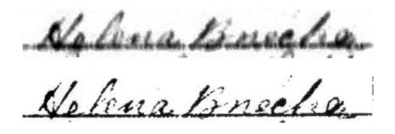

Figure 4-1 Could you transcribe this name with confidence?

Glasgow Herald
Sat 27 Jul 1867   Lanarkshire, Scotland

THE WRECK OF HER MAJESTY'S SHIP OSPREY   885 Words

66 SHIP **OSPREY**. By the arrival of the Cape mail we have detailed accounts of the
loss -of the **Osprey** (4) screw gun vessel, Conunander William Menzies. The
Osprey was on her way from the China-station for England. Having crossed the
Indian Ocean, she wa ... ?

Page 3
Miscellaneous   **Tags:** News   Buy Print   Bookmark   View

Stirling Observer
Thu 01 Aug 1867   Stirlingshire, Scotland

THE WRECK OF HER MAJESTY'S SHIP OSPREY   630 Words

66 SHIP **OSPREY**. '.By the arrival of the Cape mail We h a Â« accounts of tho loss of
the **Osprey** (4) Bcrewlâ€žÂ« etailed Commander William Menzies. The OsprevV
eSSel ' Â£er way from the China station for England. HaviÂ° n snml ed the Indian
Ocean, she wa ... ?

Figure 4-2 Optical Character Recognition – the British Newspaper Archive

Nonetheless, in manually created indexes there are some types of error which really are easily avoidable: those which are the result of poor data validation. Validation is an essential component of any data-entry project – it means checking that everything entered is, if not demonstrably correct, at least plausible. Of course, it's one thing to do this with, say, a modern postcode, where it's a simple matter to check that it is present in a list of valid postcodes or that it at least has the correct structure for a postcode. It is much harder to do the same with handwritten historical sources, particularly where surnames are involved. Even so, there have been some notable and entirely avoidable failures in major genealogical projects, which have reduced their reliability and usefulness.

Perhaps the most notorious of these was in the original release of the 1901 census, which had individuals with biologically implausible ages over 200. You'd have thought those entering the data might have had second thoughts about these themselves, but even so, given that data-entry errors are inevitable, why was there no mechanism in place to spot data which cannot possibly be correct?

In other cases, there are things that *might* be right, but are statistically so anomalous that they need individual checking. For example, all the census indexes have significant numbers of people indexed with a gender which does not seem to match with their forename. It's easy to get a name wrong in a census transcription, whether by misreading or miskeying, and sometimes the error will be down to the census enumerator. But some of the errors will be self-evident, because of gender differences in naming – it is a trivial matter to query a database for gender errors with common forenames, to flag entries that need checking.

Sometimes a lookup will suffice to trap errors: there are some strange misspellings of place-names in the census indexes (e.g. *Harimersmith* for *Hammersmith*), or some strange combinations (*Somerset, London?*). Ancestry has the Sarah Maskell, whose servant was Helena from Figure 4-1, born in *Syrian Arab Republic, Hange Common*, instead of the admittedly hard-to-read *Surrey, Ham Common* on the original. But one doesn't need to see the originals to know that these transcriptions simply must be wrong. Couldn't they have been checked against a gazetteer? Even if it was not possible to fix them immediately, could they not have been flagged as doubtful, for later investigation?

Even with forenames, one ought to be pretty suspicious of a name that is not in the forename dictionary. I suppose it's possible that England in 1891 had bearers of the forenames *Gluyabeth* or *Iomnic*, as two of the indexes would have it, but even without seeing the originals in Figure 4-3, I bet you could guess that the first ought to be *Elizabeth* and the second either *Dominic* or *Jonnie* (actually the latter). It's an obvious enough principle: even if a name is hard to make out, it's much more likely to be a badly written common name than a badly written name with no other recorded instances. From a purely pragmatic point of view, the descendants of Gluyabeth would probably guess at *Elizabeth* as a plausible transcriber's error, but hardly vice versa. There are certainly problems with the ways these names are written in the original (both seem to have too many strokes), but you would have to be absolutely sure there was no alternative other than *Gluyabeth* to put that down as your transcription.

But given that there will always be genuinely hard-to-read entries, the question is how they are treated. Techniques for editing manuscript documents to indicate uncertainties of reading were available long before the advent of computers and much work has been done by those who edit historical manuscripts on ways of indicating variants and unreadable text in electronic editions (see the Text Encoding Initiative at <**www.tei-c.org**>). So could genealogical projects not take account of this? As far as I can see, the major transcriptions used by genealogists rarely use any mechanism (and certainly nothing more sophisticated than a question mark) for indicating

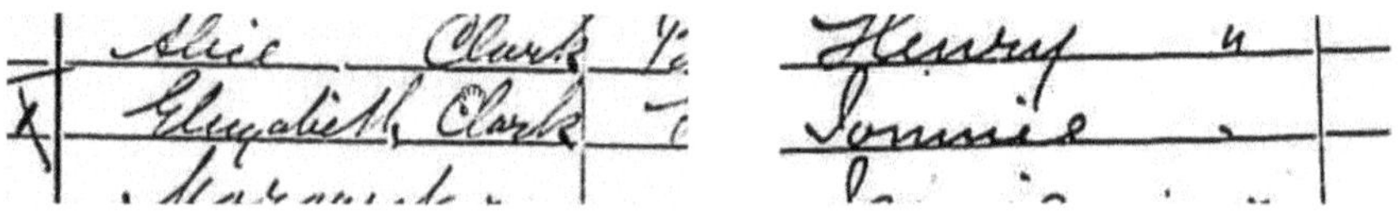

Figure 4-3 Two entries from the 1891 census for Islington

that an individual character or a word is not unambiguously decipherable, in spite of the fact that it is a common enough experience for every genealogist. The transcriber simply puts their best guess, a solution which is utterly inadequate and entirely unhelpful to the user. For example, the barely legible surname in Figure 4-1 is transcribed by Ancestry as *Boucha* and by Origins as *Bnecker*. Neither is obviously right, and both seem reasonable attempts in the circumstances. But surely neither of the transcribers in this instance can have been confident that their reading was correct. It would be much more helpful for a data provider to admit that there cannot be a definitive reading here and recognize that someone looking for *Bnecker* or *Boucha*, or a range of similar names, should be shown this entry as a possible match.

Why don't the electronic transcriptions do this? Because, to be fair, it's actually quite difficult to do. Having complicated ways of indicating doubtful characters is all very well, but it has two unwelcome repercussions. For a start you would have to teach your transcribers how to use them and check that they were doing so correctly and consistently. Then you would have to modify your search engine to retrieve these entries when something close enough was entered. The real solution then, is to have good techniques for identifying loose matches, and all the data services give you the option of choosing a less exact match, in ways which are discussed later in this chapter (p. 39).

But all this points to another issue which underlies much of the difficulty of finding people in online genealogical databases – they do not distinguish clearly between a transcription and an index. The job of a transcriber is to reproduce exactly the letters that can be identified on the original page, that of the indexer to make things findable. The problem with *Gluyabeth* only arises in a transcription. With a proper *index* the answer is simple: you link this entry to both *Elizabeth* and *Gluyabeth*. An index is a finding aid, and it is much better for it to give occasional false positives than for it to regularly ignore obvious, not to mention more likely, alternative readings.

This question also arises very noticeably in the representation of place-names, and *Guildford* in Surrey is a good example. There are two obvious alternative spellings one might expect to find: *Guilford* and *Gilford*, and both do in fact occur in records. The question is: how should these be treated? The transcription approach is the simplest – just record what is written. But the problem with this is that the user has to try all the alternatives. The index approach is more complex: either the spelling can be normalised or there can be multiple index entries. Either way, in a search for someone born in *Guildford*, Surrey, you should also find those whose birthplaces are recorded as *Guilford*, Surrey or *Gilford*, Surrey. Normalisation can be risky, though: there is actually a *Guilford* (in Pembrokeshire) and a *Gilford* (in County Down). Also, it does something that indexers and transcribers are rightly keen to avoid: interpreting the records. That's the genealogist's job! But while it is not legitimate to *transcribe Guilford* as *Guildford*, there can be no harm in *indexing* a single record under both *Guilford* and *Guildford*.

But if normalizing can be problematic, multiple index entries can be hard work – how far should one expect indexers to go to list alternative spellings? In fact, it depends: in the case of county names, it really shouldn't be a challenge. There are only 53 historic counties in England and Wales. We know what they are, we know their recognized alternative names (*Shropshire* and *Salop*, for example), and likely spelling variants are easily guessed (*Surrey* and *Surry*). There is no reason why county names should not be normalized or the variants correctly matched: the user shouldn't have to guess whether a census enumerator happened to use *Devon* or *Devonshire*. In fact some sites go further: they don't even run the risk that users might get the county spelling wrong, but offer a drop-down list for you to select from. Perhaps the real problem is not that the various sites take different and legitimate approaches, but that it is not always obvious which approach they take.

So how good should we expect the online indexes to be? When the GRO placed the tender for the DOVE project (p. 68) it specified a maximum error rate of 0.5 per cent. This sounds quite small, but in a large project it would mean a *lot* of records with errors. If this error rate requires that 99.5 per cent of *records* should be completely correct, that would still mean one million civil registration records with an error in one field or another. More likely, it means 99.5 per cent of *fields* should be error-free, which would result in around one million wrong surnames, another million wrong forenames, etc. You may think, therefore, that 99.5 per cent sets the bar too low, but for the censuses at least, where some comparative statistics have been compiled, none of the commercially available indexes gets anywhere near this figure.

For *Census: The Expert Guide* I analysed the indexing errors for two sample enumeration books, across three major data services, the work, therefore, of six individual transcribers. In each case, I checked the accuracy of three fields (forenames, surnames and birthplaces), giving a total of 18 different error-rate figures. The individual figures (online at <www.spub.co.uk/census/tables/>) are not really of any importance: they're several years old and based on a tiny and not remotely representative sample. But they show clearly that our expectations of accuracy should not be set too high. Only four of these error rates fell below 3 per cent, while in *seven* cases the error rate was over 10 per cent. That means at least one wrong forename, one wrong surname and one wrong birthplace per census enumeration page.

Since I excluded all the cases where the original was so illegible that there could be no single correct version, these were all errors that were in principle avoidable. There seemed to be four main sources of error:

- Transcribers did not sufficiently take account of the writing habits of the original enumerator – Victorian capital letters may sometimes be florid, but they are normally consistent in any one hand throughout an enumeration book.
- Transcribers were often ignorant of the names of surrounding parishes or districts and failed to recognize them; a transcriber sometimes could not even recognize the name of the enumeration district itself when it turned up as a birthplace!
- Transcribers seemed very ready to transcribe something completely implausible when there was a much more obvious alternative —*Daud* for *David*, *Stabel* for *Isabel*.
- Transcribers were not always properly trained or supervised. One transcriber treated all dittos as meaning 'the same as the head of the household', even if there was a different name in-between. The result was that over 40 per cent of individuals in that enumeration district were indexed with a completely wrong surname that was not just a garbled version of the correct name.

These figures suggest that for the GRO's digitizers to hit their target of a 0.5 per cent error rate would be a genuine cause for congratulation. But it is also important to note the census error rates cannot necessarily be applied to all online data. There is a whole category of material which ought to be much more accurate: records transcribed by individual genealogists or family history organizations. These are not produced under commercial time pressures and those involved tend to be experienced indexers who are very much more familiar with the nature of the records and highly motivated to produce accurate work. And, of course, the number of records will be a fraction of the 20 million or so in a census, which makes quality control much easier.

On the whole, my view is that there are relatively simple error checking and quality control measures which could be implemented with only a bit more trouble. Genuine indexes rather than searchable transcriptions would solve many problems about uncertain readings, but might bring additional complications. And of course, we have to accept that there will always be an irreducible core of illegible words – there are many cases where the ink on an original document is too faint to give any certain letters at all – and we simply have to live with these and find ways around them.

On a more positive note, though, it is worth remembering that although all indexes are subject to error, the great virtue of online indexes is that mistakes can be corrected. In printed or CD-ROM publications this sort of error removal can only be undertaken if and when a subsequent edition is produced, but the systematic errors in the 1901 census were dealt with reasonably promptly. All the data services have a mechanism for users to submit details of errors and suggest corrections, though how (and how promptly) these are dealt with varies between services. Ancestry, for example, does not modify the original transcription, but allows users to add 'updates' (there is a 'View/Add Alternate Info' link on the page for each record). These are not checked but are included in search results and indicated as such. Findmypast, on the other hand, checks submissions (made from the 'report transcription error' link in the image viewer) and modifies the data if the correction is accepted.

Also, one must be pragmatic: as long as an error does not prevent you actually locating an individual, then checking against the digitized image or the original record will provide the correct information. That means errors in gender or occupation may not be very significant – as long as you don't specify these in a search, that is. On the other hand, large errors in ages and misspellings of surnames and birthplaces may well make someone effectively unfindable. Even with fuzzy name-matching facilities, you may need to be imaginative in your searching if your initial search fails. Also, as with any transcription or index, a failure to locate an individual in an online index does not permit you to draw negative inferences.

The great advantage of the censuses in particular is that there are several independent indexes available on a pay-per-view basis, so if you cannot find an individual on your preferred subscription service, there is a low-cost alternative. Unfortunately, this is not the case for most other datasets.

Searching online records

Even if the online indexes and transcriptions were perfect, there would still be potential problems in locating an individual in a set of digital records. For a start, many of the records themselves are incomplete and flawed in various ways. The gaps in census records are generally well documented, but those for parish registers and many older records are often hard to pin down. Also, you start every search with a certain amount of prior information, but it's quite possible for that information to be inaccurate or at least incomplete. Sometimes our ancestors lied or were forgetful when giving information to officials; in other cases perhaps the evidence or over-reliance on the memory of an ageing family member has led you to make an assumption that turns out to be wrong. These two problems are in fact less of an issue when working with original records – you will almost always notice an entry in, say, a parish register that is similar to but not exactly what you expected. In an electronic index, though, too precise a formulation of your search may have the effect of making that entry invisible.

Techniques for getting the best results when searching census indexes, which are generally the most complex online records, are discussed in detail in Chapter 5 of *Census: The Expert Guide*, but it is easy enough to summarize the main techniques for more satisfactory searching:

- Always be prepared to assume that some of the information you have may be wrong or may have been recorded incorrectly, a corollary of which is –
- The more fields you search on, the less likely you are to find the record you are looking for.
- Searching on fewer fields will find more, perhaps not very similar records but will run less risk of missing the right record.
- Don't be too pedantic about surname spellings – these were highly variable before the standardization of the written language and universal literacy.

Name matching

This last point arises from one of the fundamental problems of searching online indexes to genealogical records: names have in the past been subject to much more variation than we are now used to. Add to that the contemporary idiosyncrasies when a name was written down and the possibility of modern mistranscription, and it is clear that searching for individuals in historical records can be far from straightforward.

There is no definitive online (or indeed offline) source to help you to decide whether surname X is in fact a variant of surname Y, or what variant spellings you can expect for a particular name. However, if a name has been registered with the Guild of One-Name Studies the Guild's online register at <**www.one-name.org/register.shtml**> may give some indication of major variants, and it will be worth contacting the person who has registered it. Posting a query about variants on one of the many surname mailing lists and query boards (see Chapter 18) would also be a sensible step.

The search forms for online records almost always have some mechanism for choosing either an exact or a looser ('fuzzy') match with what you type in the search box. In some cases, that's all they do, without any indication how matches are made; in other cases a site will use an explicit method for deciding which variants to include. FamilySearch and Ancestry take the former approach and their default is a fuzzy match – there is a check-box for you to tick if you instead want an exact match. Otherwise, the main possibilities are the following:

Wildcards: many systems allow you to use a 'wildcard', generally an asterisk, to stand for any number of letters (including none), so Brook* would find Brook, Brooke, Brooks, Brookes, Brooker, Brookbank, Brookshaw, etc. Those with Scots ancestors will find this useful to search simultaneously for 'Mac' and 'Mc' names with M*c. On some sites you can also use a question mark to stand for a single character. In general, though, you cannot use a wildcard at the beginning of a name.

Soundex: a venerable system with considerable limitations, which assigns a four-character code to each surname and regards two surnames as matching if they have the same code. Details of Soundex can be found at <**www.archives.gov/research/census/soundex.html**> and some of its shortcomings are described in my article 'Soundex – can it be improved?' at <**www.spub.co.uk/cig/605christian.pdf**>. ScotlandsPeople is the only major UK site to use it.

NameX: a more modern, proprietary system works by taking the name you are starting with and giving every other name a *score* based on how closely it matches. This allows you, in principle, to look at only close matches or to include more distant ones. Image Partners, who developed NameX, have a demo on their site at <**www.namethesaurus.com/Thesaurus/**>.

One general problem, though, is not solved by any of these methods: florid initial letters are easy to mistranscribe and this will often lead to name forms that cannot in any way be regarded as 'variants'.

The Thesaurus of British Surnames is a project to develop an online thesaurus of British surname variants. The ToBS website at <**www.tobs.org.uk**> does not have details of individual variants but has a number of resources relating to the issues of surname matching, including papers on the problems of identifying surname variants, and a comprehensive bibliography on the subject. Origins has a good discussion of the problems of identifying surname variants in historical records in its page on NameX at <**www.originsnetwork.com/namex/aboutnamex.html**>.

In January 2012, Ancestry, WeRelate and Behind The Name announced a joint project to provide for improved surname matching in the form of an open-source database of name variants. The database can be searched at <**www.werelate.org/wiki/Special:Names**> and you can add variants to the search results for any name. There does not seem to be any quality control on new submissions. There is more information about the project at <**www.werelate.org/wiki/WeRelate:Variant_names_project**>.

A particular issue for those with Irish ancestors is that many modern surnames are anglicized forms of Irish-language surnames. Indeed it may be impossible to trace an Irish ancestor in the Irish censuses (see p. 95) without knowing the original Irish form, not something which can normally be guessed at by a non-Irish speaker. The best resources on Irish surnames are found on Library Ireland at <**www.libraryireland.com/Names.php**>. This has seven, mainly nineteenth-century, works on Irish names. 'Some Anglicised Surnames in Ireland' gives the Irish form for each anglicized name, while 'Irish Names and Surnames' gives the anglicized forms for Irish originals. Wikipedia's 'Irish name' article has a list of about 200 names, with variants and anglicized forms.

FamilySearch

While most of the large sites offering a range of genealogical records are commercial, one of the most significant is entirely free: the LDS Church's FamilySearch site at <**www.familysearch.org**>. The site first went live way back in 1999 with the International Genealogical Index (IGI). This is a worldwide collection of church records, mainly baptisms, including millions of entries for the British Isles. This was followed in 2003 by the 1881 Census Index for England and Wales.

In 2006 FamilySearch launched a project called FamilySearch Indexing, in which all the microfilms of genealogical records in the Family History Library (see p. 221), including therefore all the parish register material in the IGI, would be indexed from scratch by volunteers for making available online. The first fruits of this came in 2008, when a pilot version of a new FamilySearch site went live for testing, and in 2011 the new site replaced the old at <**www.familysearch.org**> (Figure 4-4).

The old site remains accessible at <**www.familysearch.org/eng/**> even though most of the data seems to be available on the new site. Needless to say, this is by far the most ambitious genealogical indexing project ever attempted and no doubt will take many years to complete. So far over 500 million records have been indexed.

On the new site the genealogical records are in the 'Historical Records Collection' and cover a wider range than just church and census records –

Figure 4-4 FamilySearch home page

among the material already on the site are school, workhouse and probate records.

The majority of the collections on the site form well-defined record sets from a particular source, which for the UK is usually from an individual county (e.g. Cheshire Bishop's Transcripts or West Glamorgan Electoral registers). But a few of the datasets are actually the material from the International Genealogical Index (IGI) and related sources, divided into national collections for England, Wales, Scotland and Ireland. However, an important change has been made to this material: it originally included not only the results of official transcription efforts but also unverified (and in practice often inaccurate) submissions from individual church members. These now all seem to have been removed, making the quality of the data much higher. This does not mean it's wholly reliable, though – just while trying some test searches, I came across a load of entries for Leominster, Sussex (it's in Herefordshire!) and Pervensey, Sussex (for 'Pevensey').

If you are new to the site, it is useful to get an overview of what's available by using the 'Browse by location' options lower down the page. This will give you a list of all the countries in each region, from which you can select the one you want. All English records are under 'United Kingdom' though Wales, Scotland, Ireland, the Channel Islands and the Isle of Man have separate entries. For all but the UK there are so far only a handful of collections. (See Figure 4-5.)

For the newly indexed collections, there is wide variation in what each offers, based on how far the work on a particular project has progressed and the terms of any agreement with the original repository, but there are three basic patterns: an index alone, an index with a link to an image of the original record, and an unindexed series of document images. In the longer term all the images will eventually be accompanied by indexes, but the reverse may not be the case – where FamilySearch does not own the rights to a set of images, it may be unable to make them publicly available. In the case of some of the censuses, the indexes have been supplied by commercial partners and links for the images take you to the relevant commercial site, where registration and payment will be required. (This limitation does not apply if you are accessing the site from a Family History Center.)

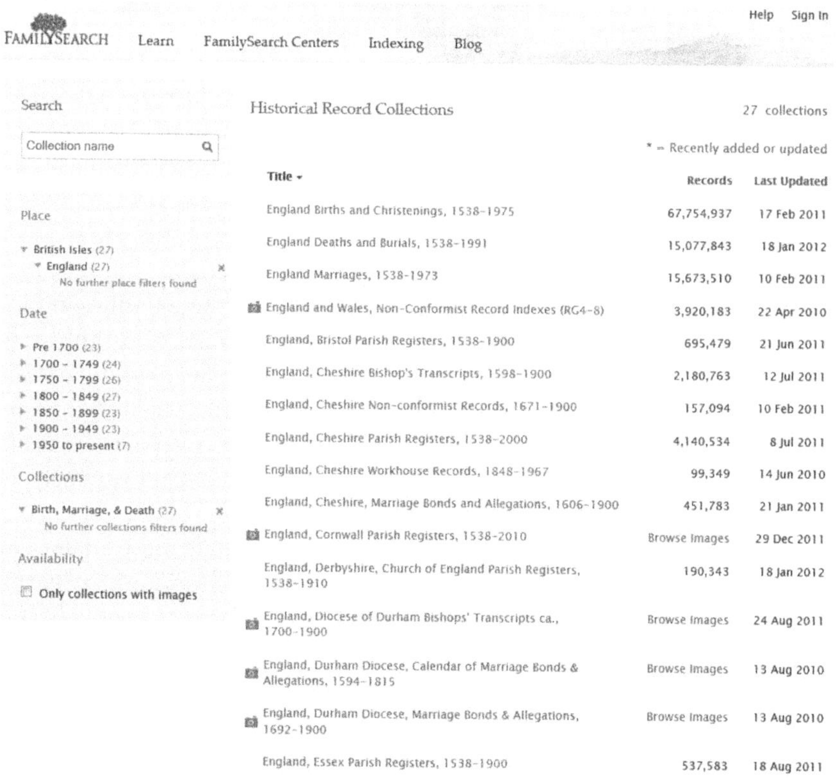

Figure 4-5 FamilySearch: UK Historical Record Collections, Birth, Marriage and Death collections

Although you can search records just by entering forename and surname on the FamilySearch home page (Figure 4-4), this will search all 850 or so data collections on the site from over 60 different countries. Since this includes 320 million entries from UK and US censuses, any English or Celtic surname will inevitably be very frequent. Even so, this *can* be useful: it can be a way to trace people who you suspect might have migrated; and for a one-name study it is a quick method of establishing which countries a surname is found in. But unless an ancestor has a reasonably unusual name, it is better to narrow down the search by using the 'Search by Life Events' or 'Search by Relationships' filters. The first of these allows you to enter a place, though if you're searching *all* the data this is less useful than you might think: if you enter, say 'Wales' in the 'Place' field, you will not only get some Welsh parish register entries, but any UK or North American census where Wales is the place of residence or place of birth. Unfortunately, there is no way to search only the British Isles records, or just those for, say, Scotland. But if you know where you ancestors came from, you are in any case much better off searching the collections for the individual nations of the British Isles and narrowing down with a county.

There is one important caveat about the dates given for these collections: when it says, for example, 'Parish registers 1538–2000', that does not mean that this is the coverage for every parish in the area, just the date of the earliest and most recent records. For a start, many parishes do not have records going back as early as 1538, and in some smaller parishes the church will still be currently using a register which was begun decades ago and has therefore not yet become available for filming. In addition, the site is a work in progress: these dates apply to the whole of the material in the collection, but the work is being done in phases and indexing is not necessarily complete. However, the wiki page for the collection (follow the 'Learn more' link on the search page or any search results page) may give more detail of the dates so far under the heading 'Collection Time Period'. Where a collection is just available as images, there is no problem seeing the exact coverage because the way the material is organized will reveal what is included. Unfortunately, the wiki page for each collection does not list exactly which parishes have so far been covered for which dates, but the FamilySearch Indexing Updates page on the wiki at <**www.familysearch.org/learn/wiki/en/FamilySearch_Indexing_Updates**> gives latest details of the percentage of each collection completed. A very rough idea of the dates covered for a particular place can be gained by doing a search on place-name only, as discussed on p. 101. This will certainly show the earliest and latest records, though gaps in the coverage may not be readily apparent.

The FamilySearch Indexing collections are missing one very useful feature: once you have a set of search results there is no easy way to download the information, whether for an individual record or for a whole set of search results, something which would be particularly useful if you have many ancestors in a parish or county and, of course, for one-name studies. This was always possible on the older site and given that its absence must be a source of irritation to most long-term users, one must hope the feature has just not yet been implemented.

FamilySearch is not just a home to the Historical Records Collection and it contains much other material, notably the wiki and the online lectures and courses discussed in Chapter 2, and the pedigrees submitted by individual genealogists, which are discussed in Chapter 14.

Among the other material that is particularly worth looking at:

- the home page for FamilySearch Indexing at <**indexing.familysearch.org**> has details of the project;
- the FamilySearch Blog at <**familysearch.org/blog**> publishes news of recent developments on the site;
- the FamilySearch Labs at <**labs.familysearch.org**> showcase potential new facilities which are still in development.

The individual categories of record on the site are discussed in the relevant later chapters, and, since church records are still the main thing that users want to search, a more detailed look at how to use the historical record collections is provided in Chapter 7.

The commercial data services

The following chapters cover the various types of record and look at sites relevant for each. But there are a number of major commercial sites which have datasets drawn from a variety of different records, and these are discussed here for convenience. All the sites mentioned are constantly adding to their data, sometimes on a monthly basis, so you will almost certainly find there is a wider range of data than mentioned here. Prices, on the other hand, have tended to be very stable, and are not likely to be much higher than those quoted.

The sites described here are all mature services and most offer facilities beyond their data collections which space does not permit coverage of here. In particular, they offer community facilities like discussion forums and shareable family trees. It should be easy to discover what additional features the sites offer, and they can sometimes be used without payment, though you will undoubtedly need to complete some form of registration.

The details given below are based on what is available on the sites in March 2012 but I have included mention of some datasets which I have not seen but which are already in preparation and should be released in the following months.

Payment systems

There are major data collections such as FreeBMD (see p. 70) and FamilySearch (see above) which do not charge for access to their material, and there are smaller free collections which are maintained by volunteer efforts or have some source of public funding. But generally there is a charge for access to larger collections of digital records. There are three basic methods that sites use to levy their charges: subscription, pay-per-view and online shop.

Initially sites tended to be pay-per-view, and Ancestry UK was the sole data service which was launched with a subscription-only system. This was almost certainly because these services tended to start with just a small number of datasets – Findmypast, for example, initially had only the BMD indexes. Also, I suspect they were unsure whether the UK's notoriously stingy genealogists would be prepared to commit themselves to an annual charge. But for heavier users a subscription is much more economical, and as the sites have added more and more data, this option has become more attractive both for the companies and for the users.

Now things are much more mixed. Of the major data services discussed later in this chapter, only ScotlandsPeople and two sites specifically targeted at the less experienced and perhaps less committed family historian, Genes Reunited and RootsUK, are exclusively pay-per-view. One of the reasons for this shift is that the data services have started offering things like scanned trade directories where it makes no sense to charge users for each page viewed. Origins went over completely to subscription some years ago, though it is planning to re-introduce a pay-per-view option in 2012, while Ancestry, as a requirement of its census licences from The National Archives, has introduced a pay-per-view option.

In pay-per-view systems you pay, in principle, for each item of data viewed. However, it is problematic to collect small amounts of money via credit and debit cards, not to mention tedious for users to complete a new financial transaction for each individual record they want to view. Therefore, all such systems require you to purchase a block of 'units' or 'credits' in advance, which are then used up as you view data. Generally units are available only in discrete amounts, and work with either real or virtual vouchers for round sums of money. There is usually a time limit, which means you could have units unused at the end of your session. You won't be able to claim a refund, but in some cases you can carry forward unused portions of a payment to a subsequent session.

In an online shop, whether it's for genealogical data or for physical products, you add items to a virtual 'shopping basket' until you have everything you want, and pay for all of them in a single transaction at a virtual 'checkout'. Only then can you download the data you have paid for. Such a procedure would make little sense for individual data entries, but is a good way of delivering entire electronic documents, so it is ideal for the wills available from The National Archives or ScotlandsPeople (see Chapter 8). It also allows items to be priced individually, though these two services in fact charge at a flat rate.

An overview of the current charging systems for the major commercial data services in the UK is shown in Table 4-1.

A useful table comparing the data and facilities offered by the four main data services was published by *Who Do You Think You Are? Magazine* and is available at <**www.thegenealogist.co.uk/images/index/wdytya_j12_comparisonchart.jpg**>

Origins

Origins at <**www.origins.net**> was the first UK genealogy data service, and its website comprises three distinct services: British Origins, Irish Origins, and Scots Origins.

British Origins at <**www.britishorigins.com**> went live at the start of 2001 (under the name English Origins) and currently includes the following main categories of material:

- the National Wills Index
- England and Wales censuses for 1841, 1861 and 1871
- marriage and burial indexes from parish registers and previously published indexes
- apprenticeship records
- militia lists
- civil court records for the 17th and 18th centuries

During 2012 the site will be adding monumental inscriptions and poor law records, and continuing to expand the scope of the National Wills Index.

The records on British Origins will mostly be of use to those who have already got some way with their pedigree, as many of the datasets only go up to the mid-nineteenth century. Unlike most other data services, Origins does not have civil registration records and is not aiming at a complete collection of censuses. The range of records for London, Middlesex and Surrey makes this site especially valuable to those with ancestors from the City and the modern Greater London area.

Irish Origins at <www.irishorigins.com> offers a wide range of Irish datasets, of which the most significant are Griffith's Valuation (1847–1864) and other census substitutes, a substantial collection of wills from the thirteenth to the nineteenth century, and electoral registers from the 1830s. There are also militia records, passenger lists, and nineteenth century trade directories.

Table 4-1 Commercial data services in the UK: subscription prices and facilities (March 2012)

Site	Name of subscription	Duration	Cost	Monthly cost	Datasets
Ancestry	Essentials	1 month	£10.95	£10.95	UK BMD + census
		1 year	£83.40	£6.95	
	Premium	1 month	£12.95	£12.95	All UK + Ireland records
		1 year	£107.40	£8.95	
	Worldwide	1 month	£18.95	£18.95	All records
		1 year	£155.40	£12.95	
Findmypast	Foundation	6 months	£49.95	£8.33	BMD + census
		12 months	£79.95	£6.66	
	Full	6 months	£69.95	£11.66	All records
		12 months	£109.95	£9.16	
	1911 Census Only	6 months	£39.95	£6.66	1911 census
		12 months	£59.95	£5.00	
Origins	British Origins	72 hrs	£7.00	—	UK records
		1 month	£9.50	£9.50	
	Irish Origins	72 hrs	£6.00	—	Ireland records
		1 month	£9.50	£9.50	
	Total Access	72 hrs	£8.00	—	All records
		1 month	£10.50	£10.50	
		1 year	£55.00	£4.58	
The Genealogist	Starter	3 months	£14.95		BMD, census, landowners
		6 months	£28.95	£4.83	
		1 year	£54.95	£4.16	
	Gold	3 months	£24.95		BMD, census 1841–1901, wills, parish records etc.
		6 months	£44.95	£7.49	
		1 year	£78.95	£6.58	
	Diamond	1 year	£149.95	£12.50	All records
Familyrelatives	Subscription	1 year	£30.00	£2.50	All records
Genes Reunited	Platinum	1 month	£19.95	£19.95	All records
		6 months	£50.00	£8.33	
		1 year	£80.00	£6.67	

Table 4-2 Commercial data services in the UK: pay-per-view prices (March 2012)

Site	Type and name of access	No. credits	Duration	Cost	Cost per credit	Typical record costs *(for pre-1911 census unless otherwise noted)*
Ancestry	Pay-as-you-go	12	14 days	£6.95	58p	1 credit
	Pay-as-you-go voucher	10	14 days	£5.75	58p	
Findmypast	PayAsYouGo	60	90 days	£6.95	12p	transcript: 5 credits image: 3 credits
		280	365 days	£24.95	9p	
Genes Reunited	Pay-per-view	50	30 days	£5.00	10p	record or image: 5 credits
		200	90 days	£17.95	9p	
1901 Census Online	Pay-per-view	500	7 days	£5.00	1p	transcript: 50 credits image: 75 credits
1911 Census	Pay-per-view		*identical to Findmypast*			(1911 census) transcript: 10 credits image: 30 credits
The Genealogist	Pay-per-view quarterly	75	3 months	£14.95	20p	search: 1 or 2 credits transcript or image: 3 credits
	Pay-per-view quarterly	175	3 months	£24.95	14p	
	Pay-per-view annual	800	12 months	£55.95	7p	
	BMD Index	50	90 days	£5.00	10p	(no census) BMD images: 1 credit
		200	1 year	£14.95	7p	
Roots UK	Pay-as-you-go	100	unlimited	£5.00	5p	advanced search: 5 credits transcript or image: 5 credits
		400	unlimited	£14.95	4p	
Familyrelatives	Pay-per-view	60	90 days	£6.00	10p	(no census) search results: 2 credits/page image: 1 credit
		150	90 days	£12.00	8p	
ScotlandsPeople	Pay-per-view	30	90 days	£7.00	23p	search results: 1 credit/page Image: 5 credits

Among the further datasets planned are the records of the Royal Ulster Constabulary from The National Archives and a collection of around 200 directories covering the period 1751 to 1900.

At the time of writing Scots Origins offers free searches of christenings and marriages from the IGI (see p. 100) and a place-name search for the 1881 census. But Origins plans to develop this into another subscription service with indexes to all the Scottish censuses and a number of other Scottish datasets, with the first material being released sometime in 2012.

Origins was originally a pay-per-view service but it moved to a subscription system in July 2004. There are a variety of subscriptions: 72 hours or one month for British or Irish Origins, with an additional annual option for the 'Total Access' subscription. The prices are given at <**www.originsnetwork.com/signup-info.aspx**>. If you just want to try the site, the 72-hour subscriptions are relatively expensive, and the one-month option is only a third more for much longer access. Origins have announced, however, that they will be re-introducing a pay-per-view option during 2012. At the time of writing, no payment details were available for Scots Origins, nor how this will integrate with other subscriptions.

There are, broadly speaking, three different types of result you may get from a search on Origins. In the case of many of the indexes, you will probably get all the available information. For other records, Origins has a scan of the original document, which you will be able to view. Finally, for some of the records, the index provides a document reference and you can place an online order for a copy of the document to be made and posted to you (or, of course, you can simply visit the relevant repository). There is a separate charge for these copies as they are made by the supplying organization, not Origins itself.

While the number of search fields is more limited than some other services, they will certainly be enough for most purposes. The site uses the NameX surname-matching system (see p. 40), which has the useful feature that you can select how close a match needs to be. The site's indexes have a good reputation for accuracy.

ScotlandsPeople

The Scottish civil registration indexes were the first genealogical records in the UK to be put online by a government agency, when Scots Origins opened its electronic doors in 1998 to provide the data on behalf of GROS. In 2002, the contract for the online service was awarded to Scotland Online, who now provide it on the ScotlandsPeople site at <**www.scotlandspeople.gov.uk**>. In 2008 Scotland Online took over Findmypast (see below) and changed its name to Brightsolid.

The site was initially designed just to supply the civil registration, census and parish records, but has now expanded its brief to cover all national records, including those previously on the National Archives of Scotland's Scottish Documents site at <www.scottishdocuments.com>, which no longer carries records itself.

ScotlandsPeople offers the following Scottish records:

- civil registration;
- censuses indexes and images;
- church records from the old parish registers, 1553–1854;
- Catholic registers, mostly from the nineteenth century but with some earlier records;
- wills and testaments, 1513–1901;
- coats of arms.

Almost all of this data is exclusive to the site, though Ancestry and Findmypast have their own indexes to some of the Scottish censuses, but without images.

This is a pay-per-view system and you purchase access in blocks of 30 credits for £7. An initial search is free of charge, but this only tells you how many hits your search produces. Each page of search results costs you one unit and includes a maximum of 25 entries, while viewing an image costs five units. In addition to viewing the scanned registers online, you can order a copy of the relevant certificate for £10. This is paid for separately and does not come out of your prepaid units. The absence of a subscription option is an issue for heavy users of the site, especially since you have to pay for each page of search results, which discourages more speculative searching.

The wills and coats of arms are not part of the pay-per-view system but are sold via an online shop (see p. 118).

The site keeps a record of all search results and certificates that you have paid to view, and these can be retrieved at any time, not just during the session in which they were first accessed. You therefore don't need to pay to return to the site to review material you have already paid for, even if you have run out of valid units. You can also download the list of all the records you have viewed in a number of formats

Unfortunately the quality of some of the images is rather poor by the standards of the other data services discussed here: most of the records are black and white, rather than greyscale like photographs (see Figure 5-6). This makes for difficulties in reading some of the poorer quality originals, particularly as they are scanned at only 200 dots per inch. More recently added records, including the 1911 census and the Catholic records, are much more satisfactory: they are in colour and at higher resolution, and can be downloaded in JPEG format. The fact that you have a range of different viewers to choose from is also very welcome.

Ancestry

The Ancestry.com website <www.ancestry.com> is the largest commercial collection of genealogical data. It holds over 25,000 separate datasets, many of them derived from printed materials which may be more or less difficult to find outside a major genealogical library. Ancestry is a long-established US company, and started to host UK data in 2002 with the launch of Ancestry UK at <www.ancestry.co.uk>, offering a subscription covering the UK data only. At the start of 2012, the UK data amounts to around 1,000 datasets.

Among the main records for the British Isles are:

- England and Wales civil registration indexes
- England and Wales census indexes linked to images
- Scotland census indexes without images
- parish and/or probate register extracts
- Pallot's Baptism and Marriage Indexes
- military records
- passenger lists and migration records
- a number of historic books and newspapers

The list of datasets available on Ancestry UK is in the 'Card Catalog' at <search.ancestry.co.uk/search/cardcatalog.aspx>: use the filter options in the left-hand column to see what is available for a particular country or type of record.

Ancestry has traditionally been a subscription service, and a quarterly or annual payment provides unlimited access to *all* databases included in the particular subscription package. There are three levels of subscription:

- Essentials membership: civil registration, census records, WWI military records for the UK; no parish registers or Irish records
- Premium membership: all UK and Ireland records
- Worldwide membership: all Ancestry datasets for all countries

With the introduction of the UK censuses in partnership with The National Archives, a pay-per-view option was introduced, with a payment of £6.95 permitting 12 page views within a 14-day period. This system covers not just the census, but all datasets on the site. If you use the pay-per-view option, you can extend it to a quarterly or annual subscription by paying the difference.

Ancestry offers a 14-day free trial offer, but if you sign up for this you should be aware that a full subscription will be charged automatically to your credit card if you do not cancel before the end of the trial period. Free access to Ancestry's UK data is available from many public libraries, from the Society of Genealogists and from the public computer facilities at The National Archives.

For Americans with UK ancestors, there is a subscription option at the main site which includes both US and UK records. Ancestry's Australian site at <**www.ancestry.com.au**> includes UK records in all subscriptions.

Although Ancestry is a commercial service, some of the material is free of charge. For example, FreeBMD's GRO index data is available here as well as on FreeBMD's own website (see p. 70). Some of the non-record facilities on the site are also available without subscribing.

The site has extremely flexible search facilities, and a striking feature is that searching does not require a surname. This can be very useful if looking for a woman under an earlier or later married name, or if you have simply failed to find the right person searching on the expected surname. While you can choose exact or loose search, with the latter, the site orders results by its own ranking system, which is far from transparent. Ancestry's image quality is generally good and its image viewer has a range of useful options. The site has suffered from some notable lapses in data validation in its census indexes (see p. 33), but the flexibility of the search does help to compensate for errors.

A useful blog is the Ancestry Insider at <**ancestryinsider.blogspot.com**>, which offers an 'unofficial, unauthorized view' of Ancestry.

Findmypast

Findmypast at <**www.findmypast.co.uk**> went live in April 2003, under the name 1837online, offering the GRO indexes. Since then, the company has expanded its material considerably, and in 2008 it was taken over by Brightsolid (see above) and became involved in the project to digitize the 1911 census. At the end of 2009, the Office of Fair Trading approved Brightsolid's acquisition of Friends Reunited, which meant that it took over Genes Reunited. The site offers:

- England and Wales civil registration indexes
- censuses (England and Wales complete, the Scottish censuses are being added)
- parish registers
- migration records (including passenger lists, passport applications and convict transportation)
- a wide range of military records
- occupational records, including apprentices and the Merchant Navy
- poor law records
- school records

The Scottish census indexes are to be completed during 2012, and partnership with the British Library will see the addition of newspapers (see p. 198), electoral registers, and India Office records.

The site operates both subscription and a pay-per-view (they call it 'PayAsYouGo') systems, and the prices are given at <**www.findmypast.co.uk/ payment-step1.action**>. The three different subscription options give access to different datasets: the 1911 Census only subscription, as you'd expect, gives access to only this dataset; the Foundation subscription covers all census and civil registration records; the Full subscription covers all records. The only real benefit of the 1911 only subscription is for those who do subscribe to another data service which does not yet have the full 1911 census. There is a 14-day free trial of the Foundation subscription data.

Findmypast also operates the distinct 1911 census site at <**www.1911census.co.uk**> (see p. 90) and pay-per-view units purchased on either site are available at the other. In May 2011, Findmypast launched a dedicated site for Irish records at <**findmypast.ie**> in association with Eneclann, an Irish company with a genealogy research and data publishing background. Prices are at <**www.findmypast.ie/payments/subscription**>. The site is still very new and the initial records include:

- Griffith's valuation
- many Irish directories
- passengers lists
- prison registers and Petty Sessions records

Material to be added during 2012 includes 13 million cases from Petty Sessions Court Registers and civil registration records.

The company has an Australian site at <**www.findmypast.com.au**>, a US site at <**findmypast.com**>, and also runs a dedicated pay-per-view site with passenger lists only, Ancestorsonboard, at <**www.ancestorsonboard.com**>.

The range of search facilities is very comprehensive for all the datasets, with both basic and advanced searches for the census records as well as the ability to search on a census reference.

Genes Reunited

With its pedigree database and contact service, Genes Reunited at <**www.genesreunited.co.uk**> is best known as a social networking site, and this aspect of the site is covered in Chapter 14 (p. 233). In 2006, it added the 1901 Census index followed by further data collections, licensed from The Genealogist. Brightsolid's acquisition of Friends Reunited in 2010 meant that it took over Genes Reunited. The data collections are few in number compared to the sites discussed above:

- England and Wales census indexes
- England and Wales civil registration
- WWI and WWII deaths
- passenger lists and other overseas records
- The British Newspaper Archive

These indexes and images are identical to their equivalents on Findmypast with the exception of the 1901 census – Genes Reunited still offers the original 1901 census index and not the separate index created by Findmypast.

The site's pricing appears complicated since it combines subscription and pay-per-view options. First, all data is available on a pay-per-view basis. Second, there is a Platinum subscription which covers the same material as Findmypast's Foundation subscription, with unlimited access to all civil registration and census records (as well as the contact service), though you need to use pay-per-view for other records. The Standard subscription does not cover records at all – it only covers the contact service. However, the site offers images of the original GRO index books free to all users, though the individual names are not indexed.

In spite of the duplication between Genes Reunited and Findmypast, the two sites are really aimed at different types of user. Genes Reunited, with subscriptions for only the core genealogical records and very basic search facilities, is clearly designed for the relative beginner, mainly perhaps the person who has uploaded a family tree for their immediate family and wants to start looking at nineteenth-century records. Certainly, once you need to move beyond civil registration and census records, Findmypast's Full subscription is the better value for money, and its more flexible search options are ideal for the more experienced family historian.

The Genealogist

The Genealogist at <**www.thegenealogist.co.uk**> is a data service run by S&N Genealogy Supplies, well known as a software retailer and publisher of genealogical records on CD-ROM. It provides a wide range of resources, including:

- England and Wales civil registration indexes
- England and Wales census indexes
- parish registers, both transcripts and scans of published indexes
- non-conformist records
- an extensive collection of trade and professional directories
- military records

Additional records in the pipeline include major newspapers and an expanded range of Welsh parish registers.

There are a range of payment options:

- Subscription with unlimited access to records – but three different subscriptions each offer a different selection of records, from the starter (civil registration and census records) to the Diamond (all records).
- BMD Index, a combination subscription/pay-per-view option with a limit of 50 credits for 90 days.
- Personal Pay-as-you-go option.

Full details are available from <www.thegenealogist.co.uk/nameindex/products.php> and the choice of datasets is shown at <www.thegenealogist.co.uk/compare.php>.

The civil registration records are also made available on The Genealogist's BMDindex site at <www.bmdindex.co.uk>, which operates a pay-per-view system. They also run a separate site BMDregisters at <www.bmdregisters.co.uk>, which contains non-conformist and non-parochial birth and burial records, described on p. 109.

The Master Search offers not only a person search but also, for the census records, family and address searches. A particularly interesting option is the facility to search for family members solely on the basis of their forenames, which is a novel way to get round seriously illegible surnames in census records. Apart from the Master Search, there are also separate, tailored search facilities for the individual categories of record.

Roots UK

The Genealogist also runs RootsUK at <www.rootsuk.com>. This site is targeted more at the relative newcomer and offers only the data that those starting their family history will need, along with much simpler search facilities. This makes the site ideal for the relative novice but probably too limited for the experienced genealogist. The data available comprises:

- civil registration
- England and Wales census records 1841–1901
- 2005 London electoral roll

All indexes and images are identical to those on The Genealogist, but the site offers only pay-per-view access, though initial searches are free. The basic search facilities are very basic (just forename and surname), but for each set of records there is a more flexible advanced search.

Familyrelatives

Familyrelatives was launched at the end of 2004 at <**www.familyrelatives.com**>. It started off with just the civil registration indexes, but now has a much wider range of material. The site's datasets include:

- England and Wales civil registration indexes
- trade and professional directories, including many for Scotland
- scans of printed parish register transcriptions
- military records
- Irish wills and other Irish records

Additions during 2012 are planned to include both Australian and US material, as well as divorce and convict records.

Familyrelatives operate both a subscription and a pay-per-view system. The latter gives access to the civil registration records and some of the military and parish records. A comparison of the two options is provided at <**www.familyrelatives.com/information/info_detail.php?id=120**>.

Other sites

The sites discussed above are, at the start of 2012, the most important commercial data services for UK genealogy, but they are not the only ones, and a number of local or specialized collections are mentioned in later chapters.

There are two sites specifically for Ireland (in addition to the Irish sites of Origins and Findmypast, mentioned above). The Irish Family History Foundation has a data service at <**www.rootsireland.ie**>, with over 188 million records, of which over three-quarters are church records. The site operates a pay-per-view system costing a rather expensive €5 per record. Searching is free, though you have to register. One significant limitation is that if you do not specify a year in your search, only the first 10 results are shown. AncestryIreland is run by the Ulster Historical Foundation at <**www.ancestryireland.com**>. It has birth, death and marriage records for County Antrim and County Down available on a pay-per-view basis, with free searches but, again, a rather expensive charge of £4 to view a record. There are many other types of record available to members of the Ulster Genealogical and Historical Guild, subscription to which costs £30 per annum.

The only real competitor to Ancestry in terms of worldwide coverage is the US-based World Vital Records at <**www.worldvitalrecords.com**>. While there is a US-only subscription, access to the UK datasets requires a World Collection Membership at $119.40. All the UK data are licensed from other companies, including military records and passenger lists from British Origins, and the England and Wales censuses from Findmypast. The site is probably not worth considering if you only have ancestors from the British Isles, but for an American family with some roots in Britain or Ireland, it could be very useful.

Document services

The data services discussed above mainly offer individual entries from much larger sets of records, but an alternative way of making records available is to offer a scan of a whole document for a one-off payment, via an online shop rather than by subscription or pay-per-view.

ScotlandsPeople in fact offers this alongside its pay-per-view service. For the Scottish wills and coats of arms, you pay a flat rate for a digital scan. In these cases, there is no transcription, just an index to help you identify the correct document. Once paid for, you can download a PDF file with scans of all the pages in the original combined in a single document.

While The National Archives does not run its own data service, and instead licenses its records to commercial partners, it does have an electronic document download facility as part of the Discovery service (see p. 210). This is not aimed solely at genealogists but at all those who need to consult its records. It therefore includes things like Cabinet papers and Ministry of Defence UFO reports. The categories of document of most interest to family historians include:

- a range of army records, particularly relating to medals, but including WAAC service records;
- navy records, including many service records;
- wills and death duties, including Prerogative Court of Canterbury wills 1384–1858;
- aliens registration cards.

Most documents cost £3.50 to download, but medal cards are £2.

A commercial document service is The Original Record at <www.theoriginalrecord.com>, which has a very sizeable collection of indexed scans of printed records. Many of them are lists which are not available elsewhere on the web and may only be found in specialist libraries. The site does not offer a master listing, you can only find out what is available by selecting one of the decades between 1000 and 1950 to see what it contains. But, for example, the decade 1900–1909 includes:

- Boys entering Sherborne School (1904)
- Associate Members of the Institution of Civil Engineers (1904)
- Outstanding soldiers of the 10th (The Prince of Wales' Own Royal) Hussars (1881–1901)

- Missing Next-of-Kin and Heirs-at-Law (1900)
- Nottingham borough officers and officials (1836–1900)

Unfortunately, there are two things which make the site less useful than it first appears. First, the search facility permits search on surname and date range only. This is perhaps inevitable given the many different types of sources, but it makes it very difficult to be sure a match is the person you are looking for, so you may therefore end up paying for many more documents than you actually need. Second, given that uncertainty, the price per document of £4 or more seems rather high. An annual subscription, with unlimited record downloads costs £100.

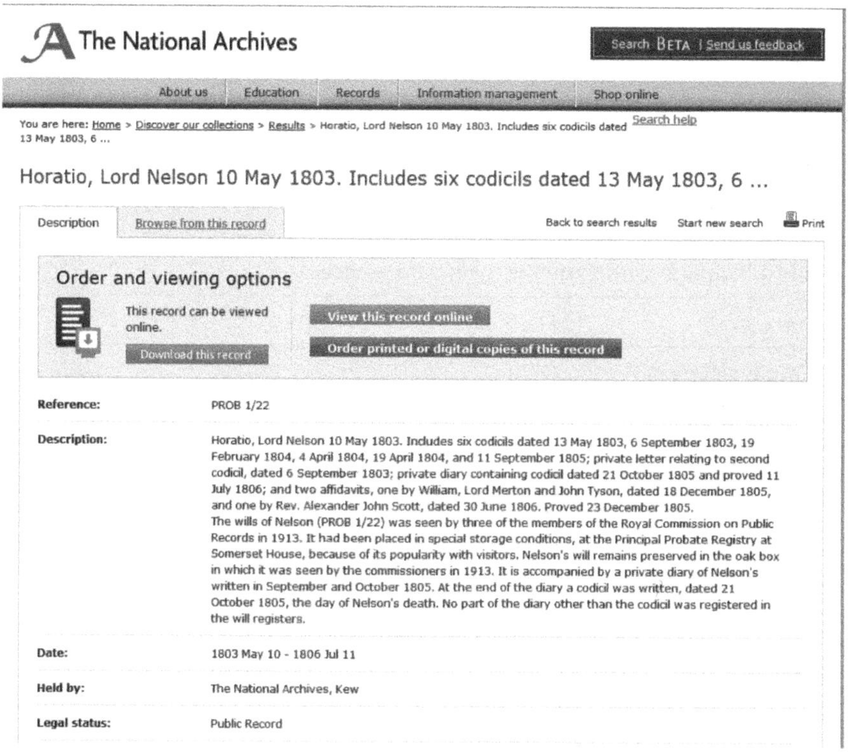

Figure 4-6 The National Archives' Discovery service: entry for the will of Horatio Nelson

Image formats and viewers

One issue that faces anyone using online services that provide images of original records is the file format of the image and the viewer needed to view them. You might think that you don't want and indeed don't need to worry about this. But it is in fact one of the main sources of problems in the data services. Even if you can see the image without problems in your browser, are you sure that when you save it to your hard disk, you have software on your machine that can display the image? Will you be able to crop or enhance it in order to suit your own particular requirements?

It would be easy to fill 20 pages with discussion of the online services' image facilities and how to make the most of them. Here, I will just look at the main image formats and some of the issues with the image viewers the sites use. Note that several of the data services offer alternative viewers or file formats (ScotlandsPeople offers six!), and in some cases different datasets use different image formats.

Record images on these sites are, on the whole, monochrome, since most of them have been created by digitizing microfilms made often many years ago. However, more recently filmed material, such as the 1911 census, has been created directly from the original records with digital cameras, and is in colour. Table 4-3 below shows the image formats used by the main commercial services.

Table 4-3 Image formats on the main data services

Ancestry	Flash, JPG
Familyrelatives	DjVu
Findmypast	DjVu, Flash
Genes Reunited	PDF, JPG
Origins	TIFF
ScotlandsPeople	PDF, Flash, direct viewer (JPG), direct download (TIFF), Java Applet, ActiveX (Internet Explorer only)
The Genealogist	PDF

Adobe Acrobat (PDF)

Adobe Acrobat is, at first sight, a pretty unproblematic format. It is not in fact an image format at all, rather a *document* format which can incorporate images. It is often referred to as 'PDF', which stands for 'portable document format', and Acrobat files always end in the extension *.pdf*. Its particular advantage for genealogical records is that it can combine many images in a single file, each on its own page. This makes it ideal for multi-page documents like a will, which can be downloaded in one file containing a separate image of each page.

To view Acrobat files you need the Adobe Acrobat Reader. Acrobat files are so widely used on the web that unless you are an internet novice using a new-ish computer, you will almost certainly have the software installed already. If not, it can be downloaded free of charge from Adobe's home page at <**www.adobe.com**>. When you install it, your browser will automatically be configured so that it knows to use the reader when it comes across an Acrobat file, and it will display the document within the browser window.

Once you have downloaded a PDF file (click on the 'Save a copy' icon at the top left of the reader window), you can view it again by clicking on its icon – this will automatically start the Acrobat reader.

The problem with Acrobat files comes when you want to manipulate the images. You might think you won't want to do this, but at some point you will certainly want to extract from a page just the bit you need; or you may want to adjust the contrast or brightness to see if you can read something that looks illegible. But since PDF is not a graphics format, you cannot simply load it into a graphics program to carry out these tasks. And the Acrobat Reader cannot save a file in any other format.

The way around the problem is:

1. click on the snapshot tool in the toolbar at the top of the Acrobat Reader window;
2. click with the cursor on any corner of the area you want to extract;
3. drag the cursor until the highlighted rectangle encloses the area you want;
4. release the mouse button.

At this point an image of the selected area has been saved on the Clipboard, and you should be able to paste it into your graphics editor.

JPG

JPG or JPEG is probably the most widely used graphics file format on the web. Browsers can display JPG images without additional software, and any graphics editor can be used to edit them. However, the data services do not simply display the JPG image in the browser window, but it is loaded into a special viewer page which has a range of controls at the top for things like zoom, rotate image and save.

TIFF

The TIFF format is a very common image format for professional graphics work, but is not that common on the web, and browsers cannot display TIFF images without special software. ScotlandsPeople only offers TIFF as a download format, in fact. Any graphics editor, however, should be able to deal with TIFF files.

Origins recommends that you install a free viewer called AlternaTIFF, and the 'can't view image?' link at the bottom of every image display page brings up information about this and how to install it. In fact, even if your browser already has a plug-in which displays TIFF images, it may be worth installing AlternaTIFF since it offers several useful tools for viewing: zooming, panning, printing and saving are all catered for. If you are using a Mac, you should find that a TIFF image is displayed automatically using Apple's QuickTime plug-in, though this does not offer any image controls to zoom or print the page. Origins' help page on image viewing at <**www.originsnetwork.com/ helpimages.aspx**> covers all aspects of viewing the site's TIFF images.

Flash

Flash is used by Ancestry and Findmypast, and is one of ScotlandsPeople's options. It is a very widely used file format, particularly for animation, and you may well have the player software installed already. If not it can be downloaded free of charge from Adobe's home page at <**www.adobe.com**>, just like the Acrobat Reader. When you save an image from the Flash player, it is saved in JPG format (see above).

DjVu

DjVu (pronounced like *déjà vu*) is a fairly exotic graphics format and you may well never have encountered it before, which means that before you can view the images, you will need to install the DjVu viewer. Familyrelatives uses it for all images; on Findmypast it is the Enhanced Viewer and brings a number of advantages over Flash, most notably much improved download speed.

There is no need to repeat here the instructions on how to install this, which will be found on the two sites (at <**www.findmypast.co.uk/helpadvice/ faqs/djVu-viewer/**> and <**www.familyrelatives.com/information/info_ detail.php?id=40**>). But you need to be aware that there are potential installation difficulties, depending on your browser and its configuration, so it really is a good idea to refer to the relevant help page first, and not just after you encounter a problem.

The DjVu viewer does have one significant problem: very few graphics editors can deal with images in this format, so you may be unable to edit the images with the graphics software you normally use. There are two solutions:

1. Ignore the 'Save Image' button and instead right-click on the image, then select 'Export to File'. From the drop-down file type list, ignore DjVu and

select BMP. This is the standard Windows Bitmap format, which any graphics program should be able to deal with.

2. Find a graphics program which supports the DjVu image format. For example, you can download the IrfanView graphics viewer for Windows, free from <**www.irfanview.com**>, and this has a DjVu plug-in which can also be downloaded.

You don't need to worry about this unless you want to edit a DjVu image; you will still be able to view the saved images – clicking on the file name in an Explorer window on the PC will load the image in a standalone version of the DjVu viewer.

Which data service?

It would be nice to make a firm recommendation as to the best of the data services discussed on the previous pages, or give them comparative scores. However, it would be very difficult to justify doing so.

For a start, it will depend on your genealogical needs and your budget. If you are on a tight budget, then you will probably want to stick to the sites with pay-per-view options rather than subscriptions. If you are already quite advanced with your family tree, you will probably want to avoid the more basic services and go for a site with a wider range of records and more sophisticated searching. All of these sites have their fans and their critics. Often people simply prefer the search facilities or the interface on one site rather than another. Many of the sites offer additional facilities, particularly the ability to maintain an online family tree, which might sway you one way or another.

The other problem is that even if you are reading this book very soon after it comes off the press, one or more of the sites will have improved facilities and additional datasets which may increase its usefulness to you.

One thing that is certainly impossible is to say much about the quality of the data. The quality is highly dependent on the nature of the original records and with many records indexed from microfilm rather than the original, poor quality filming can limit the quality of even the most diligently indexed records. Also, while the major sites all do significant amounts of digitization and indexing in-house, they all also license existing datasets from elsewhere, so the quality of one set of records is no guide to the quality of another. Even where direct comparisons can be made, most obviously in the census records, it would be quite impossible to take a large enough sample for a statistically meaningful result.

The three sites that suit both beginners and advanced users are Ancestry, Findmypast and The Genealogist. Origins is not really aimed at those just starting their research but is designed more for those who want to move beyond the obvious core records. If you're a relative beginner and don't (yet) need anything beyond civil registration and census records, then RootsUK and Genes Reunited are worth looking at. Origins and Familyrelatives probably have the best collections of Irish data, though Findmypast Ireland will no doubt be catching them up. Ancestry clearly has the largest number of datasets overall. Perhaps the only thing that can be said with certainty, for the moment at least, is that if you are researching Scottish ancestors, you will need to use ScotlandsPeople.

While in the long term, for the serious family historian, a subscription is obviously the best option overall, initially it may be worth using the free trial and cheaper pay-per-view options to get a feel for the sites which have what you want.

Free access

An issue which may definitely influence your choice may be the availability of free access. The three main commercial services all have library subscriptions available to institutions, and it may be that your local public library offers one or other of these services to ticket holders free of charge.

Other than that, there are two physical locations which offer some free access on-site:

- The National Archives' cyber café offers free access to all datasets on commercial services which are licensed from them.
- The Society of Genealogists has an 'open access area' where non-members can use the Society's computer facilities to access several of the data services covered in this chapter. Details are at <**www.sog.org.uk/library/ openaccess.pdf**>.

While these may not provide everyday access if you live far from London, their locations do mean that you can combine using online data services with a research trip to consult other records.

Common problems

It is not uncommon for users to experience problems with commercial genealogy sites, as indeed with all e-commerce sites. This is nothing to do with the security concerns people have about online payments (these are addressed in Chapter 18), but relate to the web browser and how it is configured. While it is not possible here to cover every eventuality, most of these problems arise from a readily identifiable set of facilities used by commercial websites, and are more or less straightforward to solve. Sites that use such facilities usually provide information on what is required – see, for example, The National Archives' 'Technical settings' page for its document service at <**www.nationalarchives.gov.uk/documentsonline/ help/help-technical.asp**> – and you should normally see a warning if some required facility is absent from your configuration.

The main features which cause problems are:

Cookies

A 'cookie' is a piece of information a website stores on your hard disk for its own future use. This is how a site can 'remember' who you are from one visit to the next. However, browsers can be configured to reject cookies, and some people do this to preserve their internet privacy. This will make pay-per-view sites and online shops unusable – in fact any site that requires some sort of login will only work with cookies enabled. If you are concerned about cookies, you can configure your browser to accept only those sites you specify. The online help for your browser should tell you how to check whether cookies are enabled. Most sites that require cookies will also give instructions.

JavaScript

This is a scripting language which, among other things, makes it possible for a web page to validate what the user enters in an online form (checking, for example, that you haven't left some crucial field blank) before the information is submitted. You will be unable to use sites that require this if JavaScript is disabled. The online help for your browser should tell you how to check whether JavaScript is enabled, and how to ensure it is. Most sites that require it will also give instructions.

Java

Java is a programming language which allows programs (called 'applets', i.e. small applications) to run on any type of computer as long as it has software installed which can understand the language. This allows for programmable websites. Java facilities (referred to as a 'Java virtual machine') are normally installed and enabled automatically when you install a new browser, but can be disabled. Individual websites download their own applets to your machine – you will often see a grey box saying 'loading' in the browser window while an applet is being downloaded. The online help for your browser should tell you how to check whether Java is enabled, and how to ensure it is.

Plug-ins

A 'plug-in' is a small utility program which a web browser uses to display material which it can't handle with its own built-in facilities. A number of plug-ins are fairly standard (for example, Flash and QuickTime) and may well be on your machine already. But some commercial sites have their own plug-ins for viewing images of documents – this is the case for the 1901 Census site, ScotlandsPeople and Findmypast. A plug-in needs to be downloaded before it can be run. This will usually take significantly longer than a normal web page to download, but once the plug-in is installed you won't need to repeat the process. The National Archives site has a useful page on plug-ins at <**www.nationalarchives.gov.uk/help/technical-plugins.htm**>, with links so you can download some of the most common.

Compatibility
Although the web is based on open standards, browsers do not all implement these as fully and consistently as they might. Also, some website designers insist on using features that only work properly on a particular browser (usually Internet Explorer). The only way around problems from this source is to have a recent version of your preferred browser and, if that is not Internet Explorer, a copy of that too. Since all the main browsers can be downloaded free, there's no real reason not to have the latest version, unless your computer is running an old operating system or has limited memory or disk space. However, older and less compliant versions of Internet Explorer are dropping out of use and IE is no longer so dominant in the browser market, so the number of sites which work properly with it alone has fallen considerably.

If you have any difficulties with online data services, there will always be a variety of help available. Sites selling data should always have a help page, and perhaps a separate technical help page which spells out hardware and/or software requirements. You are very likely to find a FAQ ('Frequently Asked Questions') page. As a last resort there should always be an email address to contact for assistance, and there may also be a telephone helpline.

Incidentally, for a commercial, official or major volunteer-run site, it is a good idea to mail the webmaster if you find pages that don't display properly in your browser.

5

CIVIL REGISTRATION

Birth, marriage and death certificates are generally the first official documents the family historian encounters. In an ideal world – for the genealogist at least – all of them would be online. But privacy concerns make it unlikely that full certificate details for 'recent' events will be easily accessible on the web, and so far only a small percentage of the 'historical' certificates, those from Scotland, are available online.

But even where certificates are not online, there is much information about birth, death and marriage records on the web to help you identify and order paper certificates, including a wide range of sites with the civil registration indexes, which hold the information you need to apply for a paper certificate.

Divorce is under the jurisdiction of the courts rather than the registration service and is therefore covered with other records of the civil courts on p. 127.

England and Wales

Civil registration of births, marriages and deaths started in England and Wales on 1 July 1837, and the original certificates are held in duplicate by the original local register office and by the General Register Office (GRO), which in 2008 became part of the Home Office's Identity and Passport Service (IPS). The original certificates are not yet available online, but copies can be ordered from the GRO via the web, by post or phone. The indexes to the certificates can all be consulted online on free or commercial sites.

The GRO no longer has its own website, but has pages on the government website Directgov with the unhelpfully long URL <**www.direct.gov.uk/en/ Governmentcitizensandrights/Registeringlifeevents/**>. The rather more user-friendly address <**www.direct.gov.uk/gro**> automatically redirects you to this page.

In addition to information about ordering certificates, the site has two articles aimed at genealogists. 'Using the General Register Office to research family history' contains basic information, designed for those new to genealogy, about the GRO indexes, and it links to a document showing exactly which pieces of information are contained in the birth, marriage, and death *indexes* at different periods. 'Researching family history using official records' takes this further, with details of what information is on the *certificates* themselves and various other registers held by the GRO.

The GRO does not yet have a data service – the planned project for making certificates available online has been repeatedly delayed, and this is discussed below. However, there is an online service for ordering certificates, which is still on the old GRO site at <**www.gro.gov.uk/gro/content/certificates/**> (covering England and Wales only). In order to use the online ordering system you need to log in, and if you register (rather than using a one-off guest login) your details will be stored for future use and will not have to be re-entered for subsequent orders. If you do not already know the GRO index reference for the event, you will need to give quite detailed information including the exact date and place of the event. This is fine if it's your own birth certificate, but for deceased ancestors you are unlikely to have the complete and accurate information required for this, so before ordering a certificate you will need to refer to one of the services discussed below to establish the index reference for a particular certificate.

There are also pages about civil registration on the IPS website at <**www.homeoffice.gov.uk/agencies-public-bodies/ips/civil-registration/**> but this material is at the level of policy rather than practical information for genealogists.

Beyond these sites, there are many unofficial sources of information on general registration which will be helpful for initial orientation. Genuki has a page devoted to civil registration in England and Wales at <**www.genuki.org.uk/big/eng/civreg/**>. Barbara Dixon's Registration Certificate Tutorials site at <**home.clara.net/dixons/Certificates/indexbd.htm**> describes how to order certificates and gives a detailed description of the fields on the three types of certificate. Another useful guide is Kimberley Powell's 'Civil Registration in England and Wales. How to Get Birth, Death & Marriage Certificates' at <**genealogy.about.com/od/england/a/bmd.htm**>.

In addition to the mainland records, the GRO holds records of events registered by UK nationals overseas. They mainly comprise records for the armed forces and events notified to British consuls or UK High Commissioners, but they also include births and deaths at sea, for example.

Digitization of certificates

While Scotland, as described later in this chapter, has had most of its civil registration records online since 1998, the story for England and Wales has been a very different one. The process has been long and tortuous, and hardly reflects well on the GRO, with plenty of controversy and still no firm end in sight.

As early as January 2002, a government white paper *Civil Registration: Vital Change* proposed moving to an online certificate service. After the initial proposals ran into objections, both genealogical and parliamentary, in 2005 the GRO eventually launched the DOVE (Digitization of Vital Events) project. This aimed to digitize all birth, marriage and death records up to 2006, and the contract for the project was awarded to Siemens. Meanwhile, the closure of the Family Records Centre in Islington went ahead, partly justified by the claim that, with all the records imminently online, there was no need for GRO indexes to have a physical home. In January 2007, it was announced that online searching of the indexes would be available from early 2008. But then, in July 2008, the GRO announced that, with roughly half the work done, the contract with Siemens had expired and was not being renewed. In 2009, they announced that it was reviewing the whole matter, and future progress would apparently depend on whether 'the business case confirms that sufficient benefits will result from digitization'. In November 2011, it was announced on the IPS's website that the project, now called 'Digitization and Indexing', had actually been on 'pause status' since September 2010 but in 2012 the IPS would be coming to a decision on the future. Given that half of the work is still to be done, we must assume that the certificates will not be available online until 2015 at the very earliest.

If any decision has been made by the time you read this, you should find an official announcement on the IPS's 'Modernising civil registration' page at <**www.homeoffice.gov.uk/agencies-public-bodies/ips/civil-registration/ modernising-civil-registration/**>, and new developments (or the lack of them) are widely discussed on genealogy blogs (see p. 383) and discussion forums (Chapter 18).

The GRO indexes

In 1998, in the absence of any official programme to digitize either the original certificates or the GRO indexes, a volunteer project called FreeBMD secured official permission to transcribe the indexes over 100 years old for free online access. In 2003, the GRO announced a completely open policy – any organization which has purchased the microfiche indexes is now free to transcribe or digitize the original pages and make them available online, free or charged, with no cut-off in years of coverage. This has provided impetus for a number of online services offering digitized images of the original indexes.

While the older indexes are contained in physical books, scans of which are available online, the material from 1984 onwards is rather different: the GRO has electronic records from this date, held in a number of databases. It has permitted these, too, to be made available online. The advantage of the

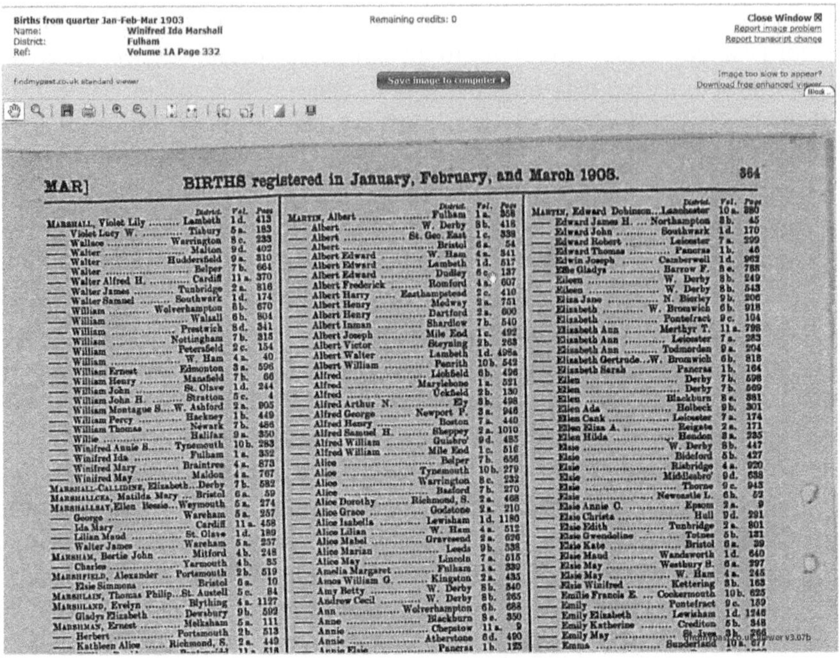

Figure 5-1 An image of the original GRO indexes (Findmypast)

databases over the older material is that entries can be searched for individually – rather than having to look at a series of pages in the hope of identifying the correct entry, you can search the whole range of years at once. However, most of the services described below have now actually transcribed all or most of the pre-1984 indexes.

The GRO ceased to supply indexes to third parties after 2005, and these can only be consulted in person at seven libraries around the country, listed on the 'Using the General Register Office to research family history' article mentioned above.

FreeBMD

FreeBMD is one of the most successful collaborative projects the genealogy world has seen. It has a massive group of over 11,500 volunteers, who either transcribe the indexes from digital images in planned extractions or simply submit entries from their own extractions along with the surrounding entries. It has two sites: <www.freebmd.org.uk> is the home site, and there is also a copy on RootsWeb at <freebmd.rootsweb.com>, which can be useful in periods when the main site is busy and therefore slow to respond to searches. Also, Ancestry includes FreeBMD data up to 1915 in its general BMD search (see below).

By the start of 2012, the project's database had reached 210 million distinct records. The original plan was to capture all the nineteenth-century entries and this has more or less been achieved. The data is in fact largely complete up to 1938, with significant inroads already made into the 1940s and 1950s, particularly for marriages and deaths. Up-to-date information on the percentage of coverage for each year and each type of event will be found at <**www.freebmd.org.uk/progress.shtml**>, and it is a good idea to check this before carrying out a search – even for the nineteenth century there are one or two years with small gaps still to be filled.

All the entries so far transcribed can be searched online. A comprehensive search page (Figure 5-2) allows you to search for a specific person in a chosen place and date range, or to extract all the entries for a particular surname.

Figure 5-2 shows a search for the marriage of Frederick Marshall in London between 1885 and 1890. Figure 5-3 shows the results of this search. On the results page, clicking on the links in the 'district' column will take you to information on the registration district, while following the link in the 'page' column brings up a list of all the events on that page in the original register (*not* the index). The reason this is useful is that, in the case of a marriage, *one* of the other names on that same page will be the name of the spouse. In this case, Figure 5-4 shows that Frederick must have married either Harriett Ann Bishop (as he in fact did, they are my great-grandparents) or Cecilia Julia Stevenson. And of course the other of these ladies will have

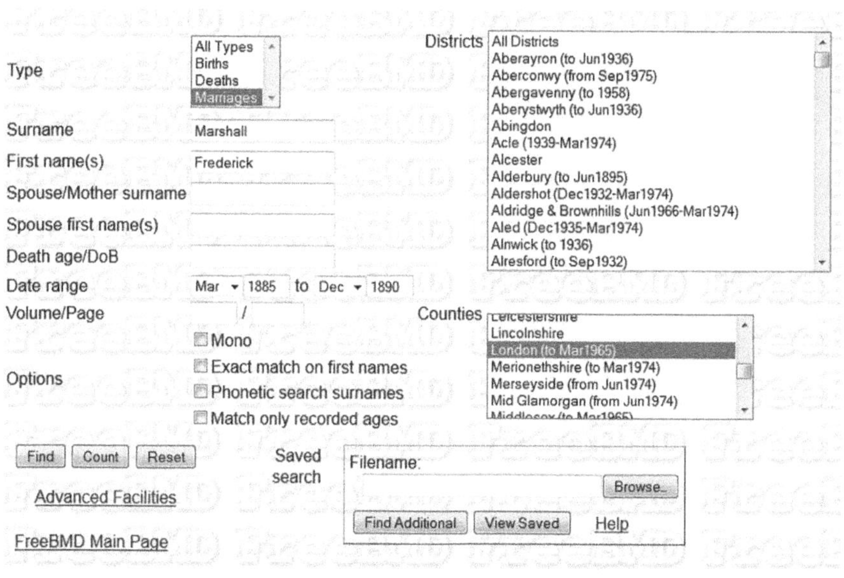

Figure 5-2 Searching FreeBMD

married John Alfred Parker. If you have already found this family in a later census, and know the husband's name and the wife's forename, it means you should be able to establish a wife's maiden name without even ordering the marriage certificate.

| Search for | *Type:* Marriages | *Surname:* Marshall | *First name(s):* Frederick |
| | *Start date:* Mar 1885 | *End date:* Dec 1890 | *County:* London |

Whilst FreeBMD makes every effort to ensure accurate transcription, errors exist in both the original index and the transcription. Y reference given from a copy of the index before ordering a certificate. If an entry has the symbol 🔍 next to it you can view the s which the transcription was made in order to verify the reference. Click on the 🔍 symbol to view the scan.

If you are SURE that our transcription(s) below differs from the GRO index, you can submit a correction request by clicking on the in question.

Surname	First name(s)	District	Vol Page	
	Marriages Dec 1885 (>99%)			
Marshall	Frederick	Islington	1b 532	Info 🔍
	Marriages Jun 1886 (>99%)			
MARSHALL	Frederick	St. Geo. H. Sq.	1a 816	Info 🔍
	Marriages Dec 1886 (>99%)			
Marshall	Frederick	Fulham	1a 443	Info
	Marriages Mar 1888 (>99%)			
Marshall	Frederick William	Fulham	1a 362	Info 🔍
	Marriages Jun 1888 (>99%)			
Marshall	Frederick	Mile End	1c 777	Info 🔍
Marshall	Frederick Charles	Pancras	1b 173	Info 🔍
	Marriages Jun 1889 (>99%)			
Marshall	Frederick William	St. Olave	1d 492	Info 🔍
	Marriages Sep 1890 (>99%)			
MARSHALL	Frederick	Pancras	1b 312	Info 🔍
	Marriages Dec 1890 (>99%)			
Marshall	Frederick Octavius	Camberwell	1d 1311	Info 🔍

Figure 5-3 FreeBMD search results

Surname	First name(s)	District	Vol Page	
	Marriages Mar 1888 (>99%)			
BISHOP	Harriett Ann	Fulham	1a 362	Info 🔍
Marshall	Frederick William	Fulham	1a 362	Info 🔍
Parker	John Alfred	Fulham	1a 362	Info 🔍
STEVENSON	Cecilia Julia	Fulham	1a 362	Info 🔍

Figure 5-4 Identifying a spouse in FreeBMD

A very useful feature is the ability to save a search and re-run it at any time. When you repeat a saved search, you see only new records that have been added since you saved. One limitation you may encounter with a common name is that the maximum number of search results for any search is 3,000 records.

Although the main focus of the project is the transcription of indexes, FreeBMD also makes digitized images of the original index pages available free of charge. There is no search facility for this – once you have selected the type of event, the year and quarter, and the initial letter of the surname, it is up to you to judge where in the pages for that letter your surname occurs. In some cases, therefore, you may need to view several images to get the right one. The site gives you several image formats to choose from: PDF, GIF, JPG and TIFF. Of these, the JPG is the largest, with files around 3Mb in size. The GIFs are around 450Mb and the other formats around half that.

FreeBMD is always looking for new volunteers, and details of what is involved can be found on the website. You can keep up to date with the progress of the project by joining the FreeBMD-News-L mailing list – subscription information will be found at <**lists.rootsweb.ancestry.com/ index/intl/UK/FreeBMD-News.html**>.

Commercial indexes

The complete set of GRO indexes up to 2005 is available on many of the commercial data services. With the progress of FreeBMD up to the 1930s and the expansion of other data on these services, you are no longer likely to be choosing your data service mainly on the basis of their GRO indexes as was the case perhaps five years ago. For that reason, only the differences in coverage (rather than price, search facilities, etc.) are discussed here.

All the services included here offer:

- the GRO's own searchable databases for events from 1984 onwards
- images of the original index books for the pre-1984 period with a search that enables you, more or less precisely, to locate the page image for a particular quarter which has the entries for a particular surname.

The problem with the latter material is that, unless you know exactly when an event was registered, you will have to check the index page image for each quarter individually. For that reason, the data services have all created their own databases of the individual entries from the period before 1984 for at least part of the material.

- Findmypast and Genes Reunited have all pre-1984 entries individually indexed.

- The Genealogist and BMDindex have births from 1950 and marriages from 1837 individually indexed; the remaining birth entries and all the death entries should be completed early in 2012.
- Familyrelatives has a searchable index for the period 1866–1920.
- Ancestry has the FreeBMD index for 1837–1915, and its own index for 1916–1983.

The Genealogist, BMDindex, Findmypast and Genes Reunited all include the overseas records mentioned on p. 68.

Local BMD projects

While all the sites mentioned so far are national in coverage, there are a number of projects centred on local register offices. These go under the generic name UKBMD, and links to all local BMD projects will be found on Ian Hartas's UKBMD site at <**www.ukbmd.org.uk**>.

It's not just that these sites supplement the national datasets. An important difference between these and all the national sites mentioned above is that they work from the original local registration records and so will be largely free of the errors that dog the GRO indexes. (The latter were made from copies of the original registrations, putting them at two removes from the originals.) If your family comes from one of the parts of the country covered, these should be used in preference to the services mentioned in the previous sections.

The first of these projects was CheshireBMD at <**cheshirebmd.org.uk**>, a collaboration between Cheshire County Council, Wirral Metropolitan Borough, and the Family History Society of Cheshire.

Cheshire aims to have all index entries for births, marriages and deaths online for the period 1837–1950. The site has detailed information on the coverage so far for each registration district, and makes the ordering of certificates very straightforward – a link from each search result brings up a form for printing off, with the certificate reference (though not the other details) already filled in (Figure 5-5). The Cheshire site already has over six million entries available for searching.

So far seven similar projects have taken a lead from the example of Cheshire, and use the same website design and software:

- BathBMD at <**www.bathbmd.org.uk**> has just over one million entries.
- BerkshireBMD at <**www.berkshirebmd.org.uk**> contains around 550,000 records.
- Cumbria at <**www.cumbriabmd.org.uk**> contains around 525,000 records.

Cheshire BMD

Births,Marriages and Deaths on the Internet

Births	Marriages	Deaths
2,997,364	1,059,100	2,059,864

Last updated: 06 January 2012

In the results below, the reference number will be a link. Clicking on this link will add your choice to a summary list on a new page. From this summary page you will be able to review all your search results and you will find links to printable application forms which can be used to order the certificate for the index entry. Full details of the charges and the Register Office address can be found on the form.

Cheshire Birth indexes for the years: 1851

Surname	Forename(s)	Sub-District	Registers At	Mother's Maiden Name	Reference
EDWARDS	(boy)	Chester Cathedral	Cheshire West		CAT/13/13
EDWARDS	(boy)	Malpas	Wrexham		ML/5/98
EDWARDS	Ann	Congleton	Cheshire East		CON/11/60
EDWARDS	Ann	Eastham	Cheshire West		EAS/6/52
EDWARDS	Ann	Hawarden	Flintshire East - Hawarden		HAW/4/76
EDWARDS	Ann	Hawarden	Flintshire East - Hawarden		HAW/4/79
EDWARDS	Ann	Hawarden	Flintshire East - Hawarden		HAW/4/84
EDWARDS	Ann	Nantwich	Cheshire Central		NA/08/090
EDWARDS	Ann	Nantwich	Cheshire Central		NA/08/100
EDWARDS	Anne Elizabeth	Daresbury	Halton		DAR/5/48
EDWARDS	Arthur Herbert	Stretford	Trafford		STR/6/31
EDWARDS	Betsey	Dukinfield	Tameside	SCHOFIELD	DUK/26/92
EDWARDS	Charles Edward	Dukinfield	Tameside	EDWARDS	DUK/28/96
EDWARDS	Charlotte	Birkenhead	Wirral		BIR/19/68
EDWARDS	Daniel	Malpas	Wrexham		ML/6/1
EDWARDS	Edmund Bushell	Neston	Wirral		NES/4/92
EDWARDS	Edward	Hawarden	Flintshire East - Hawarden		HAW/4/88
EDWARDS	Eliza	East Macclesfield	Cheshire East		EMC/13/225

Figure 5-5 CheshireBMD search results

- LancashireBMD at <www.lancashirebmd.org.uk> contains just over 15 million records.
- NorthWalesBMD at <www.northwalesbmd.org.uk> has around 2.3 million records.
- StaffordshireBMD at <www.staffordshirebmd.org.uk> has over 2.7 million records.
- WestMidlandsBMD at <www.westmidlandsbmd.org.uk> has almost 2.5 million records.
- WiltshireBMD at <www.wiltshirebmd.org.uk> has around 520,000 records.
- YorkshireBMD at <www.yorkshirebmd.org.uk> has over 5.3 million entries to date.

Quite a number of other local authorities are developing indexes on similar lines, sometimes with the help of local family history societies. Links to all these projects will be found on UKBMD by clicking on the 'Local BMD' button on the left of the page. There is also a link to UKBMD's 'multi-region search'. NortheastBMD at <www.northeastbmd.org.uk> provides a gateway to all projects covering the north east of England.

There is wide variation in the coverage of these various services – some are complete or nearly so, others do not cover all events or the full period since 1837 – so it is a good idea to check the details of coverage before spending time searching for an entry.

Register offices and registration districts

While the LocalBMD projects are very useful, they will not be much help if you do not know where an event was registered. Also, if you want to order a certificate from a local registrar, you will need to know which office to approach. For both these reasons knowledge of registration districts is valuable, and there is extensive information available online.

For historical information about registration districts (up to 1930), Genuki has a set of pages prepared by Brett Langston at <**www.ukbmd.org.uk/ genuki/reg/**> which provide comprehensive details about registration districts in England and Wales, giving:

- name of the district;
- date of creation;
- date of abolition (if before 1930);
- names of the sub-districts;
- the GRO volume number used for the district in the national indexes of births, marriages and deaths;
- an alphabetical listing of the parishes, townships and hamlets included within its boundaries (if a district covered parts of two or more counties, the areas in each county are listed separately);
- the name(s) of the district(s) which currently hold the records.

There is an alphabetical list of districts at <**www.ukbmd.org.uk/genuki/reg/ districts/**>, with links to lists for individual counties, and if you are not sure what registration district a particular place is in, you can download a place-name index in PDF format from <**www.ukbmd.org.uk/genuki/places/**>.

Genuki also has tables matching the GRO volume numbers to registration districts at <**www.genuki.org.uk/big/eng/civreg/GROIndexes.html**>. The names and current contact details of individual register offices will also be found on Genuki, at <**www.ukbmd.org.uk/genuki/reg/regoff.html**>. This lists includes email addresses and links to the websites. It also links to any LocalBMD sites which include that registration district.

The GRO has the same information (for England only, not Wales), but ordered by county. Unfortunately the URL is a 100-character monster; instead follow the 'Download Index of County Information' link on the GRO's 'Using the General Register Office to research family history' page mentioned at the start of this chapter.

Alternatives to civil registration records

With the increasing number of parish registers available online for England and Wales (see Chapter 7), it may sometimes be possible to bypass civil registration records of marriages and instead use church records: the church's record of a post-1837 wedding will be exactly the same as the GRO's. If you have already identified a marriage in the GRO indexes, it will be worth investigating whether any church records for the relevant area are online for that date. Many of the registers available at Medway's CityArk site, for example, go well into the twentieth century (see p. 105).

In fact, because of the way the GRO's index volumes for marriages are arranged, it is possible, in principle at least, to work out from the volume and page number given for an event precisely which church the marriage was conducted in. The Marriage Locator at <**www.marriage-locator.co.uk**> attempts to do exactly that for the period 1837–1911. The data is somewhat patchy, but the site has over 250,000 entries.

Scotland

In Scotland, general registration dates from 1 January 1855. The General Register Office for Scotland (GROS) is the official online source of information about these records. In April 2011, it was merged with the National Archives of Scotland to form a new body, National Records of Scotland, with a website at <**www.nrscotland.gov.uk**>. However, until the new NRS website is in place, the old GROS site at <**www.gro-scotland.gov.uk**> remains in operation.

Genuki's 'Introduction to Scottish Family History' at <**www.genuki.org.uk/big/sct/intro.html**> has information on civil registration in Scotland, and GROS has a page 'Family Records' at <**www.gro-scotland.gov.uk/famrec/**> with basic information about what records are held and where they are. It also provides a list of local register offices with contact details at <**www.gro-scotland.gov.uk/files1/registration/reglist.pdf**>. Links to websites are not provided in this listing, but the domain name given in the email address (the part after the @) prefixed with *www.* will probably get you to the local authority website which hosts the pages for the local registration service. GROS also has a list of parish and registration districts available in PDF or Excel spreadsheet format from <**www.gro-scotland.gov.uk/famrec/list-of-parishes-registration-districts.html**>.

The situation with the Scottish general registration records is much better than that for England and Wales. The indexes to births, marriages and deaths are available, along with images of the older records, via the pay-per-view system at ScotlandsPeople (described in detail on p. 50). The site currently offers indexes for all civil registration records ('Statutory Records') from 1855 to the present. Images of the original records are available for:

- births 1855–1911
- marriages 1855–1936
- deaths 1855–1961

Each year, coverage is extended by a further year, with the new data added just after New Year. See <www.scotlandspeople.gov.uk/Content/ Help/index.aspx?r=554&413> for up-to-date details of the coverage. Where certificates are not available online, the indexes provide the information needed to order a certificate (called an 'Official Extract' in Scotland) from GROS. The GROS website provides ordering information at <www.gro-scotland.gov.uk/famrec/bdm.html>.

As well as the Statutory Records, the site also includes a range of other, minor categories of civil registration records, such as overseas and army registrations. Details are given on the 'Record Types & Examples' pages, accessed via the 'About our records'. These pages also list exactly what

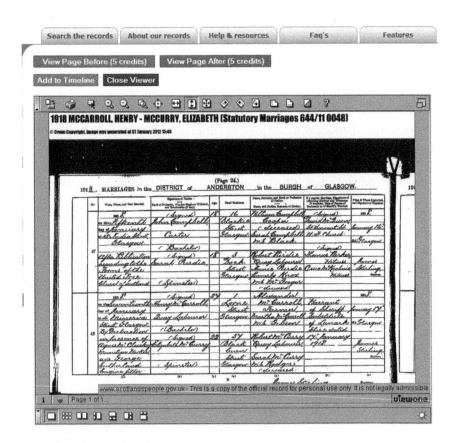

Figure 5-6 A marriage register image at ScotlandsPeople

information to expect on the records from various periods, with images of typical records (the images, alas, are in TIFF format, so you will need to download them and view them in a graphics viewer rather than in your browser).

Back in 2008 news from GROS suggested the likelihood was that some time in the not too distant future the Scottish civil registration records would also be available on other commercial sites. But at the time of writing, almost four years on, there seems to be no sign of this happening.

The University of Glasgow has an extensive and informative website devoted to the history of general registration in Scotland in The Scottish Way of Birth and Death at <**www.gla.ac.uk/departments/scottishwayofbirthanddeath/**>.

Ireland

In Ireland, registration of Protestant marriages dates from 1 April 1845, while full registration began on 1 January 1864. The records for the whole of Ireland up to 31 December 1921 are held by the Registrar General in Dublin, who also holds those from that date for the Irish Free State and then the Republic of Ireland. It has a website at <**www.groireland.ie**>. The equivalent records for Northern Ireland are held by the General Register Office (Northern Ireland), GRONI. As in the UK, GRONI no longer has an independent website, and all the material is on nidirect, the government services website for Northern Ireland, resulting, I'm afraid, in some truly mammoth URLs. The main GRO page on nidirect is at <**www.nidirect. gov.uk/gro/**>.

For the Republic, certificates can be ordered online from the Health Service website at <**www.hse.ie/eng/services/find_a_service/bdm/certificates_ie**>. Northern Ireland's certificate ordering service is on nidirect and has a 152-character URL: from the GRONI home page at <**www.nidirect.gov.uk/ gro/**> follow the link to 'Ordering certificates'. GRONI's fee is significantly higher (£14 rather than €10), so for the period before partition, you will be better off ordering certificates from the Republic.

A list of Irish registration districts, which are based on Poor Law Unions, is provided by Sean Murphy at <**homepage.eircom.net/~seanjmurphy/gro/ plus.htm**> and by ConnorsGenealogy <**www.connorsgenealogy.com/ districts.htm**>, which includes the volume numbers and links to a map of registration districts at <**www.connorsgenealogy.com/RegDist.htm**>.

From-Ireland has a page devoted to Civil Registration at <**www.from-ireland.net/irish-civil-registrations/Civil-Records-Explanation**>, which links to some small extracts for a wide range of registration districts at <**www.from-ireland.net/gene/district.htm**>.

Sean Murphy's very useful Guide to the General Register Office of Ireland at <**homepage.tinet.ie/~seanjmurphy/gro/**> covers all aspects of civil registration in Ireland, though it has not been updated since 2002 and is therefore not the place to look for latest developments.

Digitization

While Scotland had already solved the issues of online access to historical civil registration records by the end of the last century, it seems as if the Irish authorities, North and South, are a long way behind, and there is no official civil registration data for Ireland currently available on the web. In the Republic, a consultation document *Bringing Civil Registration into the 21st Century* at <**www.groireland.ie/images/consultation.pdf**> was published by the government in May 2001. In October 2003 they announced the official launch of the 'government approved modernization of the civil registration service', with the promise that 'Further developments within the modernized Civil Registration Service will include the introduction of automated genealogy/family research facilities and the provision of a range of services over the Internet'. In September 2011, in a written answer in the Irish parliament (see <**www.kildarestreet.com/wrans/?id=2011-09-14.1461.0**>), the responsible minister indicated that the bulk of the project had been completed, but, that with current budgetary constraints, the end was still some four years away. Also, there seems to be, in spite of the 2003 announcement, no firm commitment to putting any records online, which will in any case apparently require additional legislation.

The Genealogical Society of Ireland's page (on its old website) devoted to civil registration proposals at <**www.dun-laoghaire.com/genealogy/civreg.html**> provides a highly critical account both of the detail of the proposals and of the failure to make progress. The Council of Irish Genealogical Organisations reports on its own campaign to secure improvements to civil registration and access to the records in the Republic at <**www.cigo.ie/campaigns_gro.html**>.

The first signs of progress in Northern Ireland came in a consultation document *Civil Registration in the 21st century*, published in October 2003, which revealed that all the indexes had been electronically indexed. The Registrar General's Annual Report for 2009 announced (and that for 2010 repeated) 'significant progress in the digitizing of paper based records'. While it expects the digitization project to be 'on target for completion in early 2011', this covers only the in-house use of the data and does not seem to constitute a commitment to make any data available online.[1] Indeed the

---

1   The 2010 report is linked from <www.nisra.gov.uk/demography/default.asp50.htm> – the relevant material is in Appendix 5.

GRO's aims include only the production of 'certified copies' and make no mention of public access to electronic records.

All in all, it seems that not only has progress both sides of the border been slow, but a public online service is not regarded as a priority.

Indexes

While the official digitization projects are still some way from completion, there has been at least some progress in making the indexes available online.

In 2009, FamilySearch (see p. 41) announced the addition of the Irish civil registration records at the pilot of the new website, and these are now at <**www.familysearch.org**> – from the home page select 'Europe' under the 'Browse by Location' heading, then 'Ireland' and 'Ireland, Civil Registration Indexes, 1845–1958'. In fact, only the Republic of Ireland is covered for the whole period and there are no records for the North after 1921. Also, while the information on the site (click on 'Learn more' on the search page) carries no indication that this material is incomplete, I found that a great many entries I had previously extracted from the microfilm indexes were missing from the online index.

The original launch was on the pilot site before the new FamilySearch went live, and it linked an image of the relevant index book page to each entry. However, at the time of writing, the images are *not* available on the new site, though one would hope that they will be added at some point in the future.

The same indexes are available on Ancestry at <**search.ancestry.co.uk/search/db.aspx?dbid=2572**>. One advantage of Ancestry's index is that for each marriage entry you can get a list of the other names on the original page of the register, which allows you to look for the names of probable spouses.

Findmypast's Irish site at <**www.findmypast.ie**> is due to add civil registration records during 2012 (see p. 54).

Local transcripts

In the absence of any national programme of digitization for Irish registration records, there are nonetheless a few local and partial transcription projects.

The only coherent project I am aware of is Waterford County Library's online index to local death registrations, with full transcriptions of the original certificates, at <**www.waterfordcountylibrary.ie/en/familyhistory/deathregisters/**> as part of its electronic catalogue.

The following have small collections of registration data transcribed:

- From-Ireland has some small extracts for a wide range of registration districts at <**www.from-ireland.net/records/**>. Alternatively you can view those for an individual county by selecting the relevant province from <**www.from-ireland.net/county/**>.

- Margaret Grogan has a range of transcriptions for County Cork, mostly for individual places, at <**freepages.genealogy.rootsweb.ancestry.com/ ~mturner/cork/a_civil.htm**>, compiled from submissions to the Cork mailing list. You need to check each one as there is no overall search facility.
- The Ireland CMC Genealogy Record Project at <**www.cmcrp.net**> has user-submitted data which includes some civil registration records, though these are mostly individual entries rather than systematic extractions. There are separate pages for Clare, Cork, Dublin, Kerry, Limerick, Mayo, Tipperary, Waterford, Wicklow, and a single page for all other counties. Once on a county page, there are links at the top of the page to the various groups of records.

Offshore

The Isle of Man, and the individual Channel Islands (Jersey, Guernsey, Alderney and Sark) have their own civil registration starting from various dates.

The Isle of Man Civil Registry has a website at <**www.gov.im/registries/ general/civilregistry/**>, though it is mainly devoted to new registrations. The 'Contacts' button at the top of the page, though, will lead you to contact details, including an email address, enabling you to make your own enquiries. The Family History Library catalogue (see p. 221) has details of microfilmed civil registration records for the island available in Family History Centers. UKBMD (p. 74) lists two BMD projects for the Isle of Man, both named ManxBMD:

- <**www.manxbmd.com**> has indexes up to 1901 for births, 1911 for marriages and deaths, with scans of the official index pages for the remaining years.
- <**www.manx-bmd.co.uk**> is a much smaller project, with mainly marriage and a few death entries indexed.

The Superintendent Registrar for Jersey has web pages at <**www.gov.je/ Government/Departments/HomeAffairs/Departments/ SuperintendentRegistrar/Pages/**>, though there is no information about accessing records. The States of Guernsey website at <**www.gov.gg**> appears to have no information about civil registration at all.

The Priaulx Library on Guernsey has a list of 'Channel Islands Civil Records on Microfilm' at <**www.priaulxlibrary.co.uk/images/library/ CHANNEL-ISLAND-CIVIL-RECORDS.pdf**>.

The late John Fuller's 'Channel Islands Genealogy' page at <**www.rootsweb.ancestry.com/~jfuller/ci/volunteers.html**> mentions some volunteers prepared to do lookups in the Guernsey death registers.

Certificate exchanges

Although current GRO rules specifically forbid family historians from putting scanned certificates online,[2] the BMD Certificate Exchange at <**bmd-cert-exch-site.ourwardfamily.com**> provides a means for those with unwanted certificates, presumably purchased in error, to pass them on to another genealogist. The site has around 4,400 certificates. For Scotland, there is the Scotland BDM Exchange at <**www.sctbdm.com**>, which has almost 80,000 entries, though this includes some entries from parish registers. The site is free. A much more limited facility for Ireland, with just over 1,000 certificates, will be found at <**vicki.thauvin.net/chance/ireland/bmd/**>.

Overseas

If you have ancestors who were immigrants or emigrants, you may need access to other countries' civil registration services. There is no single way of getting this information for every country, but there are two good places to look for links. GenWeb (see p. 25) has sites for over 100 different countries, and the index of countries at <**www.worldgenweb.org/countryindex.html**> will take you to the relevant regional GenWeb site. Even if there is no civil registration information, there will often be a message board where you can ask. It also makes sense to check the relevant country or regional page on Cyndi's List at <**www.cyndislist.com**>. Sections devoted to individual countries will also be found on the pages for:

- Births & Baptisms <**www.cyndislist.com/births/**>
- Death Records <**www.cyndislist.com/deaths/**>
- Marriages & Divorce <**www.cyndislist.com/marriages/**>

The Research Guidance leaflets for individual countries at FamilySearch (see p. 9) should also contain information on civil registration records.

Don't expect other countries to be as far on the road to complete digital records as Scotland is, but you may be lucky. Some states in English-speaking parts of the world have indexes online. For example, New South Wales has an online index to historical registration records at <**www.bdm.nsw.gov.au/familyHistory/searchHistoricalRecords.htm**>, and British Columbia has a similar service at <**www.bcarchives.gov.bc.ca/textual/governmt/vstats/v_events.htm**>. For births, both of these sites list only events over 100 years ago, but more recent marriages and deaths are included. For the US, Cyndi's List has detailed information for each state (under the heading 'Records'), at <**www.cyndislist.com/usvital/**>.

2 'Guidance – Copying of Birth, Death, Marriage and Civil Partnership Certificates', online at <**www.nationalarchives.gov.uk/documents/information-management/copying-bmd-certificates.pdf**>.

6

CENSUS

A census has been taken every 10 years since 1801, except in 1941, and names of individuals are recorded from the 1841 census onwards. The significance of these records for genealogists is that they provide snapshots of family groups at 10-year intervals. More importantly, from 1851 onwards they give a place of birth, which is essential information for individuals born before the start of general registration: in combination with an approximate date of birth calculated from the person's age, this makes it possible to trace the line back to the parish registers.

The 1911 census is different in a number of respects from the earlier censuses. Most notably, the individual household schedules, written and signed by the head of household him- or herself, have been preserved (Figure 6-3). The form also contains fertility information: for each couple, the number of years married, the total number of children born and the number still living. There are a number of other forms showing details of the dwelling and of other buildings in the street.

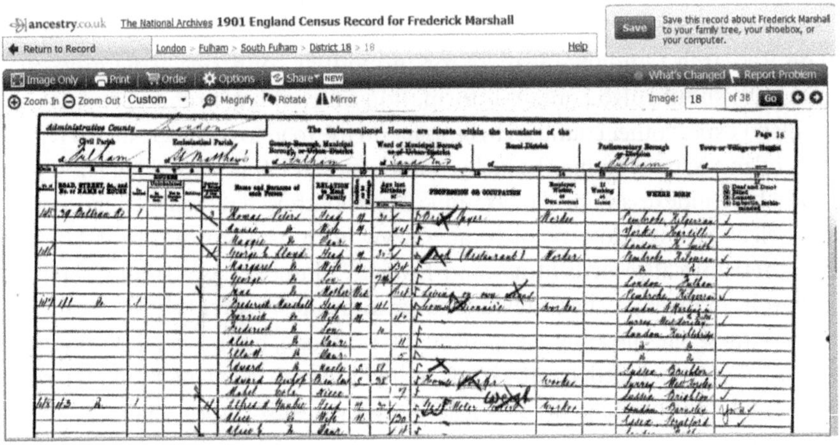

Figure 6-1 A page from the 1901 census (Ancestry)

The censuses are probably the most voluminous and the most complex genealogical records to go online, and with so many sites offering large amounts of census data, this chapter can only aim to give an overview and a brief look at the main sites offering census indexes. *Census: The Expert Guide* gives much more detail, including a step-by-step guide to each of the commercial services.

General information

There are a number of starting points for official information on the census. The National Archives' research guide on 'Census returns' at <**www.nationalarchives.gov.uk/records/research-guides/census-returns.htm**> has basic details and links to commercial indexes. The GenDocs site shows exactly what information was recorded in each column of the census forms for each census from 1841 to 1901 at <**homepage.ntlworld.com/hitch/gendocs/census.html**>.

If you are not familiar with census records and the way they are referred to, the British-Genealogy site explains piece numbers, folio numbers and schedules at <**www.british-genealogy.com/resources/census/**>. This is essential information if you are to refer to a census record as a source in your pedigree.

Genuki has pages on the census for:

- England and Wales: <**www.genuki.org.uk/big/eng/CensusR.html**>
- Scotland: <**www.genuki.org.uk/big/sct/Census.html**>
- Ireland: <**www.genuki.org.uk/big/irl/#Census**>

Talking Scot's pages devoted to the Scottish census are at <**www.talkingscot.com/censuses/census-intro.htm**>, though they do not yet include 1911.

All census records for England and Wales are catalogued in The National Archives' catalogue at <**www.catalogue.nationalarchives.gov.uk**>. Even if you are using an online census index this may be useful as it provides a way of establishing the piece number(s) for a particular place in each census.

Histpop at <**www.histpop.org**> is a site devoted to the history of the British population, and holds an enormous number of official documents relating to the censuses, including the population abstracts and the final census reports. For the population of individual counties and towns, see A Vision of Britain Through Time at <**www.visionofbritain.org.uk**> (p. 254), which has graphs of population change between 1801 and 2001. Following the 'Census reports' link on the home page will take you to the site's many census reports and a 1977 official *Guide to the Census Reports*, which 'outlines the history of the census and describes how coverage of various topics has developed'.

Digitizing census records

While we seem doomed to an interminable wait for civil registration records to go online, there has been enormous progress in putting census records on the web. Scotland was the first to put census indexes and images online, when the 1881 census index and images for the 1891 census were released in August 2001. The 1901 census for England and Wales, digitized by The National Archives and defence contractor QinetiQ, went online in January 2002. While the immense demand initially caused the site to crash, this at least showed the huge potential interest, and the result was that by April 2006, all the censuses for England, Wales and Scotland from 1841 to 1901 were available on the web. Even Ireland, the laggard in getting genealogical records online, completed its digitization of the surviving census records by the summer of 2011.

The 1911 census for England and Wales was expected to be available to the public from January 2012. The fact that it was released in advance of that date is the result of a request from Guy Etchells under the Freedom of Information Act, initially refused by The National Archives. But in December 2006 the Information Commissioner ruled that, as long as certain sensitive items of information were concealed, there was no reason why the records could not be made available. Although Guy's initial request was for access to the record for a single household, The National Archives decided more or less immediately that it would digitize the whole 1911 census for release in 2009. The contract for the project was awarded to Scotland Online (now called Brightsolid), the company behind ScotlandsPeople. With the subsequent takeover of Findmypast by Brightsolid in 2008, Findmypast became involved in the project, and on 13 January the first batch of data went online with Findmypast's branding. Since then, The Genealogist has launched its own complete index to this census, and Ancestry's index is being released in stages with completion expected during 2012. The 1911 census for Scotland, not affected by the FOI request, was launched, as had been expected, on its 100th anniversary in April 2011.

This means that all publicly available census records for the British Isles are online, in many cases with several distinct indexes.

Free census indexes

While you will need to use the commercial services as the only ones which provide images of the original records – you will need to consult these to check the index entries – there are three major sites which provide census indexes free of charge, and many local indexes.

FamilySearch

FamilySearch has census indexes for all the published censuses of England and Wales. The 1881 Census Index was in fact created in the

1980s by the Genealogical Society of Utah (GSU) and the Federation of Family History Societies. This was published first on microfiche and then on CD-ROM, and it is the index used for 1881 on all the commercial sites. The remaining years are all provided by arrangement with Findmypast and Origins. The images for these records are available on FamilySearch only if you are accessing it from a Family History Center; otherwise you are taken to the Findmypast site, where you will need to subscribe or purchase pay-per-view credits.

At the time of writing, the indexes for 1871 and 1881 are only partially available, with at least 80 per cent of the records still to be added. The 1881 Census Index is still available on the old FamilySearch site at <**www.family search.org/eng/Search/frameset_search.asp**>. (You need to search 'All Resources', with '1881' in the Year field and 'England' or 'Wales' in the Country field; selecting 'Census' just takes you back to the new site.)

Apart from the missing records, there are significant limitations in these indexes. The first is that the search options themselves are quite restricted, certainly compared to what is available on Findmypast. Second, on all the censuses apart from 1881, the results do not show the full details – the street address is not given, and in some cases not even the place of residence or the remaining household members (Figure 6-2).

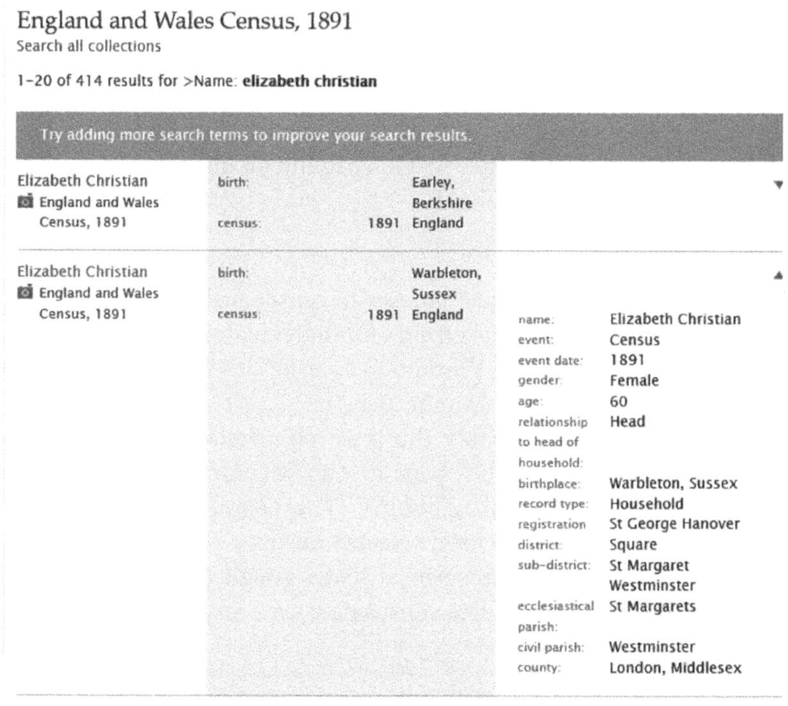

England and Wales Census, 1891
Search all collections

1–20 of 414 results for >Name: **elizabeth christian**

Try adding more search terms to improve your search results.

Elizabeth Christian	birth:	Earley, Berkshire	▼
England and Wales Census, 1891	census:	1891 England	

Elizabeth Christian	birth:	Warbleton, Sussex	▲
England and Wales Census, 1891	census:	1891 England	

name:	Elizabeth Christian
event:	Census
event date:	1891
gender:	Female
age:	60
relationship to head of household:	Head
birthplace:	Warbleton, Sussex
record type:	Household
registration district:	St George Hanover Square
sub–district:	St Margaret Westminster
ecclesiastical parish:	St Margarets
civil parish:	Westminster
county:	London, Middlesex

Figure 6-2 Search results for the 1891 census at FamilySearch

If you are already subscribed to Findmypast, FamilySearch's census indexes do not bring any benefits. However, if you are using Ancestry or The Genealogist, the ability to search for an otherwise unfindable individual in another index free of charge will sometimes be useful.

FreeCen

FreeCEN at <**freecen.rootsweb.com**> is a comprehensive volunteer project which aims to provide a free index to all censuses for England, Wales and Scotland from 1841 to 1891. Work so far has concentrated on the 1861 and 1891 census, and there is still a very long way to go. However, some counties are complete or nearly complete for individual census years. In particular, Cornwall has been almost entirely indexed, while for the 1841 census all Scottish counties are complete. By March 2012, the site had transcribed almost 21 million records. Usefully, it gives details of exactly which piece numbers are covered, and there is a status page for each county currently being transcribed, linked from <**freecen.rootsweb.com/project.htm**>.

FHS Online

FHS Online at <**www.fhs-online.co.uk**> is run by S&N Genealogy Supplies, who also run The Genealogist, as a platform for family history societies to publish their data. The site hosts 49 free county census indexes, though they do not necessarily cover the whole county for a particular census year.

Access is free, though you need to complete a registration in order to carry out searches. Search facilities are very basic – just name and age – and the results give only the area and The National Archives' census reference, not the address. However, once you have found an individual, you can get a complete listing of the household.

Local indexes

There are countless other small indexes to census material on the web. You will find much census material on sites for individual villages or parishes, and even on some FHS sites. The Workhouses site at <**www.workhouses.org.uk**> has census extracts for many workhouses.

Census Finder has probably the most comprehensive set of links to local transcriptions on its UK page at <**www.censusfinder.com/united_kingdom.htm**>, organized by county. The Genuki county and parish pages will also have links to local census indexes.

Another useful site is freecensus at <**sites.google.com/site/freecensus/**> which has a table linking to free census data for every county in the British Isles.

The commercial services

All the main commercial data services listed on p. 45ff. offer census records on a subscription or pay-per-view basis. In addition, there are dedicated sites for the 1901 census and the 1911 census of England and Wales at <www.1901censusonline.com> and <www.1911census.co.uk> respectively.

Table 6-1 shows what they offer as of January 2012.

Table 6-1 Census indexes on the commercial data services (January 2012)

	England & Wales	Scotland
Ancestry	1841–1901; 1911 in progress	1841–1901 no images
Findmypast	1841–1911	1841–1871 no images
GenesReunited	1841–1911	
Origins	1841, 1861, 1871	
RootsUK	1841–1901	
The Genealogist	1841–1911	
ScotlandsPeople		1841–1911
1901 census	1901	
1911 census	1911	

The table is provisional in that there are two current developments at the time of writing, which should be complete by the time you read this: Ancestry should have finished creating its index for the 1911 census, and Findmypast should have 1881–1901 census indexes for Scotland. Once these are complete, there are no more census records to digitize until 2021.

In spite of the many commercial sites offering censuses data, the number of *distinct* sets of census indexes is in reality much smaller. For a start, The Genealogist and RootsUK are both run by S&N Genealogy Supplies with identical data but different search facilities. Second, Genes Reunited, 1901 Census Online and the 1911 census site are all run by Findmypast and use the same census indexes, except that Findmypast has its own separate index to the 1901 census. Findmypast and Origins have cross-licensed some of their indexes, so that all those available at Origins are identical to those at Findmypast. Finally, all the 1881 censuses indexes of England and Wales take the free FamilySearch index (p. 87) as their basis, and this is normally not charged for on pay-per-view sites. Broadly speaking, then, there are only three groups of indexes for England and Wales:

- Ancestry
- Findmypast, Genes Reunited, 1911 Census, and Origins
- The Genealogist and RootsUK

This is important because, if you can't find someone in the census index on one site and want to try another, there is no point in using one with an identical index.

For details of the main data services, see Chapter 4. The two dedicated census sites are discussed below.

1901 census

The 1901 Census site at <www.1901censusonline.com> contains the original 1901 census index launched in 2002 and also offers civil registration indexes. The site operates a pay-per-view system, with 500 credits costing £5. Searches are free, but viewing an individual or household record costs 50 credits (50p) and viewing the census image costs 75 credits (75p). Credits are valid for the very short period of seven days. The search options are extensive, including person, address, place, institution, vessel and reference number searches.

While the census index on this site is historically important, the absence of any other censuses on the site means it is not likely to be your first choice for searching the 1901 census. However, if you have been unable to find someone in another 1901 index, the extensive search options make this a useful backup option.

1911 census

The 1911 Census site is at <www.1911census.co.uk>. The site runs a pay-per-view system, though it is more expensive than the other pay-per-view census sites: the household listing costs 10 credits (i.e. £1), and the census images 30 credits (£3). The justification for the higher costs is that the amount of material to be transcribed is much greater and instead of a single image to view, you get a whole bunch of them, photographed in colour, not just digitized from microfilm. The site is run by Findmypast and the same index is available on Findmypast and Genes Reunited, both of which offer a much wider range of material.

As with the 1901 census site, since there's only a single census on the site there's no reason for this to be your first port of call for the 1911 census, now that other sites have indexes to this census. But it will be useful under two circumstances: if you have been unable to find someone in that census on Ancestry, The Genealogist or RootsUK (assuming their 1911 indexes are complete by the time you read this); or if you are a seasoned family historian and have already exhausted the earlier censuses. The extensive search

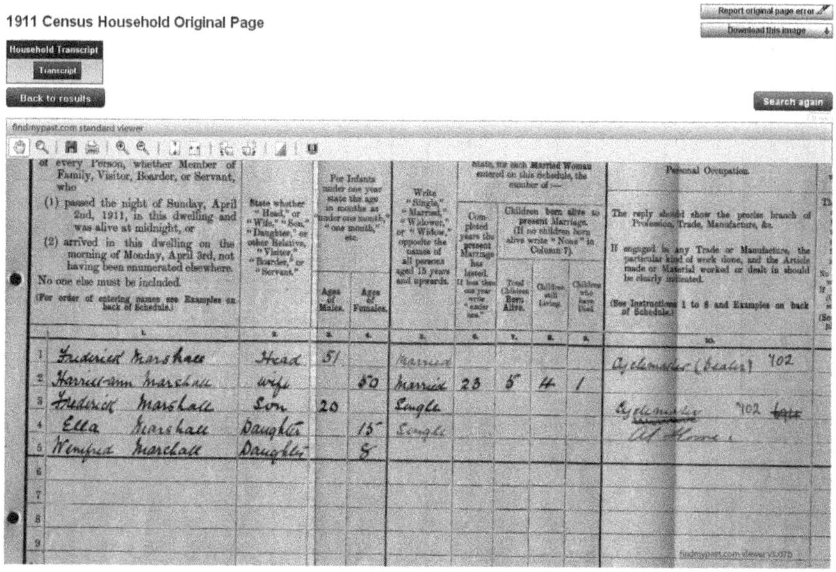

Figure 6-3 1911 Census: household schedule (Findmypast)

options may also make it a good alternative if you have been using Genes Reunited and been unable to find someone with that site's more basic search facilities.

Searching the censuses

The process of census searching on the commercial services is generally quite similar, and the flowchart in Figure 6-4 gives an overview of the typical process. The search options of the individual sites are shown in Table 6-2. If you are a pay-per-view customer, you will have credits deducted for seeing the individual and household records and the image. Only ScotlandsPeople differs very significantly from the others: you have to pay to see each page of search results, and it does not offer a transcription of an individual record or household, but goes straight from the list of search results to the page image.

In addition to the general advice on searching on p. 38, there are some particular issues that arise when searching online census indexes.

Ages are particularly problematic, and not just because our ancestors could not be relied on to know how old they were. On many of the original census forms ages were subsequently crossed through as a way of marking that an individual had been counted. Because almost all modern census indexes are based on digitized monochrome microfilm, these annotations, quite distinct on the original records, often make the age difficult to read with certainty (see Figure 6-5, from the 1891 census for Essex Road, Islington). Another problem is that many of the search forms ask you to

Table 6.2 Census search

	Ancestry	Findmypast	Genes Reunited	1901 census		1911 Census	TheGenealogist	RootsUK	Origins	Scotlands People	Ireland	FamilySearch
Search type	Advanced	Advanced	Standard	1901 advanced	1841–91 standard	Advanced	Advanced	Advanced	Standard	Standard	Standard	Standard
Name fields	2	3	2	3	2	3	2	2	2	2	2	2
Name variants	Custom	NameX	Wildcards only	Wildcards only	Wildcards only	None	Custom	Custom	NameX	Soundex		Custom
Age	Birth year	Birth year	Birth year	Birth year	Birth year	Birth year	Age	Age or Birth year	Age range	Age range	Age	Birth year
Birthplace	✓	✓	Place keywords	✓		✓	County	County	County/country			County
Residence	1 field, more addable	8 fields		10 fields	Keywords	County, district, place	County, district, address	County	County, parish	County or city, district	County, district, street	Place
Occupation		✓				✓	✓	✓				
Gender	✓	✓		✓		✓	✓			✓	✓	
Marital status		✓				Year of marriage						
Relation to head		✓				✓	✓					
Family members	1 field, more addable	1 member				List first and last names	Separate family forename search			1 additional forename		Head
Keyword	✓					✓	Separate keyword search					
Address search	Yes – by leaving name field blank	Separate address search		Separate address search	Separate address search (beta)	Separate address search	Separate address search				Browse	Spouse, parents
Reference		Separate ref. search				✓						

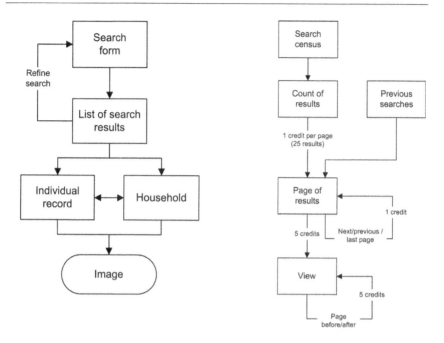

Figure 6-4 Typical census search process (right: Scotlandspeople)

enter not an age but a birth year. But because the censuses were taken between March and June it is in fact impossible to calculate accurately a person's year of birth from the age given in a census (even assuming the person did actually know his or her age). For this reason, it is advisable not to search an exact birth year but always allow at least one year either side. If this doesn't work, try leaving out the age altogether: it's quite possible for a 1 or a 7 to have been mistaken by the transcriber for a crossing-off, turning a 72-year old into a 2-year old.

With a common name, you may be very tempted to try and narrow down your search by giving an occupation known from, say, a marriage certificate. This *may* work. But quite apart from the fact that your ancestor may have changed jobs, there can be many different way to express the same occupation. Also, like ages, occupations were often partially overwritten with pen strokes or annotations when the forms were analysed, as you can see in from Figure 6-1, and so are particularly liable to be mistranscribed.

As to the gender field, there is generally no good reason to search on it – the indexes have many gender errors and most forenames from the period are unambiguously male or female, making the gender field redundant. The only real use is when you are searching without a forename (say, if you

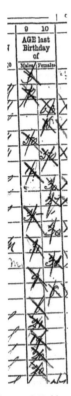

Figure 6-5 Hard-to-read ages in the 1891 census

haven't been able to find someone under the name you were expecting) and want to keep the number of search results manageable.

More detailed discussion of census search techniques will be found in Chapter 5 of *Census: The Expert Guide*.

Ireland

The National Archives of Ireland have a brief page of information at <**www.nationalarchives.ie/genealogy/ censusrtns.html**>, as has the PRONI at <**www.proni.gov. uk/your_family_tree_series_-_02_-_1901_census.pdf**>. A good guide to the Irish censuses, detailing what is missing and what has survived, is available on the Fianna site at <**www.rootsweb.ancestry.com/~fianna/guide/ census.html**>.

Until recently, the situation with the Irish censuses has been very different from that for the rest of the British Isles. Until the end of 2007 there was no official or commercial site offering images of Irish census records, and the only indexes were those made for individual counties or towns by volunteers. Of course, the situation with the records themselves is also very different – almost no Irish census records survive for the nineteenth century. On the other hand, the 1901 and 1911 censuses have been publicly accessible in Ireland since the 1980s, so the irrelevance of the privacy issues that have controlled the timing of their digitization in England, Wales and Scotland ought to have seen them digitized sooner rather than later, one would have thought.

But in December 2005 the National Archives of Ireland joined Library and Archives Canada to announce a project to digitize the two surviving Irish censuses, and make them available online free of charge. In December 2007 the first fruits of this collaboration, the 1911 Census for Dublin, went online at <**census.nationalarchives.ie**>. By June 2010 the 1901 and 1911 censuses were available in their entirety.

The next Irish census due for release is that for 1926, the first one conducted by the newly formed Irish Free State (there was no census in 1921 because of the war between the Irish and Britain). As in England, there is a movement to reduce the closure period for the next census from 100 years to 75, which would make it immediately available. A campaign by the Irish genealogy world, led by the Council of Irish Genealogical Organisations (CIGO) – see <**www.cigo.ie/campaigns_1926.html**> – has resulted in a commitment from the Irish Government in its 2011 programme to 'enable publication of the

1926 census'.[1] That initial commitment gave no timescale for the actual digitization, but the Minister for Arts, Heritage and the Gaeltacht has since stated in a written answer to the Irish parliament that 'it is my intention to have the census returns digitised and made available on-line as a 1916 centenary project, subject to resources and the resolution of legal and other issues'. In March 2012 it was confirmed that the necessary legislation had received Cabinet approval and should be passed within four months, with only the issue of funding to be resolved.

Census of Ireland 1901/1911

On the official Irish census site at <**census.nationalarchives.ie**>, the search allows you to specify name, age in 1911, the townland or street and, if you know it, the district electoral division (DED, the equivalent of the British enumeration district). The initial search results (Figure 6-6) show name, address, age and gender, but the absence of birthplace in this listing may mean you cannot immediately identify the correct individual. However, since it costs nothing to look at the images of the household schedules (Figure 6-3), this hardly matters.

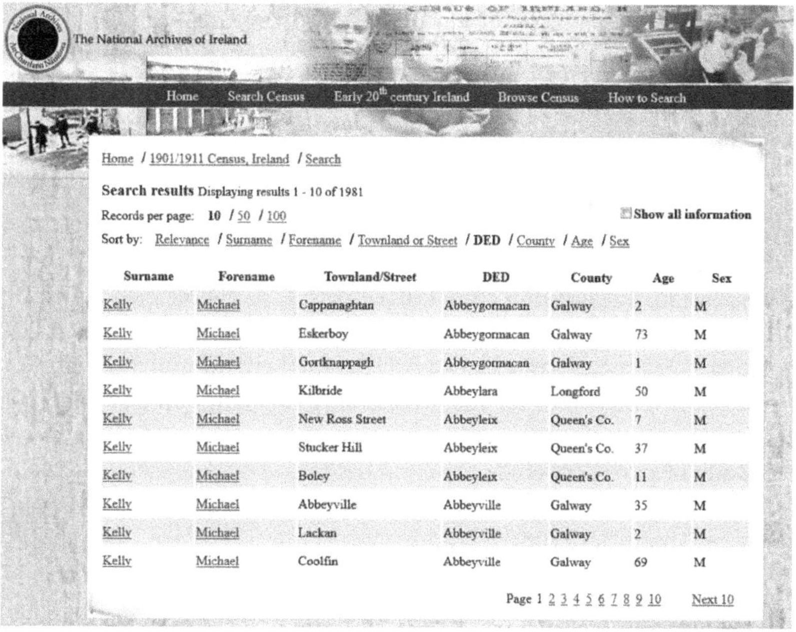

Surname	Forename	Townland/Street	DED	County	Age	Sex
Kelly	Michael	Cappanaghtan	Abbeygormacan	Galway	2	M
Kelly	Michael	Eskerboy	Abbeygormacan	Galway	73	M
Kelly	Michael	Gortknappagh	Abbeygormacan	Galway	1	M
Kelly	Michael	Kilbride	Abbeylara	Longford	50	M
Kelly	Michael	New Ross Street	Abbeyleix	Queen's Co.	7	M
Kelly	Michael	Stucker Hill	Abbeyleix	Queen's Co.	37	M
Kelly	Michael	Boley	Abbeyleix	Queen's Co.	11	M
Kelly	Michael	Abbeyville	Abbeyville	Galway	35	M
Kelly	Michael	Lackan	Abbeyville	Galway	2	M
Kelly	Michael	Coolfin	Abbeyville	Galway	69	M

Figure 6-6 Ireland 1911 census: search results

1 See p. 56 of the document at <**www.taoiseach.gov.ie/eng/Publications/Publications_2011/Programme_for_Government_2011.pdf**>.

From the search results, clicking on the name takes you to a page listing the entire household, and this has links to the images. Alongside the image of the household return, the site provides all the other forms (enumerator's abstract, house and building return, out-office and farm-steading return) in PDF format, one file per return, and the images open in the Acrobat viewer (see p. 60).

Where those in the household are Irish speakers, the household return will be in Irish, using the Irish script, and with the Irish forms of names (e.g. *Seághan* for *John*, *Séamus* for *James*). However, the head of household's name, anglicized, will be in the index as this occurs on the cover of the household return. So the playwright Sean O'Casey appears in the 1911 census as Seághan Ó Cathasaigh in the household of his brother Michael Casey. Female family members will usually have the traditional feminine form *Ni* before their surname rather than Ó. See p. 293 for resources to help with the Irish language.

Ireland's National Centre for Gecocomputation has a useful online map to help with identifying locations: its 'Population Change 1841–2002' map, available from <**ncg.nuim.ie/redir.php?action=projects/famine/explore**>, allows you to select a county and then see a map of the DEDs. If you tick the 'Background Mapping' option, the boundaries are superimposed on a modern street map or satellite photograph.

Local indexes

There are a number of sites with census data for individual counties, though their usefulness is now diminished because of the official site. But they may nonetheless prove useful if you have trouble finding an individual on the NAI site.

In the Republic of Ireland some data from the 1901 census is online at <**www.leitrim-roscommon.com/1901census/**>. Available data covers all or part of the following six counties: Roscommon, Leitrim, Mayo, Sligo, Wexford, Westmeath and Galway. Data for Leitrim and Roscommon is essentially complete, but for the others, only small amounts of material are present. A table gives detailed information about which individual parishes are wholly or partly covered.

Census Finder has links to many local transcriptions for Ireland at <**www.censusfinder.com/ireland.htm**>. While these are mainly for the 1901 census with some material for 1911, they include some surviving fragments of nineteenth-century censuses.

Irish Origins (p. 47) has the surviving records of the 1851 census for Dublin. Because of the amount of Irish census material destroyed, the so-called 'census substitutes' are important. One of the most important census substitutes, Griffith's Valuation, is discussed in Chapter 8, p. 123. Fianna has a useful guide to these at <**www.rootsweb.ancestry.com/~fianna/**

guide/cen2.html>, while the National Archives of Ireland has a briefer description at <**www.nationalarchives.ie/genealogy/valuation.html**>. The PRONI has similar information leaflets on valuation records and tithe applotment books linked from <**www.proni.gov.uk/index/family_history/ family_history_key_sources.htm**>.

Overseas

It is not possible to deal here with census data for countries outside the British Isles, but Cyndi's List provides links to census sites around the world at <**www.cyndislist.com/census-worldwide/**>.

The census data on FamilySearch includes the 1880 US census and the 1881 Canadian census, and there is a large amount of US census data online at Ancestry.com <**www.ancestry.com**>, which, for UK users, requires a worldwide subscription (see p. 52).

Census Links at <**www.censuslinks.com**> has links to census transcriptions for a number of countries, including most of Western Europe.

7

CHURCH RECORDS

Before the introduction of General Registration in 1837, church records of baptisms, marriages and burials are the primary source for the major events in our ancestors' lives. Unfortunately, there is very much less data online for parish registers than for the civil registration and census records covered in the previous chapters, and there are good reasons why this should be so.

The national records are centrally held and recorded on forms which ensure that the structure of the data is consistent and very obvious. They all date at the earliest from the 1830s, and they have generally been kept in fairly good conditions. All this makes digitizing and indexing them a manageable, if mammoth, task.

But for parish registers, there is much more variety. First, in England and Wales at least, they are not held centrally, so no one body can be approached to put them online. Second, there is a huge variation in their format and preservation, the more so because they cover the whole period since the sixteenth century. And, third, while most genealogists soon become comfortable with nineteenth-century handwriting, the same cannot be said of the writing in some of the eighteenth-century registers, never mind those from the sixteenth century. Although many parish registers have been transcribed and published in print or typescript, getting the requisite permissions simply to digitize and index these from the hundreds of individuals and groups concerned would be a substantial task. Indeed, the right to transcribe and publish parish register material seems to be legally unclear, with some clergy refusing to allow transcription. All this conspires to make the prospect of a comprehensive collection of online parish registers for England and Wales much more distant than it is for civil registration. Nevertheless, a growing body of data is available in online indexes, as well as information that will help you to identify what parish registers remain. One welcome development is that there are an increasing number of digital images of parish registers available online. But you will not be able to do all your parish register research online – a visit to record offices will remain essential.

If you are unfamiliar with parish registers, British-Genealogy has a useful set of pages on English Parish Registers at <**www.british-genealogy.com/ parish-registers/english-registers.html**>. These describe the information given for baptism, marriage, and burial entries at different periods and have some examples of original documents. The tutorials discussed in Chapter 2 will also have information on using parish registers. For help with the handwriting found in older registers, refer to the material on p. 289ff.

Parish churches

The most important church records, in earlier times even for Roman Catholic or Nonconformist families, are those of the Established Church. The easiest way to identify which church is most likely to have baptized, married or buried your ancestors, is Genuki's Church Database at <**www.genuki.org.uk/big/churchdb/**> described on p. 256. The Church of England's A Church Near You site at <**www.achurchnearyou.com**> will find the nearest present-day CofE churches to a given location, shown in Figure 7-1. There is a marker for each church, with a key to the right – clicking on either brings up a brief statement about the church. Notice that the map also shows the parish boundaries.

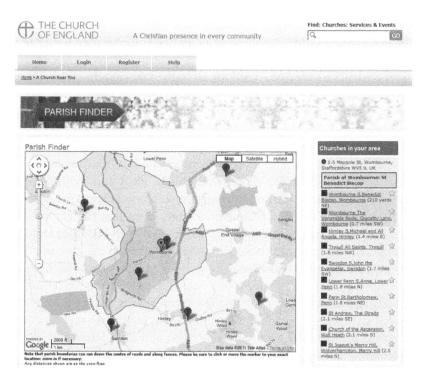

Figure 7-1 A Church Near You: Wombourne, Staffordshire

The UK Church directory at <**www.findachurch.co.uk**> provides similar facilities for the whole of the British Isles (including the Republic of Ireland) and includes other denominations, though the information about some of the churches is minimal and it is not always obvious which is the main CofE parish church.

The official websites for the Anglican churches of the British Isles also have details of their individual churches, though naturally they are orientated towards the present-day parishes. The relevant sites are:

- Church of England <**www.cofe.anglican.org**>
- Church in Wales <**www.churchinwales.org.uk**>
- Church of Ireland <**www.ireland.anglican.org**>
- Church of Scotland <**www.churchofscotland.org.uk**>
- Scottish Episcopal Church <**www.scotland.anglican.org**>

Many individuals have placed pictures of parish churches online, and these are discussed under 'Photographs' on p. 306.

FamilySearch

The major online resource for all UK parish records is the FamilySearch site at <**www.familysearch.org**>, discussed on p. 41ff.

When searching for parish records, either you can search one of the newer collections from the FamilySearch Indexing project, each of which covers a particular type of record for an individual city, diocese or county, or you can search one of the older collections covering a whole country. The newer collections should always be used for preference as they are likely to be more accurate, but even for the places covered, some records are provided at present solely in the form of digital images of the original documents. As of March 2012, there are indexes for Bristol, Cheshire, Derbyshire, Dorset, Essex, and Warwickshire. There are images only and no indexes for Cornwall, the Diocese of Durham, Lancashire, Norfolk, and Yorkshire.

While the new material will be preferable, given that the FamilySearch Indexing project still has a long way to go, you will still be reliant largely on the material that was on the old FamilySearch site. On the new site this is presented in the form of 'national' collections of births/baptism, marriages and death/burials for England, Wales, Scotland, Ireland, the Isle of Man, the Channel Islands and Great Britain. These records are mostly from the IGI (see p. 42), 'controlled extractions' from the original parish registers, which are mostly for baptisms, with some marriages and a few burials.

Figure 7-2 shows the start of the results for a search on a name and county in the England Births and Christenings records (the search terms are shown in bold above the results table).

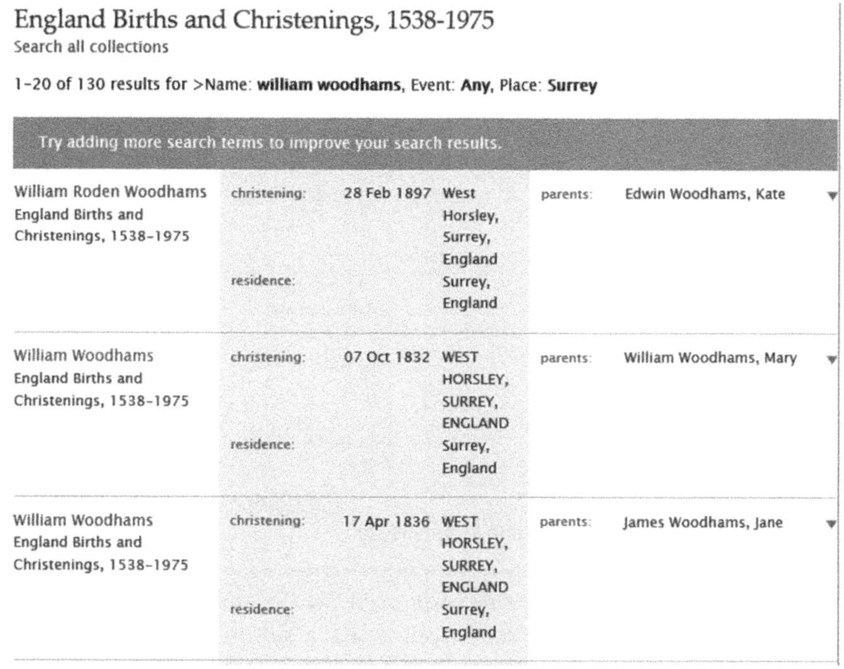

England Births and Christenings, 1538-1975
Search all collections

1-20 of 130 results for >Name: **william woodhams**, Event: **Any**, Place: **Surrey**

Try adding more search terms to improve your search results.

William Roden Woodhams England Births and Christenings, 1538-1975	christening: residence:	28 Feb 1897	West Horsley, Surrey, England Surrey, England	parents:	Edwin Woodhams, Kate ▼
William Woodhams England Births and Christenings, 1538-1975	christening: residence:	07 Oct 1832	WEST HORSLEY, SURREY, ENGLAND Surrey, England	parents:	William Woodhams, Mary ▼
William Woodhams England Births and Christenings, 1538-1975	christening: residence:	17 Apr 1836	WEST HORSLEY, SURREY, ENGLAND Surrey, England	parents:	James Woodhams, Jane ▼

Figure 7-2 FamilySearch search results in England Births and Christenings

You can see more details of each entry either by clicking on the arrow at the top right of each record, which expands the record on the same screen (as in Figure 6-2), or by clicking on the name, which opens up a new window (Figure 7-3).

You can see *all* the records for a particular place by doing a search with the name fields left blank, selecting 'Any' from the 'Add a Life Event' filter and putting a place-name in the 'Any' field. The place-name needs to be spelt exactly as in the records, though you can use the asterisk as a wildcard to represent any characters.

As mentioned in Chapter 4, the new FamilySearch site does not so far provide any way of downloading data. But if you are using the older collections, you can simply repeat a search on the *old* site at <**www.familysearch.org/eng/ search/frameset_search.asp**>, which does have a download facility: from a list of search results, you can select an individual record or a group of records to download in GEDCOM format (see p. 357), ready to be imported into your genealogy database.

Batch numbers

Although the default search of these national record sets is the whole country, you can, as discussed, narrow it down by adding a filter which includes a county or place-name. Likewise in the recently indexed county record sets.

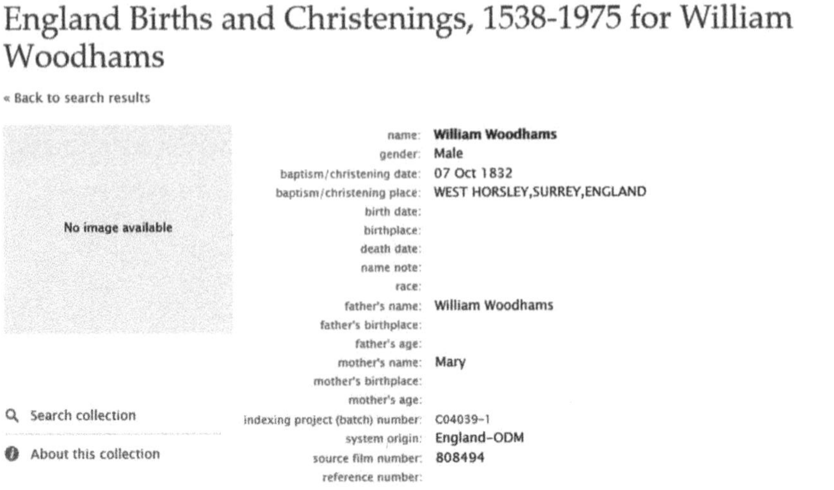

England Births and Christenings, 1538-1975 for William Woodhams

« Back to search results

No image available

name:	**William Woodhams**
gender:	Male
baptism/christening date:	07 Oct 1832
baptism/christening place:	WEST HORSLEY,SURREY,ENGLAND
birth date:	
birthplace:	
death date:	
name note:	
race:	
father's name:	William Woodhams
father's birthplace:	
father's age:	
mother's name:	Mary
mother's birthplace:	
mother's age:	
indexing project (batch) number:	C04039–1
system origin:	England-ODM
source film number:	808494
reference number:	

Q Search collection

ℹ About this collection

Figure 7-3 An individual record in FamilySearch

But if you are using the older records from the IGI there is an easy way to see other records from the same source. Each set of transcriptions for a particular parish has a 'batch number' and when you look at an individual record (either by clicking on the person's name, which opens a new page, or by clicking on the down-arrow to the right (which just expands the entry on the same page) this batch number is cited. On the individual page (Figure 7-3) the batch number is a link, and clicking on it will bring up a list of all the other entries. With the 'source film number', incidentally, you can go to a Family History Center and view the microfilm of the original parish register. Each batch is generally for an individual physical volume of the registers, so there are separate batches for baptisms and marriages where a parish kept these in separate books. The batch numbers also provide a handy way to discover exactly which records are in the batch, information which is not provided anywhere on the FamilySearch site itself – a search on the batch number with name fields blank will retrieve all the records in the batch.

A very useful tool for exploiting batch numbers is Hugh Wallis's 'IGI Batch Numbers – British Isles and North America' site at <**freepages.genealogy. rootsweb.ancestry.com/~hughwallis/IGIBatchNumbers.htm**>. This gives for each county a list of parishes and the batch number for that parish, with details of the type of records covered and the dates. Less well-known but more comprehensive and up-to-date is Steve Archer's 'FamilySearch: a Guide to the British batches' at <**www.archersoftware.co.uk/igi/**>, which also has the advantage of indicating how many entries there are in a batch. Both of these sites provide links which initiate a search on the relevant batch number in the

Historical Records Collection at FamilySearch, and you can leave the surname field blank to get a complete listing of the entries.

You can also find batch numbers by doing a 'Place Search' in the Family History Library Catalogue and looking at the 'Title Details', as explained on p. 221. Genuki has step-by-step instructions on how to do this at <**www.genuki.org.uk/big/FindingBatchNos.html**>.

The Global Gazette has a detailed article by Fawne Stratford-Devai, 'The LDS FamilySearch Website: Using The Batch Numbers', at <**globalgenealogy.com/globalgazette/gazfd/gazfd36.htm**>, which explains what the batch numbers are and how to use them. It also provides links to batch number information for a number of countries.

Bear in mind that the batch number information on these sites is unofficial, and should not be regarded as authoritative. Also note that for many parishes there will be more than one batch number.

Other free collections

FreeReg at <**freereg.rootsweb.com**> is another volunteer project, like FreeBMD and FreeCEN, which aims to put UK genealogy data online 'to provide free internet searches of baptism, marriage, and burial records, which have been transcribed from parish and Nonconformist church registers in the UK'. At the beginning of 2012, the project had over 18 million records, around half of which are marriages. Of course, this is only a tiny percentage of the likely total number of records, but even so it will be worth checking. The 'Counties and Parishes' page shows the date of the earliest registers for each parish and the years which have been covered.

UK Genealogy Archives have digitized a large number of printed parish register transcriptions, all linked from <**www.uk-genealogy.org.uk/Registers/**>. These include Phillimore's marriages for over 500 parishes. Coverage is very variable with much for some counties (Lancashire, Somerset, Wiltshire) but little or nothing for others (Hertfordshire, Kent). The site does not provide an index, though some of the individual volumes do.

Local resources

Many local family history societies have created indexes to parish records for their own county or area, and a number of these are being made available via the commercial data services, discussed in the next section. But there are also projects by record offices and volunteer groups to put church records online, either as indexes or as images of the original registers.

Kent seems to be doing particularly well in this regard. Medway's CityArk project includes images of parish registers from the Diocese of Rochester. The CityArk home page is at <**cityark.medway.gov.uk**> and the link to 'Parish Registers Online' will take you to the records. There is no single link to the image database; instead, at the bottom of this long page, is a list of parishes with a link for each. You then just page through the collection of images in search of the entry you want, exactly as you would do with microfilm. The images themselves are rather large and you may want to use your browser's zoom-out facility (Figure 7-4).

Alongside this, there are single-parish projects for two Kent villages. The Woodchurch Ancestry Group have a free index to the registers for the parish of Woodchurch at <**www.woodchurchancestry.org.uk**>, with full transcriptions of the individual entries, including names of witnesses. The entries go up to the 1980s. And Penshurst has put images of all its registers up to 1812 online on the village website at <**www.penshurst-online.co.uk/ penshurst_registers_ly.html**>.

Essex Ancestors is a subscription service from Essex Record Office at <**seax.essexcc.gov.uk/EssexAncestors.asp**> which includes images of the county's parish registers. The site provides detailed information about the records, sufficient to enable you to identify the right image for a particular parish and date, but the records themselves are not indexed. Subscriptions range from £5 for 24 hours up to £75 for a year.

The Norfolk Transcription Archive has a large collection of parish records for the county at <**doun.org/transcriptions/**>. A surname index links to pages with all the entries for each name, which then links to the transcript for the relevant parish. Rather bizarrely, only years are given, not full dates.

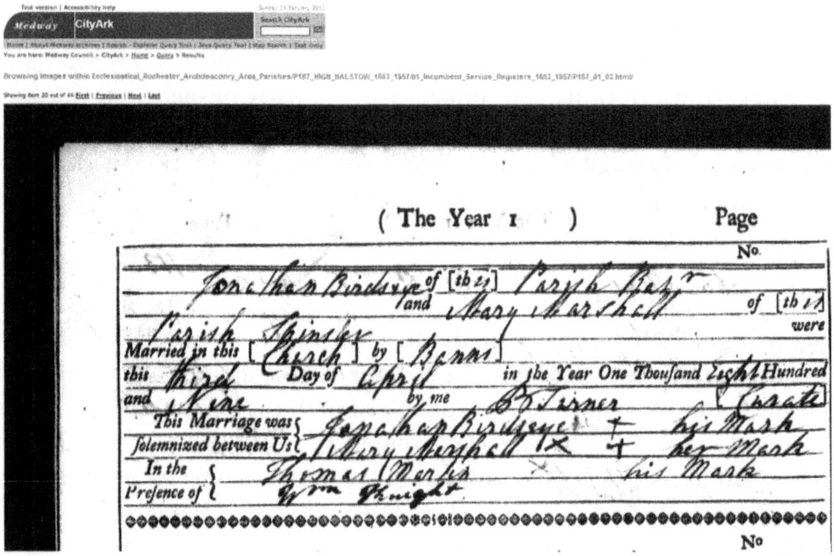

Figure 7-4 Medway's CityArk: a page from a marriage register (1809)

Commercial data services

Although the commercial data services are better known for their national datasets, they are increasingly adding parish register indexes to their offerings. These are sometimes created by the companies themselves, particularly where they are based on scans of printed parish register indexes, but there are also indexes created by third parties, often family history societies and individual transcribers.

The Genealogist (see p. 105) has parish register indexes for over 1,700 English parishes, plus a small number for Aberdeenshire and Brecknockshire. Some are original transcriptions, others derived by indexing printed books. A very useful feature of the transcription database is that from a baptism you can get a listing of other children of the same parents, and from a marriage you get a list of potential children extracted from the baptisms for the same parish. To see the full list, go to <**www.thegenealogist.co.uk/ nameindex/ai_content.php**> and follow the two 'Parish Records' links. Welsh coverage is to be expanded in 2012.

British Origins, described on p. 47, has a number of parish record indexes available online, mainly for marriages:

- Dorset Marriage Index 1538–1856 (over 500,000 names)
- Surrey Marriage Index 1500–1846 (nearly 540,000 names)
- Webb's London Marriages 1538–1837 (nearly 200,000 names)
- York Marriage Bonds and Allegations Index 1613–1839 (over 300,000 names)
- City of London Burials 1781–1904 (36,000 records)

Findmypast (see p. 53) has a parish records collection based mainly on indexes created by family history societies. In particular, it has the National Burial Index, the index of over 13 million burial records transcribed by local family history societies under the co-ordination of the FFHS. Details of the county coverage will be found at <**www.ffhs.org.uk/projects/nbi/ nbi-coverage.php**> – the list on this page links to a detailed list of individual parishes. Among the other parish record indexes available on the site are:

- City of London burials 1742–1904
- London docklands baptism records 1712–1933
- West Middlesex Marriage Index 1538—1837
- Boyd's London Burials 1538–1872
- Boyd's Marriage Index 1538–1840
- Boyd's 1st Miscellaneous Series 1538–1775
- Faculty Office Marriage Licence Allegations 1701–1850
- Vicar-General Marriage Licence Allegations 1694–1850

Ancestry at <www.ancestry.co.uk> (see p. 52) has parish register material in the Parish and Probate Record collection available on Ancestry UK. Details of the coverage will be found in the list of UK databases at <www.ancestry.co.uk/search/locality/dbpage.aspx?tp=3257> under the 'Birth, Marriage and Death, including Parish' heading. The site generally does not give precise source information for this material, only the general statement 'Electronic databases created from various publications of parish and probate records'. However, it seems likely that many of these records are taken from printed parish register indexes. Two important indexes available on Ancestry are Pallot's baptism and marriage indexes for England, covering the period 1780–1837, the originals of which are held by the Institute of Heraldic and Genealogical Studies. These have 200,000 baptisms and 1½ million marriages, mainly from Middlesex and the City of London, but with some material from other counties. An important component of this material are the nine million or so parish register entries from the London Metropolitan Archive, covering the period 1538 to 1812, accompanied by images of the original documents. These can be searched from <search.ancestry.co.uk/search/db.aspx?dbid=1624>.

Familyrelatives at <www.familyrelatives.com> (see p. 57) has online indexes to material from around 80 of the volumes of Phillimore's Marriage Registers, published in the early twentieth century.

The Parish Register Transcription Society is a non-profit volunteer group with searchable indexes to a selection of parish registers for each English county. For most counties coverage is as yet quite small scale, with perhaps a dozen parishes covered, but there is substantial material for Hampshire, Lincolnshire, Norfolk and West Sussex. For some counties there are also books, such as trade directories. The site at <prtsoc.frontisgroup.com> runs a pay-per-view service with individual records costing 20p to view.

Scotland

Unlike England and Wales, Scotland has collected most of its parish registers in one place, the GROS. All the births/baptisms, banns/marriages and deaths/burials dating from 1553 to 1854 (the start of general registration) are available online at ScotlandsPeople <www.scotlandspeople.gov.uk> (see p. 50). The site has an index and page images of the Old Parish Registers, as they are called. There is general information on these registers at <www.scotlandspeoplehub.gov.uk/research/old-parish-registers-1553-1854.html>, and this page has links to a 'List of OPRs' which in turn links to a number of files in PDF format covering individual counties or groups of counties.

Because all the registers are held centrally and have all been digitized, you will not find the wide range of other indexes and transcriptions that is found in the case of England and Wales, though some of the commercial data services include small amounts of Scottish material among the resources discussed above. You may also find some printed indexes to Scottish parish registers in the digitized books discussed in Chapter 12.

The Anglo-Scottish Family History Society has compiled a Scottish Strays Marriage Index, i.e. an index of marriages that took place outside Scotland, where at least one of the partners was born in Scotland. The index is available free of charge as a series of PDF files at <www.anglo-scots.mlfhs.org.uk>.

Ireland

Ireland differs from the other parts of the British Isles in that the relative importance of the established church, the Church of Ireland, is much less.

The National Archives of Ireland has information about Irish church records at <www.nationalarchives.ie/genealogy/church.html> and PRONI has a guide to Northern Ireland church records at <www.proni.gov.uk/your_family_tree_series_-_03_-_church_records.pdf>, covering all denominations. The National Library of Ireland has guides to Roman Catholic Parish Registers at <www.nli.ie/en/parish-register.aspx> (irritatingly, these PDF documents do not display in your browser window but get downloaded to your hard disk).

Useful information can be found online about the location of church records. IrelandGenWeb at <www.irelandgenweb.com> and NorthernIrelandGenWeb at <www.rootsweb.ancestry.com/~nirwgw/> have county pages which often include details of the parishes whose registers have been filmed by the LDS. Fianna has a convenient list of LDS microfilm numbers for Irish parishes at <www.rootsweb.ancestry.com/~fianna/county/ldspars.html>, though of course this information can also be gleaned from the Family History Library catalogue (see p. 221).

A major development in access to Irish parish records was the launch at the end of 2009 by Ireland's Department of Tourism, Culture and Sport of the Irish Genealogy site at <www.irishgenealogy.ie>, which provides free access. The site represents a mammoth project, and areas covered so far are Counties Carlow, Cork, and Kerry, and Dublin City, including both Roman Catholic and Church of Ireland registers, as well as a number of Presbyterian records. There are links to detailed lists of dates and parishes included from <www.irishgenealogy.ie/record_list.html>. In some cases, images of the records are available on the site in PDF format.

The Irish Family History Foundation's Roots Ireland site at <www.rootsireland.ie> has a large collection of indexes for both Roman Catholic and Church of Ireland registers available on a pay-per-view basis (with initial searches free). Detailed information on the dates and parishes covered can be found by following the 'Online Sources' link on the home page, then 'List of Sources' and selecting a county from the drop-down list.

FamilySearch has some Irish records: around five million births and baptisms, and 423,000 marriages. Unfortunately, there is no detailed information about the sources of these collections (though individual records are fully sourced), so it is not possible to tell in advance of searching whether you are likely to find the record of a particular event.

There are several other places to look for Irish material:

- The Irish Ancestors site has links to online resources for individual counties at <**www.irishtimes.com/ancestor/browse/links/counties/**>, which includes some parish register material.
- The Genuki county pages for Ireland, linked from <**www.genuki.org.uk/big/irl/**>, have sections devoted to Church Records.
- RootsWeb has a small number of user-submitted databases with Irish parish register material listed at <**userdb.rootsweb.ancestry.com/regional.html**> – note there are two sections for Ireland, one of which is under 'United Kingdom'. Some of these are *very* limited in scope and just cover particular surnames.
- The Ulster Historical Foundation has around 1½ million records for County Antrim and County Down on its pay-per-view service at <**www.ancestryireland.com/database.php**> – charged at £4 per record it is rather expensive, though initial searches are free. The site does not give any indication of the denominations and parishes covered.

The Roman Catholic Church

The official websites for the Roman Catholic Church in the British Isles are:

- England and Wales <**www.catholic-ew.org.uk**>
- Scotland <**www.bpsconfscot.com**>
- Ireland <**www.catholicireland.net**>

The National Archives has a research guide on 'Catholic Recusants' at <**www.nationalarchives.gov.uk/records/research-guides/catholics.htm**>, which gives a guide to the relevant official records. Some of the records are grouped with Nonconformist registers in TNA's record series RG4, which is available online at BMDregisters – see below. The Catholic Record Society at <**www.catholicrecordsociety.co.uk**> is the main publishing body for Catholic records, while the Catholic National Library has a guide to its collections at <**www.catholic-library.org.uk**>. The Catholic Archives

Society has a website at <www.catholicarchivesociety.org> and the Scottish Catholic Archives at <www.scottishcatholicarchives.org.uk>.

Information about the Catholic Family History Society will be found at <www.catholic-history.org.uk/cfhs/>, and the Catholic History site at <www.catholic-history.org.uk> also hosts three regional Catholic FHS websites.

Scotland's Catholic parish registers, as well as those for the Catholic Bishopric of the Forces, are available online at ScotlandsPeople with an introductory page at <www.scotlandspeople.gov.uk/Content/Help/index.aspx?r=554&1375>. Because of the varied dates of the records, it is worth checking the list of extant records at <www.scotlandspeople.gov.uk/content/images/ScotlandsPeople%20CPR%20Missions.pdf> if you fail to find an event recorded.

For Ireland, the Fianna website has a guide to the nation's Roman Catholic records at <www.rootsweb.ancestry.com/~fianna/county/parishes.html> taken from Brian Mitchell's *A Guide to Irish Parish Registers*.

Useful links for the British Isles will be found on the Catholic Genealogy site at <www.amateur-genealogist.com/catholic_genealogy.htm>. Cyndi's List has almost 250 links to Catholic resources at <www.cyndislist.com/catholic/>.

The websites of the libraries and archives discussed in Chapter 13 are worth checking for information about local Catholic records.

Nonconformist churches

The British Isles are home to many Protestant denominations outside the Established Church. The Spartacus Internet Encyclopaedia has a brief history of the most important religious groups at <www.spartacus.schoolnet.co.uk/religion.htm>, with links to details of individual reformers and reform movements. Wikipedia has substantial articles on the main groups both worldwide and in Britain. Its 'Nonconformism' page lists the main denominations and links to other relevant historical articles.

Cyndi's List has individual pages devoted to Baptist, Huguenot, Methodist, Presbyterian and Quaker materials, and links to many other relevant resources on the 'Religion and Churches' pages at <www.cyndislist.com/religion/>.

For details of the records for England and Wales, consult TNA's research guide 'Nonconformists' at <www.nationalarchives.gov.uk/records/research-guides/nonconformists.htm>. The records themselves are held in four document series at TNA:

- RG4: Early Registers (authenticated by the Non-Parochial Registers Commissioners) of births, baptisms, deaths, burials and marriages. They cover dates from 1567 to 1858.
- RG5: Early Birth Certificates from the Presbyterian, Independent and Baptist Registry and from the Wesleyan Methodist Metropolitan Registry. They cover dates from 1742 to 1840.
- RG6: The Society of Friends' (Quakers) Registers, Notes and Certificates of Births, Marriages and Burials ranging from 1578–1841.
- RG8: GRO Registers of Births, Marriages and Deaths surrendered to the Non Parochial Registers Commission of 1857, and other registers and church records.

Each of these is available online, indexed and with page images, at The Genealogist (p. 55). If you're not already subscribed to The Genealogist, you can get access to these records on the dedicated BMDregisters' pay-per-view service at <**www.bmdregisters.co.uk**>, which is run by The Genealogist. Basic information about the content of each will be found in BMDregisters' help pages and there is much more detail in TNA's Discovery service (see p. 210) – simply enter the series reference in the search box. When viewing the record for an individual congregation, the 'View this record online' link will take you to BMDregisters.

For Scotland and Ireland, look at Sherry Irvine's article 'Protestant Nonconformity in Scotland' at <**www.genuki.org.uk/big/sct/noncon1.html**>, while Fianna has guides to Baptist, Methodist, Presbyterian and Quaker Records in Ireland linked from <**www.rootsweb.ancestry.com/~fianna/county/churches.html**>.

GenDocs has lists of London churches for a number of Nonconformist denominations on its 'Victorian London Churches' page at <**homepage.ntlworld.com/hitch/gendocs/churches.html**>.

Societies which are relevant for those with Nonconformist ancestors are:

- The Quaker Family History Society <**www.qfhs.co.uk**> which has details of Quaker records and their location, with a page for each county.
- The Baptist Historical Society at <**www.baptisthistory.org.uk**>, which has no general genealogical material but does have information on Baptist ministers.

There are a number of libraries which specialize in Nonconformist material. The John Rylands University Library in Manchester has a strong Nonconformist collection, particularly for the Methodist Church. A description of the main resources will be found at <**www.library.manchester.ac.uk/searchresources/guidetospecialcollections/atoz/subjectgroups/theology/**>, and the home page of the Methodist Archives and Research

Centre is at <www.library.manchester.ac.uk/searchresources/ guidetospecialcollections/methodist/>.

Dr Williams's Library is an essential repository for those researching English Nonconformist ancestors. Its website at <**www.dwlib.co.uk**> has information about the library and its holdings, as well as a family history area with a brief introduction to Nonconformist records and an explanation of which denominations are and are not covered by the library. The ARCHON Directory at <**www.nationalarchives.gov.uk/ archon/**> (see p. 205) has an entry for the Library with links to the materials catalogued in the National Register of Archives, including papers relating to around 200 clergymen. The Library's Surman Index (*not* 'surname'), which comprises 32,000 typed cards with information on the careers of Congregational and English Presbyterian (later Unitarian) ministers for England and Wales, is available free on the website of Dr Williams's Centre for Dissenting Studies, hosted by Queen Mary, University of London, at <**surman.english.qmul.ac.uk**>.

The official Quaker website has information about the collections in the Library at Friends House at <**www.quaker.org.uk/library/**>, which includes a guide to the Library's genealogical sources.

Municipal burials and cremations

Originally, all burial records were parish records, and will be found among online parish registers. However, with the rise of urban cemeteries in the Victorian era, this has increasingly not been the case, and burial records are now more often municipal than ecclesiastical. Lists of cemeteries and crematoria in an area should be available on the website of the relevant local authority along with information on how to access the records.

Deceased Online at <**www.deceasedonline.com**> was launched in 2008 to provide a central database of burial and cremation records for the whole of the British Isles, though so far there is no material for Wales or Ireland. The free search provides basic details: name, date of burial or cremation, and the name of the cemetery or crematorium. If you subscribe or purchase pay-per-view credits you can see fuller details, including the deceased's date of birth, address and occupation, as well as the location of any grave. While the monumental inscription records discussed in the next section are based on volunteers inspecting individual gravestones, which in many cases are not easy to read, the data for Deceased Online is submitted directly by participating cemeteries and crematoria and should therefore be highly accurate. As of March 2012, the site has around 3 million entries from two dozen authorities, with another 1.7 million records from 18 further authorities in preparation.

There is quite a lot of relevant material online for London. GenDocs has a list of Victorian London Cemeteries at <**homepage.ntlworld.com/hitch/ gendocs/cem.html**>, with addresses and dates. The London Burial Grounds site at <**www.londonburials.co.uk**> has details of many London burial grounds. For the City of London Cemetery and Crematorium, there is no online index but scans of all the pages of the original records are available online at <**www.cityoflondon.gov.uk/burialRegisters/**>.

Manchester has its own free searchable database at <**www.burialrecords. manchester.gov.uk**>, though there is a charge for images of the records. The Sheffield General Cemetery Trust has indexed the first 6,000 burials and details of plot owners in the city's principal Victorian cemetery at <**www.gencem.org**>.

Two of the largest cemeteries on the island of Ireland have online databases. The Glasnevin Trust, which runs Dublin's main cemetery and several others in the city, has an online database of around 1½ million records at <**www.glasnevintrust.ie/genealogy/**> on a pay-per-view basis, priced at €3 for a standard entry. The extended search at €8 gives details of all other burials in the same grave. Belfast City Council has an online database with around 360,000 records for three of the city's cemeteries going back to 1869 at <**www.belfastcity.gov.uk/burialrecords/search.asp**>. Access to the records is free.

Alongside these official sites, there are, of course, volunteer projects for particular cemeteries. For example, Toxteth Park Cemetery Indexes at <**www.toxtethparkcemetery.co.uk**> covers two Liverpool cemeteries.

The British Association for Cemeteries in South Asia cares for and records European cemeteries wherever the East India Company set foot. Its website at <**www.bacsa.org.uk**> gives details of the published records.

Monumental inscriptions

While monumental or memorial inscriptions (MIs) are not official records, their close connection with the deceased means that they can provide family information not given by a death certificate, and can make up for a missing entry in a burial register. Similar information can come from obituaries, which are covered on p. 203.

The best starting point for cemeteries and MIs is Guy Etchells's Tombstones & Monumental Inscriptions site at <**www.framland.pwp. blueyonder.co.uk**>. This aims to 'provide a photographic record of the various churches, churchyards and cemeteries for the benefit of those genealogists who live some distance away', but it also has a comprehensive collection of links to related sites for the UK and other English-speaking countries, as well as links for war memorials. Cyndi's List has a 'Cemeteries

& Funeral Homes' page at <www.cyndislist.com/cemeteries/> with a number of links for UK sites and many general resources for cemeteries.

There are countless small volunteer transcriptions. For example, the England Tombstone Project at <**www.rootsweb.ancestry.com/~engcemet/**> has transcriptions for a number of cemeteries including four from London. Interment.net at <**www.interment.net**> has collections of MI transcriptions for some UK cemeteries. These are individual user-submitted records, and only some of the materials represent complete transcriptions for a cemetery or churchyard. Cornish Cemeteries at <**freepages.genealogy.rootsweb. ancestry.com/~chrisu/cornwall/cornwall.htm**> has material for around a dozen cemeteries and churchyards in Cornwall. Norfolk Epitaphs at <**epitaphorigins.info**> has transcriptions for around 70 parishes in the county.

A large collection of Scottish MIs (90,000 records from 150 cemeteries) is available on Deceased Online, discussed above. The material was compiled by volunteers and includes photographs of headstones.

Apart from the general resources mentioned above, good ways to see if there is anything for a particular place or church is to look at the relevant Genuki parish page if there is one, or simply use a search engine to find pages with the place-name and the phrase "monumental inscriptions".

British-Genealogy has pages on recording and publishing memorial inscriptions at <**www.british-genealogy.com/resources/graves/**>. For help with Latin inscriptions, see p. 291.

There are many mailing lists relating to cemeteries and monumental inscriptions. Those most relevant to the British Isles are:

- UK-CEMETERIES, subscription details at <**lists.rootsweb.ancestry.com/ index/intl/UK/UK-CEMETERIES.html**>
- MI-ENGLAND at <**lists.rootsweb.ancestry.com/index/intl/ENG/ MI-ENGLAND.html**>
- SCOTLAND-CEMETERIES at <**lists.rootsweb.ancestry.com/index/intl/ SCT/SCOTLAND-CEMETERIES.html**>
- SCT-TOMBSTONE-INSCRIPTIONS at <**lists.rootsweb.ancestry.com/ index/intl/SCT/SCT-TOMBSTONE-INSCRIPTIONS.html**>
- IRELAND-CEMETERIES at <**lists.rootsweb.ancestry.com/index/intl/ IRL/IRELAND-CEMETERIES.html**>
- IRL-TOMBSTONE-INSCRIPTIONS at <**lists.rootsweb.ancestry.com/ index/intl/IRL/IRL-TOMBSTONE-INSCRIPTIONS.html**>

War memorials are discussed in Chapter 10.

8

PROPERTY, TAXATION AND THE LAW

The foregoing chapters have looked at the three core types of genealogical record, the ones which, in principle at least, provide a record for every person who has lived in the British Isles for the last 450 years. But there are, of course, many other types of record of interest to the family historian, and these are covered in this and the following four chapters.

One problem when you start to look for other types of genealogical record is that you cannot be sure in advance whether there will actually *be* any records pertaining to a particular ancestor. Not everyone served in the military, made a will or was convicted of a crime; many occupations left little or no documentation. In particular, in the female line there may be very few records of this sort before the twentieth century.

But the particular advantage where these records have been digitized is that they can be checked very quickly. You might not be able to justify spending a day in a record office going through a whole sheaf of documents in the uncertain hope that an ancestor might be mentioned. But there's no reason not to check these records if there is an online index.

These chapters look at the most useful sites for the most important types of record, but there is much more than can be covered here. The commercial data services have significant collections of material from sources other than civil registration, census and parish registers, as indicated in the sections devoted to each site in Chapter 4. Where there are official records, the websites of the national or local repositories will give details of any large-scale plans for digitization (see p. 208ff.). But even where there are no such plans, many individuals and groups are publishing small collections of data from other records online. These tend to be piecemeal indexes and transcriptions, rather than the publication of complete national datasets, and some are discussed under 'Local and social history' in Chapter 16. In addition, the archives and libraries discussed in Chapter 13 have details of other records which may or may not have been digitized.

Wills

Wills are an important source for family historians and there has been a considerable increase in the number of wills available online in the last few years. Wills have been proved in many different places, and locating the right source for the potential will of a particular ancestor can sometimes be difficult, so if you are not familiar with historical probate records it is a good idea to look at the general information before looking for a specific will.

Although wills and probate records are specifically property records – they record what the testator intended to happen to his or her property after death – their importance extends beyond this. Because they indicate an approximate death date, they can provide a substitute for a missing burial record, and they are also valuable for clarifying family relationships. Indeed, apart from rare personal diaries and letters, they are the only major documentary source likely to give information about the personal relations between our ancestors and their families.

England and Wales

My 'Introduction to Wills' at <**www.origins.net/help/resarticle-willsPC.aspx**> provides a concise overview of the topic, but for detailed information about wills in England and Wales the best starting points are the 'Probate Records' pages for the two nations on the FamilySearch wiki at <**www.familysearch.org/learn/wiki/en/England_Probate_Records**> and <**www.familysearch.org/learn/wiki/en/Wales_Probate_Records**>. The National Archives has three guides on wills and death duties, all linked from the 'Looking for a person?' page at <**www.nationalarchives.gov.uk/records/looking-for-person**> but the information provided is very brief. More useful is the research guide 'Wills and probate records' at <**www.nationalarchives.gov.uk/records/research-guides/wills-and-probate-records.htm**>, and the 'Probate records' article in the Your Archives wiki at <**yourarchives.nationalarchives.gov.uk/index.php?title=Probate_records**> which gives a lot of background.

Probate records since 1858 are under the jurisdiction of the Probate Service, which has pages on the Courts and Tribunals Service website at <**www.justice.gov.uk/guidance/courts-and-tribunals/courts/probate/**>. There is a page on 'Probate Records and Family History' at <**www.justice.gov.uk/guidance/courts-and-tribunals/courts/probate/family-history.htm**>. A 2004 review of probate business by the former Court Service (now in the Government Web Archive at <**hmcourts-service.gov.uk/cms/files/rop-final-report.pdf**>, 5 July 2007) concluded that the full Probate Calendar from 1858 onwards should be online by April 2006, but so far this has failed to materialize. However, Ancestry has a

National Probate Calendar database, which is a searchable index to the printed indexes of wills and administrations for the period 1861–1941. The search results link to scans of the original index books, which give basic details of the grant of probate or administration.

Before 1858, wills were proved in ecclesiastical courts (mostly in local archdeaconry and diocesan courts) and there is no national repository for these records. This means that you need to establish which court a will is proved in before you can find it. In principle, the will should be in the relevant diocesan record office, which will almost always be the county record office.

Origins has a useful article on 'Probate before 1858' at <**www.origins.net/ help/resarticle-wills-pre1858.aspx**>, which will give you some idea of how to decide which court may be relevant for a particular ancestor. FamilySearch also has useful material relating to English probate jurisdictions. The search facility at <**www.familysearch.org/eng/Library/FHL/probate.asp**> will tell you which courts had jurisdiction for a particular place, though so far it covers only London and Essex. The 'England Jurisdictions, 1851' map on FamilySearch at <**maps.familysearch.org**> (see p. 272) includes an overlay which shows which ecclesiastical jurisdiction a particular parish was in (though note this is for England only, not Wales).

For locating pre-1858 wills online, there is only one place to start: TNA's Your Archives wiki has an article on 'Online Probate Indexes' at <**yourarchives.nationalarchives.gov.uk/index.php?title=Online_Probate_ Indexes**> which details all the online will indexes for individual counties or jurisdictions. There are four major collections with national coverage:

- The National Archives' Discovery service offers images of over one million wills from the Prerogative Court of Canterbury, the largest probate court for England and Wales, for the period 1384–1858. Each will costs £3.50 to download, regardless of length. Details are at <**www.nationalarchives.gov.uk/documentsonline/wills.asp**>.
- Origins is in the process of building up a National Wills Index, searchable from <**www.nationalwillsindex.com**>, which combines a number of pre-existing indexes, such as those of the British Record Society, along with new digitizations. It currently includes over 3.2 million names, with 90 per cent of English counties represented.
- Ancestry has a database of just under two million 'Extracted Probate Records' at <**search.ancestry.co.uk/search/db.aspx?dbid=1610**> derived from a variety of sources. (The site also has some much smaller datasets of will calendars and probate inventories from individual probate courts.)
- The National Library of Wales has a free index to its probate collection in Welsh Wills Online, with over 190,000 records, available at <**cat.llgc.org.uk/ cgi-bin/gw/chameleon?skin=profeb&lng=en**>.

Note that The National Archives is the only one of these four which provides the wills themselves; the others are indexes and you will need to consult the relevant repository to see the original documents. However, the National Wills Index in some cases includes a detailed summary of the will.

The Your Archives listing also includes will digitization and indexing projects for many individual English counties, and many CRO websites have material devoted to their will collections.

Beyond the CROs there are a number of smaller volunteer-based sources. For example, Maureen Rawson has many Kent will transcripts and some inventory indexes at <**freepages.genealogy.rootsweb.ancestry.com/~mrawson/probate.html**>, and the Norfolk Family History Society has an index of around 600 Norfolk wills at <**www.norfolkfhs.org.uk/resources/wills/willstranscripts.asp**>. The Castle Donnington Wills site at <**www.oldwills.co.uk**> has wills for just the area around Castle Donnington in Leicestershire.

Findmypast has two related resources:

- Index to Death Duty Registers 1796–1903 – see <**www.findmypast.co.uk/helpadvice/knowledge-base/wills-divorces/**>.
- Great Western Railway Shareholders 1835–1932 at <**www.findmypast.co.uk/great-western-railway-shareholders-search-start.action**>, which are mostly records of share transfers on the death of a shareholder.

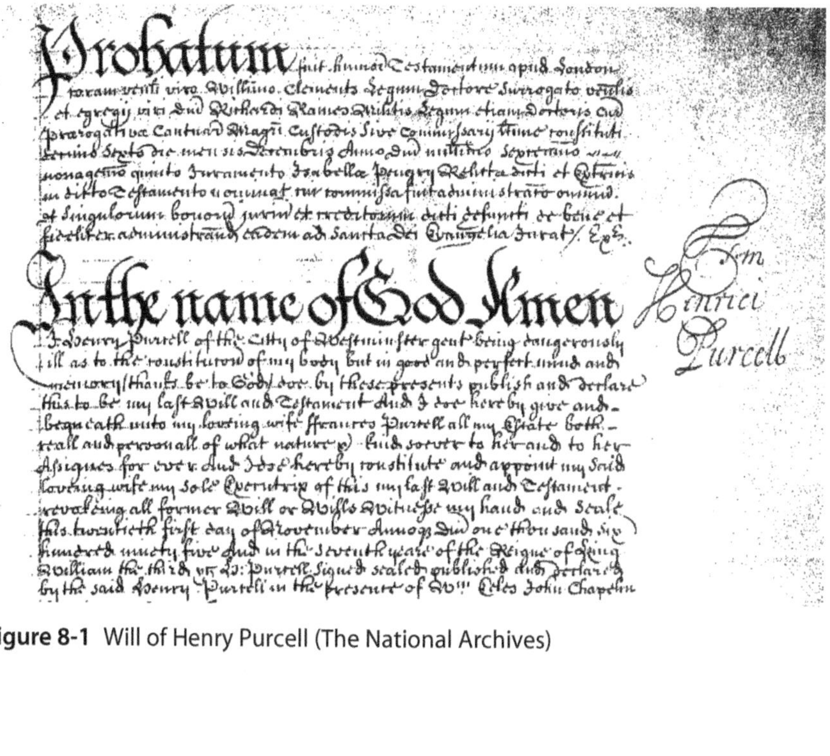
Probatum

In the name of God Amen

I Henry Purcell of the City of Westminster gent being dangerously ill as to the constitution of my body but in good and perfect mind and memory (thanks be to God) doe by these presents publish and declare this to be my last Will and Testament And I doe hereby give and bequeath unto my loving wife Frances Purcell all my Estate both reall and personall of what nature or kind soever to her and to her Assignes for ever And I doe hereby constitute and appoint my said loving wife my sole Executrix of this my last Will and Testament revoking all former Will or Wills Witnesse my hand and Seale this twentieth first day of November Annoq Dni one thousand six hundred ninety five And in the seventh yeare of the Reigne of King William the third &c: H: Purcell Signed sealed published and declared by the said Henry Purcell in the presence of Wm Eccles John Chaplin

Henrici Purcell

Figure 8-1 Will of Henry Purcell (The National Archives)

Disputes about inheritance formed a major part of the business of the Chancery Courts, whose records are discussed at the end of this chapter.

Scotland

There are guides to Scottish wills and testaments on the National Archives of Scotland site at <www.nas.gov.uk/guides/wills.asp> and on ScotlandsPeople at <www.scotlandspeople.gov.uk/Content/Help/index.aspx?r=554&407>.

All Scottish wills from 1513 to 1901 are available online at ScotlandsPeople (see p. 50). The site offers a free index of over half a million entries in the Registers of Testaments, and scans of the wills can then be purchased online and downloaded. Unlike the other material on ScotlandsPeople, the wills are not part of the pay-per-view system, but cost £5 each via an online shop (all wills costs the same, regardless of length). The index entries themselves give quite detailed information about testators.

The site also has some examples of wills from each 50-year period covered by the index. On the 'Wills & Testaments' page click on the period you want in the right-hand panel under the 'Wills & Testaments' heading. For those unfamiliar with Scottish probate records and terminology, the FAQ pages at <www.scotlandspeople.gov.uk/content/faqs/> provide a comprehensive introduction to all aspects of the records under the heading 'Property & Inheritance'. There is also an explanation of the various Scottish courts with a role in probate. Further help is available in the 'Research Tools' area (under 'Help & Other Resources'), which includes material on handwriting, abbreviations found in wills, and occupations.

Wills and testaments after 1901 are not available online and details of how to obtain them are given on the NAS page mentioned above.

Ireland

A good overview of wills and probate in Ireland will be found on the Irish Ancestors site at <www.irishtimes.com/ancestor/browse/records/wills/>, and PRONI has a useful set of pages on wills in Northern Ireland at <www.proni.gov.uk/index/search_the_archives/will_calendars/about_wills.htm>. In the Republic of Ireland, probate affairs are managed by the Probate Office, whose web page at <www.citizensinformation.ie/en/justice/courts_system/probate_office.html> provides basic information and has a link to the page for the Personal Application Section of the Probate Office (112-character nonsense URL!).

There are three national indexes to Irish wills:

- Irish Origins at <www.irishorigins.com> has four sets of indexes to Irish Wills, including the Irish Wills Index 1484–1858 covering over 100,000 wills held at the National Archives of Ireland and those published by Phillimore.

- Ancestry UK also has the Phillimore indexes – details at <**www.ancestry. co.uk/search/db.aspx?dbid=7287**>.
- PRONI has a Will Calendar Search for counties of Northern Ireland at <**applications.proni.gov.uk/DCAL_PRONI_WillsCalendar/ WillsSearch.aspx**>, which includes a concise abstract of each will and in some cases an image of the original documents.

You can also expect to find local transcriptions done by volunteers. For example, there is an index to wills for the Diocese of Raphoe, Donegal at <**freepages.genealogy.rootsweb.ancestry.com/~donegal/wills.htm**>, while Ginni Swanton has scanned images of the Phillimore index to Irish Wills for the Dioceses of Cork and Ross at <**www.ginnisw.com/Indexes%20to%20 Irish%20Wills/Thumb/Thumbs1.htm**>. Other sites with Irish wills can be found from the UK and Ireland page in the 'Wills and Probate' category of Cyndi's List at <**www.cyndislist.com/wills/uk/**>, or by using a search engine.

Land and taxation

Property records are important in showing a place of residence before the start of the census or where, as in Ireland, census records are missing. Even those too poor to own property may be recorded as occupiers, though of course only a head of household will be given. However, most older property records are not strictly property records at all. Rather they are generally records of tax assessments *based on* land ownership and occupation, which was the norm before the permanent introduction of income tax in 1842. They, therefore, do not necessarily give much information about the property held other than its acreage or rateable value, which nonetheless may help to indicate the status of an ancestor in the locality. The 1911 census (see p. 90) is the only general national source to give much information about the properties occupied by our ancestors.

It is not possible here to look at all classes of property and taxation records, only to draw attention to some of the most useful resources available online. The FamilySearch wiki has an article 'Introduction to Tax Records in England' at <**www.familysearch.org/learn/wiki/en/Introduction_to_ Tax_Records_in_England**> which provides an introduction, and a fairly comprehensive Wikipedia article on the 'History of the English fiscal system' discusses many of these taxes in their historical context.

The National Archives has a research guide on 'Taxation records before 1689' at <**www.nationalarchives.gov.uk/records/research-guides/**

taxation-before-1689.htm>, and there are individual guides to Hearth Tax, Land Tax and Tithe Records linked from <**www.nationalarchives.gov.uk/ records/atoz/t.htm**>.

The E179 Database at <**www.nationalarchives.gov.uk/e179/**> is a catalogue of taxation records. It does not contain any information about individuals, its sole function being to identify the relevant documents for a particular place, tax and period.

The National Archives of Scotland has a guide to Scottish taxation records at <**www.nas.gov.uk/guides/taxation.asp**>.

Many property and taxation records are held at local level, so it is worth checking the relevant county record office website for information. There are few national projects in this area, but many small transcriptions for individual parishes. Also, many of these records have been published in book form by the various record societies, so a search of the digital book archives described in Chapter 12 is recommended.

Tithes

Tithe records, and in particular the nineteenth-century tithe maps, are important sources for both owners and occupiers of land. A very thorough discussion of tithe records will be found in The National Archives' research guide 'Tithe Records: A Detailed Examination' at <**www.nationalarchives.gov.uk/ records/research-guides/tithe-records.htm**>. The National Library of Wales also has comprehensive pages on this topic at <**www.llgc.org.uk/ index.php?id=549**>. County record office websites often give information about tithe maps and schedules in their collections, and these are obvious candidates for digitization. Devon and Worcester have projects to index their tithe maps – these both have mammoth URLs of 100 or so characters, so follow the links on the site for this book or search from the county council home pages at <**www.devon.gov.uk**> and <**www.worcestershire.gov.uk**> respectively. Cornwall Record Office has a Tithe Project in development, though this still has some way to go and there are no materials online as yet. Details will be found at <**www.cornwall.gov.uk/default.aspx?page=14666**>.

A major tithe records project is the University of Portsmouth's Tithe Survey of England and Wales at <**tiger.iso.port.ac.uk:7785/www/web. html?p=tithe_intro**>, which also offers data for 15 parishes.

There are many individual transcriptions of tithe schedules. For example:

- Tithe Titles for Kelsall, Cheshire <**www.the-dicksons.org/Kelsall/kelsall/ tithespg.htm**>
- Tithe Book of Bolton with Goldthorpe, 1839 <**www.genuki.org.uk/big/ eng/YKS/Misc/Transcriptions/WRY/BoltonGoldthorpeTitheBook Index.html**>

The best way to find them is probably to search on the word 'tithes' or the phrase 'tithe map' and the relevant place-name.

Lay subsidy and land tax

There have many property-based taxes levied on the population since the Middle Ages which have left records, notably the irregularly raised lay subsidy and the later land tax. It is not possible to aim at any sort of comprehensive list of online resources, as there seem to be no national resources devoted to these taxes, but rather many small transcriptions and indexes for particular localities. The simplest way to see if there is any relevant material online is to search on the name of a tax and the county of interest. A few examples:

- British History Online has various lay subsidy records linked from <**www.british-history.ac.uk/catalogue.aspx?gid=53**>.
- Genuki Devon at <**genuki.cs.ncl.ac.uk/DEV/**> has a number of transcriptions of land tax records for Devon parishes, while Genuki Pembrokeshire has many extractions from tax records, mainly land tax, for the parish of Monkton at <**www.genuki.org/big/wal/PEM/ Pemtax1.html**>.
- The Sussex Record Society at <**www.sussexrecordsociety.org**> has transcriptions of the Lay Subsidy Rolls for the county of Sussex 1524–1525 and the 1747 Window Tax.
- The 1662 Hearth Tax Returns for Ploughley Hundred in Oxfordshire are indexed at <**www.whipple.org/oxford/ploughley_100_hearth_ tax_1662.html**>.

Land ownership and occupation

There are records of land ownership which are not tied to taxation. The 1873 Returns of Owners of Land list all those who owned more than an acre of land. A complete set of scans of the printed records for England, Wales, Scotland and Ireland are available to Familyrelatives subscribers at <**www.familyrelatives.com**> (see Figure 8-2). The Irish return, dated 1876, is also available to Ancestry UK subscribers – see <**www.ancestry.co.uk/ search/db.aspx?dbid=48475**>. The return for Wales can be seen free on the Welsh site the Ogre at <**www.cefnpennar.com/1873index.htm**>, which has those for Scotland and Ireland available via paid download.

There are also several online transcriptions for individual counties. The most extensive of these is available in the UK Genealogy archives at <**uk-genealogy.org.uk/cgi-bin/DB/search.cgi?action=loadDB&DB=1**>, which has over 30,000 records for the counties of Anglesey, Brecknock, Cardigan, Leicester, Worcester, Oxford, Stafford, Middlesex, Rutland and

DERBY.

Population in 1871	. . .	379,394.
Inhabited Houses	. .	78,309.
No. of Parishes	. .	331.

Name of Owner.	Address of Owner.	Extent of Lands.	Gross Estimated Rental.	Name of Owner.	Address of Owner.	Extent of Lands.	Gross Estimated Rental.
		A. R. P.	£ s.			A. R. P.	£ s.
Abbott, Josiah	Wirksworth	10 2 7	30 14	Allison, William	Whitwell	1 3 11	46 10
Abbott, Mary	Breaston	1 3 24	27 –	Allport, James J.	Littleover	6 – 26	120 16
Abbott, Ruth	Breaston	.1 3 24	27 –	Allsop, Charles	Foston	46 3 29	77 17
Abel, John	Matlock	3 1 3	6 1	Allsop, Charles	Turnditch	72 2 10	128 10
Abell, Hy.	Kniveton	21 3 23	30 9	Allsop, Charles	Wirksworth	16 2 31	46 13
Abell, Hy.	Wirksworth	1 3 1	4 12	Allsop, Miss D.	Chesterfield	7 – 19	10 16
Abell, John	Belper	2 – –	1 9	Allsop, Eliza	Dethick Lea	10 – 14	27 –
Abell, John	Bonsall	20 3 17	51 1	Allsop, Elizabeth	Kniveton	7 – –	12 16
Abell, John	Wirksworth	1 5 1	4 12	Allsop, Ellen	Wirksworth	2 – –	33 6
Abell, John & William	Hulland Ward	12 – 9	15 4	Allsop, Francis	Parwich	32 1 2	64 19
Abell, Martha	Bonsall	2 1 25	4 6	Allsop, George	Brassington	1 2 9	6 12
Abell, William	Darby	–	261 5	Allsop, George	Parwich	32 1 2	64 19
Abell, William	Rutland Ward	12 – 22	16 17	Allsop, Griffith	Nottingham	1 – 17	11 2
Abney, Rev. E. H.	Derby	129 3 34	388 12	Allsop, Hannah	Ballidon Moor	29 2 2	40 8
Abney, Mrs.	Measham	102 1 3	252 8	Allsop, Hannah	Hognaston	5 2 35	12 17
Adams, Bakewell	Church Broughton	6 – 1	49 16	Allsop, John	Hulland	33 2 17	48 19
Adams, George	Boylestone	1 2 –	18 –	Allsop, John	Parwich	7 – 20	9 11
Adams, John	Alstonefield	5 2 12	6 9	Allsop, John & William	Higham	3 1 24	4 12
Adams, John	Church Gresley	3 1 38	84 9	Allsop, Luke	Orich	10 2 13	40 19
Adams, John	Hilton	5 2 16	34 18	Allsop, Mrs.	Brassington	31 1 24	68 11
Adams, Josh.	Kirk Langley	1 – 32	12 1	Allsop, Richard	Nottingham	6 3 3	18 –
Adams, Robert	Middleton	12 2 22	29 9	Allsop, Ruth	Bonsall	2 – 34	·3 18
Adams, Robert Edward	Ivon Brook	10 3 19	17 12	Allsop, Samuel	Wirksworth	7 – 2	40 10
Adams, Samuel	Ockbrook	5 1 11	21 –	Allsop, Sarah	Bonsall	5 – 1	9 8
Adams, Sarah	Hatton	10 3 21	59 13	Allsop, Thomas	Brassington	2 – 5	6 10
Adcock, John	Chesterfield	24 2 35	66 16	Allsop, Thomas	Wardlow	11 3 9	16 12
Adcock, Mrs.	Melbourne, near Derby	1 – 35	10 –	Allsop, William	Foston	68 1 56	97 1
Adcock, William H.	Melbourne	4 3 13	96 16	Allsopp, Hy.	Repton	1 3 16	26 10

Figure 8-2 The Return of Owners of Land, 1873 (Familyrelatives)

Hertford. The 'Explanatory Statement' from the original publication, which explains a great deal about the survey, is included at <uk-genealogy.org.uk/OwnersofLand.html>. Further county extracts include:

- Oxfordshire: <www.genoot.com/eng/oxf/landowners/>
- Norfolk: <www.thornburypump.myby.co.uk/1873/>
- County Carlow: <www.rootsweb.ancestry.com/~irlcar2/Carlow_1871.htm>

The National Farm Surveys of England and Wales, 1940–1943 are described in a National Archives research guide at <www.nationalarchives.gov.uk/records/research-guides/farm-survey.htm>.

The most famous survey of property holdings, though few of us can trace our pedigrees back that far, is the Domesday Book. The National Archives has information about it at <www.nationalarchives.gov.uk/documents online/domesday.asp>. Open Domesday has the entire work available online at <domesdaymap.co.uk> as a set of entries for the individual places, with an image of the original manuscript and summary of the details.

Another medieval source, going up to the Tudor period, are the feet of fines, which are legal records of land purchase. Chris Phillips's Medieval English Genealogy site has a list of feet of fines published (whether in print or online) for each English county at <www.medievalgenealogy.org.uk/fines/counties.shtml>. The site itself has transcriptions and images for some counties, while the Anglo-American Legal Tradition website at

<aalt.law.uh.edu> has images of many others. However, the latter provides only images of the original documents written in Latin, and provides no index or transcription. British History Online has transcription of the records for a number of counties and periods at <**www.british-history.ac.uk/subject.aspx?subject=5&gid=90**>.

Medieval English Genealogy has a great deal of information about similar records at <**www.medievalgenealogy.org.uk/sources/public.shtml**> with many links to online materials.

Griffith's Valuation

For Ireland, the nineteenth-century property records are all the more important because of the destruction of census records. The sites referred to for Irish census material in Chapter 6 have information on these records, usually under the heading 'Census substitutes'. Among the most important is Griffith's Valuation, also called the Primary Valuation, and there is a range of material from this source online.

Ask About Ireland has a free index at <**www.askaboutireland.ie/griffith-valuation/**> with images of the original index pages and a pop-up of the accompanying maps. To identify the relevant plot on the map you need to locate the townland under which an ancestor is listed and look for the map reference given in the index's left-hand column. The Irish Origins site at <**www.irishorigins.com**> has an index to Griffith's Valuation and images of the original documents.

There are also many local transcriptions, and links to these will be found on the Genuki pages for Ireland at <**www.genuki.org.uk/big/irl/**> and on the Ireland pages of Census Finder at <**www.censusfinder.com/ireland.htm**>.

The PRONI has a guide to Irish valuation records at <**www.proni.gov.uk/your_family_tree_series_-_04_-_valuation_records.pdf**> and James R. Reilly's article 'Is There More in Griffith's Valuation Than Just Names?' at <**www.leitrim-roscommon.com/GRIFFITH/Griffiths.PDF**> shows just how much information can be extracted from these records.

Insurance records

Useful sources of information on property in London are the surviving fire insurance policies. The Guildhall Library holds records for many insurance companies, and over 50,000 policies from the Sun Fire Office for 1808 to 1839 have been indexed. The index can be found on the Access to Archives website at <**www.nationalarchives.gov.uk/a2a**>, and detailed instructions on using it are available at <**www.history.ac.uk/gh/sun.htm**>. The index comprises the name and address of the policyholder, his occupation or status and the location of property insured. There is general information on the Guildhall Library's fire insurance records at <**www.history.ac.uk/gh/ fire.htm**>.

Crime

The official records of the courts and the prison system contain much information about the individuals who came into contact with the law and are generally held by The National Archives. TNA's 'Looking for a person?' page at <**www.nationalarchives.gov.uk/records/looking-for-person**> links to sub-pages on bankrupts and debtors, civil litigants, criminal trials and convictions, prisoners and transportees, with information on what records are available. More detailed information is provided by a wide range of research guides which are linked from <**www.nationalarchives.gov.uk/ records/atoz/**> – look under the keywords 'crime and criminals' and 'courts of law'.

The most important online records for those tried for a crime are The National Archives' Criminal Registers for the period 1791 to 1892, which have been digitized and indexed by Ancestry at <**search.ancestry.co.uk/ search/db.aspx?dbid=1590**>. While the information given in the registers is very basic – name, when and where tried, crime and sentence – these records will at least indicate whether it will be worth looking for an ancestor in other court and prison records. Ancestry also has the Prison Hulk Registers and Letter Books, 1802–1849, searchable from <**search.ancestry.co.uk/search/ db.aspx?dbid=1989**>. Again, details are minimal, but indicate that other records will be worth seeking out.

A resource providing much more detail, albeit for only a minority of criminal ancestors, is the Proceedings of the Old Bailey site at <**www.oldbaileyonline.org**>, which contains detailed accounts of almost 200,000 trials from 1674 to 1913, with transcriptions and scanned images from the contemporary printed proceedings. Sophisticated search facilities allow trials to be selected by keyword, name, place, crime, verdict and punishment, or you can browse the trials by date. The text of each trial also contains the names of defendants, victims, witnesses, jurors and judges, which can be found via the name search, so the site is not only of interest to those with criminal ancestors.

In addition to the records themselves, the site has extensive background material about particular communities, which will be of general interest:

- Black Communities
- Gypsies and Travellers
- Homosexuality

- Irish London
- Jewish Communities
- Huguenot and French London
- Chinese Communities

Additional background includes material on the various types of verdict and punishment. Even if you don't think you have criminal ancestors, this site is worth visiting for the insight it provides into urban life in the period.

The Newgate Calendar was a popular eighteenth-century work with information on notorious criminals, and there are a number of versions online including <**www.exclassics.com/newgate/ngintro.htm**>. Capital Punishment UK at <**www.capitalpunishmentuk.org**> is a sited devoted to all aspects of the subject and has extensive information on those executed in the British Isles.

Records relating to crime and punishment in Scotland are held by the NAS (see p. 213), which has a very comprehensive page on 'Crime and Criminals' at <**www.nas.gov.uk/guides/crime.asp**>.

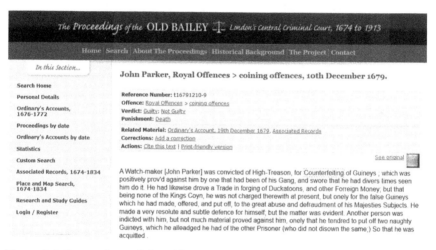

Figure 8-3 Proceedings of the Old Bailey

There are a number of online databases relating to particular courts and gaols :

- For Aylesbury Gaol, Buckinghamshire has an online database of nineteenth-century prisoners at <**www.buckscc.gov.uk/bcc/archives/ea_libprisoners.page**>.

- Warwickshire County Record Office has a Calendars of Prisoners Database covering the courts at Warwick, Birmingham and Coventry between 1801 and 1900, with details of over 30,000 prisoners. The database can be searched by crime and residence as well as by surname. The URL is a 94-character monster – see the website for this book for a link.
- The National Library of Wales has a Crime and Punishment database at <**www.llgc.org.uk/sesiwn_fawr/index_s.htm**>, with details of crimes and criminals included in the gaol files of the Court of Great Sessions in Wales from 1730 until its abolition in 1830.
- For Dumfries and Galloway there is a database of the Jail Books (1714–1788) and the Bail Bond Registers (1775–1810) at <**www.dgcommunity.net/ historicalindexes/jail.aspx**>.

For general information on prisons, the Rossbret Prisons website is an essential resource. This has a list of prisons organized by county with historical information and details of the relevant records. However, the site is now only available at the Wayback Machine with the URL <**www.institutions.org.uk/prisons/**> (15 November 2010).

There is a PRISONS-UK mailing list, details of which will be found at <**lists.rootsweb.ancestry.com/index/intl/UK/PRISONS-UK.html**>. Historic Herefordshire Online has material on the county's prisons at <**www.smr.herefordshire.gov.uk/post-medieval/prisons/prisons_index.htm**>.

The resources discussed here mostly relate to the modern period. The National Archives has research guides at <**www.nationalarchives.gov.uk/ records/atoz/**> on earlier courts such as the Court of Requests and the Star Chamber. However, you are unlikely to find material relating to individual cases online except where they have been published in print and are available in one of the digital book archives discussed in Chapter 12.

Cyndi's List has a page devoted to 'Prisons, Prisoners & Outlaws' at <**www.cyndislist.com/prisons/**>, though many of the UK links relate to policing rather than to criminals. Genuki (see p. 18) lists relevant resources under the headings 'Court Proceedings' and 'Correctional Institutions' on national and county pages. There are many resources online relating to convict transportation to the colonies, and these are discussed in Chapter 11. Materials relating to the legal profession and the police are covered in the following chapter.

Civil courts

While an increasing number of records for the criminal courts and prisons are online, and are fairly straightforward to use, the records of the civil courts are highly complex and have been little digitized as yet. Their importance for genealogists lies in the immense amount of personal and family detail that may have been recorded in, for example, a dispute about an inheritance. Again the records are held by The National Archives, whose website is the best place for an overview of the courts and their work. The 'Looking for a person?' page at <**www.nationalarchives.gov.uk/records/ looking-for-person**> has links to pages on bankrupts and debtors, and civil litigants. In-depth research guides for this area include:

- Bankrupts and Insolvent Debtors: 1710–1869
- Bankruptcy Records After 1869
- Chancery proceedings: equity suits before 1558
- Chancery proceedings: equity suits from 1558
- Assizes: key to series for English civil trials 1656–1971

all linked from <**www.nationalarchives.gov.uk/records/research-guide-listing.htm**>. The Equity Pleadings database at <**www.nationalarchives.gov.uk/ equity/**> is a catalogue of over 30,000 equity cases in Chancery 1606–1722, which can be searched by person or place.

The commercial data services have a number of sets of Chancery records online. Ancestry has a Calendar of chancery proceedings: bills and answers filed in the reign of King Charles the First at <**search.ancestry.co.uk/search/ db.aspx?dbid=28535**> and British Chancery Records, 1386–1558 at <**search.ancestry.co.uk/search/db.aspx?dbid=7919**> with 270,000 records. Origins has two datasets, both linked from <**www.origins.net/ BOWelcome.aspx**>:

- Charles I Chancery Index 1625–1649 (82,000 cases)
- Inheritance Disputes Index 1574-1714 (over 26,000 lawsuits)

Since 1665, bankruptcies have been announced in the *London Gazette* (see p. 197), and may well also be recorded in the commercial press (see Chapter 12).

Since 1858, divorces have been under the the jurisdiction of the High Court, and The National Archives' 'Looking for records of a divorce' page at <**www.nationalarchives.gov.uk/records/looking-for-person/divorce.htm**> gives details of the relevant records (none of which are online). Before 1858, divorces were effected by various means under various jurisdictions. TNA's research guide 'Divorce records before 1858' at <**www.nationalarchives.gov.uk/ records/research-guides/divorce-before-1858.htm**> covers the range of possibilities.

▌ Church courts

The records of the church courts, apart from those relating to probate discussed at the start of this chapter, are probably under-exploited by genealogists, though the fact that they dealt, among other things, with matrimonial matters, and disputes between clergy and parishioners (often about tithes) mean they can often be of interest. Their preoccupation with immorality is the reason they are popularly referred to as 'bawdy courts'. Basic information about them will be found in Else Churchill's article on the BBC History site at <**www.bbc.co.uk/history/ familyhistory/next_steps/adv_06_church_courts_01.shtml**> and Origins' article at <**www.origins.net/help/aboutbo-churchcourts.aspx**>.

So far there are few of these records online. British History Online has an index and list of London Consistory Court Depositions for 1586–1611 at <**www.british-history.ac.uk/source.aspx?pubid=1274**>, and origins has London Consistory Court Depositions Index 1700–1713 at <**www.origins.net/help/aboutbo-lccd.aspx**>

In 2011, the Borthwick Institute launched a website with the Cause Papers in the Diocesan Courts of the Archbishopric of York 1300–1858 at <**www.hrionline.ac.uk/causepapers/**> with detailed background information about the work of the courts. The index includes the names of all those named in a case – as plaintiff, defendant or witness – and indicates the type of case. For some, there are images of the papers for the case, though these are quite forbidding, since they are in Latin and written in secretary hand. The site also has details of the relevant records for the whole of the province of York.

9

OCCUPATIONS

Occupational records do not form a coherent category. There are state records only where people were employed by the state itself or where the government sought to regulate qualifications and employment. Otherwise each trade or industry kept its own records. Of course, many of our ancestors, especially those who worked the land, have left no record of their employment at all, other than in the occupation column of a census or a certificate.

Occupational terms

Given that most agricultural and early industrial occupations are now marginal if not actually obsolete, it is not uncommon to encounter unknown terms for occupations in historical records.

The definitive reference work for occupational terminology in any period is the *Oxford English Dictionary* (Figure 9-1). Accessing the online edition at <**www.oed.com**> is described on p. 186.

The most comprehensive listing of occupational terms for the early twentieth century is the Ministry of Labour's 1927 *Dictionary of Occupational Terms,* based on the terms used in the 1921 census, which has something like 30,000 entries and descriptions. It also classifies occupations, so that you can see all the jobs involved in, say, basket-making. Unfortunately, it is a rare publication and is not available online, but it has been published by the Open University on CD-ROM, and this may be available in libraries. The *OED* uses this as one its own sources for occupational terms.

A similar US work, The *Dictionary of Occupational Titles,* published by the US Department of Labor in 1971, is available online at <**www.occupationalinfo.org**>, though, of course, you will need to exercise considerable caution if using this to interpret an eighteenth-century British occupation.

The other material available online is, by comparison, very concise. Brief explanations of terms for past occupations are provided in John Hitchcock's

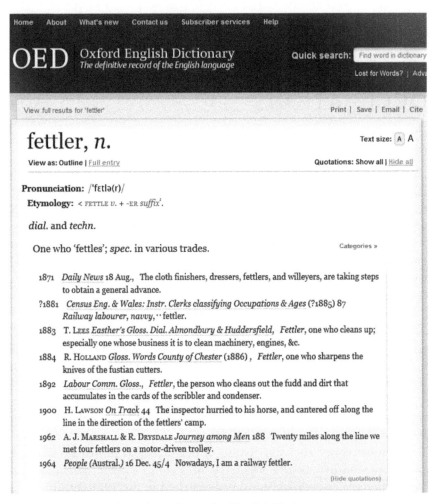

Figure 9-1 An entry from the online *Oxford English Dictionary*

'Ranks, Professions, Occupations and Trades' page at <**homepage. ntlworld.com/hitch/gendocs/trades.html**>, which has around 1,600 occupational terms. The 'Dictionary of Ancient Occupations and Trades, Ranks, Offices, and Titles' at <**freepages.genealogy.rootsweb.ancestry. com/~dav4is/Sources/Occupations.html**> is a smaller collection of around 750 terms, with the emphasis on the sixteenth and seventeenth centuries. Olive Tree's list of 'Medieval And Obsolete English Trade And Professional Terms' at <**olivetreegenealogy.com/misc/occupations. shtml#med**> may be useful, especially since it includes medieval Latin terms for many occupations, and some older English spellings. Rodney Hall's 'Old Occupation Names' at <**rmhh.co.uk/occup/**> is also useful.

For specifically Scottish terminology, look at Scots Family's 'Old Occupations in Scotland' page at <**www.scotsfamily.com/occupations.htm**>.

There is a substantial collection of terms for a single industry in the Pottery Jobs Index at <**www.thepotteries.org/jobs/**>.

If you need to clarify an occupation shown in the 1911 census, you can look up the three-figure codes in the original census documentation available from Histpop at <**www.histpop.org**> (see p. 85). On the 'Browse' menu, select 'TNA Census Other', then 'Census of England, Wales and Islands in the British Seas, 1911', then 'Occupation tables. Code sheet' – see Figure 9-2. This won't tell you what the job involves but will allow you to see how it fits into a particular industry. It can also help you identify similar jobs, which can be useful if an ancestor has different occupations given in different sources. (You will need to use the +2 Zoom option to make the text legible.)

If you have ancestors in manufacturing or trade, you may also find the Dictionary of Traded Goods and Commodities, 1550–1820 site at <**www.british-history.ac.uk/source.aspx?pubid=739**> useful in identifying precisely what your ancestor made or sold.

XIII.

(1) Cabinet Makers	751	751
French Polishers	752	752
Upholsterers	753	753
House and Shop Fittings Makers	754	754
Undertakers ; Funeral Furniture Makers	755	755
Wood Carvers ; Carvers and Gilders	756	756
Willow, Cane, Rush—Workers ; Basket Makers	757	757
Dealers in Works of Art	758*	758
Furniture &c. Dealers	759*	759
(2) Sawyers ; Wood Cutting Machinists	761	761
Lath, Wooden Fence, Hurdle—Makers	762	762
Wood Turners	763	763
Wooden Box, Packing Case—Makers	764	764
Coopers ; Hoop—Makers, Benders	765	765
Cork, Bark—Cutters, Workers	766	766
Other Workers in Wood	767	767
Timber, Wood, Cork, Bark—Merchants, Dealers	768*	768

Figure 9-2 Occupation classifications in the 1911 census

▌ General information

The National Archives has material on occupations in its 'Looking for a person' section at **<www.nationalarchives.gov.uk/records/looking-for-person>**, with pages devoted to the following occupations and professions for which there are state records:

- Apprentices and masters
- Civil or Crown Servants
- Clergy
- Coastguard
- Customs officers
- Excise officers
- Famous people
- Lawyers
- Patients, doctors and nurses
- Police
- Railway workers
- Teachers and pupils
- Workhouse inmates and staff

These lead to pages with links to online information, relevant research guides and details of the relevant records at TNA.

The Modern Records Centre at the University of Warwick holds records relating to 'labour history, industrial relations and industrial politics'. While it has not put any records online, the main genealogy page at **<www2.warwick.ac.uk/services/library/mrc/subject_guides/family_history/>** has links to genealogical guides for the following occupations:

- Blacksmiths, Forge & Smithy Workers
- Boilermakers
- Bookbinders
- Bricklayers
- Brushmakers
- Bus & Cab Workers
- Carpenters
- Carvers
- Compositors
- Decorators
- Gilders
- Ironfounders
- Joiners

- Lithographic Workers
- Miners
- Painters
- Papermakers
- Picture-frame Makers
- Plasterers
- Printing Workers
- Quarrymen
- Railwaymen
- Seamen
- Shipwrights & Shipbuilders
- Steam Engine Makers
- Stonemasons
- Telegraphists
- Tramway Workers
- Typefounders
- Woodworkers

The India Office area of the British Library website has an extensive set of pages relating to occupations in British India at <**www.bl.uk/reshelp/ findhelpregion/asia/india/indiaofficerecordsfamilyhistory/occupations/ occupations.html**> with details of the relevant records in its collections.

There is as yet little occupational data available on the commercial data services apart from a small amount for the professions (see below). The only significant sets of general occupational records online are for apprenticeships:

- Origins has the London City Apprenticeship Abstracts 1442–1850 (100,000 records with 300,000 names of apprentices, their parents, and masters).
- Findmypast has:
  - the Apprentices of Great Britain 1710–1774 (350,000 records, about 20 per cent of which relate to Scotland);
  - local apprenticeship records for Dorset, Lincolnshire, Manchester and Somerset.

Information about the City of London Livery Companies will be found on the Corporation of London site at <**www.cityoflondon.gov.uk/Corporation/ LGNL_Services/Leisure_and_culture/Local_history_and_heritage/ Livery/**>, which has links to the companies' own websites. The Institute of Historical Research has a project to make a database of Livery Company membership records for the period 1500–1900 available online. The data should be available in spring 2012 and details are at <**www.history.ac.uk/ projects/livery-company**>.

In the case of self-employed tradesman or craftsman, it will be worth checking trade directories – see p. 189 – which may well bring the benefit of establishing a workplace address.

Cyndi's List has a page of resources relating to occupations at <**www.cyndislist.com/occupations/**> and many other pages which have information on occupations related to particular topics – for example, the 'Prisons' page at <**www.cyndislist.com/prisons**> includes links to police history websites.

Individual industries and occupations

There are many sites devoted to individual occupations, sometimes with just historical information, sometimes with a database of names. Unfortunately, it is not possible here to do more than cite a few examples, but you can find many other links to sites for individual occupations on Cyndi's List and among my own public bookmarks at <**delicious.com/ petex/occupations**>.

Examples of the sites with individual names include:

- the Database of Sugar Bakers and Sugar Refiners at <**www.awer. clara.net/intro.html**>
- the Biographical Database of British Chemists at <**www5.open.ac.uk/ Arts/chemists/**>
- the Coalmining History Resource Centre at <**www.cmhrc.co.uk**>, which has lists of mines at various dates, reports from an 1842 Royal Commission on child labour in the mines, and a database of mining deaths with 90,000 names (Figure 9-3)
- the Institute of Historical Research's lists of Office Holders in Modern Britain at <**www.history.ac.uk/publications/office/**> cover those employed by the Crown since Tudor times
- Corkcutters in England at <**corkcutter.info**>, with information on the corkcutting industry and a database of corkcutters
- the British Book Trade Index, hosted by the University of Birmingham at <**www.bbti.bham.ac.uk**>, an index of people who worked in the book trade in England and Wales up to 1851. There is a similar project for Scotland run by the National Library of Scotland at <**www.nls.uk/ catalogues/scottish-book-trade-index**>

For many occupations, records are very limited until you get to the twentieth century. The learned professions are a major exception, and these

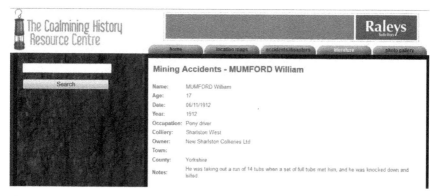

Figure 9-3 The Coalmining History Resource Centre

are treated separately below. Likewise, any service in the army or navy will have left some, perhaps even many, records for an individual, and these are discussed in Chapter 10. Otherwise, the occupations most likely to have left records are the professions, where formal qualifications and professional bodies are involved. It is always worth checking the website of any relevant professional body, since it may well provide some indication of what records are available and other information on tracing individuals. For example, the Royal College of Nursing has an area of its site devoted to archives at <www.rcn.org.uk/development/rcn_archives> with a section on 'genealogy and research advice'. It also has copies of historical nursing journals for 1888–1956, in which many individuals are named. The Royal Institute of Chartered Surveyors has a guide to its Library and a page on family history at <www.rics.org/site/scripts/documents_info.aspx?documentID=479>. It is worth checking ARCHON (see p. 205) for details of the archives of such professional bodies.

On the whole, there are few substantial collections of professional records online, but there are two notable datasets created by the Society of Genealogists and available on Findmypast:

- Teachers' Registrations at Origins, which give details of nearly 100,000 people who taught in England and Wales between 1870 and 1948 – see <www.findmypast.co.uk/search/teachers-registrations/>.
- Civil Service Evidence of Age records 1752–1948 at Findmypast – see <www.findmypast.co.uk/civil-service-evidence-of-age-search-start.action>.

Ancestry has two important occupation collections:

- Railway Employment Records 1833–1963 at <search.ancestry.co.uk/search/db.aspx?dbid=1728> from The National Archives.

- British Postal Service Appointment Books, 1737–1969 <**search. ancestry.co.uk/search/db.aspx?dbid=1933**> from the British Postal Museum and Archive (Figure 9-4).

The Genealogist has around 20 sets of occupational records, including:

- Biographical Dictionary of the Judges of England, 1066–1870;
- Roll of Army Medical Staff, 1727–1898;
- Biographia Dramatica – a biographic record of actors, playwrights and their works from the 1500s to 1811.

It is also worth checking record office sites for local data collections, such as:

- Lancashire's database of the police officers of the Lancashire County Constabulary, 1840–1925, and some borough police forces at <**www.lancashire.gov.uk/education/record_office/records/police.asp**>.
- Warwickshire's Victuallers Database, which gives details of the county's victuallers in Warwickshire 1801–1828 taken from quarter session records. Unfortunately, this is another instance of a monster nonsense URL – instead start from the council home page at <**www.warwickshire.gov.uk**> and search for 'victuallers', or follow the link on the website for this book.

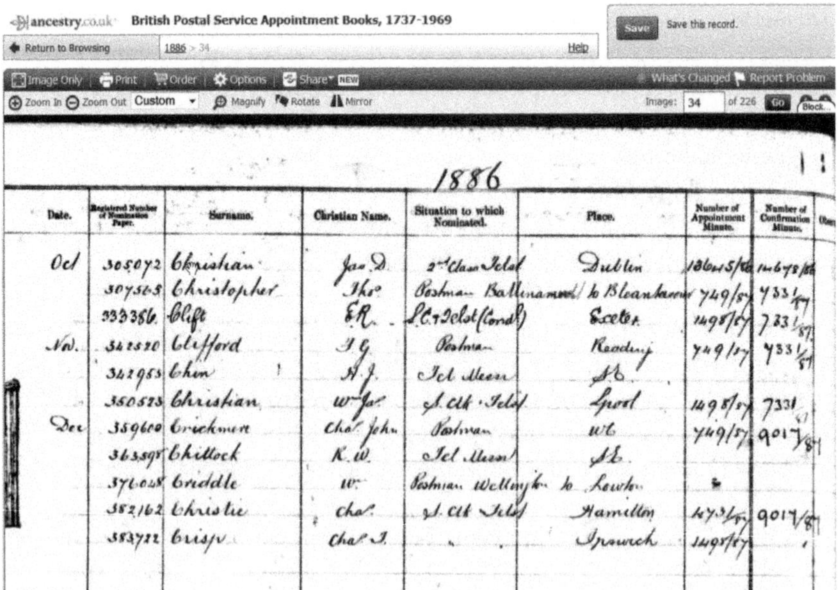

Figure 9-4 British Postal Service Appointment Books at Ancestry

Local directories (see p. 189ff.) often carry lists for individual trades, and you may well find an entry for a self-employed tradesmen or craftsmen. Appointments and promotions in the civil service, even at the lowest clerical grades, including, for example, postmen, should be recorded in the *London Gazette* – see p. 197.

There are a number of mailing lists devoted to occupations. They are listed at <**www.rootsweb.ancestry.com/~jfuller/gen_mail_occ.html**>, and those most relevant to UK family historians are:

- BLACKSMITHING
- BRITISH-HATTERS
- CANAL-PEOPLE and ENG-CANAL-PEOPLE
- CIRCUS-FOLK
- COALMINERS
- DOCTORS-NURSES-MIDWIVES
- ENG-PUBS-INNS
- ENG-THAMESWATERMEN
- HM-CUSTOMS-EXCISE
- HM-CUSTOMS-WATERGUARD
- LIGHTHOUSE-KEEPERS
- MUSIC-OCCUPATIONS
- ORGAN-BUILDERS
- PAPER-MILLS-MAKERS
- POLICE-UK
- POSTALWORKERS-UK
- RAILWAY-UK
- SCOTLAND-TINKS-HAWKERS
- SCOTTISH-MINING
- THEATRE-UK
- TOWNCRIERS-UK
- UK-COALMINERS
- UK-PHOTOGRAPHERS
- UK-WATCHMAKERS
- VIOLIN-MAKERS
- WOODWORKERS

Many of these are hosted by RootsWeb, where details and archives will be found – most are linked from <**lists.rootsweb.ancestry.com/index/other/ Occupations/**> but others from <**lists.rootsweb.ancestry.com/index/intl/ ENG/**>. British-Genealogy has a general 'Occupations' discussion forum as well as forums for specific occupations:

- Actors & Artistes
- Apprentices
- Bakers
- Canals and Watermen
- Carpenters, Wheelwrights, etc.
- Clergymen
- Coastguards and Customs Officers
- Cordwainers, Shoemakers, Saddlers, etc.
- Husbandmen, Yeoman, etc.
- Labourers
- Licensed Victuallers, Innkeepers, etc.
- Mariners and Ships
- Medical Occupations
- Miners
- Occupations – general forum
- Photographers and old photographs
- Policemen
- Railwaymen
- Smiths
- Stone Masons & Builders
- Tailors and Dressmakers
- Teachers

All are linked from <**www.british-genealogy.com/forums/forumdisplay.php/ 36-Occupations**>.

There are even a few societies devoted to the history of trades and occupations. In the case of the railways, for example, there is the Railway Ancestors Family History Society, with a website at <**www.railwayancestors.org.uk**>, while the London & North Western Railway Society has a Staff History Group. Its web pages at <**www.lnwrs.org.uk/SHG/**> offer a family history research guide and a database of staff members (Figure 9-5).

Resources relating to merchant seamen are discussed along with those for the Royal Navy, on p. 149. Photographers are covered on p. 309.

The learned professions

While records for individual trades and occupations are generally sparse and fortuitous, those for the learned professions are much more copious, well organized and, in many cases, available in print.

Most of the relevant material is, of course, specific to a particular profession, but there are a number of general sources to check. Directories, for example, often have lists of self-employed professionals.

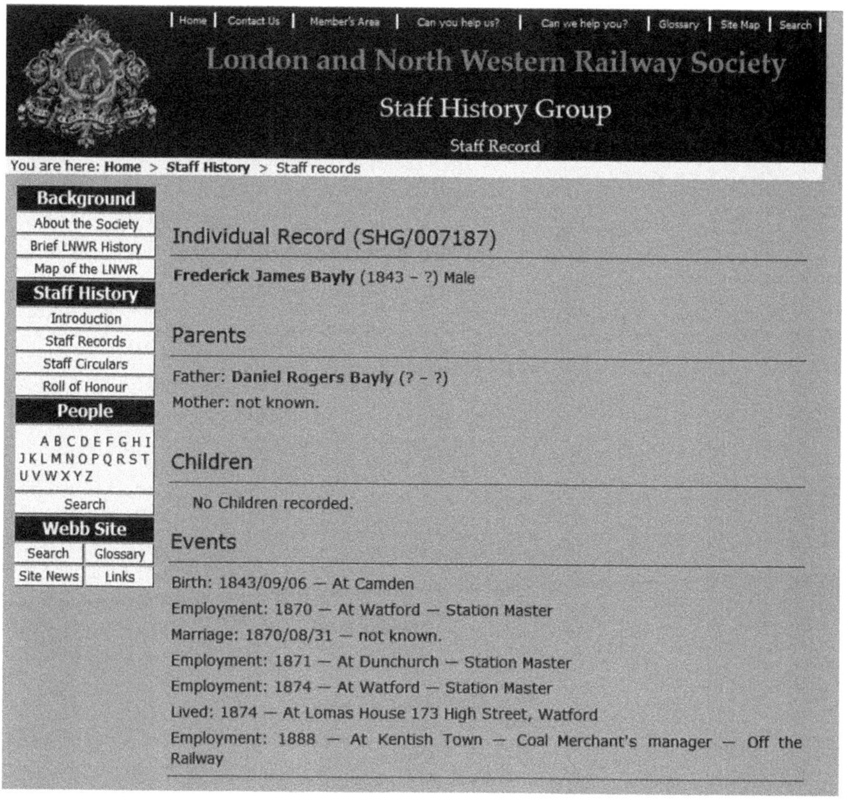

Figure 9-5 The Staff Database for the L&NWR

Figure 9-6, from the Historical Directories site (p. 189), shows an example – a list of local dentists from Kelly's 1895 directory for Gloucestershire. All the professional entries here give an address, and many indicate qualifications. In some cases, specific days are listed for surgeries in particular towns.

Some professions have their own directories, such as the clergy's *Crockford's Clerical Directory*. The digital book archives discussed in Chapter 12 may have scans of individual volumes; otherwise a search of the library catalogues mentioned in Chapter 13 will locate a physical copy. The Society of Genealogists, for example, has a considerable collection of such directories, and all are listed in their online catalogue (see p. 222). The professional directories available on the commercial data services are discussed under the relevant profession below.

The learned professions are so called because they require a university degree. This means that the records of the ancient universities can be looked to for information on individual ancestors. For Cambridge, Venn's *Alumni Cantabrigienses*, covering the period 1261–1900, is on the Internet Archive

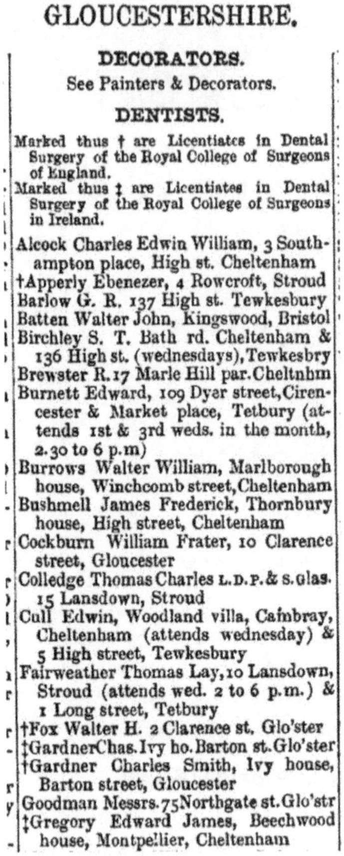

GLOUCESTERSHIRE.

DECORATORS.

See Painters & Decorators.

DENTISTS.

Marked thus † are Licentiates in Dental Surgery of the Royal College of Surgeons of England.

Marked thus ‡ are Licentiates in Dental Surgery of the Royal College of Surgeons in Ireland.

Alcock Charles Edwin William, 3 Southampton place, High st. Cheltenham

†Apperly Ebenezer, 4 Rowcroft, Stroud

Barlow G. R. 137 High st. Tewkesbury

Batten Walter John, Kingswood, Bristol

Birchley S. T. Bath rd. Cheltenham & 136 High st. (wednesdays), Tewkesbry

Brewster R. 17 Marle Hill par. Cheltnhm

Burnett Edward, 109 Dyer street, Cirencester & Market place, Tetbury (attends 1st & 3rd weds. in the month, 2.30 to 6 p.m)

Burrows Walter William, Marlborough house, Winchcomb street, Cheltenham

Bushmell James Frederick, Thornbury house, High street, Cheltenham

Cockburn William Frater, 10 Clarence street, Gloucester

Colledge Thomas Charles L.D.P. & S.Glas. 15 Lansdown, Stroud

Cull Edwin, Woodland villa, Cainbray, Cheltenham (attends wednesday) & 5 High street, Tewkesbury

Fairweather Thomas Lay, 10 Lansdown, Stroud (attends wed. 2 to 6 p.m.) & 1 Long street, Tetbury

†Fox Walter H. 2 Clarence st, Glo'ster

‡Gardner Chas. Ivy ho. Barton st. Glo'ster

†Gardner Charles Smith, Ivy house, Barton street, Gloucester

Goodman Messrs. 75 Northgate st. Glo'str

‡Gregory Edward James, Beechwood house, Montpellier, Cheltenham

Figure 9-6 Dentists in Kelly's 1897 directory of Gloucestrshire (Historical Directories)

at <www.archive.org/details/texts/>. A search for the title will bring up a list of volumes; alternatively just follow the links from Wikipedia's 'Alumni Cantabrigienses' article. It is also available to Ancestry subscribers at <www.ancestry.com/search/db.aspx?dbid=3997>. A free database is in preparation by John Dawson and this is available at <venn.lib.cam.ac.uk>.

The equivalent publication for Oxford, Foster's *Alumni Oxonienses*, is also available on the Internet Archive at <www.archive.org/stream/alumnioxoniense00fostgoog>. Again, Ancestry has made the material available to subscribers, at <www.ancestry.co.uk/search/DB.aspx?dbid=8942>. Bob Sanders has a page devoted to 'Oxford University Alumni with Cardiff & Vale Of Glamorgan Connections' at <www.angelfire.com/ga/BobSanders/ALUMNOX.html>. Familyrelatives at <www.familyrelatives.com> has not only the *Alumni Oxonienses*, but also the *Alumni Dublinenses*, which lists staff and students of Trinity College, Dublin 1593–1846. Findmypast Ireland (see p. 54) also has this latter work, while Google Books (see p. 184) has *A catalogue of graduates who have proceeded to degrees in the University of Dublin*, going up to 1868.

If you know which college an ancestor attended, you may find useful information about the available records by consulting the college website. Balliol College Oxford, for example, has a comprehensive page devoted to tracing past members at <**archives.balliol.ox.ac.uk/Past%20members/ trace.asp**>.

The legal profession

For the legal profession, a useful place to start is The National Archives' site, which has a 'Looking for records of a lawyer' page at <**www.nationalarchives.gov.uk/ records/looking-for-person/lawyer.htm**> and a research guide to 'Lawyers: Records of Attorneys and Solicitors' at <**www.nationalarchives.gov.uk/ records/research-guides/attorneys-solicitors.htm**>.

The Law Society has a guide on 'How to Trace Past Solicitors' with a 167-character URL – use a search engine to search on this phrase or follow the link on the website for this book.

The Inner Temple is another useful site. Its Admissions Database at <**www.innertemple.org.uk/archive/itad/**> has entries covering the period 1547 to 1850. The Admissions Database home page also has links to a list of bibliographical sources for lawyers and information on 'Legal Education to 1850'. The site has a number of historical articles and those of most use to genealogists are 'The Inns Of Court And Inns Of Chancery And Their Records' and 'The admission of overseas students to the Inner Temple in the 19th century' – search for 'historical articles' from the home page at <**www.innertemple.org.uk**>.

The commercial data services do not as yet have much in the way of records for lawyers. The exception is The Genealogist which has several Law Lists, and a Biographical Dictionary of the Judges of England for 1066 to 1870 available under its Diamond subscription.

Medicine

The medical profession has a range of professional bodies to which an ancestor may have belonged, and the websites of these are worth looking at. The Royal College of General Practitioners has a guide to 'Tracing Your Medical Ancestors' at <**www.rcgp.org.uk/default.aspx?page=93**>, which includes information on former colonies. Although it does not itself hold any personal records, the British Medical Association has information on 'Tracing a doctor for historical research' on its 'Tracing a doctor' page at

<www.bma.org.uk/patients_public/tracingadoctor.jsp>. The older medical establishments all have historical material in their libraries and archives, which may include the publications and perhaps even personal papers of members, so it will be worth consulting any online catalogue.

The Guildhall Library has information using its own holdings in 'Sources For Tracing Apothecaries, Surgeons, Physicians And Other Medical Practitioners At Guildhall Library' at <www.history.ac.uk/gh/apoths.htm>, but this page will also be of use for doctors outside the capital.

Munk's Roll is a collection of obituaries of members of the Royal College of Physicians, and the College has an online index to it at <**munksroll. rcplondon.ac.uk**>. Ten volumes have been printed, covering the period from the founding of the College to 1997, and all of these are included in the online index, with detailed biographies for a number of members.

A list of those granted medical licences by the Archbishop of Canterbury is available as a PDF file on the Lambeth Palace Library site at <**www.lambethpalacelibrary.org/files/Medical_Licences.pdf**>. The licences cover the period 1535–1775.

The commercial data services have a number of resources for medical ancestors. Ancestry has a complete run of the quadrennial UK Medical Registers of the General Medical Council for 1859–1959 at <**www.ancestry.co.uk/search/ DB.aspx?dbid=33538**>, which can be browsed (the entries are in alphabetical order) or searched, though since the index has been created by optical character recognition it is not entirely reliable. Findmypast has three medical registers: the 1925 *Dental Surgeons Directory*, the 1858 *Medical Directory For Ireland* and the 1913 *Medical Register*. Familyrelatives has a series of medical registers covering the period 1853 to 1943.

DOCTORS-NURSES-MIDWIVES is a mailing list for those with ancestors in the medical profession, details of which will be found at <**lists.rootsweb.ancestry.com/index/other/Occupations/DOCTORS-NURSES-MIDWIVES.html**>.

Further links will be found on the 'Medical & Medicine: Doctors and Nurses' page on Cyndi's List at <**www.cyndislist.com/medical/doctors**>. The Library of the Wellcome Institute at <**library.wellcome.ac.uk**> has links to more general material on the history of medicine.

The Church

Among the useful guides for anyone starting to investigate clerical ancestry is the Guildhall Library's introduction to 'Sources For Tracing Clergy And Lay Persons' at <**www.history.ac.uk/gh/clergy.htm**>. Although the main focus is London, much of the information is relevant to all ancestors in the Established Church. Lambeth Palace Library has a guide to 'Biographical sources for Anglican clergy' at <**www.lambethpalacelibrary.org/files/ Clergy_Guide.pdf**>.

By far the most important online resource is the Clergy of the Church of England Database project (CCEd) at <**www.theclergydatabase.org.uk**>, which aims to document the careers of all Church of England clergymen between 1540 and 1835. The project is still in progress, but it already has details of around 120,000 individuals on the website. Information about the dates and dioceses covered so far will be found at <**www.theclergydatabase.org.uk/ upgrade/content.html**>. For each individual the database gives details of his university degree (if known) and a list of appointments, with links to information on sources (Figure 9-7).

The *Fasti Ecclesiae Anglicanae* list English bishops and higher clergy up to 1857 and are available on British History Online – follow the 'Ecclesiastical & religious' link on the home page at <**www.british-history.ac.uk**>. They are organized by diocese and locating an individual may be easier if you use the indexes provided by the Institute of Historical Research at <**www.history.ac.uk/publications/fasti**>. The first two volumes (of seven) of the equivalent publication for Scotland, the *Fasti Ecclesiae Scoticanae*, are indexed and transcribed at <**www.dwalker.pwp.blueyonder.co.uk/ Ministers%20Index.htm**>. Vol. VII is available (catalogued as Vol. 10) on the Internet Archive at <**www.archive.org/stream/fastiecclesiaesc00scot**>, and it will be worth keeping an eye out for other volumes appearing on this site.

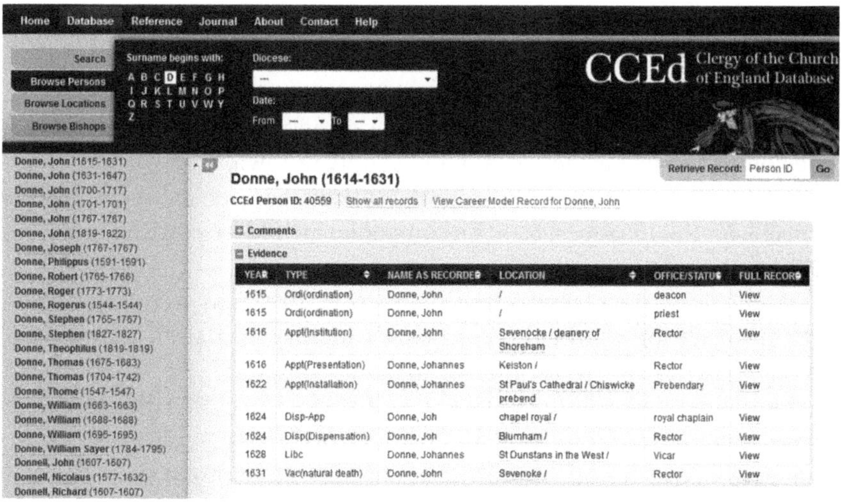

Figure 9-7 The entry for the poet John Donne in CCEd

CHURCHMEN-UK is a mailing list for those interested in clerical ancestors – details will be found at <**lists.rootsweb.ancestry.com/index/other/Occupations/CHURCHMEN-UK.html**>, and British-Genealogy has a 'Clergymen' discussion forum at <**www.british-genealogy.com/forums/forumdisplay.php/39-Clergymen**>.

Mundus at <**www.mundus.ac.uk**> describes itself as a 'gateway to missionary collections in the UK', and will be worth checking if you have missionary ancestors. The site provides information on over 400 collections of overseas missionary materials held in institutions in the United Kingdom, including collections of personal papers. The International Mission Photography Archive is described on p. 305.

For ministers outside the established church, see the links for other denominations in Chapter 7.

Company records

If you think that an ancestor may have worked for, or even owned, a particular company, it will be worth trying to find out whether there are any surviving records. Unless the company is still in existence, and perhaps even then, the records are likely to be in a repository, in which case they should show up in the National Register of Archives at <**www.nationalarchives.gov.uk/nra**> (see p. 207). The NRA's 'Corporate name' search will identify such records, and in many cases link to an A2A record (see p. 206). For example, Figure 9-8 shows the beginning of a substantial page in A2A describing the records of Berger Jenson and Nicholson Limited of Hackney. Lower down the page is a complete history of the company, and a list of the individual documents, which include staff records.

The NRA also has a Business Index Advanced Search, which helps you to find companies by business sector and county or town.

The Business Archives Council of Scotland has details of the records available for the 100 oldest Scottish companies at <**oldestscottishcompanies.wikispaces.com**>.

Of course, in the case of a large company, there may well be a website with information about the company's history and staff records. For example, although it is not an official company site, there is 'an electronic history of J. Lyons & Co. and some of its 700 subsidiaries' at <**www.kzwp.com/lyons/**>. This has a 'Pensioners' section including hundreds of death notices, obituaries of notable senior staff and lists of the company's war dead. RBS has a dedicated company history wiki, RBS Heritage Online, at <**heritagearchives.rbs.com**>. The 'Sources for family history' page at <**heritagearchives.rbs.com/wiki/Sources_for_family_history**> is the best place to start for guidance on records of genealogical interest, such as staff registers and war memorials.

A The National Archives

Search the archives   Search ▸
Advanced search

| About us | Education | Records | Information management | Shop online |

You are here: Home > Search the archives > Access to Archives > Records

Access to Archives
Part of the UK archives network

Hackney Archives Department
▸ Berger Jenson and Nicholson Limited

BERGER, JENSON AND NICHOLSON, PAINT MAKERS RECORDS

The hierarchical structure of this catalogue is shown below. See the entire contents of the catalogue

Reference	D/B/BER
Covering dates	1783 - 1986
Held by	Hackney Archives Department
Extent	1.68 m²
Conditions of access	Open (Board minutes closed for twenty years from date of last entry in volume)
Archival history	A large part of these records were surveyed by the Business Archives Council in 1981, when they were held at the Company's headquarters at Berkeley Square. The records were subsequently moved to Hoechst House in Hounslow. Some of the records had been placed in the care of the Publicity Manager, Roger Tamplin, who collected other material from subsidiary and absorbed companies. Not all the records included in the BAC survey have survived, but more recent material, including board minutes were included in the deposit.
Source of acquisition	Acc 1988/6
Creators	Berger Jenson and Nicholson Limited, 1960-1988
Related information	The local history collection includes copies of the 1910 history and A Notable Record, 1910, together with the history by Armitage to 1914 (2/7/44/45, 51), though there is a copy of the Armitage work that contains an additional chapter in the records (2/7/53). Also in the printed collection is Jeffery Farnol's Portrait of a gentleman in colours: the romance of Mr Lewis Berger (1935), described by Armitage as

Figure 9-8 Corporate records in A2A

The website for Guinness's Dublin tourist attraction, the Storehouse, has a Trace Your Guinness Roots section at <**www.guinness-storehouse.com/en/ GenealogySearch.aspx**> giving details of over 20,000 staff with dates of birth and dates of joining.

Familyrelatives has four volumes of the *Directory of Directors* for the period 1897 to 1946.

▊ Trade unions

In the case of nineteenth-century or later workers, there may be information on individual ancestors in the records of the trade unions. Records for the thousands of individual unions which preceded the growth of the large amalgamated unions of the present should be sought in the online catalogues of the local record offices (see Chapter 13). But for general information about trade union records and family history the site to visit is Trade Union Ancestors at <**www.unionancestors.co.uk**>. This not only lists the more than 5,000 unions which have existed over the last 200 years, but provides family trees showing the 'genealogy' of the modern national unions, which may help to identify the likely location of surviving records. There are also brief histories of a number of unions, with lists of officers.

A partner site, Chartist Ancestors at <www.chartists.net>, will be of interest to those with activist ancestors in the 1840s, and contains lists of names from newspapers, court records and petitions.

The Trades Union Congress Library Collections are deposited at the London Metropolitan University, and details will be found on its website at <www.londonmet.ac.uk/services/sas/library-services/tuc/>.

10

THE ARMED FORCES

Even before the mass conscription of the two World Wars, the army and the navy provided an occupation or a career for large numbers of men from all strata of society. There can be few British families without some ancestors who served in the forces.

Because of this, military records have been high on the list for indexing and digitization. The National Archives itself has made them a major focus of its digital document service (p. 58), and all the major commercial data services offer a range of military records. There are many sites dedicated to those who have fallen in war, particularly the First World War. Also, the widespread interest in military history means there are a host of well-informed non-commercial sites, which, even if they do not list individual names (and are often not graphically appealing), provide useful historical information.

General information

There are two official sites for information on the armed forces and their records: The National Archives and the Ministry of Defence (MoD). Linked from 'Looking for a person?' at <**www.nationalarchives.gov.uk/records/looking-for-person/**>, The National Archives has pages giving basic information on how to trace ancestors in the forces, covering some three dozen categories of service, under the headings 'Army', 'Navy', 'Air', 'Marines', and 'PoWs and conscientious objectors'. TNA's extensive series of research guides at <**www.nationalarchives.gov.uk/records/atoz**> provide more detail on individual classes of record, how they are organized and how to locate and understand them. The site also has a separate set of pages on military history linked from the 'Looking for a subject?' page at <**www.nationalarchives.gov.uk/records/looking-for-subject/**>. These cover particular wars, regiments and squadrons, and medals.

The MoD site at <**www.mod.uk**>, while mainly devoted to the present-day forces, has detailed pages on the location of recent service records, and provides many contact addresses. Each branch of the services has its own website within the MoD's internet domain: <www.royalnavy.mod.uk>, <www.army.mod.uk> and <www.raf.mod.uk>. Beyond these central bodies, there are the individual regiments, ships, squadrons and other units, many of which have their own web pages with historical information. The easiest way to find these is from the official site for the relevant arm of the services, which has links to its constituent units. The MoD site does not offer information about individuals, but the page on 'Making a Request for Information held on the Personnel Records of Deceased Service Personnel' at <www.mod.uk/DefenceInternet/AboutDefence/WhatWeDo/Personnel/ServiceRecords/> gives details of how to apply for copies of service records for all branches of the services where they have not already been lodged at The National Archives.

Genuki has pages devoted to Military Records at <www.genuki.org.uk/big/MilitaryRecords.html> and Military History at <www.genuki.org.uk/big/MilitaryHistory.html>. Cyndi's List has a page devoted to UK & Irish Military at <www.cyndislist.com/uk/military/>, which covers all branches of the services, while her 'Military Resources Worldwide' page at <www.cyndislist.com/military-worldwide> has more general material. There are individual collections of links for the two World Wars at <www.cyndislist.com/ww1/> and <www.cyndislist.com/ww2/>. UKMFH has over 1,200 links covering all aspects of UK military family history at <www.ukmfh.org.uk>, including over 130 museums.

The *London Gazette* (p. 197) contains details of officer appointments in the armed forces, and the text search facility on the site at <www.gazettes-online.co.uk> can be used to do a name search.

The Scots at War site at <www.scotsatwar.org.uk> concentrates mainly on the twentieth century. It has a Commemorative Roll of Honour with service and biographical information on Scottish servicemen.

Britains [*sic*] Small Wars at <www.britains-smallwars.com> covers the period from 1945 up to the present and has extensive information about each war, including in many cases lists of casualties. British Armed Forces and National Service 1947–1963 at <www.britisharmedforces.org> is a site with historical information about the period of national service, the various units active in the period, and 'Servicemen's Tales' from both national service conscripts and regular servicemen.

There are quite a few sites devoted to particular wars or battles, such as Electric Scotland's pages on the Battle of Culloden <www.electricscotland.com/history/culloden/>. Some are devoted to a war as a whole, such as the Trenches on the Web site at <www.worldwar1.com>, which is subtitled 'An Internet History of The Great War'. While you can locate such sites by using a search engine, it will often be less time-consuming to start by looking for an article on the engagement on Wikipedia, which will have links to recommended sites and sources.

RootsWeb has a number of mailing lists devoted to particular wars, including:

- NAPOLEONIC
- CRIMEAN-WAR
- BOER-WAR
- WORLDWAR2
- GREATWAR
- WW1-UK
- KOREAN-WAR

WW20-ROOTS-L is devoted to 'genealogy in all twentieth century wars'. Details for all these lists can be found by using the 'Find a mailing list' search at <**lists.rootsweb.ancestry.com**>.

British-Genealogy has discussion forums devoted to the following conflicts:

- English Civil War
- Napoleonic Wars
- American War of Independence
- Crimean War
- Boer War
- World War 1
- World War 2

Links to these will be found at <**www.british-genealogy.com/forums/**>.

▌ The Royal Navy and merchant navy

Although the merchant navy is not an arm of the state, it has long been subject to government regulation. There has always been movement between the Royal Navy and the merchant fleet, and many ancestors will have served in both. For those reasons, they are treated here together.

The official Royal Navy site at <**www.royalnavy.mod.uk**> has separate sections for each branch of the service, including ships, submarines, the Fleet Air Arm, the Royal Marines and naval establishments, all linked from the 'The Fleet' menu on the home page. Unfortunately, the extensive 'History' section is no longer available on the site, but it is preserved on the Government Web Archive – search for <**royalnavy.mod.uk/history/**> (25 August 2010). There is no material specifically on family history.

The National Maritime Museum has over 70 research guides devoted to maritime history on the Royal Museums Greenwich site at <**www.rmg.co.uk/ researchers/library/research-guides/**>. Two of these are devoted specifically to tracing ancestors in the Royal Navy and merchant navy, and there is a general introduction to 'Tracing family history from maritime records', but others that will be of interest are the guides to passenger lists, shipping companies, *Lloyd's List*, press gangs, and uniforms and medals.

Genuki has a page of merchant marine links at <**www.genuki.org.uk/big/ MerchantMarine.html**>, while the Royal Navy is included in its Military Records and Military History pages mentioned above.

A site with a substantial collection of naval resources is Paul Benyon's 'Late 18th, 19th and early 20th Century Naval and Naval Social History' at <**www.pbenyon.plus.com/Naval.html**>. It includes extracts from many different types of source, from Navy regulations to newspaper reports, and many include names of individual seamen.

The MARINERS mailing list is for all those whose ancestors pursued maritime occupations, worldwide. The list has its own website at <**www.mariners-l.co.uk**> with sections devoted to individual countries, as well as more general topics such as wars at sea, and shipping companies. The site also has a guide to ranks in both the Royal and merchant navy at <**www.mariners-l.co.uk/GenBosun'sLocker.html**>. The MERCHANT-MARINE mailing list covers Merchant Marines of all countries involved in the Second World War, and details will be found at <**lists.rootsweb.ancestry. com/index/other/Military:_Naval/MERCHANT-MARINE.html**>. There is also a BRITISH-MARINERS list – details at <**lists.rootsweb.ancestry.com/ index/other/Occupations/BRITISH-MARINERS.html**>.

In addition to the NMM's site at <**www.rmg.co.uk/national-maritime-museum/**>, almost 300 maritime museums in the British Isles are listed at <**people.pwf.cam.ac.uk/mhe1000/museums.htm**>.

Records

Since the majority of naval records are held by The National Archives, one of the best places to find out about them is the collection of online research guides at <**www.nationalarchives.gov.uk/atoz**>, where the relevant materials are grouped under 'Royal Navy', 'Merchant seamen' and 'Merchant shipping'. The 'Looking for a person?' at <**www.nationalarchives.gov.uk/ records/looking-for-person/**> has links to introductory material about naval records.

For a more discursive guide to naval records, Fawne Stratford-Devai's articles on the Global Gazette site are recommended, 'British Military Records Part 2: THE ROYAL NAVY' at <**globalgenealogy.com/ globalgazette/gazfd/gazfd48.htm**> and 'Maritime Records & Resources' in two parts, at <globalgenealogy.com/globalgazette/gazfd/gazfd50.htm> and <globalgenealogy.com/globalgazette/gazfd/gazfd52.htm>. Among other things, these articles have very useful lists of some of the main groups of records which have been microfilmed by the LDS Church and can therefore be consulted at Family History Centers. (Note, however, that these articles have not been updated for sometime and many of the external links are no longer correct.)

Other guides to tracing seafaring ancestors include Bob Sanders's site at <www.angelfire.com/de/BobSanders/Site.html>, which has an extensive collection of material on 'Tracing British Seamen & their ships', including not only naval occupations but also Fishermen, Customs & Excise Officers and Coastguards. Len Barnett has what he calls 'a realistic guide to what is available to those looking into merchant mariners' careers' at <www.barnettmaritime.co.uk>.

The National Archives' Discovery service (p. 58) offers around a dozen series of naval service records, including:

- Royal Marines Service Records (ADM 159)
- Registers of Seamen's Services (ADM 139, ADM 188)
- Royal Naval Division service records (ADM 339)
- Royal Naval Officers' Service Records (ADM 196)
- Naval Officers' Service Record Cards and Files (ADM 340)
- RNVR service records from WW1 (ADM 337)
- Royal Naval Reserve Service Records (BT 164)
- WRNS: Women's Royal Naval Service (ADM 318, ADM 336)

Naval records available on other commercial sites include:

- Findmypast: Royal Naval Division 1914–1919 and Merchant Navy Seamen records 1835–1857
- Origins: Trinity House Calendars 1787–1854
- Ancestry: British Naval Biographical Dictionary, 1849, and Royal Naval Division Casualties of The Great War, 1914–1924, Navy Lists for 1908 and 1914
- The Genealogist: a dozen Navy Lists drawn from the period 1806–1938.
- Familyrelatives: World War I and II Royal Navy Deaths (1913–21 and 1935–50)

The National Library of Scotland has digitized and donated to the Internet Archive 100 volumes of The Navy List covering the periods of the two World Wars. All volumes are linked from <www.archive.org/details/

nlsnavylists> (Figure 10-1). Familyrelatives has around 20 Navy List volumes, mainly from the twentieth century.

There are many data transcriptions relating to seamen to be found on websites run by individuals. For example, Bob Sanders has an index to O'Byrne's *Royal Navy Biography* of 1849 with details of Royal Navy officers on six separate pages, linked from his site mentioned above, as well as many other small data collections. The Naval Biographical Database is an ambitious project at <**www.navylist.org**> to 'establish accurate biographical information on those individuals who have served, or supported the Royal Navy since 1660'. So far the site has details of around 21,500 people and 5,000 ships. The site is basically free, though there is a charge for more detailed information.

The National Archives has a Trafalgar Ancestors database, launched on the 200th anniversary of the battle, at <**www.nationalarchives.gov.uk/trafalgarancestors/**>, with over 18,000 names drawn from a wide range of sources. There is much further information about the battle and about Nelson. The Age of Nelson at <**www.ageofnelson.org**> has a complete Navy List for the period of the Napoleonic Wars. It also has a project to trace

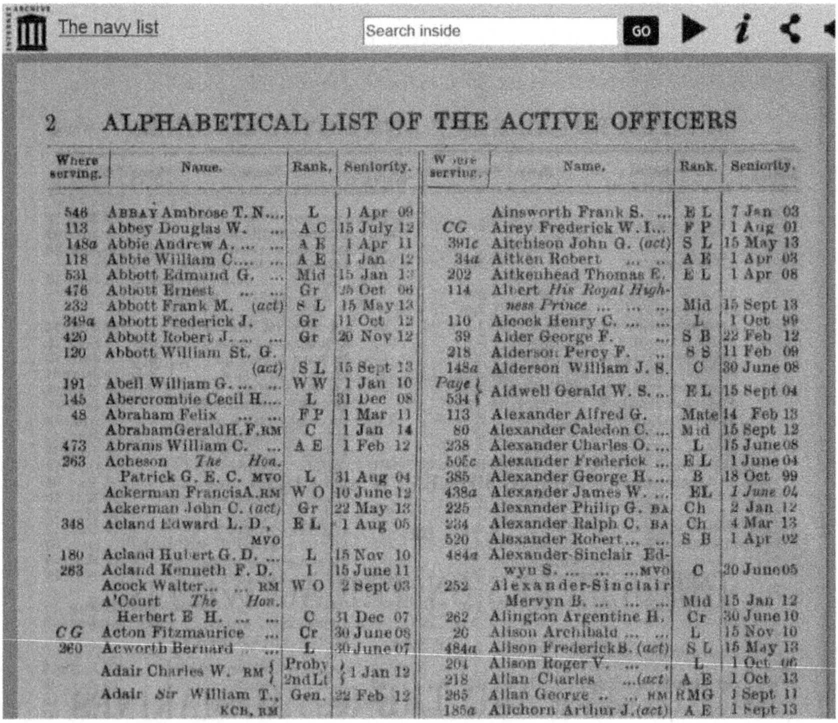

2 ALPHABETICAL LIST OF THE ACTIVE OFFICERS

Where serving.	Name.	Rank.	Seniority.
546	ABBAY Ambrose T. N....	L	1 Apr 09
113	Abbey Douglas W. ...	A C	15 July 12
148a	Abbie Andrew A.	A E	1 Apr 11
118	Abbie William C.... ...	A E	1 Jan 12
531	Abbott Edmund G. ...	Mid	15 Jan 13
476	Abbott Ernest	Gr	25 Oct 08
232	Abbott Frank M. (act)	S L	15 May 13
349a	Abbott Frederick J.	Gr	11 Oct 12
420	Abbott Robert J.	Gr	20 Nov 12
120	Abbott William St. G. (act)	S L	15 Sept 13
191	Abell William G.	W W	1 Jan 10
145	Abercrombie Cecil H....	L	31 Dec 08
48	Abraham Felix	F P	1 Mar 11
	Abraham Gerald H. F. RM	C	1 Jan 14
473	Abrams William C. ...	A E	1 Feb 12
263	Acheson *The Hon.* Patrick G. E. C. MVO	L	31 Aug 04
	Ackerman Francis A. RM	W O	10 June 12
	Ackerman John C. (act)	Gr	22 May 13
348	Acland Edward L. D., MVO	E L	1 Aug 05
180	Acland Hubert G. D. ...	L	15 Nov 10
263	Acland Kenneth F. D.	I	15 June 11
	Acock Walter... ... RM	W O	2 Sept 03
	A'Court *The Hon.* Herbert E. H.	C	31 Dec 07
CG	Acton Fitzmaurice ...	Cr	30 June 08
260	Acworth Bernard	L	30 June 07
	Adair Charles W. RM	Proby 2nd Lt	1 Jan 12
	Adair *Sir* William T., KCB, RM	Gen.	22 Feb 12

Where serving.	Name.	Rank.	Seniority.
	Ainsworth Frank S. ...	E L	7 Jan 03
CG	Airey Frederick W. I...	F P	1 Aug 01
391c	Aitchison John G. (act)	S L	15 May 13
34a	Aitken Robert	A E	1 Apr 03
202	Aitkenhead Thomas E.	E L	1 Apr 08
114	Albert *His Royal Highness Prince*	Mid	15 Sept 13
110	Alcock Henry C.	L	1 Oct 99
39	Alder George F. ...	S B	22 Feb 12
218	Alderson Percy F. ..	S S	11 Feb 09
148a	Alderson William J. S.	C	30 June 08
Page 534	Aldwell Gerald W. S. ...	E L	15 Sept 04
113	Alexander Alfred G.	Mate	14 Feb 13
80	Alexander Caledon C. ...	Mid	15 Sept 12
238	Alexander Charles O. ...	L	15 June 08
505c	Alexander Frederick ...	E L	1 June 04
385	Alexander George H....	B	18 Oct 99
438a	Alexander James W. ...	EL	*1 June 04*
225	Alexander Philip G. BA	Ch	2 Jan 12
234	Alexander Ralph C. BA	Ch	4 Mar 13
520	Alexander Robert... ...	S B	1 Apr 02
484a	Alexander-Sinclair Edwyn S. ... ... MVO	C	30 June 05
252	Alexander-Sinclair Mervyn B.	Mid	15 Jan 12
262	Alington Argentine H.	Cr	30 June 10
26	Alison Archibald	L	15 Nov 10
484a	Alison Frederick B. (act)	S L	15 May 13
204	Alison Roger V.	L	1 Oct 06
218	Allan Charles ...(act)	A E	1 Oct 13
265	Allan George .. ... RM	RMG	1 Sept 11
185a	Allchorn Arthur J. (act)	A E	1 Sept 13

Figure 10-1 The Navy List, January 1914 (Internet Archive)

the descendants of those who fought at Trafalgar, as well as its own Trafalgar Roll.

Among the sites devoted to merchant seamen is Irish Mariners at <**www.irishmariners.ie**>, which contains an index of around 23,000 Irish-born merchant seamen, extracted from records in the Southampton Civic Archives for the period from late 1918 to the end of 1921. A particular interest of these records is that they include photographs. Welsh Mariners at <**www.welshmariners.org.uk**> has a database of 23,500 Welsh merchant seamen, 1800–1945, and over 3,000 men active in the Royal Navy 1795–1815, which therefore includes Welshmen at Trafalgar.

A major undertaking is the Crew List Index Project (CLIP) at <**www.crewlist.org.uk**>. The site does not list names of individuals, but it has a wealth of information about crew lists, and how to locate them, including indexes of the lists held at The National Archives and in local record offices.

Ships

There are a number of sites relating to the ships rather than the seamen who served on them, and these can be useful for background. For example, Gilbert Provost has transcribed details of vessels from *Lloyd's Register of British and Foreign Shipping* from 1764 up to 2003 at <**users.xplornet.com/~shipping/ Lloyds.htm**>. Michael P. Palmer maintains the Palmer List of Merchant Vessels at <**www.geocities.com/mppraetorius/**>, which has descriptions of hundreds of merchant vessels, compiled from a variety of sources. Both sites provide names of masters and owners as well as information on the ships themselves. Steve Johnson provides a 'photographic A to Z of British Naval warships, submarines, and auxiliaries from 1880 to 1950s' at <**freepages. misc.rootsweb.ancestry.com/~cyberheritage/**>. Through Mighty Seas at <**www.mightyseas.co.uk**> is devoted to the merchant sailing ships of the North West and the Isle of Man and has histories of over 950 vessels.

If you suspect that an ancestor was on a naval vessel, either in port or at sea, on census night in 1901, you should find Jeffery Knaggs's index to the location of Royal Navy ships at <**homepage.ntlworld.com/jeffery. knaggs/RNShips.html**> of interest. Bob Sanders has a similar list of Ships in UK Ports for the 1881 census at <**www.angelfire.com/de/ BobSanders/81Intro.html**>.

The army

The official army site at <**www.army.mod.uk**> has information about the present-day service, and the pages on 'British Army Structure' at <**www.army.mod.uk/structure/structure.aspx**> give an overview of how the army is organized. It has a listing of all current divisions, brigades, corps and regiments. There is limited historical information on these pages.

Records

The National Archives' 'Looking for a person?' page has links to introductory material on tracing army ancestry and there is more detailed guidance on the records in the research guides. Genuki has a page devoted to British Military History at <**www.genuki.org.uk/big/MilitaryHistory.html**>, and an article by Jay Hall on 'British Military Records for the 18th and 19th Centuries' at <**www.genuki.org.uk/big/MilitaryRecords.html**>. There is a useful article by Fawne Stratford-Devai devoted to 'British Military Records Part 1: The Army' in *The Global Gazette* at <**globalgenealogy.com/ globalgazette/gazfd/gazfd44.htm**>.

The National Archives Discovery service is the main source of information for all service records for individual solders. In some cases, it includes the names of individual soldiers from documents in class WO 97, which comprises discharge papers for the period 1760–1854 (Figure 10-2). TNA has a range of army records available for paid download, listed at <**www.nationalarchives.gov.uk/documentsonline/army.asp**> and including:

- Campaign Medal Index Cards, WW1 (WO 372)
- Selected WW1 and Army of Occupation War Diaries (WO 95)
- Women's (later Queen Mary's) Army Auxiliary Corps service records (WO 398)
- Royal Marines Service Records (ADM 159)
- Prisoner of War interviews and reports, WW1 (WO 161)
- Recommendations for Honours and Awards (WO 373)
- Waterloo Medal Book (MINT 16/112)
- First World War Nursing Service Records (RAIL 235/516)

Among the records available on the commercial data services are:

- Findmypast: British Army Service Records 1760–1915 (includes WO 97, mentioned above), De Ruvigny's Roll 1914–18, Waterloo medal roll 1815 and other army lists 1656–1888
- The Genealogist: various Army Lists 1806–1938
- Ancestry: WWI Medal Rolls Index Cards, Pension Records and Service Records, 1914–1920; Scottish Soldiers in Colonial America
- Familyrelatives: World War I and II Army Deaths (1913–21 and 1935–50)

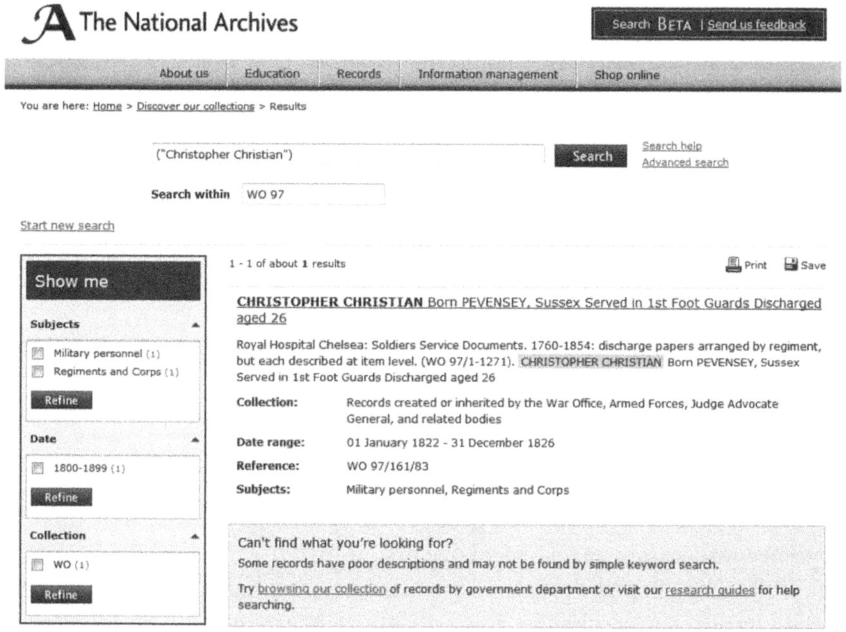

Figure 10-2 A search result in the Soldiers Service Documents (WO97)

The National Roll of the Great War is available at both Findmypast and Ancestry.

The National Library of Scotland has deposited scans of around 200 volumes of Hart's *Army List* with the Internet Archive at <**www.archive.org/details/nlsarmylists**>, covering the periods 1840–1918 and 1938–46.

Regiments

While the army website has information on the present-day structure, over the centuries the regiments have not been very stable in either composition or naming. In particular, the last few decades have seen an extensive series of regimental mergers. Since the crucial piece of information about any ancestor in the army is the regiment or unit he served in, you are likely to need historical information for the specific period when an ancestor was in uniform. The essential resource for regimental history is T. F. Mills's Land Forces of Britain, the Empire and Commonwealth site at <**www.regiments.org**>. The site closed down in 2008 but is preserved at the Wayback Machine (29 January 2008). The site not only provides detailed background information on the regimental system, but also lists the regiments in the army in particular years since the eighteenth century.

An alternative comprehensive source of information on regiments is Wikipedia's 'List of British Army regiments' article, which gives the present-day regiments and has links to equivalent lists for a number of earlier dates, as well as a useful list of regimental nicknames. There are, as you would expect, quite extensive articles on the individual regiments.

For details of the regiments active in the Indian subcontinent, the Families In British India Society Wiki (see p. 178) is a good source. The entry point for all articles on military subjects is at <**wiki.fibis.org/index.php? title=Category:Military**>. The site also has details of the East India Company's military presence in India.

Many individuals have put up pages on particular regiments, sometimes in relation to a specific war or engagement. There is no single comprehensive listing of these, but you should be able to find them by entering the name of the regiment in a search engine.

There is a very active britregiments mailing list, details of which will be found at <**groups.yahoo.com/group/britregiments/**>. Note that this is a military rather than genealogical discussion forum.

While the Wikipedia article on an individual regiment generally includes a photograph of a cap badge, this will not help if you need to identify an unknown regimental cap badge. But, there are plenty of illustrations on the sites of commercial dealers – just do a search on 'army cap badges'. There is a discussion forum devoted to the topic, the British & Commonwealth Military Badge Forum, at <**www.britishbadgeforum.com/forums/**>. If you want to know what uniform an ancestor wore, or are trying to identify a photograph, the illustrations from two booklets by Arthur H. Bowling on the uniforms of British Infantry Regiments 1660–1914 and Scottish Regiments 1660–1914 are online at <**members.upnaway.com/~obees/soldiers/brit_uniforms/ buframe.html**>. Otherwise, you will need to browse through some of the online photographic collections, such as Photographs of Soldiers of the British Army 1840 to 1920 at <**www.members.dca.net/fbl/**>.

The Army Museums Ogilby Trust's site at <**www.armymuseums.org.uk**> has details of 136 museums, which can be located by name or by geographical area. For each museum, there is a link to its website if there is one. The National Army Museum in Chelsea has a website at <**www.national-army-museum.ac.uk**>. A list of Scottish military museums is provided on the Scottish Military Historical Society's website at <**www.scottishmilitaryresearch.org.uk/ page6.htm**>. Regimental museums can also be found via the regiment's page on the army website.

▌ The Royal Air Force

The official RAF site is at <**www.raf.mod.uk**>, with a list of squadrons and stations linked from the 'Organisation' page at <**www.raf.mod.uk/**

organisation/>. The History section at <**www.raf.mod.uk/history/**> offers historical material on individual squadrons and stations, with images of squadron badges, and details of battle honours and aircraft. If you have an ancestor who took part in the Battle of Britain, you will want to look at the operational diaries at <**www.raf.mod.uk/history/battleofbritain 70thanniversary.cfm**>. Contact details (non-electronic) for RAF Personnel records are given at <**www.raf.mod.uk/links/contacts.cfm**>.

So far, Familyrelatives at <**www.familyrelatives.com**> seems to be the only commercial data service with RAF-specific collections, offering Second World War RAF Deaths, and RAF lists for 1920, 1922, 1929 1949 and 1954. The National Archives has a small number of records for the RAF, linked from <**www.nationalarchives.gov.uk/documentsonline/airforce.asp**>, including Royal Air Force Officers' Service Records (AIR 76) and WRAF service records (Series AIR 80) for the First World War.

Although not strictly RAF records, Ancestry's collection of Royal Aero Club Aviators' Certificates, 1910–1950 at <**search.ancestry.co.uk/search/ db.aspx?dbid=1283**> will include details of many who had been or were to be RAF pilots in the two World Wars. This collection includes around 28,000 index cards and 34 photograph albums.

The RAF Museum has a website at <**www.rafmuseum.org.uk**>, and the pages for the museum's Department of Research & Information Services at Hendon have information on archive and library material at <**www.rafmuseum.org.uk/research/**>.

There do not seem to be any genealogical mailing lists specifically for the RAF, though the general lists for twentieth-century wars mentioned on p. 149 above will cover RAF interests.

Medals

The National Archives has five main research guides on medals and their records, all linked from <**www.nationalarchives.gov.uk/records/atoz**>:

- Medals, British armed services: campaign medals and other service medals
- Medals, British armed services: gallantry medals, further information
- Medals, British armed services: gallantry medals
- Medals: Civilian gallantry
- Merchant Seamen: Medals and Honours

An increasing number of the records relating to medals are available for download and are listed at <**www.nationalarchives.gov.uk/ documentsonline/**>, which currently includes:

- WWI Campaign Medal Index Cards (WO 372)
- Recommendations for Honours and Awards (WO 373)
- WWI Merchant Seamen Medal Cards
- WWII Medals issued to Merchant Seamen (BT 395)
- The Victoria Cross Registers (WO 98)

The first of these is particularly important since it includes almost all who served overseas, including many whose service records do not survive.

Ancestry has a database of the Silver War Badge Records, 1914–20 for around two million individuals at <**search.ancestry.co.uk/search/ db.aspx?dbid=2456**>. This was awarded to 'all military personnel who had served at home or overseas since 4 August 1914 and who had been discharged because of wounds or illness'. The records give enlistment and discharge dates, and unit discharged from, which again can substitute for lost service records.

Details of gallantry awards were posted in the *London Gazette*, which can be searched at the Gazettes Online website, described in more detail on p. 197.

There are many other sites devoted to medals, though mostly without information on recipients. In particular, Wikipedia has an extensive set of pages devoted to British military medals and awards. The most general starting page is 'Military awards and decorations of the United Kingdom', but for a specific medal, just type the name of the medal into the search box on the home page at <**en.wikipedia.org**>. For the Victoria Cross, George Cross, George Medal and Military Medal, there are pages listing the recipients and linking to biographies with details of the action for which the award was made. Stephen Stratford has information on gallantry medals, with photographs, at <**www.stephen-stratford.co.uk/ gallantry.htm**>.

Google's image search at <**images.google.com**> (see p. 343) will quickly find images of a particular medal. Medals of the World has an extensive collection of images of medals and ribbons for many countries at <**www.medals.org.uk**> (Figure 10-3). A handy 'Medals of Great Britain' page with images of the gallantry and campaign medals of the First World War is at <**www.gwpda.org/medals/britmedl/britain.html**>.

The MoD Medal Office has details of all medals available to living veterans at <**www.mod.uk/DefenceInternet/DefenceFor/Veterans/ Medals/**> and the 'British Armed Forces Medals Booklet' has images of all gallantry and campaign medals awarded since the start of the Second World War.

United Kingdom: Abyssinian War Medal

Figure 10-3 Medals of the World

Commemoration

There are many online resources which commemorate those who served in the armed forces and particularly those who fell in action.

Commonwealth War Graves Commission

The most important collection of online data relating to twentieth-century service personnel who gave their lives is that held by the Commonwealth War Graves Commission (CWGC) at <**www.cwgc.org**>. This was one of the first major databases of genealogical significance to go online when it was launched in 1998, and contains the names of 1.7 million members of the Commonwealth forces who died in the First and Second World Wars.

For all those listed there is name, rank, regiment and date of death, with details either of place of burial or, for those with no known grave, of commemoration. The burial information gives not only the name of the cemetery but also the grave reference and instructions on how to get to the cemetery. Some records have additional personal information, usually including the names of parents and the home address. With many cemeteries holding the dead from particular battles and campaigns, there is often historical information which puts the death in its military context. The database also includes information on 60,000 civilian casualties of the Second World War, though without details of burial location.

The initial search form on the home page allows you to specify surname, initials, the service (i.e. army, navy, etc.) and war. However, unless you have an unusual surname, this will almost certainly give you an unwieldy number of results, so it is better to use the Advanced Search which allows you to enter a wide range of additional details, including rank, regiment, any gallantry award and a date range. The 'Regiment' search field only works, though, if you enter the name of an individual regiment – if you enter, say, 'artillery', you will get a drop-down list of artillery regiments to choose from, which unfortunately does not help if all you know is that an ancestor was 'in the artillery'. One thing to watch out for is that if you enter a full forename rather than an initial, you need to select the 'Forename' check-box, otherwise you will get no results at all. But any search on a forename includes in the results all forenames beginning with the same letter, so the forename option does not in fact narrow down your results, as you can see from Figure 10-4, the results of a search for the record of my great uncle Frederick George Marshall. This is a manageable set of six results but if you get dozens or even hundreds of results, which will often be the case if you have only a name to search on, you can sort them on any column. The 'Filter Results' form in the left-hand panel makes it easy to refine your search if you get too many or too few results.

Each name in the search results links to a page giving the details for the soldier (see Figure 10-5). In this instance, in addition to the basic details of rank, regiment and date of death, the record shows the names and address of his parents, which makes it possible to be sure of identification. The bottom part of the screen gives details of the cemetery and grave or memorial, which often includes information on the particular engagements. The 'Find out more' link brings up a page of cemetery details, with further links to plans and photographs. For each cemetery there is a complete list of casualty records.

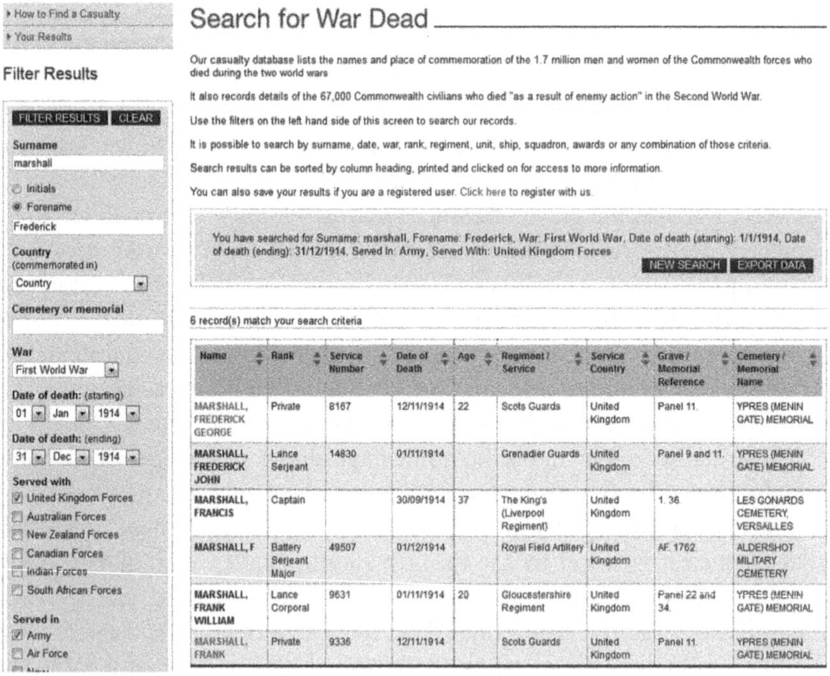

▸ How to Find a Casualty
▸ Your Results

Filter Results

FILTER RESULTS | CLEAR

Surname: marshall
Initials
Forename: Frederick
Country (commemorated in): Country
Cemetery or memorial
War: First World War
Date of death: (starting) 01 Jan 1914
Date of death: (ending) 31 Dec 1914
Served with: United Kingdom Forces; Australian Forces; New Zealand Forces; Canadian Forces; Indian Forces; South African Forces
Served in: Army; Air Force

Search for War Dead

Our casualty database lists the names and place of commemoration of the 1.7 million men and women of the Commonwealth forces who died during the two world wars

It also records details of the 67,000 Commonwealth civilians who died "as a result of enemy action" in the Second World War.

Use the filters on the left hand side of this screen to search our records.

It is possible to search by surname, date, war, rank, regiment, unit, ship, squadron, awards or any combination of those criteria.

Search results can be sorted by column heading, printed and clicked on for access to more information.

You can also save your results if you are a registered user. Click here to register with us.

You have searched for Surname: marshall, Forename: Frederick, War: First World War, Date of death (starting): 1/1/1914, Date of death (ending): 31/12/1914, Served In: Army, Served With: United Kingdom Forces

NEW SEARCH | EXPORT DATA

6 record(s) match your search criteria

Name	Rank	Service Number	Date of Death	Age	Regiment/Service	Service Country	Grave/Memorial Reference	Cemetery/Memorial Name
MARSHALL, FREDERICK GEORGE	Private	8167	12/11/1914	22	Scots Guards	United Kingdom	Panel 11.	YPRES (MENIN GATE) MEMORIAL
MARSHALL, FREDERICK JOHN	Lance Serjeant	14830	01/11/1914		Grenadier Guards	United Kingdom	Panel 9 and 11.	YPRES (MENIN GATE) MEMORIAL
MARSHALL, FRANCIS	Captain		30/09/1914	37	The King's (Liverpool Regiment)	United Kingdom	1. 36.	LES GONARDS CEMETERY, VERSAILLES
MARSHALL, F	Battery Serjeant Major	49507	01/12/1914		Royal Field Artillery	United Kingdom	AF. 1762.	ALDERSHOT MILITARY CEMETERY
MARSHALL, FRANK WILLIAM	Lance Corporal	9631	01/11/1914	20	Gloucestershire Regiment	United Kingdom	Panel 22 and 34.	YPRES (MENIN GATE) MEMORIAL
MARSHALL, FRANK	Private	9336	12/11/1914		Scots Guards	United Kingdom	Panel 11.	YPRES (MENIN GATE) MEMORIAL

Figure 10-4 Commonwealth War Graves Commission search results

Because the search results sometimes give only the initials of the individuals, it can be quite time-consuming to search for someone whose regiment is unknown, though in some cases an age is given. Unfortunately, next of kin is not always named, so for common names you may need ultimately to look at service records to confirm the identity of a particular entry.

A useful feature, particularly for one-namers, is the ability to download the entire results table in a format which can then be opened in a spreadsheet or database.

A separate project, but one being carried out in association with the CWGC, is the War Graves Photographic Project <**www.twgpp.org**> which aims to 'photograph every war grave, individual memorial, MoD grave and family memorial of serving military personnel from WWI to the present day'. In January 2012, the site had around 1.7 million names in its database (Figure 10-6). Photos of the headstones can be ordered.

In addition to the CWGC data, the Officers Died site at <**www.redcoat.info/ memindex3.htm**> lists officers killed in a whole range of wars from the North American Wars of the eighteenth century to Afghanistan in 2009, compiled from various books, casualty lists, medal rolls, newspapers, and memorials.

Casualty details

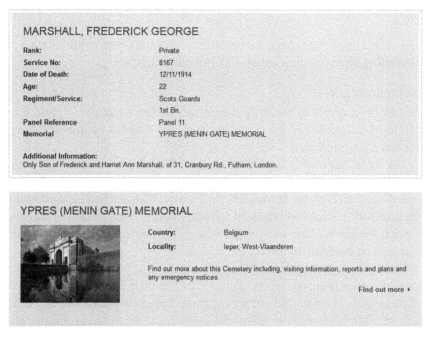

Figure 10-5 Commonwealth War Graves Commission individual record

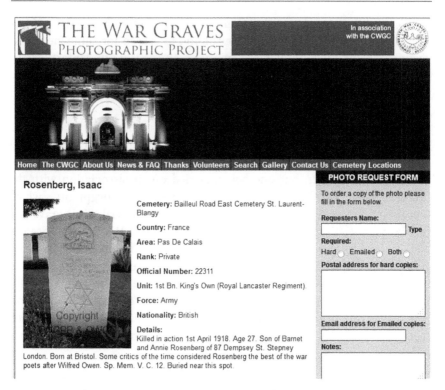

Figure 10-6 The War Grave Photographic Project: the war poet Isaac Rosenberg

The same site has pages devoted to Soldiers [*sic*] Memorials at <www.angelfire.com/mp/memorials/memindz1.htm>.

War memorials

Perhaps as a result of the 90th anniversary of the Armistice, a significant development in the last few years has been the number of sites devoted to domestic war memorials.

The main national project is the Imperial War Museum's UK National Inventory of War Memorials at <www.ukniwm.org.uk>. The main database lists around 60,000 war memorials with details of appearance, location and the number of names recorded. Individual names are not currently listed on the site, though the data were prepared for a now defunct Channel 4 site and may well be available in future.

The equivalent project for Ireland, the Irish War Memorials Project, has a site at <www.irishwarmemorials.ie>. The site includes many photographs of memorials and often the names of those commemorated and any other text. In addition to a list of memorials, which can be sorted geographically, there is a list of names and regiments.

The Scottish National War Memorial at <**www.snwm.org**> has databases of over 200,000 names of Scottish casualties from the two World Wars and the period since 1945.

World War One Cemeteries at <**www.ww1cemeteries.com**> is designed as a guide to the cemeteries of the two World Wars. For each cemetery, it generally has a description and photograph; for some there are lists of names, while for others there is just a list of the regiments represented.

Roll of Honour at <**www.roll-of-honour.com**> is a site dedicated to listing those commemorated on war memorials, organized by county. For each memorial the site gives not only the names of the individuals but also, where available, personal details drawn from the CWGC records (p. 159) or other publications. There are photographs for many of the memorials. The site does not confine itself to those who died, nor to the World Wars, but includes the Boer War and more recent conflicts such as the Falklands.

Alongside these national projects, there are countless local sites, such as:

- Newport's War Dead at <**www.newportsdead.shaunmcguire.co.uk**> and Cwmbran and District's War Dead at <**www.cwmbransdead. shaunmcguire.co.uk**>
- Dover War Memorial Project at <**www.doverwarmemorialproject.org.uk**>.

Not only towns and cities, but individual institutions may have details of their war dead on the web. For example:

- The Bata company's Reminiscence and Resource Centre has details of its fallen employees at <**www.batamemories.org.uk/MAIN/ENG/00-EN-Pages/07-Worldwar.html**>.
- The Department for Business, Innovation & Skills (the DTI, as was) had a section of its website devoted to the 300 staff from the department's wartime predecessors who died in the wars. It includes basic biographical details for each individual, including, in some cases, the enumeration of the family in the 1901 census. The material is now hosted in The National Archives Web Archive but can be most easily accessed from <**www.bis.gov.uk/about/who-we-are/war-memorial**>.

Some have rolls of honour listing all those who served, not just those killed. For example:

- The University of Glasgow's Roll of Honour at <**www.universitystory. gla.ac.uk/ww1-intro/**> has a database of 4,500 staff and students who served in the First World War. For over 200 of them, there are biographies drawn from the university's records.

- Aviva has databases of employees of its predecessor companies for both world wars at <**www.aviva.com/about-us/heritage/**>, recording both the casualties and gallantry awards.
- The Internet Archive has the Roll of Honour of The Commercial Bank of Scotland Limited, 1914–1918 at <**www.archive.org/details/ RollOfHonourOfTheCommercialBankOfScotlandLimited1914-1918**>.

11

MIGRATION AND COLONIES

Former British colonies are genealogically important for British and Irish family history for three reasons: they have been the destination of emigrants from the British Isles (both voluntary and otherwise), the source of much immigration, and a place of residence and work for many British soldiers, merchants and others.

There is not space here to deal with internet resources relating to the individual countries, or to overseas records unrelated to immigration or emigration, but good places to start are Cyndi's List at <**www.cyndislist.com**>, which has individual pages for all the countries or regions, and the GenWeb site for the country at <**worldgenweb.org**> (see p. 25). Genuki has links relating to both emigration and immigration at <**www.genuki.org.uk/big/ Emigration.html**>. Resources relating to child migration are covered in 'Adoption and child migration' on p. 195.

For the official British records of emigration, The National Archives site has a range of resources. The 'Looking for a person?' page at <**www.nationalarchives.gov.uk/records/looking-for-person/**> has a heading 'Migrants and passengers' linking to individual pages for Naturalised Britons, Emigrants, Internees, Immigrants, Passengers, and Passports. The research guide on 'Emigrants' is a comprehensive guide to official records of emigration, at <**www.nationalarchives.gov.uk/records/ research-guides/emigration.htm**>. The equivalent guide on immigration is at <**www.nationalarchives.gov.uk/records/research-guides/immigrants.htm**>.

While TNA's material concentrates on the official records, broader coverage of immigration to Britain is provided by the Moving Here site at <**www.movinghere.org.uk**> (Figure 11-1). This has sections devoted to Caribbean, Irish, South Asian, and Jewish immigration to England over the past two centuries as well as the subsequent history of the immigrant communities. The site has a catalogue of resources as well as general historical material and individual historical testimony. There is specifically genealogical information for each of these immigrant groups in the 'Tracing Your Roots gallery' at <**www.movinghere.org.uk/galleries/roots/**>. These

Figure 11-1 Material on South Asian migration from MovingHere

sections also include material on those who went from Britain to work in the colonies.

Wikipedia has a wealth of articles relating to the history of British colonies, which will provide some historical background and have useful bibliographical pointers. For example, there are over 200 articles on the history of New South Wales, listed at <**en.wikipedia.org/wiki/Category:History_of_New_South_Wales**>, which include pages devoted to individual convict ships. The best way to find such material is to start from the main page on the history of the particular modern country or from the 'British Empire' article. There are also articles on immigration into individual countries.

The National Library of Scotland has details of material held by the library relating to emigration from Scotland in its Scots Abroad databases at <**digital.nls.uk/emigration/**> and has a substantial listing of non-NLS resources, both in Britain and overseas, for Scottish emigration at <**digital. nls.uk/emigration/resources/**>.

There is a Museum of Immigration at Spitalfields in London which has a website at <**www.19princeletstreet.org.uk**>. The British Empire & Commonwealth Museum in Bristol has a website at <**www.empiremuseum.co.uk**> with information on the museum and its collections. The Migrations Museum Network at <**www.migrationmuseums.org**> has details of over two dozen migration museums around the world.

UntoldLondon at <www.untoldlondon.org.uk> 'tells you where to look for the history of all of London's races and faiths', with details of and links to relevant material in archives and museums via the 'Collections' menu.

There are a number of general mailing lists relating to migration from and within the British Isles, including:

- ENGLISH-EMIGRANTS <lists.rootsweb.ancestry.com/index/other/ Ethnic-English/ENGLISH-EMIGRANTS.html>
- WELSH-EMIGRANTS <lists.rootsweb.ancestry.com/index/other/ Ethnic-Welsh/WELSH-EMIGRANTS.html>
- IRISH-IN-UK <lists.rootsweb.ancestry.com/index/other/Ethnic-Irish/ IRISH-IN-UK.html>, with a website at <www.connorsgenealogy.com/ IrishUK/>
- IRISH-SCOTS <lists.rootsweb.ancestry.com/index/other/Ethnic-Irish/ IRISH-SCOTS.html>

British-Genealogy has discussion forums for emigration and Jewish Roots at <www.british-genealogy.com/forums/>, and TalkingScot has discussion forums for Scottish emigration (including that to other parts of the British Isles) at <www.talkingscot.com/forum/> under the heading 'Scots Abroad'.

There are also local resources relating to immigrant groups, and these are often part of a local history site, particularly in the case of major cities. For example, the PortCities sites at <www.portcities.org.uk> have material on the slave trade for Bristol and Liverpool, while for London there are individual sections devoted to the roles of Chinese, Scandinavian, Jewish, Bengali, Goan, Swahili, Somali and Portuguese communities in the life of the port. The Old Bailey Proceedings site has some very substantial articles about individual immigrant communities in the capital at <www.oldbaileyonline.org/static/Communities.jsp>.

One problem in finding online resources relating to immigration is that search engines will find predominantly materials relating to current immigration practices and issues, and it is much more difficult to identify historical materials by this method. For that reason, it is generally more productive to follow the links from the specialist genealogical and historical sites mentioned in this chapter.

Passenger lists

Key general records for emigration from the British Isles are passenger lists, and there are a number of sites with information about surviving passenger lists, or with data transcribed from them. Cyndi's List has a 'Ships and

Passenger Lists' page at <www.cyndislist.com/ships>. Among other information, this has links to many passenger lists and lists of ship arrivals. Passenger lists specifically for emigration to North America and Australia are covered in more detail below.

The Immigrant Ships Transcribers Guild at <www.immigrantships.net> has transcribed over 11,000 passenger lists and is adding more all the time. These can be searched by date, by port of departure, port of arrival, passenger name or captain's name. In addition to its own material, the 'Compass' area of the site at <immigrantships.net/newcompass/pcindex.html> has an enormous collection of links to other passenger list sites.

The Scottish Emigration Database at <www.abdn.ac.uk/emigration> contains the records of over 21,000 passengers who embarked at Glasgow and Greenock for non-European ports between 1 January and 30 April 1923, and at other Scottish ports between 1890 and 1960.

Ancestorsonboard at <www.ancestorsonboard.com> is Findmypast's pay-per-view passenger list site, with 24 million records derived from The National Archives' Outward Bound Passenger Lists (series BT 27, Figure 11-2). These records are also accessible from the main site at <www.findmypast.co.uk>, which has, additionally, UK Passport Applications 1851–1903. All these records are also available on Genes Reunited.

Ancestry UK has a large number of databases relating to migration, many drawn from published works on English, Scots and Irish migration to North America. While most of the material discussed here concerns those leaving the British Isles, Ancestry also has a database of UK Incoming Passenger

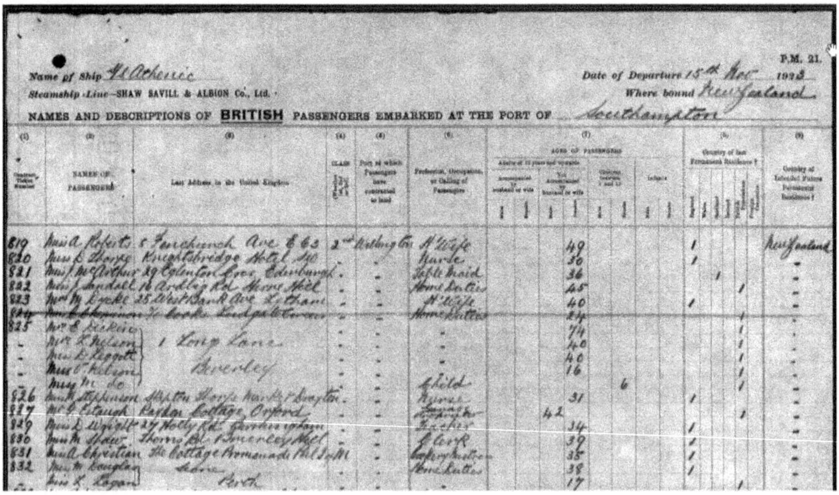

Figure 11-2 Passengers travelling to New Zealand, 1927 (Findmypast)

Lists, 1878–1960, drawn from The National Archives' BT 26 series and Alien Arrivals, 1810–1811, 1826–1869 from various TNA document series. There is a name search, and you can also browse the records by port, year and ship. This material is not just a source for immigrants – it also captures those returning from working abroad. All of these are listed in the Ancestry Card Catalogue at <search.ancestry.co.uk/search/CardCatalog.aspx> – use the 'Filter by Collection' option to select 'Immigration & Travel'.

Origins has British and Irish Passenger Lists for 1890 and 1891 (see <www.origins.net/help/aboutbo-passenger.aspx>) which include ships to North American destinations. This dataset comprises the records in BT 27, also found on Findmypast, supplemented by additional Canadian records. This is available to both British Origins and Irish Origins subscribers, but Irish Origins also has passenger lists for ships returning to Britain and Ireland from North America between 1858 and 1870 from the National Archives of Ireland (see <www.origins.net/help/aboutio-migration.aspx>).

There are a number of mailing lists for emigrant ships, but the most general is TheShipsList, which has its own website at <www.theshipslist.com>. SHIPS_FROM_ENGLAND has similar coverage, though with an emphasis on the British Colonies of North America – details are at <lists.rootsweb. ancestry.com/index/other/Immigration/SHIPS_FROM_ENGLAND.html>. Other lists relating to emigration and immigration will be found at <www.rootsweb.ancestry.com/~jfuller/gen_mail_emi.html>.

The Americas

The earliest British migrants to North America were either voluntary settlers or transported convicts, though American independence eventually put a stop to the latter. Of course, independence did not put a stop to immigration from Britain and particularly Ireland.

In addition to the North America section in its general emigration guide, mentioned above, The National Archives has two research guides on the UK's official records relating to British North America and the United States, linked from <www.nationalarchives.gov.uk/records/research-guide-listing.htm>: 'America and West Indies: Colonies before 1782' and 'American Revolution'.

The US National Archives and Records Administration (NARA) has comprehensive information on US immigration records at <www.archives.gov/research/immigration/> and naturalization records at <www.archives.gov/research/naturalization/>.

For other links relating to emigration to North America, the best starting point is the 'Immigration and Naturalization' page on Cyndi's List at <www.cyndislist.com/immigration>.

US sites of course have a wealth of data relating to immigrants. For the early period of settlement, Ancestry at <www.ancestry.com> has several databases in addition to the passenger lists mentioned above:

- Immigrants to New England 1620–33
- Irish Quaker Immigration into Pennsylvania
- New England Founders
- New England Immigrants, 1700–75
- New England Irish Pioneers
- Scots-Irish in Virginia

A number of immigration datasets are included in a subscription to Ancestry's UK record collection, but for most a subscription to the US Discovery Collection or the Worldwide Membership is required (see p. 52).

There are many sites devoted to the earliest settlers. Pilgrim Ship Lists at <www.packrat-pro.com/ships/shiplist.htm> has details of over 7,100 families and 250 ships between 1602 and 1638. There are also sites devoted to particular groups of settlers, such as Caleb Johnson's MayflowerHistory.com at <www.mayflowerhistory.com>. Wikipedia has details for many individual *Mayflower* settlers and indeed has many articles relating to the early settlement of North America and notable individual settlers.

In addition to the general passenger list sites mentioned above, there are a number of major databases for ships carrying immigrants to the USA. NARA has a page at <www.archives.gov/research/immigration/passenger-arrival.html> devoted to 'Ship Passenger Arrival Records and Land Border Entries' (not all of which, of course, constitute immigration) covering the various types of record. The most significant databases are:

- Castle Garden at <www.castlegarden.org>, which has an online searchable database of 11 million immigrants from 1820 to 1892.
- The Ellis Island Passenger Arrivals (the American Family Immigration History Center) at <www.ellisislandrecords.org> has a searchable database of more than 22 million passengers who entered America through Ellis Island between 1892 and 1924. (Requires registration, free of charge.)
- Irish Famine Passenger Records in NARA's Access to Archives Databases (AAD) at <aad.archives.gov/aad/series-list.jsp?cat=GP44> lists around 600,000 passengers who arrived in the Port of New York, from 1846–1851.

A smaller index, The Immigrant Servants Database at <www.immigrantservants.com> includes details of over 18,000 immigrants identifiable from published records as indentured servants up to 1820.

Harvard has more general historical materials relating to post-independence immigration (i.e. not records of named individuals) at <**ocp.hul.harvard.edu/immigration/**> on its 'Immigration to the United States, 1789–1930' site.

Needless to say, Cyndi's List has hundreds of further links relating to immigration to the United States at <**www.cyndislist.com/immigration/**>.

There is less material online for Canada. Marjorie Kohli's Immigrants to Canada site at <**www.ist.uwaterloo.ca/~marj/genealogy/thevoyage.html**> has an extensive collection of material, and links to many related resources. The National Archives of Canada has information on immigration and citizenship at <**www.collectionscanada.gc.ca/genealogy/022-908-e.html**>, covering both border entry and passenger lists. There is a pilot online database for the passenger list records for the years 1925–35 at <**www.collectionscanada.gc.ca/databases/immigration-1925/index-e.html**>. The inGeneas site at <**www.inGeneas.com**> also has a database of passenger lists and immigration records: the National Archives of Canada Miscellaneous Immigration Index is free; the index to other material can be searched free, but there is a charge for record transcriptions.

Resources relating to the British Home Children settled in Canada will be found on p. 251.

Latin America has been a much less significant destination for British settlers, but the Glaniad site at <**www.glaniad.com**> provides information on the Welsh in Patagonia. TNA's Your Archives wiki has a detailed list of the official documents relating to this group of emigrants at <**yourarchives. nationalarchives.gov.uk/index.php?title=Welsh_Colony_in_Patagonia**>. Information on emigration to Argentina and Uruguay will be found on the British Settlers in Argentina site at <**www.argbrit.org**>, which has extracts from both local Protestant church registers and a range of other records.

Australasia

After the United States gained their independence from Britain in 1783, a new destination was required for the undesirables sentenced by the courts to transportation.

There are extensive materials online relating both to convict transportation to Australia, and to later free emigration to Australia and New Zealand. Good starting points are the Australia and New Zealand pages on Cyndi's List at <**www.cyndislist.com/Australia/**> and <**www.cyndislist.com/ new-zealand/**> respectively. Another worthwhile site is the Australian Family History Compendium, which has a list of online sources at <**www.cohsoft.com.au/afhc/**>. For information on the official records held by the British state, see The National Archives' Research Guides.

The University of Wollongong has a database of the First Fleet convicts <**firstfleet.uow.edu.au**>, with details of crime and conviction, and much supporting material about the fleet. The First Fleet 1788 site at <**www.jag10. freeserve.co.uk/1788.htm**> includes officials and marines as well as convicts, and also lists the provisions carried on the supply ships. Convicts to Australia at <**convictcentral.com**> has extensive material on the transported convicts, including the names of all those on the first, second, and third fleets, and details of later convict ships to the various states. Convict Records of Australia at <**www.convictrecords.com.au**> has a searchable and browsable database of the convicts in the Convict Transportation Register (HO 11) at the UK National Archives.

The National Archives of Ireland has a database of Transportation Records 1788–1868 at <**www.nationalarchives.ie/topics/transportation/ search01.html**> (Figure 11-3) along with information on the transportation of Irish convicts at <**www.nationalarchives.ie/genealogy/ transportation.html**>.

Australian government agencies have much information relating to convicts and free settlers online. The National Archives of Australia (NAA) website at <**www.naa.gov.au**> has a section devoted to 'Migration, citizenship and travel' at <**www.naa.gov.au/collection/explore/migration/**>, which includes information on the relevant records and their locations, with

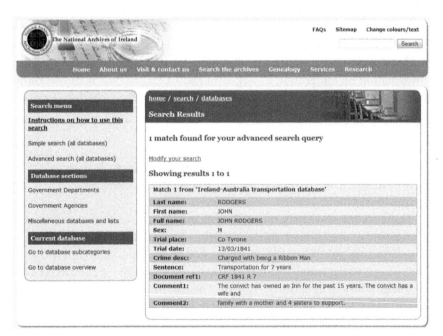

Figure 11-3 An entry from the National Archives of Ireland's Transportation Records

links to a wide range of further fact-sheets and research guides. The NAA's Record Search includes, in addition to a general name search, a Passenger Arrivals Index at <**recordsearch.naa.gov.au/Scripts/PassengerSearch.asp**> covering those arriving by ship in Fremantle and other Western Australian ports between 1921 and 1949 or arriving at Perth airport between 1944 and 1949. In the same search, you need to select 'Immigration and naturalisation records'.

FamilySearch (see p. 41) has around a dozen record collections for Australia and New Zealand, including indexes and images for the Index to Bounty Immigrants Arriving in N.S.W., 1828–1842 and New Zealand, Immigration Passenger Lists, 1855–1973.

Ancestry Australia at <**www.ancestry.com.au**> has a substantial collection of databases relating to convicts and free settlers, including:

- NSW Free Settlers, 1826–1922, with almost nine million names
- NSW Assisted Immigrants, 1828–1896, with around 450,000 names
- The List of Convicts with Particulars, 1788–1842, with physical descriptions of around 23,000 convicts
- Convict Savings Bank Books, 1824–1886
- Queensland Passenger Lists, 1848–1912, with over 300,000 names

These are also available to those with a Worldwide Membership.

Findmypast launched a data service for Australia and New Zealand records at <**www.findmypast.com.au**> in May 2010, taking over WorldVitalRecords' Australian site. There are over 600 datasets including electoral rolls and government gazettes for both Australia and New Zealand. The only material specifically related to immigration is Convict Arrivals in New South Wales 1788–1842.

There are also relevant resources on the websites of the individual states. For example, the Victoria Public Record Office has several online indexes including passenger lists and convict registers, all linked from <**www.access. prov.vic.gov.au/public/PROVguides/PROVguide023/PROVguide023.jsp**>. The Archives Office of Tasmania has a number of name indexes at <**www.linc.tas.gov.au/tasmaniasheritage/search/name-indexes/ nameindexes**> which include convicts, arrivals and naturalizations. There is also a Colonial Tasmanian Family Link Database at <**portal.archives. tas.gov.au/menu.aspx?search=8**> with about 500,000 entries about Tasmanian families. New South Wales has a large number of online indexes, half a dozen relating to immigration and five relating to convicts, linked from <**www.records.nsw.gov.au/state-archives/indexes-online/**>.

About.com has an excellent collection of links to Australian resources including 'Top Databases & Web Sites for Australian Genealogy' at <**genealogy.about.com/od/australia/tp/top_databases.-9b1.htm**>.

SCAN (see p. 206) provides material on the role of the Highland and Island Emigration Society in promoting Scottish emigration to Australia in the 1850s, together with searchable passenger lists, at <**www.scan.org.uk/ researchrtools/emigration.htm**> (note the 'r' after 'research').

The Australian Society of Archivists has a comprehensive 'Directory of Archives in Australia' at <**directory.archivists.org.au/archives/**>, with descriptions and links.

Archives New Zealand's website at <**www.archives.govt.nz**> includes a 'Migration' research guide at <**archives.govt.nz/sites/default/files/Migration_-_ A33044_0.pdf**>. The Registrar General's site at <**www.bdm.govt.nz**> has information on births, deaths and marriages but no online data.

The online Encyclopedia of New Zealand at <**www.teara.govt.nz**> has considerable material relating to settlement, with sections devoted to particular communities. There is extensive coverage of English, Scots, Welsh and Irish settlement.

There are dozens of mailing lists for Australian and New Zealand genealogy, all listed at <**www.rootsweb.ancestry.com/~jfuller/gen_mail_ country-aus.html**> and <**www.rootsweb.ancestry.com/~jfuller/gen_mail_ country-nez.html**>. The main general lists are AUSTRALIA, NEW-ZEALAND, and GENANZ, while the remainder are devoted to specific topics: AUS-CONVICTS, AUS-IMMIGRATION-SHIPS, AUS-IRISH, AUS-MILITARY, AUS-NSW-COLONIAL-HISTORY, convicts-australia, TRANSCRIPTIONS-AUS and TRANSCRIPTIONS-NZ. There are also lists for individual states, regions, and even towns.

Africa and the Caribbean

A good starting point for researching Black British ancestry is the BBC's History site, which offers an introduction to Caribbean family history by Kathy Chater at <**www.bbc.co.uk/history/familyhistory/get_started/ caribbean_01.shtml**> and the more detailed 'Researching African-Caribbean Family History' by Guy Grannum at <**www.bbc.co.uk/history/ familyhistory/next_steps/genealogy_article_01.shtml**>. Both provide historical background and the second discusses the relevant records in some detail. TNA has pages devoted to 'Caribbean Histories Revealed' at <**www.nationalarchives.gov.uk/caribbeanhistory/**>, which provides information about the region and the migrations to and from it, with an extensive collection of links and a very substantial bibliography. 'Black Presence. Asian and Black History in Britain 1500–1850' is another National Archives site at <**www.nationalarchives.gov.uk/pathways/blackhistory/**> which provides a concise introduction to the historical background of migration from the Caribbean and the Indian subcontinent.

CaribbeanGenWeb at <www.rootsweb.ancestry.com/~caribgw/> has areas devoted to each of the islands of the Caribbean. Though there are considerable differences in scope, as each island site has its own maintainer, all have message boards to make contact with other researchers, and many have substantial collections of links. You should also find information on civil registration, parish registers and other records. Another useful collection of genealogy links for the Caribbean will be found on the Candoo site at <www.candoo.com/genresources/>, including lists of relevant microfilms in the LDS Church's Family History Centers.

For the records of the slave trade the best starting point after Guy Grannum's article, mentioned above, is TNA's 'Looking for records of slavery or slave owners' page at <www.nationalarchives.gov.uk/records/looking-for-person/slaves-and-slave-owners.htm>. A research guide on 'Slavery: British transatlantic slave trade' will be found at <www.nationalarchives.gov.uk/records/research-guides/slave-trade-slavery.htm>.

As yet, few records of slavery for British colonies have been digitized, but the Slave Registers of former British Colonial Dependencies (TNA document series T 71), with almost three million names, are available on Ancestry. The Your Archives wiki has detailed information on these registers at <yourarchives.nationalarchives.gov.uk/index.php?title=Slave_registers> along with many other articles on slavery and related topics, all listed at <yourarchives.nationalarchives.gov.uk/index.php?title=Category:Slavery>, covering both the historical background and the records of the trade.

As mentioned above, the PortCities sites for Bristol and Liverpool, linked from <www.portcities.org.uk>, have material on the slave trade centred on these ports, while the London site has pages devoted to the capital's Somali and Swahili-speaking communities.

The Parliament website had extensive historical material on 'Parliament and the British Slave Trade 1600–1807' at <slavetrade.parliament.uk/slavetrade/>, published in 2007 to celebrate the bicentenary of the abolition of slavery, but this material is now available only on the Wayback Machine (8 May 2010). TNA has materials on slavery and its abolition at <www.nationalarchives.gov.uk/slavery/>.

For convict transportation to the West Indies, see The National Archives' Research Guides mentioned under 'The Americas', above.

While there is still relatively little specifically genealogical material online for those with Black British ancestry, the web offers an increasing amount of general historical information relating to black immigration and the history of black communities in Britain.

Resources relating to the BBC's *Windrush* season, broadcast in 1998, at <www.bbc.co.uk/history/british/modern/windrush_01.shtml> include a factfile and oral testimony from those who came to Britain on the *Windrush*. This is part of the 'Multiculture' area of the BBC's site which has a range of material relating to Black History and the British Empire.

It's worth using a search engine for the phrase 'black history' with the name of a town or county you are interested in. This will turn up sites such as Birmingham Black History at <www.**birminghamblackhistory.com**>, Brighton and Hove Black History at <www.**black-history.org.uk**>, or Norfolk Black History Month at <www.**norfolkblackhistorymonth.org.uk**>.

One of the most significant local projects is the Black and Asian Londoners Project (BAL), run by the London Metropolitan Archives (LMA). It aims to create an online database of Black and Asian Londoners between 1536 and 1840, with names and area of residence based on information from church registers, family papers in the LMA and material from the British Library and the India Office. The home page is at <www.**learningzone.cityoflondon. gov.uk/dataonline/lz_baproject.asp**> and the database can be searched on name, street, borough, place of origin, or occupation. The results of a search are images of the original records – Figure 11-4 shows the baptism of William Antonio, 'an African', at St Peter, Regent Square.

CASBAH is a project which aims to identify and map national research resources relevant to Caribbean studies and the history of Black and Asian peoples in Britain. The CASBAH website at <www.**casbah.ac.uk**>, while aimed primarily at academic researchers, is useful to anyone researching Black History in Britain because it provides links to around 120 other websites, particularly libraries, with relevant collections. A number of organizations have useful websites, for example the Black Cultural Archives, 'the first national institution dedicated to commemorating and celebrating the experiences of people of African and African-Caribbean descent in Britain' at <**bcaheritage.org.uk**> and the Black and Asian Studies Association <www.**blackandasianstudies.org**>.

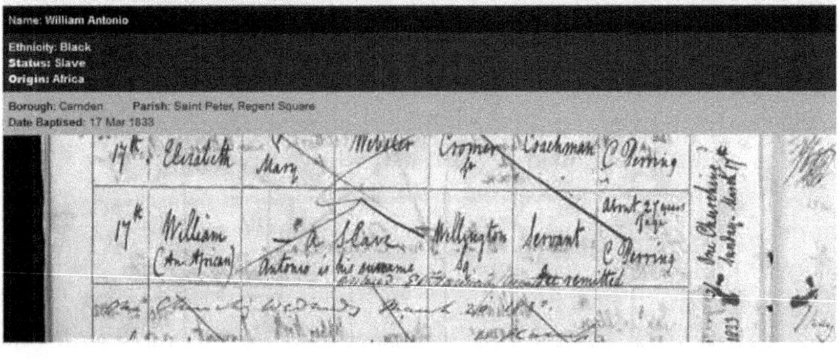

Figure 11-4 The Black and Asian Londoners database

The Open Directory's African-British page at <**dmoz.org/Society/ Ethnicity/African/African-British/**> is another starting point for web resources relating to African and Afro-Caribbean immigration into Britain, though the listing does not specialize in genealogical sources.

The Caribbean Surnames Index (CARSURDEX) at <**www.candoo.com/ surnames/**> offers a discussion forum where users can post details of the families they are researching. The postings can be read by anyone but registration (free) is required to respond, post a message yourself or contact others.

The main mailing list for West Indian ancestry is CARIBBEAN – see <**lists. rootsweb.ancestry.com/index/other/Newsgroup_Gateways/ CARIBBEAN.html**>. The GEN-AFRICAN list (see <**lists.rootsweb. ancestry.com/index/other/Newsgroup_Gateways/GEN-AFRICAN.html**>) covers the genealogy of Africa and the African diaspora. The CARIBBEAN-FREEDMEN and ENGLAND-FREEDMEN mailing lists may be of interest to descendants of freed slaves. Details of both are linked from <**lists.rootsweb. ancestry.com/index/other/Ethnic-African/**>.

There are message boards for Africa and the Caribbean on RootsWeb at <**boards.rootsweb.com/localities.africa/mb.ashx**> and <**boards. rootsweb.com/localities.caribbean/mb.ashx**> respectively, with individual boards for all the modern countries and islands. Boards for a more limited range of countries will be found at GenForum, linked from <**genforum.genealogy.com/regional/countries/**>.

India

Initially the genealogical significance of the Indian subcontinent for Britain was as the temporary home of many young men in the army, trade, or colonial administration, with those who chose to remain giving rise to an Anglo-Indian population. Since independence, that flow has been reversed.

A number of the resources mentioned in the previous section cover Asian immigration to Britain as well as Black immigration. The British Library site is one of the most useful for ancestors from the British Isles who lived or worked in India, as it includes the India Office website. This has pages for family historians at <**www.bl.uk/reshelp/findhelpregion/asia/india/ indiaofficerecordsfamilyhistory/familyresearch.html**>, with information on the various types of genealogical source. The India Office Family History Search at <**indiafamily.bl.uk**> has a database of 300,000 births, baptisms, marriages, deaths and burials in the India Office Records, mainly for Europeans, for the period 1600–1949. Following the links to 'Sources' leads to a list of the original documents extracted.

Apart from the British Library, the most important site for the British in India is that of the Families in British India Society at <**www.fibis.org**> with a free online database of selected records of the India Office and East India Company held by the British Library and elsewhere. The records include transcriptions of civil, ecclesiastical, maritime and military records covering the period from 1737 to 1947. Amongst over 700,000 records are details of ships sailing to India, and their occupants, plus births, marriages and deaths of persons in British-administrated territories in India. Many records relate to soldiers of the Indian Army and the British Army regiments which served in India. The database can be searched from <**search.fibis.org**>. The FIBIWiki at <**wiki.fibis.org**> provides research guides, lists sources, and provides general background information about the culture, society and history of India during the period of British rule.

For general and local information about British India, an invaluable resource is the 1909 edition of the *Imperial Gazetteer of India* available in the University of Chicago's Digital South Asia Library at <**dsal.uchicago.edu/reference/gazetteer/**>. It covers the whole of the Indian Empire, not just India itself, and has comprehensive introductory material as well as gazetteer entries for individual places.

Findmypast at <**www.findmypast.co.uk**> (see p. 53) has a number of datasets relating to British India, including:

- Bengal Civil Service Graduation List 1869
- India Office List 1933
- East India Register & Army List 1855
- Indian Army & Civil Service List 1873
- East India Company's Commercial Marine Service Pensions List 1793–1833

Military sites mentioned in Chapter 10 may have information about the British Army in India.

The Honorable East India Co site at <**www.honeastindiaco.com**> had birth, marriage and death notices of people who worked for or were associated with the Company, collected from various newspapers and publications. It is now available only at the Wayback Machine (7 February 2011). Wikipedia has many links to web resources relating to the company, linked from its 'East India Company' article.

The National Archives' research guide to 'Family History Sources for Indian Indentured Labour' at <**www.nationalarchives.gov.uk/records/research-guides/indian-indentured-labour.htm**> explains the practice of sending Indian labourers to sugar-producing colonies and gives guidance on the official records.

The British Library has a whole set of pages devoted to 'Asians in Britain' at <**www.bl.uk/reshelp/findhelpsubject/history/history/asiansinbritain/ asiansinbritain.html**>, including an outline of Asian immigration and contemporary material from various walks of life. TNA materials relating to Black and Asian Britons have been mentioned above.

For a general historical introduction to the British Asian community, see Wikipedia's articles on 'British Asian' and 'British Indian', which also have links to articles on related topics and individual subgroups. The first of these pages also has a list of the main South Asian communities with links to the articles for the relevant towns and cities. For the capital, PortCities London at <**www.portcities.org.uk/london/**> has material on the Bengali and Goan communities – follow the 'Port communities' link.

Local history sites for major cities are always worth checking. For example, the Liverpool Museums site hosts material on 'The Indian Presence in Liverpool' at <**www.liverpoolmuseums.org.uk/hamlyn/ip/**> with photos, biographies, and recordings of the immigrant families who came to the city in the twentieth century.

There are two genealogical mailing lists relevant to the Indian subcontinent, BANGLADESH and INDIA. Details will be found at <**lists.rootsweb.ancestry.com/index/intl/BGD/BANGLADESH.html**> and <**lists.rootsweb.ancestry.com/index/intl/IND/INDIA.html**> respectively. RootsWeb hosts genealogical mailing lists for a number of other Asian countries, listed at <**lists.rootsweb.ancestry.com/index/**>. There is also an INDIA-BRITISH-RAJ list, though this is devoted to general historical and cultural topics rather than to genealogical issues as such. Subscription details and a link to the archive of messages will found at <**lists.rootsweb.ancestry.com/ index/intl/IND/INDIA-BRITISH-RAJ.html**>.

European immigration

For guidance about immigrants to Britain from continental Europe, the best starting points are the pages for the relevant country at Cyndi's List (p. 24) and WorldGenweb (p. 25) and the general immigration sites given at the start of this chapter. However, three particularly significant groups with a distinct identity in the British Isles long after migration are covered here in more detail.

Jews

There are many sites devoted to Jewish genealogy, though not many are specifically concerned with British Jewry. A general history of Jews in Britain is provided in Shira Schoenberg's Virtual Jewish History Tour, which has a page devoted to England at <**www.jewishvirtuallibrary.org/jsource/vjw/ England.html**>. JewishGen at <**www.jewishgen.org**> is a very comprehensive site with a number of resources relevant to Jewish ancestry in the British Isles. These include an old but still useful article on researching Jewish ancestry at <www.jewishgen.org/infofiles/ukgen.txt>, and the London Jews Database <www.jewishgen.org/databases/UK/londweb.htm>, which has over 9,000 names, taken principally from London trade directories. (Jeffrey Maynard, who compiled this database, has a number of other small datasets on his Anglo-Jewish Miscellanies site at <www.jeffreymaynard.com>.) The site also hosts JCR-UK at <www.jewishgen.org/jcr-uk>, a comprehensive guide to Jewish communities and records in the UK and Ireland, with information on synagogues in each locality.

The Jewish genealogical magazine *Avotaynu* has a 'Five-minute Guide to Jewish Genealogical Research' at <www.avotaynu.com/jewish_genealogy.htm>. The National Archives has a research guide 'Anglo-Jewish History, 18th–20th Centuries: Sources in The National Archives' online at <www.nationalarchives.gov.uk/records/research-guides/anglo-jewish-history-18th-20th.htm>. The Jewish Historical Society of England at <www.jhse.org> has a few general articles and a useful 'Chronology of the Jews in Britain'. The site's bibliographies and links will direct you to further sources of information. As usual, Cyndi's List has a good collection of links at <www.cyndislist.com/jewish/>.

The Jewish Genealogical Society of Great Britain's website at <www.jgsgb.org.uk>, has a substantial collection of links to Jewish material in Britain and worldwide. *Avotaynu* has a Consolidated Jewish Surname Index at <www.avotaynu.com/csi/csi-home.htm> with over half a million names. There is a varied collection of material relating to London Jews on Jeffrey Maynard's site at <www.jeffreymaynard.com>.

FamilySearch hosts the Knowles Collection of Jewish Families, which includes a dataset for the British Isles compiled by Isobel Mordy. This can be searched from the Community Trees area of the site at <histfam.familysearch.org/learnmore.php>.

The United Synagogue website has a 'Find Your Family' section at <www.theus.org.uk/support_services/find_your_family/> with indexes of burial and marriage authorization records.

For research into the continental origins of British Jewish families the JewishGen Family Finder (JGFF) at <www.jewishgen.org/jgff/> should be of use. This is a 'database of ancestral towns and surnames currently being researched by Jewish genealogists worldwide', with around 120,000 surnames submitted by 90,000 Jewish genealogists.

For details of Jewish archives in the UK, consult the University of Southampton's 'Survey of Jewish archives in the UK and Ireland' at <www.archives.soton.ac.uk/jewish/> which gives details and locations. There are two sites devoted to particular archives:

- The Susser Archive, relating to Jews in South West England, at <www.jewishgen.org/JCR-uk/susser/>
- The Rothschild Archive at <www.rothschildarchive.org>

There are two general Jewish mailing lists: the JEWISHGEN list, hosted by JewishGen at <www.jewishgen.org/JewishGen/DiscussionGroup.htm> and RootsWeb's JEWISH-ROOTS list at <lists.rootsweb.ancestry.com/index/other/Religion/JEWISH-ROOTS.html>. John Fuller lists another three dozen mailing lists for Jewish genealogy at <www.rootsweb.ancestry.com/~jfuller/gen_mail_jewish.html>, but these are all specific to particular geographical areas, whether as sources of emigration, or as destinations of migrants. A similar list is at Cyndi's List, <www.cyndislist.com/jewish/mailing-lists/>. Only one list is specifically relevant to Jewish communities in the British Isles, the BRITISH-JEWRY mailing list, details of which are at <lists.rootsweb.ancestry.com/index/other/Ethnic-Jewish/BRITISH-JEWRY.html>. The list has its own separate website at <www.british-jewry.org.uk> with a number of small databases. There is also a Jewish Roots forum on British-Genealogy at <www.british-genealogy.com/forums/forumdisplay.php?f=187>.

The regional Jewish newspaper *The Jewish Telegraph* has a 'Roots Directory' at <jewishtelegraph.com/roots.html> where people can post contact messages.

Huguenots

Around 50,000 French protestants fled religious persecution and settled in England and Ireland in the seventeenth century. Cyndi's List has links to Huguenot resources at <www.cyndislist.com/huguenot>, while basic information on the Huguenots will be found on Olive Tree Genealogy at <olivetreegenealogy.com/hug/overview.shtml>.

The Huguenot Society of Great Britain & Ireland has a website at <www.huguenotsociety.org.uk>. The 'Family History' section has a number of research guides, which provide detailed information on the relevant records. Although the society's library, the Huguenot Library, is temporarily located at The National Archives, it will in due course return to its original home at University College, London. Details of the library holdings will therefore be found in UCL's online catalogue at <library.ucl.ac.uk> and in COPAC (see p. 220) at <copac.ac.uk>, while the archival material can be found with the UCL Archives search at <archives.ucl.ac.uk>. UCL also has general information about the Huguenot Library at <www.ucl.ac.uk/Library/huguenot.shtml>.

There are also sites with local information: the Institute of Historical Research has pages on the French Protestant Church of London at

<ihr.sas.ac.uk/ihr/associnstits/huguenots.mnu.html>, and the Church has its own French-language site at <www.egliseprotestantelondres.org.uk> with a section on the history of the Church and of French Protestants in England. The England GenWeb Project has comprehensive material on Cambridgeshire Huguenots at <www.rootsweb.ancestry.com/~engcam/ HuguenotsandWalloons.htm> with a list of surnames, and Hidden Dublin has a list of the names on the memorial tablet in Dublin's Huguenot Cemetery at <www.hidden-dublin.com/huguenot/huguenot2.html>.

The mailing list for Huguenot ancestors is HUGUENOTS-WALLOONS-EUROPE, hosted at RootsWeb. Subscription details and the message archive are at <lists.rootsweb.ancestry.com/index/other/ Religion/HUGUENOTS-WALLOONS-EUROPE.html>. The Huguenot Surnames Index at <www.aftc.com.au/Huguenot/Hug.html> will enable you to make contact with others researching particular Huguenot families.

Gypsies

There are two starting points on the web for British gypsy ancestry. The Romany & Traveller Family History Society site at <www.rtfhs.org.uk>, apart from society information (including a list of contents for recent issues of its magazine), has a page on 'Was Your Ancestor a Gypsy?'. This lists typical gypsy surnames, forenames and occupations. The site also has a good collection of links to other gypsy material on the web. The Gypsy Lore Society Collections at the University of Liverpool site at <sca.lib.liv.ac.uk/ collections/colldescs/gypsy/> has information about, and photographs of, British gypsy families as well as a collection of links to other gypsy sites.

Romani.org at <www.romani.org> is a general site devoted to the Romani people, and there is an online publication for Romani culture and history, The Patrin Web Journal, at <reocities.com/Paris/5121/>. BBC Kent has a Romany Roots site at <www.bbc.co.uk/kent/romany_roots/>. Although it has no specifically genealogical material, there are many articles on Romany history and culture, and the message board is used for genealogical queries. Another Kent site is Gypsies, Travellers And Other Itinerants In Kent at <freepages.genealogy.rootsweb.ancestry.com/~gypsy/gypsy.htm>, which includes many extracts from parish records. The Romany Wales project at <www.valleystream.co.uk/romhome.htm> has information on the Romany people in Wales, with histories of a number of individual families.

Wikipedia has a wide range of articles on Romany history and culture. The best starting point is the 'Romnichal' article. George Borrow's *Lavengro*, the well-known semi-autobiographical account of nineteenth-century gypsy life, is available at a number of electronic book sites, and there are links from the Wikipedia's 'Lavengro' article.

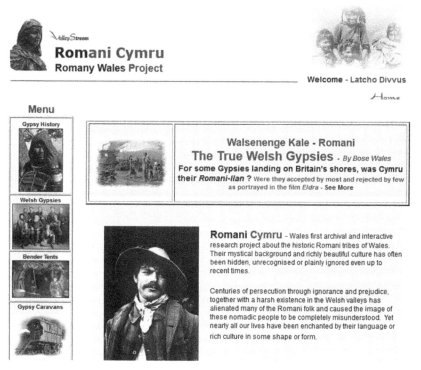

Figure 11-5 The Romany Wales Project

There is a UK-ROMANI mailing list for British gypsy family history, details of which will be found at <**lists.rootsweb.ancestry.com/index/other/Ethnic-Romani/UK-ROMANI.html**>. Ancestry's Gypsy message board will be found at <**boards.ancestry.co.uk/topics.ethnic.gypsy/mb.ashx**>. British-Genealogy has a Romanies forum at <**www.british-genealogy.com/forums/forumdisplay.php?f=424**>.

Cyndi's List has links to further genealogical resources at <**www.cyndislist.com/unique-peoples/gypsy/**> in the category 'Unique Peoples & Cultures'.

12

PRINT SOURCES

While the most important records for family historians are the usually hand-written public records, there are important sources of information in print, and not just where manuscript records have been transcribed.

▌ Books

Digital archives

A significant development in the last few years has been the start of major projects to put digitized books online. These have received some bad publicity because many books still in copyright have been digitized without the permission of the copyright owners, and major academic and public libraries have been criticized for deals with commercial organizations. But the effect for genealogists has been very beneficial in that large numbers of eighteenth- and nineteenth-century books, many of them far from easy to find, have become available online via online book archives. Those of most interest to family historians fall into two groups. First, there are many topographical works devoted to describing various parts of the country – for any town or county you should be able to find a guidebook from the early twentieth century or before. Second, there seem to be quite a few books from historical publishing societies, some of which include transcriptions of historical records, so there is plenty of chance of finding transcribed parish registers, poll books and the like on these sites.

Google is the major commercial company involved in book digitization, after Microsoft abandoned its Live Search Books programme in May 2008. Google Books at <**books.google.com**> has books both from publishers and from university libraries. Where a book comes from a publisher, you will find either that only the publication details are available with no access to the content, or that there is a 'limited preview', with perhaps 10 per cent of the pages viewable online. Even if you only get the publication details, these will help you find a second-hand copy or search the library catalogues mentioned in Chapter 13. In the case of out-of-copyright books, you should be able to download the entire book as a PDF file. The libraries who are working with Google are listed at <**books.google.com/googlebooks/ partners.html**>. They include the Bodleian Library in Oxford, a dozen of the most important US university libraries, as well as a number of European libraries. All books have been fully indexed and are visible to Google's main search engine (though not to any other search engine), so you can in fact search for individual names.

The Open Content Alliance is a non-profit group set up to create a free digital archive. Its textual material is available from the Text Archive area of the Internet Archive at <**www.archive.org/details/texts/**>. It also draws considerably on the collections of American libraries, including some of the major public libraries, though it seems to have less historical UK material than Google Books. Unlike Google Books, however, this project does not include material that is still in copyright (in the USA).

The Internet Archive is made up of a number of discrete collections, which can be searched individually. The most important of these for the family historian is the Genealogy collection at <**www.archive.org/details/ genealogy**>, which includes over 3,500 items from the National Library of Scotland at <**www.archive.org/details/nationallibraryofscotland**> and over 60,000 from the Allen County Library, one of the most significant genealogical libraries in the USA. Highlights of the NLS contribution include over 750 Scottish directories and 200 volumes of Hart's *Army List* (see p. 155).

A related but distinct project, run by the Internet Archive, is the Open Library at <**www.openlibrary.org**>, which has the primary aim of providing a web page for every book ever published. Alongside records for some 30 million books, it has scanned copies of around one million of these. The search facility on the home page allows you to restrict your search to scanned volumes.

One of the sites included in Open Content Alliance is the much older Project Gutenberg, which has its own site at <**www.gutenberg.org**>. This is a long-standing project to digitize out-of-print books, which now hosts over 25,000 texts. Although the main focus of the project has been literary texts (including translations), there seem to be quite a few Victorian works of topography and social history. For example, there is Edwin Waugh's *Home-Life of the Lancashire Factory Folk during the Cotton Famine* and E. V. Lucas's *Highways & Byways in Sussex*. It is well worth using the 'Full Text' field on the advanced search page to see if there is any text with material on places your ancestors came from. The texts are all provided in plain text form or formatted for the web. Unlike the other material in the Internet Archive, all the Project Gutenberg texts have been entered manually rather than created by optical character recognition of the scanned page images, and are therefore much more accurate.

One thing to note is that since all these sites are US-based, it is the copyright status in the United States which is relevant. This means that any book published before 1923 is regarded as out of copyright, even though such a work would, if the author died after 1941, still be in copyright in the UK in 2012.

In addition to these general book archives, there are several sites which concentrate on genealogy books. The most significant is the Family History Archives site at FamilySearch, which has a collection of over 17,000 digitized books from the Family History Library (see p. 221) and a number of other US genealogical libraries. They include many hard-to-find printed family histories, and some are even scanned typescripts. The basic search includes author, title and surname, but there is an additional option to include a full text search (though this will be rather slow and may well give you too many results to be useful). Helpfully, the initial list of matching books includes a description and the main surnames covered. The books are presented in PDF format, but cannot be downloaded as a whole – each page is a separate PDF file. If you are already on the FamilySearch site, select 'Historical Books' from the 'Search Records' menu; otherwise, go to <**www.lib.byu.edu/fhc**>.

Library Ireland has around 70 out-of-copyright books and countless articles on Irish history and genealogy at <**www.libraryireland.com**>. These include a number of works on Irish names and a growing collection of directories (see below).

The commercial data services (see Chapter 4) also tend to offer digitized reference books, though these are only accessible with a subscription to the sites. For example, Ancestry has a 'Reference, Dictionaries, and Almanacs' collection, with over 100 books relating to the UK. These can be searched without a subscription from <**search.ancestry.co.uk/search/ CardCatalog.aspx?cat=41**>. You can use the filter option in the right-hand column of this page to narrow the list down to books which include material for a particular county.

Current reference works

It is important not to overlook general reference books, not perhaps for information on individual ancestors (unless they were specially notable), but for authoritative historical and geographical information about the British Isles. While many older editions are available in digitized versions in the book archives discussed above, in many cases current editions are also available online. An important set of reference works is that published by Oxford University Press, particularly:

- *The Oxford English Dictionary* <**dictionary.oed.com**> (see Figure 9-1, p. 130)
- *The Oxford Dictionary of National Biography* <**www.oxforddnb.com**>

- *The Oxford Reference Collection* <www.oxfordreference.com>

These are available only to subscribers, and the individual subscriptions are quite hefty. However, thanks to a national agreement with the Museums, Libraries and Archives Council, most public libraries in the UK have subscriptions, and if you are a member of your local library this will almost certainly extend to access from your own computer at home. You will need a library card, as the login requires a library card number from a participating library instead of a username and password. Details should be given on the library area of your local authority website, which will probably also have links to the correct log-in pages. There is information about this scheme at <**www.oup.com/uk/academic/online/library/**> and a list of libraries at <**www.oup.com/uk/academic/online/library/available/**>. The scheme also extends to the Republic of Ireland, though I have been unable to find any details of availability.

The *Encyclopædia Britannica* <**www.britannica.com**> is widely available on the same basis. Some earlier editions are now in the public domain, in the US at least, and available free online. The 1911 edition is at <**www.1911encyclopedia.org**> as well as a number of other sites, including Project Gutenberg and the Internet Archive — see Wikipedia's article 'Encyclopædia Britannica Eleventh Edition', which also draws attention to some of the most notable problems of relying on this edition.

Electoral records

While most genealogical records, well into the twentieth century, are hand-written records of voters and electors have always been printed. The modern electoral registers, which can be used to trace living people and are discussed on p. 248, are effectively a form of census of the adult population. Before the introduction of universal suffrage in 1928, however, the further you go back the smaller the proportion of the population which was allowed to vote. Before the Reform Act of 1832, only males over the age of 21 who owned property of significant value. The Wikipedia article on 'Suffrage' is a good starting point for more detailed information on the qualifications for voting at various dates.

Electoral registers of the type we are familiar with — a list of those entitled to vote and their place of residence — came in the wake of The Reform Act and were maintained, as they are now, by local authorities. Until recently, there has been little of this material online, but in November 2011 Findmypast (see p. 53) added the Cheshire electoral registers for 1842–1900 to its collections, with material for other counties to follow during 2012. In February 2012, Ancestry (p 00) published indexes and images of the electoral registers for London 1847–1965 by arrangement with the Guildhall Library. As you can see from Figure 12-1, the earlier registers give much more detail than just an address.

Christian Name and Surname of each Voter at full length.	Place of Abode.	Nature of Qualification.	Street, Lane, or other like place in this parish, and number of house (if any) where the property is situate, or name of the property, and the name of the tenant; or if the qualification consist of a rent-charge, then the names of the owners of the property out of which such rent is issuing, or some of them, and the situation of the property
Peeke, Roger	St. Margaret's Cottage, Kilburn	Leasehold cottage and land, upwards of £50 per annum	St. Margaret's Cottage, Kilburn
Potter, William	No. 11, Montem Villas	Occupation of house and garden	No. 11, Montem Villas
Pollock, Alfred	Windmill-hill, Hampstead	House as occupier	Windmill-hill
Preedy, John	48, Adelaide-road, Hampstead	House as occupier	48, Adelaide-road
Presant, John	14, Oakley Villas	Occupation of house and garden	14, Oakley Villas
Prideaux, Thomas Symes	15, Well-walk, Hampstead	House as occupier	No. 15, Well Walk
Pratt, Samuel	47, New Bond-street	Copyhold cottages	Lower Heath—Mr. Steven and Mr. Mc Innes, tenants
Ponsford, John	8, Saint John's-park Villas	House as occupier	8, St. John's-park Villas
Procter, Joseph	No. 5, Finchley New-road, St. John's-wood	Occupier of house and garden	No. 5, Finchley-new-road, St. John's-wood
Prowett, Charles Gipps	West-end, Hampstead	House and land as occupier	West End
Randall, Richard	24, Adelaide-road, Hampstead	Leasehold house as occupier	Adelaide-road
Reed, Thomas	13, John-street, Oxford-street, St. Marylebone	Two copyhold cottages	South End Green, Pond-street

Figure 12-1 Electoral register for Hampstead, 1851 (Ancestry)

Before 1832, there are no electoral registers but published poll books record the outcome of parliamentary elections and simply give the name of the voter and which candidate(s) he voted for. (In fact poll books carry on until the introduction of the secret ballot in 1872.) Entries are grouped by polling district but precise addresses are not given. Many of these are available in reference libraries and as a result a number of them are available in the book archives discussed at the start of this chapter, particularly Google Books. Searching on the phrase "poll book" and the name of a county is the easiest way to find those which may list your ancestors.

The Society of Genealogists has an unrivalled collection of poll books, all listed in its online catalogue (see p. 222). The National Library of Ireland has added records for Irish city and country electoral registers to its online catalogue at <catalogue.nli.ie>. Entering the words 'electoral registers' and the city or county of interest will locate relevant material.

Modern electoral registers are discussed as sources for tracing living people in Chapter 14, p. 248.

Directories

For the family historian, the most important class of printed books are the nineteenth-century trade and post office directories. These provide descriptions of individual towns and villages, along with the names of some or all tradespeople and householders – the earlier directories tend to include only businesses and professional people. A large number of these have been digitized and published on CD-ROM, but an increasing number are available either complete or in part on the web. There are also directories relating to the military and the professions, but these are discussed with other occupational records in Chapters 9 and 10.

The British-Genealogy site has some general information about trade directories and how they can help with your research at <**www.british-genealogy.com/by-county/county-directories.html**>. An article by David Tippey, 'Using Trade Directories in your Research', is available at <**www.genealogyreviews.co.uk/tippey_directories.htm**>.

The major site for directories is the Digital Library of Historical Directories site at <**www.historicaldirectories.org**>. This is the fruit of a Heritage Lottery Fund project based at the University of Leicester. The aim of the project was to place online digitized trade directories from England and Wales from 1750 to 1919. It is intended to be representative rather than comprehensive, with one directory for each county and each major town for the pre-1850 period and then each later decade up to the end of the First World War. The project is now complete and offers a total of 675 directories.

You can browse by county or decade, or you can select the keyword option to do a more advanced search. This allows you to specify, if you wish, a county, a decade, a publisher, and any names or other terms (a particular occupation, perhaps). The search results list all matching directories, but do not list the pages with individual hits – you need to select the directory you want to examine. This will bring up the title page of the directory and tell you how many occurrences of your keywords there are. To examine the relevant pages, you need to click on 'Next hit' button. You can also simply browse the directory, page by page. The display shows a page at a time, and pages can be printed or saved (see Figure 12-2).

Although this is by far the largest collection of directories, there are many other sites which have material from directories. In some cases, there is simply a name index to the printed volume, such as that for Pigot's *Commercial Directory for Surrey* (1839), which is on the Genuki Surrey site at <**homepages.gold.ac.uk/genuki/SRY/**>. This provides text files with page references for names and places. While not a substitute for online versions of the directories, these listings at least indicate whether it is worth locating a copy of the directory in question. Another approach is to place scanned

Figure 12-2 Digital Library of Historical Directories: a page from *Pigot & Co.'s Directory of Yorks, Leics ..., 1841*

images on the web, along with a name index, as on Nicholas Adams's site, which provides Pigot's 1830 and 1840 directories for Herefordshire at <**freepages.genealogy.rootsweb.ancestry.com/~nmfa/genealogy.html**>. Finally, some sites offer a full transcription, with or without a name index. For Derbyshire, for example, there is Ann Andrews's transcription of all the Derbyshire entries from Kelly's *Directory of the Counties of Derby, Notts, Leicester and Rutland*, 1891, at <**www.andrewspages.dial.pipex.com/dby/kelly/**>.

There are also some partial transcriptions, usually for individual towns or cities, such as Brian Randell's material for Exeter at <**genuki.cs.ncl.ac.uk/DEV/Exeter/White1850.html**> taken from White's *Devonshire* directory of 1850. Rob Marriott and Davina Bradley's site devoted to Ashover in Derbyshire has entries for the town from six different directories at <**www.ashover.org/drct.htm**>.

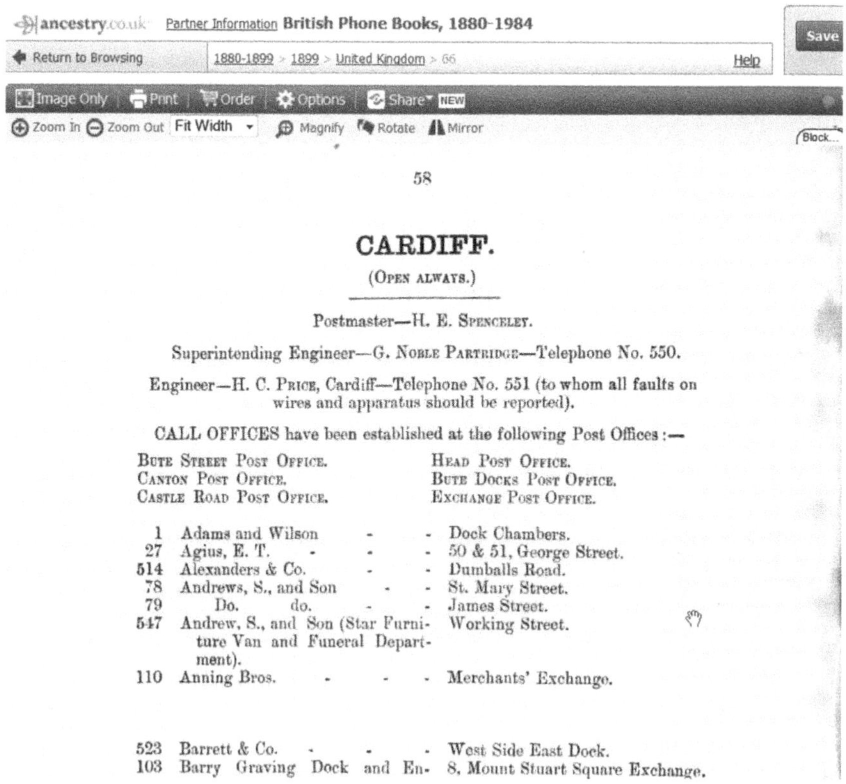

58

CARDIFF.

(Open always.)

Postmaster—H. E. Spenceley.

Superintending Engineer—G. Noble Partridge—Telephone No. 550.

Engineer—H. C. Price, Cardiff—Telephone No. 551 (to whom all faults on wires and apparatus should be reported).

CALL OFFICES have been established at the following Post Offices:—

Bute Street Post Office.	Head Post Office.
Canton Post Office.	Bute Docks Post Office.
Castle Road Post Office.	Exchange Post Office.

1	Adams and Wilson	Dock Chambers.
27	Agius, E. T.	50 & 51, George Street.
514	Alexanders & Co.	Dumballs Road.
78	Andrews, S., and Son	St. Mary Street.
79	Do. do.	James Street.
547	Andrew, S., and Son (Star Furniture Van and Funeral Department).	Working Street.
110	Anning Bros.	Merchants' Exchange.
523	Barrett & Co.	West Side East Dock.
103	Barry Graving Dock and En-	8, Mount Stuart Square Exchange.

Figure 12-3 Telephone listing for Cardiff, 1899 (Ancestry)

Since directories were compiled on a county or regional basis, the easiest way to find them online is to look at the relevant county page on Genuki. Alternatively, you could use a search engine to search for, say, [Directory AND Kelly AND Norfolk] or [Directory AND Pigot AND Lancashire] to locate the publications of the two main nineteenth-century directory publishers. (See Chapter 19 for information on search engines and formulating searches.) County record offices have good collections of local directories, so it will be worth looking at the online catalogues. With few exceptions the directories available online date from before the First World War, so for more recent directories you will almost certainly need to visit the relevant CROs or local libraries.

The British Library, of course, has many trade and post office directories, which can be located by searching the online catalogue at <**catalogue.bl.uk**> – see p. 216. Since directory titles are very varied, the best way to search is to enter the town/county and the word 'directory' in the 'Type word or phrase' field and select 'Word from title' in the 'Search by' field. You can then sort the results by year, though note that modern digitizations will be listed by the modern year of publication, not the original date of the directory

As mentioned above (p. 186), Library Ireland has a number of transcribed directories.

Three of the commercial data services described in Chapter 4 have significant directory holdings. The Genealogist at <**www.thegenealogist.co.uk**> (see p. 55) has over 200 trade and post office directories, the latest of which is for 1941. Around 50 of them are for London and include the 1677 *Little London Directory*, which seems to be the earliest directory available online. Each directory is displayed as a single PDF file.

Familyrelatives at <**www.familyrelatives.com**> (see p. 57) has around 30 post office directories for individual English counties for the period 1828–40, and half a dozen twentieth-century directories for Irish counties, and a similar number for Scotland. There is a free search which, for the English and Scottish directories, just tells you the number of hits. For the Irish directories, the results show two lines of text from a matching entry. In each case, to view the original page image you need to be a subscriber. The images are not available to pay-per-view customers.

Ancestry has a collection of 'City and County Directories 1600s–1900s', information on which is given at <**www.ancestry.co.uk/search/ db.aspx?dbid=1547**>. The site does not provide any unified listing; you can only see the individual holdings by selecting country and county from a drop-down list. There seem to be between one and a dozen directories per English county, with a few for Scotland and Wales, and one for the Isle of Man. Each directory page displays as a separate image in Ancestry's image viewer. You can browse through any directory, but there is also a name search.

The City and County Directories search does not include Ancestry's collection of 1,780 UK telephone books, which have their own search page at <**search.ancestry.co.uk/search/db.aspx?dbid=1025**>. The books come from the BT Archives, and provide 'near full county coverage for England as well as containing substantial records for Scotland, Ireland, and Wales'. They cover the period from the very first phone books in 1880 up to the privatization of British Telecom in 1984. As well as searching on a name, you can also specify a year and an address; alternatively you can browse an individual phone book. With a common surname, there may be a problem in identifying the correct individual, since usually only initials are given rather than a forename. Obviously the information is quite limited, but the ability to find an address in years other than those for which you have certificates or census records is very useful. The early books have relatively few individuals but have many business addresses, so can be used in the same way as trade directories (Figure 12-3).

An extensive collection of links to a wide variety of directories and printed lists will be found on the UKGDL site at <**www.ukgdl.org.uk**>, where they can be viewed by county or by type.

Newspapers

Only a few years ago, the only way to read historical newspapers, particularly for local titles, was to go to the British Library Newspaper Library or the reference library in the locality. Now most national papers have an online archive and the British Newspaper Archive, launched in 2011 with over half a million issues of almost 200 titles, has transformed the availability of regional and local papers.

The Genuki county pages are a good way of finding links to local newspapers on the web, and Cyndi's List has a 'Newspapers' page at <**www.cyndislist.com/newspapers**>. There are, of course, many sites relating to present-day newspapers including Kidon Media-link, which has links to the websites of UK newspapers at <**www.kidon.com/media-link/uk.php**>.

The most important site for information about newspapers is that of the British Library (BL). This has a general page for newspapers and comics at <**www.bl.uk/reshelp/findhelprestype/news/**>, which is a gateway to an extensive set of pages with links to newspaper sites on the web, including London National Newspapers, Scottish Newspapers, Irish Newspapers, English and Welsh Newspapers, Channel Islands and Isle of Man Newspapers, Newspapers Around the World, and Other Newspaper Libraries and Collections.

Most of the online newspaper archives are commercial in nature. Nonetheless, they generally offer institutional subscriptions, which means that in many cases those in Further and Higher Education will have free access via their institutions, and many local public libraries provide free access to one (or occasionally more) of these services for local residents.

Catalogues

Details of the BL's own resources are on the British Library Newspaper Collections page at <**www.bl.uk/reshelp/findhelprestype/news/blnewscoll/**>, and these comprise over 52,000 newspaper and periodical titles from all over the world, dating from the seventeenth to the twenty-first century, including all UK national dailies and most UK and Irish provincial papers.

The newspaper collection is included in the library's Integrated Catalogue at <**catalogue.bl.uk**>. You can in fact search the newspaper collections separately, though this is far from obvious the way the site is designed. The URL is a 125-character monster consisting of apparently random letters and numbers, so to get to it you need to select 'Search the Integrated Catalogue' from the catalogue home page, then 'Catalogue subset search', then 'Newspapers'. The resulting page can then be bookmarked for quicker access.

To find the newspapers for a particular town or city, you need to select 'Newspaper place' from the drop-down list in the 'Search by' field and then enter the name of the place in the field to the right. Each entry in the web catalogue contains full details of the title (including any title changes), the place of publication (the town or city, and the country) and the dates which are held. The results can be sorted by any of these fields, which means you can get a historical list of newspapers for a particular town (see Figure 12-4). Clicking on the newspaper title brings up a detailed listed of the library's holdings.

The websites for other major libraries and archives discussed in Chapter 13 will have sections on their newspaper holdings.

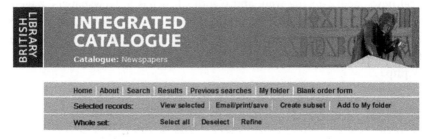

You searched for (W-newspaper place= norwich) in Newspapers. Sorted by: Date Range, then Title

Records 1 - 10 of 118
Quick tips - for this page
Seeing strange characters in some of the records?   Last Browse

#	Title	Edition	Place	Date Range
1	The Norwich Post.		England Norfolk Norwich.	1707 to 1712
2	The Loyal Packet.		England Norfolk Norwich.	1714 to 1714
3	The Norwich Gazette.		England Norfolk Norwich.	1725 to 1747
4	The Norwich Mercury.		England Norfolk Norwich.	1727 to 1949
5	The Norfolk Chronicle: or, the Norwich Gazette.		England Norfolk Norwich.	1776 to 1810
6	The Iris: or, Norwich and Norfolk Weekly Advertiser.		England Norfolk Norwich.	1803 to 1804
7	The Norfolk Chronicle.		England Norfolk Norwich.	1810 to 1810
8	The Norfolk Chronicle and Norwich Gazette.		England Norfolk Norwich.	1810 to 1921
9	The Norwich, Yarmouth and Lynn courier, and general Norfolk advertiser.		England Norfolk Norwich.	18uu to 1823
10	The East Anglian; or, Norfolk, Suffolk, and Cambridgeshire, Norwich, Lynn and Yarmouth Herald.		England Norfolk Norwich.	1830 to 1833

Figure 12-4 Search results for 'Norwich' in the Newspaper Library catalogue, sorted by date

A particularly useful programme is Newsplan. This was a lottery-funded project to microfilm historic newspapers in public collections. It comprises a number of independent regional sites, and details of the overall project and its 10 regional sub-projects will be found on the British Library's Newsplan page at **<www.bl.uk/reshelp/bldept/news/newsplan/ newsplan.html>**. This has links to the local websites, though at the time of writing, some of these links were dead. The NEWSPLAN Scotland list of newspapers is at **<www.nls.uk/about-us/working-with-others/newsplan- scotland/titles.cfm>** and is not linked directly from the main site. Figure 12-5 shows a sample record in Newsplan from the West Midlands site at **<www.newsplan.co.uk>**, which has details of 1,100 titles.

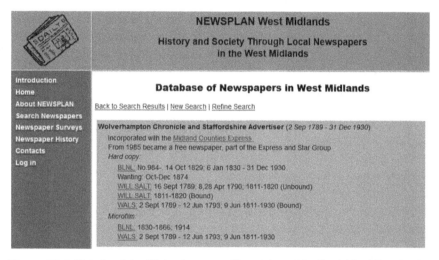

Figure 12-5 Details of the *Wolverhampton Chronicle and Staffordshire Advertiser* in Newsplan

Free archives

There are a number of broad-based historical collections as well as non-commercial projects for individual local newspapers.

The BL has made a small selection of newspapers available online in the Olive ActivePaper Archive at **<www.uk.olivesoftware.com>**, which has digitized copies of a number of editions of the:

- *Daily News*
- *News of the World*
- *Manchester Guardian*
- *Weekly Despatch*

There are a number of short runs of each paper for up to five individual years. Each newspaper page comes up as a separate image in the browser window. In this view only the headlines are easily legible, but clicking on an article brings up an enlarged version so you can read the body text. There is also a text search facility, which brings up only the individual articles. You can also download a complete edition in PDF format. In spite of the fact that the site has been running for some years, it is still effectively a demo.

The National Library of Wales has a Historic Newspapers and Journals project due to go live in 2012. This will offer free access to the text of over 700 different titles published in Wales. Details will be found at <**www.llgc.org.uk/index.php?id=4723**>.

The Internet Library of Early Journals at <**www.bodley.ox.ac.uk/ilej/**> is a joint project by the universities of Birmingham, Leeds, Manchester and Oxford to place online digitized copies of eighteenth- and nineteenth-century journals, in runs of at least 20 years. The project comprises:

- *Gentleman's Magazine*
- *The Annual Register*
- *Philosophical Transactions of the Royal Society*
- *Notes and Queries*
- *The Builder*
- *Blackwood's Edinburgh Magazine*

The Nineteenth-Century Serials Edition is a free online edition of six nineteenth-century periodicals and newspapers at <**www.ncse.ac.uk**>:

- *Monthly Repository* (1806–37) and *Unitarian Chronicle* (1832–33)
- *Northern Star* (1838–52)
- *Leader* (1850–60)
- *English Woman's Journal* (1858–64)
- *Tomahawk* (1867–70)
- *Publishers' Circular* (1880–90)

A specialist newspaper of interest to those with maritime ancestors is *Lloyd's List* and there is an index to the marine news from 1740 to 1837 at <**www.cityoflondon.gov.uk/lloydslist/**>. This can be searched on the name of a person, ship and location between chosen dates.

Google News at <**news.google.com/newspapers**> has an archive of almost 2,500 newspapers. The overwhelming majority are North American local papers and those expecting to find Welsh or East Anglian ancestors in the *Bangor Daily News* and the *Ely Echo* will be disappointed. Nonetheless, there are some significant runs of UK newspapers including 42,000 issues of the *Glasgow Herald* from 1806 to 1990. There are also shorter runs of five early nineteenth-century Edinburgh newspapers, notably the 2,000 issues of the *Edinburgh Advertiser* from 1772 to 1829. The site gives no bibliographical information.

Gazettes Online

Another important site for historical newspapers is Gazettes Online at **<www.gazettes-online.co.uk>**. This a major project to make the entire archive of the London, Edinburgh and Belfast Gazettes available on the web. These are the UK's official newspapers of record, stretching back to 1665 and containing official announcements of many types, including the award of medals, official appointments (including appointments of officers in the armed forces – see Figure 12-6) and insolvency notices. Although there is a browse option, this covers only the most recent issues; for historical material, you need to select the advanced search, in which you specify a date or date range and the words or phrases to look for. The pages are black and white scans (*not* greyscale) and are displayed in PDF format, one file to a page.

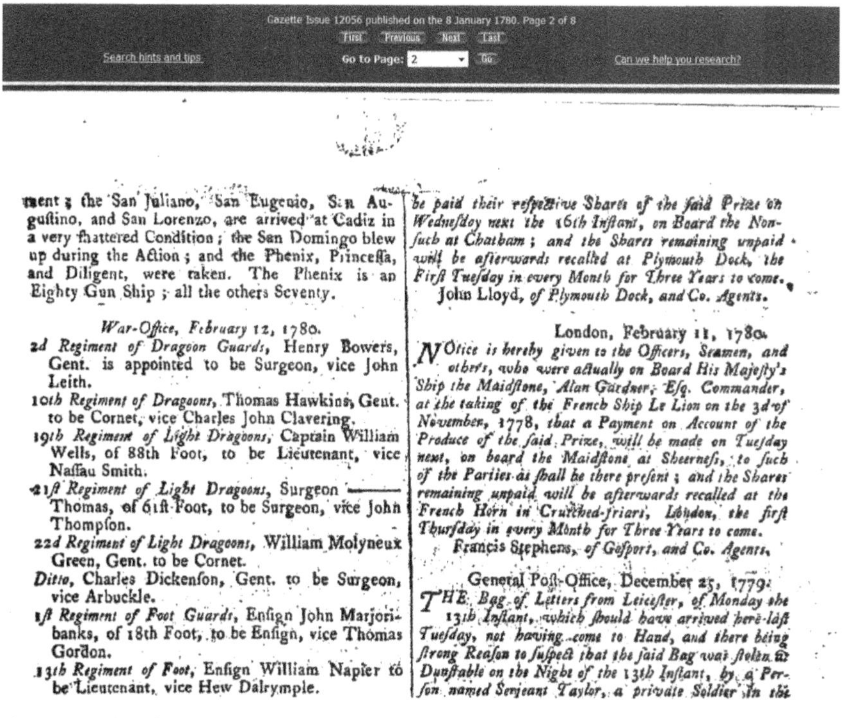

ment; the San Juliano, San Eugenio, San Augustino, and San Lorenzo, are arrived at Cadiz in a very shattered Condition; the San Domingo blew up during the Action; and the Phenix, Princessa, and Diligent, were taken. The Phenix is an Eighty Gun Ship; all the others Seventy.

War-Office, February 12, 1780.

2d Regiment of Dragoon Guards, Henry Bowers, Gent. is appointed to be Surgeon, vice John Leith.

10th Regiment of Dragoons, Thomas Hawkins, Gent. to be Cornet, vice Charles John Clavering.

19th Regiment of Light Dragoons, Captain William Wells, of 88th Foot, to be Lieutenant, vice Nassau Smith.

21st Regiment of Light Dragoons, Surgeon —— Thomas, of 61st Foot, to be Surgeon, vice John Thompson.

22d Regiment of Light Dragoons, William Molyneux Green, Gent. to be Cornet.

Ditto, Charles Dickenson, Gent. to be Surgeon, vice Arbuckle.

1st Regiment of Foot Guards, Ensign John Marjoribanks, of 18th Foot, to be Ensign, vice Thomas Gordon.

13th Regiment of Foot, Ensign William Napier to be Lieutenant, vice Hew Dalrymple.

be paid their respective Shares of the said Prize on Wednesday next the 16th Instant, on Board the Nonsuch at Chatham; and the Shares remaining unpaid will be afterwards recalled at Plymouth Dock, the First Tuesday in every Month for Three Years to come.

John Lloyd, *of Plymouth Dock, and Co. Agents.*

London, February 11, 1780.

NOtice is hereby given to the Officers, Seamen, and others, who were actually on Board His Majesty's Ship the Maidstone, Alan Gardner, Esq. Commander, at the taking of the French Ship Le Lion on the 3d of November, 1778, that a Payment on Account of the Produce of the said Prize, will be made on Tuesday next, on board the Maidstone at Sheerness, to such of the Parties as shall be there present; and the Shares remaining unpaid will be afterwards recalled at the French Horn in Crutched-friars, London, the first Thursday in every Month for Three Years to come.

Francis Stephens, *of Gosport, and Co. Agents.*

General Post-Office, December 25, 1779.

THE Bag of Letters from Leicester, of Monday the 13th Instant, which should have arrived here last Tuesday, not having come to Hand, and there being strong Reason to suspect that the said Bag was stolen at Dunstable on the Night of the 13th Instant, by a Person named Serjeant Taylor, a private Soldier in the

Figure 12-6 Military appointments in the *London Gazette*, 8 January 1780

One thing to note about the text search is that the index it uses has been created by optical character recognition and therefore contains many errors. Unlike the census, where you can try and imagine what a letter might have looked like to a transcriber, it is very difficult to predict OCR errors, since typically these are caused by unevenness in the printing and random marks on the paper (especially print-through from the other side of the sheet, as you can see in Figure 12-6). This is particularly the case with older issues.

British Newspaper Archive

In November 2011, the British Library and Brightsolid launched the British Newspaper Archive at <**www.britishnewspaperarchive.co.uk**>. This was the result of a massive digitization project and contains 'most of the runs of newspapers published in the UK since 1800'. It also includes the 50 or so titles which comprised the subscription service British Newspapers 1800–1900, which was launched in 2009 and is still available at <**newspapers.bl.uk/blcs/**>.

An annual subscription with unlimited usage costs £79.95, while shorter subscriptions are available, with some (fairly generous) usage limits for two days and 30 days, costing £6.95 and £29.95 respectively. Shortly after the initial launch, the archive was made available on the pay-per-view system of Genes Reunited (which is also run by Brightsolid), where each page view costs five credits (costing 50p). During 2012 it will be added to the material available at Findmypast.

The project was launched with over three million pages from 200 titles but in the aim is to add another 40 million pages over the next few years. Significantly, the site offers many issues that are not available to the public at the Newspaper Library because they are too fragile to produce.

You can use the site without subscribing and initial searches are free of charge. The basic search is itself *very* basic – just a single field for keywords – but the filters (on the left in Figure 12-7) allow you to narrow your search down to a single year, county or place, and a particular newspaper if you wish. The advanced search is highly flexible and should enable you to home in on particular subjects, dates and places. The site has various facilities for annotating and keeping track of what you have looked at. Pages can be downloaded (in PDF format) or printed from the BNA site, but the Genes Reunited viewer does not provide for either, and your only options are to print the browser window or capture a screenshot.

The text was created by optical character recognition, so the accuracy will vary considerably depending on the print quality of the original pages (see Figure 4-2, p. 33), and of course both personal and place-names are particularly liable to error. But the site's facility for accepting corrections

Figure 12-7 British Newspaper Archive

from users will no doubt help, and the availability of the same story across several titles should certainly mean that matters of more than just local interest are findable (again, see Figure 4-2) in spite of any errors.

Other subscription collections

Many of the larger newspapers have their own digital archives covering, in most cases, the entire run of the paper from its first to its most recent edition. These tend to be subscription services, though the options often include a 24-hour subscription for under £10. Initial searches are usually free. These archives are particularly likely to be available online via local public libraries.

Digital archives for national dailies include:

- *The Times* <**archive.timesonline.co.uk**>
- the *Guardian/Observer* <**archive.guardian.co.uk**>
- *The Scotsman* <**archive.scotsman.com**>
- the *Irish Times* <**www.irishtimes.com/search/archive.html**>

The *Jewish Chronicle* at <www.thejc.com> has an archive of issues from 1841 onwards. There is a free trial search, but full access to the archive is only for those who subscribe to the newspaper itself.

Ukpressonline at <www.ukpressonline.co.uk> offers an archive of the *Daily Mirror* and *Daily Express* for the twentieth century, with more recent runs of a number of other papers. You can search the site without subscription or registration and the search results will give you the issue and page number of any hits, but a subscription is required to see the articles. It seems that only a small number of public libraries have subscriptions, but there are also a number of personal subscription options, starting at £5.99 for 48-hour access to an individual paper – see <**www.ukpressonline.co.uk/ ukpressonline/open/services.jsp**>.

The Irish Newspaper Archives at <www.irishnewsarchive.com> holds a searchable archive of 23 Irish national and local newspapers dating back in some cases to the eighteenth century, with additional newspapers to be added. Individual subscriptions are quite expensive, starting at €10 for 24 hours, but Irish residents should find free access via their local public library. You can view the front pages free of charge, but these are not high enough resolution to read the body text.

Last Chance To Read at <www.lastchancetoread.com> focuses on around 80 less well known newspapers for the period 1710–1870, almost entirely local publications. The site lists all the papers included, but does not indicate dates of coverage. Searching is free, though you need to complete the registration process, and the search results show you a small but legible thumbnail from the original newspaper page. You then need to pay £2.50 for each page downloaded, or £3 to £5 for each newspaper, though there is a minimum charge per transaction.

Ancestry has a Historical Newspaper Collection with significant runs of three UK newspapers:

- *The Times*
- *Edinburgh Advertiser*
- *Staffordshire Sentinel*

There are also other short runs, from a single month to several years, of a dozen other newspapers. All are listed at <**search.ancestry.co.uk/search/ CardCatalog.aspx?cat=38**>. As with the reference works on Ancestry (see p. 52), you can filter this list for particular localities.

In 2012, The Genealogist will be adding newspaper indexes to its data collections, starting with the *Illustrated London News* and *The Times*.

The NewspaperArchive at <**newspaperarchive.com**> is a subscription site with around a dozen English, Scottish and Irish papers for shorter or longer runs. You can see what is available by selecting the 'Browse Available Papers' option. There is a very large collection of US papers, as well as titles from Canada, Denmark, Jamaica and South Africa.

Recent newspapers

To find the website of a current newspaper or to see which present-day local newspapers cover a particular town or area, online newspapers at <**www.onlinenewspapers.com**> is a useful resource. It has a separate page for each constituent of the British Isles, though Ireland and Scotland and Wales are listed under Northern Europe while England, the Channel Islands and Jersey are under Western Europe. Usefully, it gives the place of publication for papers with generic titles so that you can identify which of the eight different *Advertiser*s you are looking for.

There are several subscription services for recent editions of current newspapers, which may be available to you free of charge via your local public library.

Newsbank provides a full text search for a range of UK national and regional newspapers. The full list of over 250 papers is at <**www.newsbank.com/ libraries/PDF/Access%20U.K.%20and%20Ireland%20Newspapers.pdf**>, and coverage generally starts in the 1990s, though *The Times* and the *Financial Times* run from the 1980s. The exact range of newspapers available to you locally will be much smaller and will depend on the subscription options of your public library service. You can expect access at the very least to all the main national daily and Sunday newspapers, and probably any regional papers local to the area. Lancashire County Council, for example, offers the *Liverpool Echo, Manchester Evening News, Lancaster Guardian* and *Blackpool Gazette*. Libraries in Scotland will carry *The Scotsman* and those in the Republic of Ireland will include *The Irish Times* and *Irish Independent*. There may also be papers from further afield: a number of English libraries include *The Scotsman* or the *New York Times*. Slainte, a Scottish library site, has a guide to using Newsbank at <**www.slainte.org.uk/files/pdf/slic/peoplesnet/content/ newsbank.pdf**>.

UK Newsstand is a similar service operated by ProQuest, with many local library services among its subscribers. It includes around 170 papers in the UK and Ireland, though for most of these coverage does not go back beyond 2000. Unlike Newsbank, a UK Newsstand subscription gives access to all newspapers in the collection. A useful feature is that there is a separate obituary search. Aberdeen City Libraries have a guide to using UK Newsstand at <**www.aberdeencity.gov.uk/nmsruntime/saveasdialog.asp? lID=37946&sID=16231**>.

ProQuest also has a Historical Newspapers service, which includes complete runs of the *Guardian*, the *Observer*, *The Irish Times*, the *Weekly Irish Times* and *The Scotsman* as well as several of the older US newspapers. While in principle available to public libraries, subscriptions have been taken out almost exclusively in the university sector – see <**www.jisc-collections.ac.uk/ Catalogue/Overview/Index/940**> for details.

For online newspapers beyond the British Isles, see Wikipedia's 'List of online newspaper archives'.

Indexes

There are also a number of online indexes to individual editions of newspapers, particularly local papers. These are generally non-commercial and therefore inevitably limited in scope, without digital images, though some include transcriptions. Being manually compiled, they should be more accurate than the OCR-based indexes in larger collections.

- The *Belfast Newsletter* is served by an index for the period 1737–1800 at <**www.ucs.louisiana.edu/bnl/**> and a number of digitized copies for 1796–1803 on the Act of Union site at <**www.actofunion.ac.uk/news.php**>.
- There is a surname index for the *Surrey Advertiser* for 1864–67 at <**www.newspaperdetectives.co.uk**>.
- The Georgian Newspaper Project at <**www.bathnes.gov.uk/leisureand culture/recordsarchives/georgian/**> aims to abstract and index the *Bath Chronicle* for the years 1770–1800. So far the database covers 17 completed years up to 1799.
- *The Cambrian* was the first newspaper to be published in Wales, and Swansea's Cambrian Index Online at <**www.swansea.gov.uk/index.cfm? articleid=5673**> covers the newspaper in the period 1804–1930.
- North Lincolnshire has a surname index to the Star series of newspapers started on 26 October 1889 as the *North Lindsey Star*. The Star Surnames Index, covering births, marriages and deaths 1891–1959, is at <**www.northlincs.gov.uk/Leisure/libraries/familyhistory/surnames/**>.
- Richard Heaton has a collection of nearly 850 Extracts and full Transcripts of mainly English and Irish, Georgian and early Victorian Regional Newspapers <**freepages.genealogy.rootsweb.ancestry.com/~dutillieul/ ZOtherPapers/Index.html**>.

The National Library of Scotland has a 'Guide to Scottish Newspaper Indexes', which provides details of Scottish newspaper titles that have an index (not necessarily online, or even digital), along with the dates covered and the libraries that have a copy. So far it includes 183 titles and can be found at <**www.nls.uk/collections/newspapers/indexes/**>.

Am Baile (The Gaelic Village) has an index to six newspapers covering the Highlands and Islands for various dates from 1807 right up to 2002. The index can be searched from <**www.ambaile.org.uk/en/newspapers/**>. You can specify a general subject as well as individual keywords. From the search results you can send a request to the holding library for further information.

Obituaries

There are a number of sites with information about newspaper obituary notices. Cyndi's List has a page devoted to obituaries at <**www.cyndislist.com/ obituaries/**>, though almost all the sites listed relate only to the US.

Free Obituaries On-Line at <**www3.sympatico.ca/bkinnon/obit_ links6.htm**> has links to sites providing obituaries – many are newspaper sites – for Australia, Bermuda, Canada, England, India, Ireland, Jamaica, New Zealand, Scotland and the US.

The Obituary Daily Times is a daily index of published obituaries at <**www.rootsweb.ancestry.com/~obituary/**>, which has over 10 million entries, mainly from US newspapers. The site is an index only – you need to refer to the original newspaper to see the text.

Ancestry subscribers can search a substantial database of recent obituaries. The search page for the UK and Ireland material is <**www.ancestry.co.uk/ search/obit/?uk&dbid=8960**>. There is no indication of which sources are included.

Obituary Lookup Volunteers at <**freepages.genealogy.rootsweb. ancestry.com/~obitl/**> holds lists of those prepared to look up obituaries in particular newspapers or libraries. There are separate pages listing volunteers for England, Wales, Scotland and Ireland, as well as a number of other countries. However, the coverage of the British Isles is extremely limited.

RootsWeb has around 40 mailing lists for obituaries, including ENGLAND-OBITS, ENGLISH-OBITS, IRELAND-OBITS and SCOTLAND-OBITS, as well as a number for former British colonies. All are listed at <**lists.rootsweb.ancestry.com/index/other/Obituaries/**>.

Iannounce at <**www.iannounce.co.uk**> has a free database of obituaries, death notices and other family announcements from almost 500 local and regional papers in the UK and the Republic of Ireland. The site does not indicate when coverage starts, but the earliest notice I could find was from 2003. It is best to enter a name in inverted commas, otherwise you get an OR search (see p. 335) on forename and surname, which tends to produce hundreds of results. Also, the date search does not allow you to specify a year.

All national newspapers and many local papers have a website, and these will generally carry the obituaries from recent editions.

13

ARCHIVES AND LIBRARIES

Archives and libraries are often seen as the antithesis of the internet, but this is largely illusory, certainly from the genealogical point of view. Even with the growing range of British genealogical resources reproduced as images on the web, you will often need to go to the relevant record office or a suitable library to check the information you have found online against original documents (or microfilms of them). It will be years before even the *core* sources are completely available online. Technologically, it is in fact a trivial matter to take records which have already been microfilmed and put images of them online. But to be usable, such online images need to be supported by indexes, and the preparation of these requires substantial labour and investment. As mentioned in Chapter 4, delivering images via the web has implications for running costs, even where production costs are minimal.

If you are going to look at paper (or even parchment) records, then catalogues and other finding aids are essential. Traditionally, these have been available only in the reading rooms of record offices themselves, so a significant part of any visit has to be spent checking the catalogues and finding aids for whatever you have come in search of. But the web has allowed repositories to make it much easier to access information about their collections and facilities. At the very least, the website for a record office will give a current phone number and opening times. Larger sites will provide descriptions of the holdings, often with advice on how to make the most of them. Increasingly, you can expect to find catalogues online and, in some cases, even place orders for documents so that they are ready for you when you visit the repository.

All this means you can get more out of a visit to a record office, because you're able to go better prepared. You can spend more time looking at documents and less trying to locate them. And if you can't get to a record office, you will be able to give much more precise information than previously to someone visiting it on your behalf.

This chapter looks at what the major national repositories and the various local institutions provide in the way of online information.

Many repositories have been reducing levels of service in response to actual or imminent budget cuts. This has generally been seen in restricted opening hours and lower levels of staffing, and will probably have less effect on the web presence of the institutions. Even so, when no more staff cuts are possible, no doubt website running costs will be scrutinized more closely, with the potential loss of access to electronic resources. Current digitization projects should not be affected unduly, since these are in many cases externally funded. However, it is much more doubtful whether a reduced staff will have the time to develop and seek funding for new projects. The campaign against cuts in service at record offices is discussed on p. 395.

Gateways to archives

There are a number of sources of information about repositories and the archival collections they hold. The ARCHON Directory at <**www.nationalarchives.gov.uk/archon/**> acts as a gateway for all British archives. The site is hosted by The National Archives (see p. 208) and its intention is to provide 'information on all repositories in the United Kingdom and all those repositories throughout the world which have collections of manuscripts which are noted in the indexes to the UK National

Figure 13-1 The ARCHON Directory's list of repositories in the South West

Register of Archives'. There is a page devoted to each archival repository in the British Isles, including the Republic of Ireland. In addition to basic details such as contact information, opening times and a link to any website, it also provides links to catalogue entries in the National Register of Archives (see below).

There are also search facilities which make it possible to search across the directory, so, for example, you could search for all archives in a given town or county. Although it is probably easier to use the Genuki county pages to find county record offices (see p. 217), the ARCHON Directory is better for locating other repositories and archives with relevant material.

ARCHON lists only the repositories and does not list their individual holdings. For these, you need to consult Access to Archives (A2A) at <**www.nationalarchives.gov.uk/a2a/**>. This is a national project, initially funded by government and the Heritage Lottery Fund, to 'create a virtual national archives catalogue, bringing together a critical mass of information about the rich national archival heritage and making that information available globally from one source via the World Wide Web'. The project has now closed with no new material being added, but the resources created during the project remain available, containing 10.3 million records for 418 record offices and other repositories. This represents about 30 per cent of the archival collections in England and Wales.

The search allows you to look for a word or phrase (which includes names) in a specific repository, over a whole region, or indeed over all regions. You can also restrict the search to material you have not previously seen by searching only for items added since a particular date.

North of the border, the Scottish Archive Network (SCAN) at <**www.scan.org.uk**> has a similar remit, and its directory has contact details for all Scottish repositories at <**www.scan.org.uk/Directory/**>. There is an online catalogue at <**www.scan.org.uk/catalogue/**>, which provides consolidated access to the catalogues of over 50 repositories in Scotland, with over 20,000 archives. The Research Tools pages at <**www.scan.org.uk/ researchrtools/**> (note the 'r' before 'tools') include examples of documents, a glossary of Scottish terms and material on handwriting. The Virtual Vault (on the 'Digital Archive' menu) has examples of a range of Scottish records. There is also a Knowledge Base with answers to questions frequently asked in Scottish archives. Oddly, this does not have its own page but is available as a pop-up link from other pages, such as the Research Tools page, though in fact you can go to it directly at <**www.scan.org.uk/knowledgebase/**>. SCAN hosts or runs a number of other related websites, notably Scottish Handwriting, which is discussed on p. 289.

Archives Wales at <**www.archiveswales.org.uk**> is a similar site for Wales, with descriptions of over 7,000 archival collections in 21 Welsh record offices, universities, and other bodies.

The Irish Archives Resource at <**www.iar.ie**> covers 19 repositories in the Republic of Ireland, mainly city and county archives.

Alongside these national gateways, there is a regional gateway for London archives in AIM25 at <**www.aim25.ac.uk**>, which includes the records of over 100 institutions including Higher Education, learned societies, cultural organizations and livery companies within the M25.

There are two more general gateways of use to the family historian. Cornucopia at <**www.cornucopia.org.uk**> is 'an online database of information about more than 6,000 collections in the UK's museums, galleries, archives and libraries'. It does not offer 'genealogy', or even 'history', as a subject heading, but a search for 'genealogy' brings up over 200 records and 'family history' another 300 or so. The latter are almost all records from a very useful public library project called Familia, discussed below (p. 218).

The Archives Hub at <**archiveshub.ac.uk**> offers a catalogue of archives for almost 200 institutions in England, Wales and Scotland. They are predominantly universities but there are also a number of local archives and some specialist collections of interest to genealogists, such as the National Fairground Archive, the Scottish Brewing Archive and the Royal College of Surgeons.

The National Register of Archives

The National Register of Archives contains 'information on the nature and location of manuscripts and historical records that relate to British history' and has an online index at <**www.nationalarchives.gov.uk/nra/**>. This contains reference details for around 150,000 people, families and corporate bodies relating to British history, with a further 100,000 related records. The materials themselves are held in record offices, university libraries and specialist repositories. The search engine allows you to search by:

- Corporate Name – combined search of the Business Index and the Organizations Index
- Personal Name – combined search of the Personal Index and the Diaries and Papers Index
- Family Name
- Place-Name – lists businesses, organizations and other corporate bodies by place

The full details for an item in the search results include not only the repository (with a link to its ARCHON entry) but also the reference number used by the record office in question. An obvious use of the NRA is to locate the parish registers for a particular place.

It is important to note that unlike A2A, the NRA catalogue cannot be used to search for the contents of archives, only the description and location, so a search on family name will only find archives deposited by or relating to the family, not individual documents which mention someone with that surname.

National archives

The National Archives

The National Archives is the main national repository for the UK, with a website at <**www.nationalarchives.gov.uk**>. The area most relevant to family historians is the 'Looking for a person?' page at <**www.nationalarchives.gov.uk/records/ looking-for-person**> (and on the 'Records' menu). This has links to detailed pages on all the types of record at TNA which can be used to research the history of an individual under the following headings:

- Births, marriages and deaths
- Adoption
- Census
- Change of name
- Divorce
- Electoral registration
- Wills
- Migrants and passengers
- Army
- Navy
- Air
- Marines
- PoWs and conscientious objectors
- Occupations
- Criminals, bankrupts and litigants
- Merchant seamen

Each page has sections on:

- What do I need to know before I start?
- What records can I see online?
- What records can I find at The National Archives at Kew?
- What records can I find in other archives and organizations?
- What other resources will help me find information?
- In-depth research guides

By way of example, Figure 13-2 shows the 'Looking for an emigrant' page.

Figure 13-2 A typical 'Looking for...' page on The National Archives site

Similar sets of pages on 'Looking for a place? and 'Looking for a subject?' cover records relevant to local and general history.

More detailed information on The National Archives' records for individual areas of interest is provided by over 300 research guides, all linked from an alphabetical index at <**www.nationalarchives.gov.uk/ records/atoz**>. The material on the site flagged as 'educational' is mainly aimed schools, but TNA's podcasts (see p. 13), now numbering over 200, provide introductions to many of the types of record held by TNA and how to use them in genealogical research.

The 'Visit Us' pages (on the 'About us' menu) have all you need to know when visiting The National Archives, including details of opening hours. Probably the most important page if you have never previously visited is the advice on planning your visit at <**www.nationalarchives.gov.uk/visit/ before-you-visit.htm**>. There are also a number of animated guides which cover various aspects of using TNA at <**www.nationalarchives.gov.uk/ records/quick-animated-guides.htm**>.

There is an enormous amount of other material on the site that is relevant to genealogists and these resources are not described here but in the relevant chapters. The 'Catalogues and online records page' has links to TNA's various catalogues (see below), to TNA's digitized document collection (p. 58), and to the online data collections on commercial data services which are licensed from TNA.

At the time of writing TNA has a wiki at <**yourarchives. nationalarchives.gov.uk**>, which allows users to add information on the records, and has a wealth of useful material. However, this is now closed to new contributors and no further editing will be possible after September 2012, at which point it will be transferred to the UK Government Web Archive, while some of the content will be migrated to the new Discovery service described below.

TNA has a development site at <**labs.nationalarchives.gov.uk**>, which offers a preview of facilities not yet ready for full public release, both enhancements of existing resources and completely new services.

The Discovery service

In April 2012, The National Archives will be replacing its long-standing online catalogue with a new Discovery service at <**discovery. nationalarchives.gov.uk**>. Like its predecessor, this will hold details of the 11 million or so records in the collection and links to those available for download, but is designed to provide more flexibility and to make it easier to find details of the relevant records.

The records in The National Archives are catalogued with a brief alphabetic code for the originating department (e.g. ADM for Admiralty, HO for Home Office) followed by a number for the document series and a second number for the individual piece. Figure 13-3 shows the details for some of the records in series HO 8, which cover the nineteenth century prison hulks, and HO 8/1, as you can see, identifies the quarterly returns of prisoners by hulk and date.

The screen display in Figure 13-3 is the sort of thing you will see if you select the Discovery service's browse option, and it allows you to see what sort of documents are in each part of the collection. However, if you are looking for a specific document series or a specific piece, it is in fact easier to do a search on the document reference.

The initial basic search offers just a single field to enter search terms or a document reference, but a drop-down adds the possibility of adding a year and a topic — you can select any combination of topics from a list of around

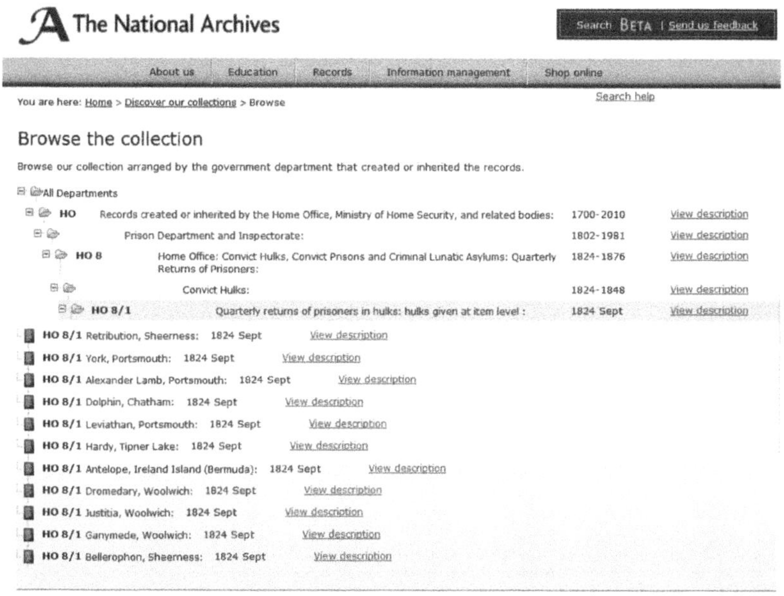

Figure 13-3 List of pieces for the class HO 8

120. The advanced search doesn't actually offer a significantly wider range of options but makes formulating a complex search much easier. The search help page shows how to formulate searches, and a particularly welcome feature is the NEAR operator, which finds cases where two words occur close to each other but not actually in a phrase. When searching for an individual, this can be a useful alternative to putting a personal name in inverted commas (or using the phrase search option on the advanced search page), as it will also find documents where the surname has been put first. If you just search on forename and surname without using one of these techniques, you will get lots of irrelevant results. In fact, you will often get a large number of results anyway, but the search results page will offer you a set of filters to refine your search by subject, date, and government department.

Figure 13-4 shows the start of the results listing from a search for the military record of my great-great-great-grandfather Christopher Christian. In this case, there are only five results so it is not difficult to spot the right one lower down the page, but selecting 'Military personnel' in the subject filter removes all the other types of record, leaving the single correct entry, shown in Figure 10-2 on page 155, which is for a record in series WO 97 (Royal Hospital Chelsea: Soldiers Service Documents). In fact, if you know you are looking for records in a particular collection, it is easiest to use the advanced search and put the reference in the 'Search within' field.

Figure 13-4 Initial search results in the Discovery service:

In themselves, the Discovery service's search and browse facilities are very straightforward to use, but they cannot simplify the organization of the actual records, which have been created independently by individual government departments over the past 900 or so years. In order to make the most of the service, particularly if you are going to do in-depth research on an ancestor's military, naval or criminal career, it can be useful to have some familiarity with the way in which the records you are looking for are organized. Of course, the subject indexing means you do not actually *have* to know anything about document references, but knowing the correct reference for the records you are interested in may save you a lot of time. In fact, all the 'Looking for …?' pages (see above) cite the relevant record classes – the 'What records can I find at The National Archives at Kew?' section of each page will have a direct link to the relevant material in the Discovery service. Genealogy books and articles which mention TNA documents will almost always tell you the document reference under which the material is catalogued, as with the military and naval records mentioned in Chapter 10. The research guides, linked from <**www.nationalarchives. gov.uk/records/atoz/**>, cover all the major series of records of interest to genealogists, and books such as *Tracing Your Ancestors in the National Archives* by Amanda Bevan and specialist works on individual subject areas (for example, *A Guide to Naval Records in the National Archives of the UK* by R. Cock and N.A.M. Rodger) are recommended reading for those planning more extensive research.

Other catalogues

In addition to the Discovery Service, there are a number of specialist catalogues on the site. Those of most interest to genealogists are:

- the E179 database of tax records, discussed on p. 120;
- the Equity Pleadings database, which currently contains details of around 30,000 Chancery Pleadings (see p. 127);
- the Hospital Database, which includes the location and covering dates of administrative and clinical records;
- the Manorial Documents Register (MDR), which shows the whereabouts of manorial documents in England and Wales, with county sections for: Berkshire, Buckinghamshire, Cumberland, Dorset, Hampshire, Hertfordshire, Isle of Wight, Lancashire North of the Sands (the Furness area, now part of Cumbria), Middlesex, Norfolk, Nottinghamshire, Shropshire, Surrey, Westmorland, the three Ridings of Yorkshire and all the Welsh counties.

All are linked from the 'Catalogues and online records page ', via the Records menu.

National Archives of Scotland

Until April 2011, the National Archives of Scotland (NAS) was an independent agency with a website at <www.nas.gov.uk>. However, the NAS and the General Register Office for Scotland have now been merged into a new body, the National Records of Scotland (NRS). In due course, the merged service will have a new website at <**www.nrscotland.gov.uk**>, but at the time of writing this has only a holding page and the NAS site retains an independent existence.

The site has a brief 'Family History' page at <**www.nas.gov.uk/ familyhistory/**> and a range of around 50 guides to the various types of record held by the NAS. There is also a 'Record guides directory', which will help you to find which guide covers a particular topic and which is very useful for those unfamiliar with the distinctive nomenclature of Scottish administration and records.

The material in the NAS is indexed in the SCAN online catalogue (see p. 206). The NAS has a number of catalogues and indexes. These are all listed at <**www.nas.gov.uk/catalogues/**> and the main catalogue is at <**www.nas.gov.uk/onlineCatalogue/**> (Figure 13-5). The records are organized by government department, which means that unless you already have a document reference, it is probably better to use the search facility than browse. The guides cite the document classes for the records covered, but unfortunately do not link directly to the relevant catalogue entries.

The NAS also maintains the Scottish Documents site at <**www.scottishdocuments.com**>, which has information on the NAS's digitization projects, and the Scottish Handwriting site at <**www.scottishhandwriting.com**>, discussed on p. 289.

THE NATIONAL ARCHIVES OF SCOTLAND
DEFINING MOMENTS IN HISTORY

Catalogue search - internet

Welcome	[Browse]	Search		Help

Browse | Summary catalogue | Top level record | Treeview

You are in: Catalogue search> Browse> Summary catalogue> Treeview

Tuesday 3 January 2012 12:46

Page options:
Print this page
E-mail this page
Previous page

Records updated:
3 January 2012

Summary catalogue treeview

HD4		Highland Emigration Society	1852-1859
expand HD4/1	HD4/1	Letterbook	Jan-Jul 1852
expand HD4/2	HD4/2	Letterbook	Jul-Nov 1852
expand HD4/3	HD4/3	Letterbook	Nov 1852-Feb 1854
expand HD4/4	HD4/4	Letterbook	Feb 1854-Jan 1859
expand HD4/5	HD4/5	List of emigrants	1852-1857
expand HD4/6	HD4/6	Promissory note book	1852-1857

Figure 13-5 The NAS catalogue

The Public Record Office of Northern Ireland

The Public Record Office of Northern Ireland (PRONI) has a website at <**www.proni.gov.uk**>. The site offers extensive information for genealogists, including descriptions of the major categories of record and about two dozen leaflets on various aspects of Irish genealogical research. There are individual leaflets on emigration to Australia, Canada, and the US. Links to all these aids are provided on the 'Records Held' page at <**www.proni.gov.uk/index/research_and_records_held.htm**>. There is also a FAQ page at <**www.proni.gov.uk/index/about_proni/frequently_asked_questions.htm**>.

There is a main family history page at <**www.proni.gov.uk/index/family_history.htm**>, which has links to the most important genealogical resources on the site.

PRONI has an online catalogue, eCatalogue, at <**www.proni.gov.uk/index/search_the_archives/ecatalogue.htm**> (there is also a prominent link on the home page). For a number of types of record, the catalogue entries include individual names – for example, private papers, criminal records, wills, land records and many other types of legal record. It is therefore worth searching the catalogue for any family name you are researching. Figure 13-6 shows the results of a search for the surname 'Blackburn'.

In addition to the catalogue, the site has several indexes of use to genealogists, including:

- the Geographical Index (for locating any administrative geographical name, with Ordnance Survey Map reference number)
- the Prominent Person Index
- the Presbyterian Church Index
- the Church of Ireland Index

The last two cover only those records which have been microfilmed by PRONI. There are plans to add other church records, and school records. All are linked from the 'Online guides and indexes' page. Unfortunately this has a 125-character URL, so either follow the link from the website for this book, or, from the PRONI home page, click on 'Search the Archives', then 'Online guides and indexes'.

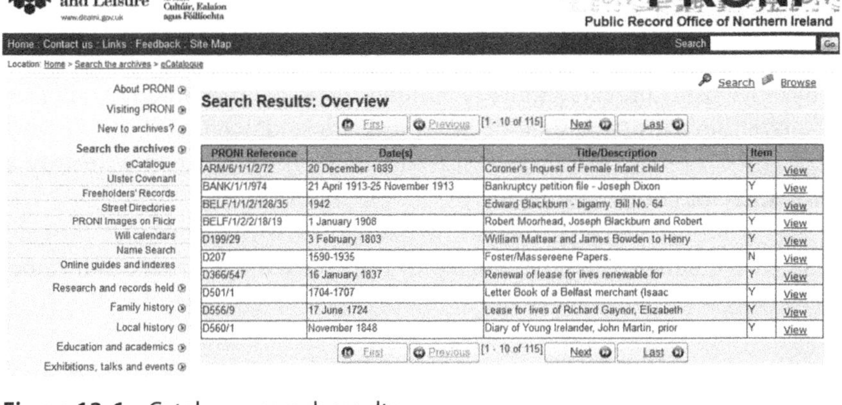

PRONI Reference	Date(s)	Title/Description	Item	
ARM/6/1/1/2/72	20 December 1839	Coroner's Inquest of Female Infant child	Y	View
BANK/1/1/974	21 April 1913-25 November 1913	Bankruptcy petition file - Joseph Dixon	Y	View
BELF/1/1/2/128/35	1942	Edward Blackburn - bigamy. Bill No. 64	Y	View
BELF/1/2/2/18/19	1 January 1908	Robert Moorhead, Joseph Blackburn and Robert	Y	View
D199/29	3 February 1803	William Mattear and James Bowden to Henry	Y	View
D207	1590-1935	Foster/Massereene Papers.	N	View
D366/547	16 January 1837	Renewal of lease for lives renewable for	Y	View
D501/1	1704-1707	Letter Book of a Belfast merchant (Isaac	Y	View
D556/9	17 June 1724	Lease for lives of Richard Gaynor, Elizabeth	Y	View
D560/1	November 1848	Diary of Young Irelander, John Martin, prior	Y	View

Figure 13-6 eCatalogue search results

PRONI has three important online databases of primary records, all linked from the home page:

- a database of half a million men and women who signed the Ulster Covenant and Declaration in 1912, with scanned images of the signatures;
- Freeholders' Records, an index of pre-1840 voter registration records;
- Will Calendars (see p. 118).

National Archives of Ireland

The National Archives of Ireland has a website at <www.nationalarchives.ie>. Among other things, this has help for beginners, information on the main types of Irish genealogical record, and a good list of links to websites for Irish genealogy, all linked from the 'Genealogy' page at <www.nationalarchives.ie/genealogy/>.

The national libraries

The UK's national library, the British Library, has a number of collections of interest to genealogists. The BL's home page is at <www.bl.uk>, while the Integrated Catalogue is at <catalogue.bl.uk>. The catalogue is also included in COPAC, discussed on p. 220.

The India Office records held by the British Library do not have their own online catalogue, but a comprehensive guide to them will be found at <www.bl.uk/reshelp/findhelpregion/asia/india/indiaofficerecords/indiaofficehub.html>. Some of the material can be found on Access to Archives <www.a2a.org.uk> – on the A2A search page select 'British Library, Asia, Pacific and Africa Collections' from the 'Location of Archives' field. The NRA at <www.nationalarchives.gov.uk/nra/> also contains entries for material in the India Office records.

The British Library's newspaper collection is discussed in detail on p. 193ff.

The National Library of Scotland has a website at <www.nls.uk>. Its main catalogue is at <main-cat.nls.uk> and various other catalogues are linked from <www.nls.uk/catalogues/>. Among these, Scots Abroad at <digital.nls.uk/emigration/> will be of interest to those descended from Scottish emigrants. The site also has an introduction to Scottish family history at <www.nls.uk/family-history/>.

The National Library of Wales website at <www.llgc.org.uk> provides links to a number of online catalogues from <www.llgc.org.uk/index.php?id=catalogues>. The most useful of these for genealogists are:

- the main catalogue
- Crime and Punishment (see p. 124)
- Marriage Bonds

The Digital Mirror area of the site includes 'Welsh Biography Online', which has information on the lives of eminent Welsh people, and links to online collections of maps and photographs.

The NLW also maintains another useful (though not genealogical) database, Wales on the Web. This is a gateway of web resources relating to all aspects of Wales and has its own website at <www.walesontheweb.org>.

The National Library of Ireland has a website at <www.nli.ie>, with a family history section at <www.nli.ie/en/family-history-introduction.aspx>. This covers all the main sources in the library which are of use to family historians, and has lists of parish registers. There are several online catalogues, searchable separately or combined, all linked from the homepage. There is also a newspaper catalogue at <www.nli.ie/newsplan/>. There are catalogues of the photographic collections, linked from the family history page. The site also hosts the web pages of the Office of the Chief Herald at <www.nli.ie/en/heraldry-introduction.aspx>.

For access to online catalogues of the UK national libraries, see the information on COPAC, p. 220, below.

County record offices

There are several ways to locate a county record office (CRO) website. Each Genuki county page provides a link to relevant CROs, and may itself give contact details and opening times. The ARCHON Directory (see p. 205) allows you to locate a record office by county or region. Finally, CROs can be found via the website of the relevant county council (you may even be able to make a guess at its URL, as it will often be something like <www.essexcc.gov.uk>).

Andrew Chapman has a set of links for county record offices in England, Scotland and Wales at <hatmandu.net/writing/cros/>. Usefully, the page includes direct links to many of the online catalogues and other digital projects. There is a similar list at <councilarchivesuk.webs.com>, which includes the offshore islands.

For the Republic of Ireland, where the term 'county archives' is used in preference to 'county record office', see the listing in ARCHON (above, p. 205), or the Genuki page for the particular Irish county.

There is a wide variation in what record offices provide on their websites. At the very least, though, you can expect to find details of location, contacts, and opening times, along with some basic help on using their material. However, most offer substantial background material on the area and specific collections, and even online catalogues. Even better, a number of CROs have undertaken substantial digitization projects, some of which are mentioned elsewhere in this book. Much of the manuscript material held by CROs is catalogued on ARCHON.

Public libraries

Public libraries, although they have little in the way of manuscript collections, have considerable holdings in the basic sources for genealogical research. For example, many central libraries have microfiche of the GRO indexes and microfilm of local census returns, as well as local printed material.

The UK Public Libraries page at <**dspace.dial.pipex.com/town/square/ ac940/ukpublib.html**> is a general site devoted to public libraries. It provides links to library websites, and to their OPACs (Online Public Access Catalogues) where these are available over the internet. However, the pages do not seem to have been updated for some time, so you may find some links no longer work. As with record offices, public library websites will be part of the relevant local authority's web presence.

The People's Network at <**www.peoplesnetwork.gov.uk**> is a site devoted to English public libraries and the 'Find a library' facility enables you to find public libraries centred on a particular postcode or place. Although focusing on English libraries, the site does have details of those in Wales, Scotland, and Northern Ireland. However, the place-name search seems to be hopelessly unreliable – it thinks that Worcester is 4.9 miles from Greenwich, and doesn't even recognize the locations where some of the listed libraries are located. In fact, it may be better to use the 'Search and Discover' facility, on the 'Discover' menu, to search on a place-name and the word 'library'. You can also use this to search for particular content within public library collections. The full list of collections covered will be found on the 'Detailed search' page at <**www.peoplesnetwork.gov.uk/discover/advanced**>, which allows you to search within any combination of collections.

A particularly useful collection to search from this page is 'Cornucopia Familia' (listed under 'UK Collections'). Familia was a major project to provide a comprehensive guide to genealogical holdings in public libraries. Unfortunately, the project lost its funding some years ago and its site has long closed down. However, Cornucopia (see p. 207) now has an archive of Familia's data for UK libraries and these will turn up with the title 'Family and Local History Resources' if you do a search on a local authority or place-name, either on the People's Network or on Cornucopia itself at <**www.cornucopia.org.uk**>. Since the information has not been updated since 2006 at the latest, phone numbers and opening times will not necessarily be up to date, but the lists of material held are probably still quite accurate. A public library may possibly have disposed of census microfilms, now that all the censuses are online, but for details of holdings of printed electoral registers, trade directories and newspapers, Familia ought still to be quite reliable. The original Familia site is accessible via the Wayback machine under <**www.familia.org.uk**> (5 July 2009) and this includes the holdings of libraries in the Republic of Ireland, which Cornucopia has not archived.

For public libraries in the Irish Republic, the country's public library portal Library.ie has links to public library websites and online catalogues at <**www.library.ie/weblog/public-libraries/**>.

A useful resource for locating individual books in public libraries is Worldcat at <**www.worldcat.org**>, a global library catalogue. If you enter a book title, it will bring up a record for the book. If you then enter your postcode, it will list the closest libraries which hold copies of the book.

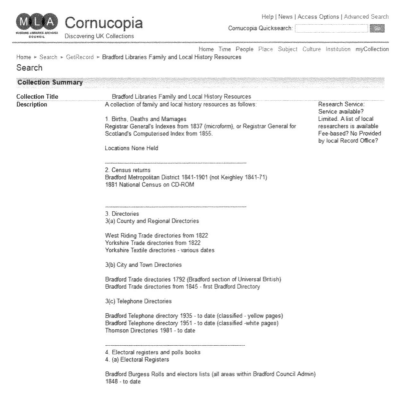

Figure 13-7 The Familia record for Bradford Public Libraries on Cornucopia

University libraries

While university libraries are not of major importance for genealogical research, all have special collections which may include personal papers of notable individuals. There are some significant university collections relating to occupational, religious and ethnic groups, some of which are mentioned in the relevant chapters of this book – for example, the gypsy collections at the University of Liverpool (see p. 182). They are also likely to have collections of local material which, while probably not of use in constructing a pedigree, may be of interest to the family historian looking for local topographical and historical information.

There is no single central index to university library holdings but COPAC is a major consortium of 60 research libraries, including the three university libraries which are also legal deposit libraries, entitled to request a copy of any book published in the UK (Cambridge University Library, the Bodleian in Oxford, and Trinity College, Dublin). It also includes the British Library, and the national libraries of Scotland and Wales (see p. 216). The COPAC website at <**www.copac.ac.uk**> provides access to a consolidated catalogue for all member institutions.

All university libraries are included on the ARCHON site at <**www.nationalarchives.gov.uk/archon/**>, which provides contact details and has catalogue entries for archival material (i.e. not books or periodicals) relating to individuals, families and organizations. The Archives Hub at <**www.archiveshub.ac.uk**> is a site which offers descriptions of archival collections in over 170 academic libraries.

University library sites do not generally cater for family historians, but the University of London's Helpers site at <**www.helpers.shl.lon.ac.uk**> is an exception in that it is specifically designed to assist with research about individuals – the name stands for 'Higher Education Libraries in your PERsonal history reSearch'. It includes a database which lists and describes the holdings in the University's colleges and institutions that may be useful in genealogical research, and has guides to using Higher Education libraries.

Bear in mind that university libraries are not open to the general public and that you will normally need to make a written application in advance in order to have access, particularly in the case of manuscript material.

Family History Centers and the Family History Library

The LDS Church's Family History Centers (FHCs), increasingly referred to as FamilySearch Centers, are valuable not just because they hold microfiche copies of the GRO indexes and other materials, but because any UK genealogical material which has been microfilmed by the Church can be ordered for viewing in a FHC, and this includes many parish registers. Also, their computer suites provide free access to some commercial genealogical data.

Contact details for FHCs are given on the FamilySearch site at <**www.familysearch.org/locations/**>. If you use the basic search, you may get no results if there's not an exact match. Unless you know there is a centre in a particular town, it may be better to search on a county name. The results are shown as a list of local centres and an interactive map.

Genuki provides a quick way to get listings from the equivalent search facility on the old FamilySearch site (see p. 41): the page at <**www.genuki.org.uk/ big/LDS/**> has links which will search automatically for all FHCs in England, Scotland, Ireland and Wales.

The key to exploiting this immense wealth of material is the Family History Library (FHL) catalogue, which can be consulted online at the FamilySearch site. The catalogue search is available by clicking on the word 'catalog' above the search boxes on the home page. This offers searches by place, surname or, for published works, author. There is also a beta version of a keyword search. Note that there is no advanced search – you can only search on one field. If you enter a place-name, the search page will validate this and convert it automatically to show the country, county and place. The search results show a list of the various types of record available for it. Figure 13-8 shows the initial results of a place search for West Horsley in Surrey, while Figure 13-9 shows the expanded entry for 'Church records', with descriptions of the various items available.

In order to find the microfilm reference for one of the entries, you need to click on it to bring up the 'Title Details' screen (Figure 13-10). This tells you the repository where the material is held (or was at the time of filming), together with the repository's reference for the material. This means you could even use the FHL catalogue as a partial catalogue to county record offices. Under the 'Notes' heading is detailed information on the microfilms relating to this item (Figure 13-10) with an exact description of what is on each film, together with the film reference which you can now use to order the film at an FHC.

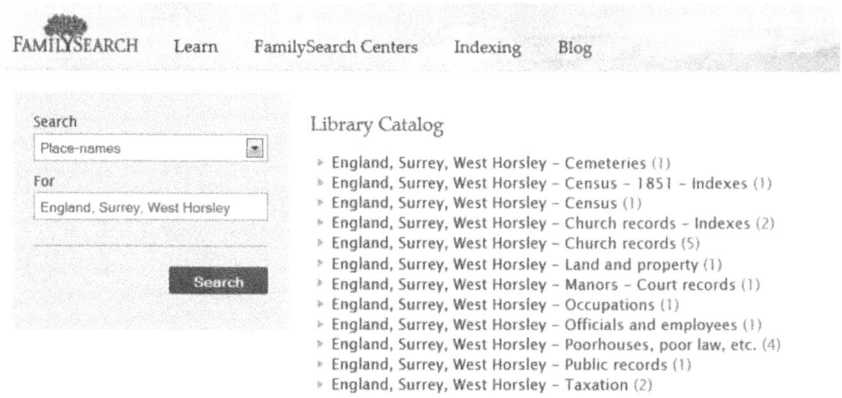

Figure 13-8 Search results for West Horsley, Surrey, in the FHL catalogue

The Society of Genealogists

The Society of Genealogists is home to the premier genealogical library in the country and its website is at <**www.sog.org.uk**>. General information about the library is at <**www.sog.org.uk/library/intro.shtml**> and there is a link to the library catalogue from <**www.sog.org.uk/sogcat/sogcat.shtml**>. There are two types of search: the default browse search takes you to the first item in the catalogue which matches your search criteria, or the more useful 'Power Search' allows you to select items based on up to three fields.

In order to use the library, you need to be a member of the Society or pay a search fee (see <**www.sog.org.uk/visit.html**>, or follow the 'How to find us' link at the foot of the page). But even if you are not in a position to use the library itself, the comprehensive nature of the Society's collections makes the catalogue a valuable guide to which parish registers, for example, have been transcribed, or what has been published on a particular surname. If you are not already familiar with the library and its catalogue, it will be worth looking at the tutorial at <**www.sog.org.uk/sogcat/intro.shtml**>, particularly if you want to search for place-names or surnames.

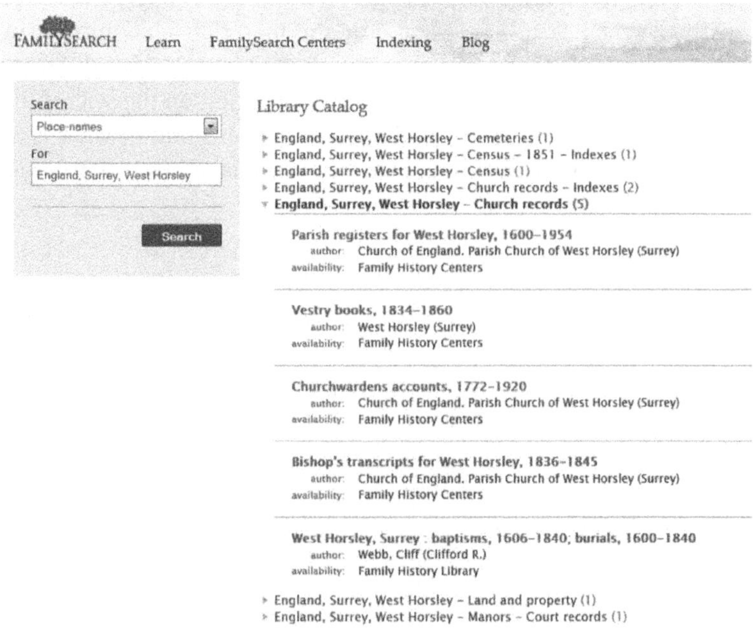

Figure 13-9 Search results for West Horsley, Surrey, in the FHL catalogue – Church records

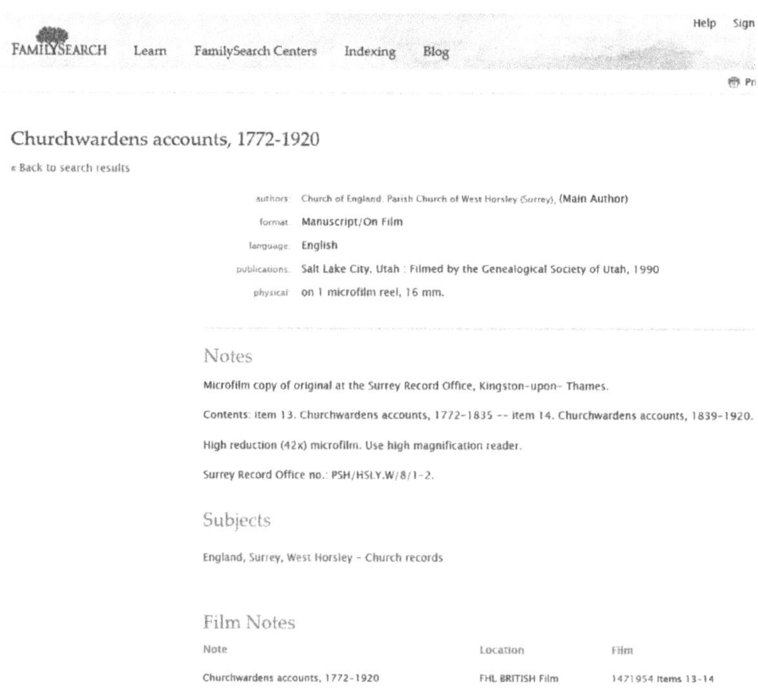
FAMILYSEARCH Learn FamilySearch Centers Indexing Blog Help Sign

Churchwardens accounts, 1772-1920

« Back to search results

authors: Church of England. Parish Church of West Horsley (Surrey), (Main Author)
format: Manuscript/On Film
language: English
publications: Salt Lake City, Utah : Filmed by the Genealogical Society of Utah, 1990
physical: on 1 microfilm reel, 16 mm.

Notes

Microfilm copy of original at the Surrey Record Office, Kingston-upon- Thames.

Contents: item 13. Churchwardens accounts, 1772-1835 -- item 14. Churchwardens accounts, 1839-1920.

High reduction (42x) microfilm. Use high magnification reader.

Surrey Record Office no.: PSH/HSLY.W/8/1-2.

Subjects

England, Surrey, West Horsley - Church records

Film Notes

Note	Location	Film
Churchwardens accounts, 1772-1920	FHL BRITISH Film	1471954 Items 13-14

Figure 13-10 FHL catalogue search Title Details

Beyond the British Isles

If you need to consult archives outside the UK and Ireland the best general starting points will be the pages for individual countries on Cyndi's List – each of these has a section headed 'Libraries, Archives & Museums', with links not only to the national archives, but also to major provincial archives. Of course, if the country is not English-speaking you may not be able to make full use of the site, but you will often find at least some basic information in English and an email address for enquiries.

The Family History Centers have microfilmed records from many countries, and searching on a country in the Family History Library Catalog will list the various types of record and what has been filmed (see p. 221).

14

SURNAMES, PEDIGREES AND FAMILIES

The resources discussed in Chapters 4 to 11 contain direct transcriptions of, or indexes to, primary genealogical sources. But alongside these are 'compiled' sources, the material put together by individual genealogists. Many people are now putting their pedigrees on the internet on a personal website – Chapter 20 explains how to do this yourself, and Chapter 19 looks at how to locate such material. But there are a number of public sites to which people can submit details of the surnames they are interested in, or even entire pedigrees, so that others can contact them. This chapter also looks at sites devoted to the genealogies of royal, noble and otherwise notable families. Finally, there is a look at general resources for finding living people.

Sites devoted to surname origins and distribution are discussed in Chapter 16.

Surname interests

One of the best ways to make progress with your family tree is to get in touch with others who are interested in the same surnames. In some cases you will end up encountering cousins who might have considerable material relating to a branch of your family, but at the very least it is useful to discover what resources others have looked at. If you find someone who is doing a one-name study, they may even have extracts from primary sources they are prepared to share with you.

Before the advent of the internet, making such contacts was quite difficult. It involved checking a range of published and unpublished sources, looking through the surname interests in family history magazines, and consulting all the volumes of directories such as the annual *Genealogical Research Directory,* which was issued in print or on CD up until 2007. You will still need to do all this, of course, not least because quite a few genealogists are still not online and this is the only way to find out about *their* researches. The SoG 's leaflet 'Has it been done before?' at <**www.sog.org.uk/leaflets/**

done.pdf> provides a comprehensive overview of the various offline resources to check. But the internet now offers a much easier way of both locating and inviting such contacts.

Surname lists

If you have already made some progress with your family history and have got back far enough to know where your ancestors were living 100 or so years before your birth, then you should check the relevant surname lists. These do not provide genealogical information as such: they are just registers of interests, like a printed research directory, and for each surname they give the contact details of the researcher who submitted it, and usually a date range for the period of interest (see Figure 14-1). Some lists also have links to the websites of submitters.

Genuki has a comprehensive listing of both the major surname lists with national coverage and those for individual counties at <**www.genuki.org.uk/ indexes/SurnamesLists.html**>.

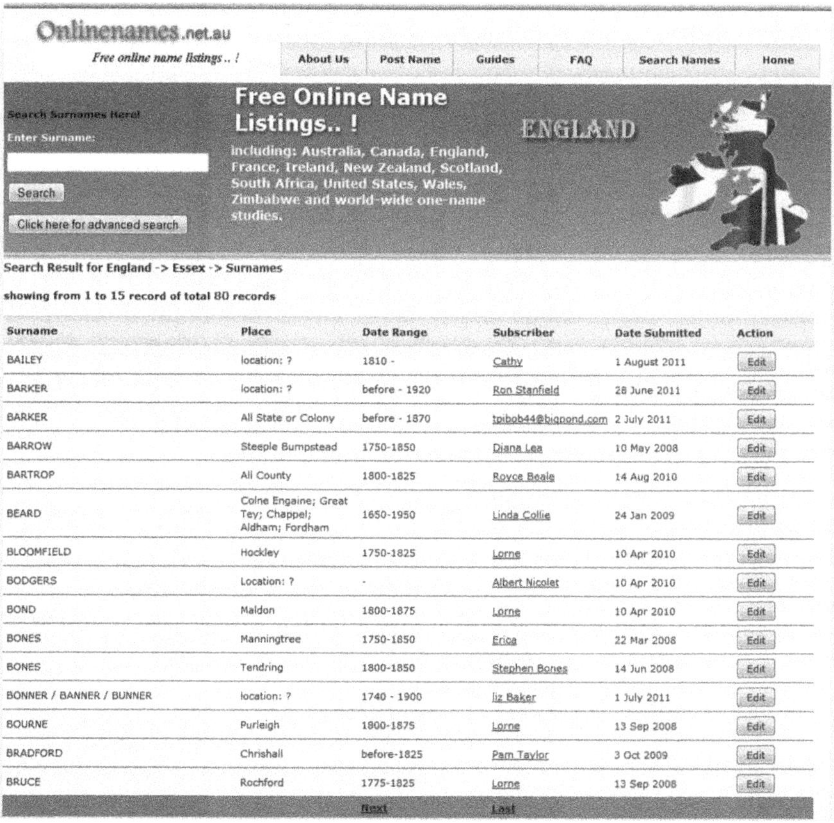

Surname	Place	Date Range	Subscriber	Date Submitted	Action
BAILEY	location: ?	1810 -	Cathy	1 August 2011	Edit
BARKER	location: ?	before - 1920	Ron Stanfield	28 June 2011	Edit
BARKER	All State or Colony	before - 1870	tpibob44@bigpond.com	2 July 2011	Edit
BARROW	Steeple Bumpstead	1750-1850	Diana Lea	10 May 2008	Edit
BARTROP	All County	1800-1825	Royce Beale	14 Aug 2010	Edit
BEARD	Colne Engaine; Great Tey; Chappel; Aldham; Fordham	1650-1950	Linda Collie	24 Jan 2009	Edit
BLOOMFIELD	Hockley	1750-1825	Lorne	10 Apr 2010	Edit
BODGERS	Location: ?	-	Albert Nicolet	10 Apr 2010	Edit
BOND	Maldon	1800-1875	Lorne	10 Apr 2010	Edit
BONES	Manningtree	1750-1850	Erica	22 Mar 2008	Edit
BONES	Tendring	1800-1850	Stephen Bones	14 Jun 2008	Edit
BONNER / BANNER / BUNNER	location: ?	1740 - 1900	liz Baker	1 July 2011	Edit
BOURNE	Purleigh	1800-1875	Lorne	13 Sep 2008	Edit
BRADFORD	Chrishall	before-1825	Pam Taylor	3 Oct 2009	Edit
BRUCE	Rochford	1775-1825	Lorne	13 Sep 2008	Edit

Figure 14-1 Essex entries from Onlinenames

Of the three main surname listing sites for the British Isles, the longest established is Graham Jaunay's Onlinenames site at <**www.onlinenames.net.au**>. This covers England, Wales, Scotland and Ireland, but does not seem to include the Channel Islands or the Isle of Man. Searches require you to enter both a country and a county, which means that you cannot do a global search. However, you can leave the surname field blank and search for all surnames within a particular county. Figure 14-1 shows the results of a search for any name in Essex. Clicking on the name in the 'Subscriber' column will bring up a 'new message' window in your email software with the email address of the person to contact, or you can read the email address from the status bar at the bottom of the browser when you move your mouse over the link. Surname interests for Australia, Canada, New Zealand, the US and a number of other countries are also included. Adding your own names to the site is straightforward and requires no prior registration. However, the first time you want to edit your entries you need to apply for a password.

UK Surnames at <**www.uk-surnames.com**> has listings for:

- All English counties, plus London and the Isle of Wight
- All Scottish counties, plus the city of Glasgow (Kinross-shire is not listed separately, but entries for the county are listed under Perth)
- 18 Irish counties
- All Welsh counties
- Channel Islands and Isle of Man (listed under England)

Alternatively you can search across all counties. The site also has listings for a small number of one-name studies. New entries are submitted via the 'My Page' page, which also allows you to see whose surname interests or place-names match yours. Contacts are made indirectly: the site does not display or provide the email addresses of contributors but you complete an online form for the site to send a message to the recipient.

The UK Genealogy Interests Directory at <**www.ukgid.com**> allows you to get a listing of interests by surname or by county. You can search and contact submitters (indirectly) without registering, but registration is required for submissions. Unfortunately, at the time of writing, there are two problems with the site: the county and user pages appear not to be working, and listings are presented in a very small window, which means details cannot be seen without scrolling.

In addition to these three national sites, there are around 40 other county-based surname lists, with a few for smaller areas. Although these lists are not formally connected with Genuki, many of them have a long-standing relationship with the relevant Genuki county page. Links to any lists relevant to a county will be found on the Genuki county page as well as on the central surname list page.

For other countries, look at the section headed 'Queries, Message Boards & Surname Lists' on the page for the country on Cyndi's List at <www.cyndislist.com>, but do not expect to find the same level of coverage as there is for the British Isles.

In addition to the county surname lists, there are a number of surname lists relevant to UK emigration and immigration. These are discussed in Chapter 11 (see p. 165ff).

Obviously, you should not just look for contacts but also consider attracting contacts yourself by submitting your own interests to the relevant national or county lists. The exact method of doing this varies from list to list: on some there is a web page with a submission form; on others you will need to email the list-maintainer. Be sure to follow the instructions, as many list-maintainers expect you to submit your interests in a particular format (to make processing of submissions easier to automate) and may ignore something sent in the wrong format.

One problem with surname lists is that someone who has made a submission may forget to update their entries if they subsequently change their email address, so you will occasionally find contact details that are no longer valid. Unfortunately there is nothing you can do about this – it is a fact of life on the internet – and there is no point in asking the surname list-manager where a particular submitter can be contacted if their stated email address is no longer valid. Needless to say, if you change your own email address, you'll need to update your details on the site.

Guild of One-Name Studies

The Guild of One-Name Studies at <**www.one-name.org**> is an organization for those who are researching all people with a particular surname, rather than just their own personal pedigree. It has a searchable Register of One-Name Studies online at <**www.one-name.org/register.html**>, which gives a contact address (not necessarily electronic) for each of the 8,000 or so surnames registered with the Guild.

Unlike the national and county lists, the surname interests registered with the Guild cover the whole world – this is, in fact, a requirement for registration. So, even though the person who has registered a particular one-name interest may not have ancestors in common with you, there is still a good chance that they have collected material of interest relating to your surname. In particular, a Guild member is likely to have a good overview of the variants of their registered surname. This makes the Guild's list of surnames worth checking even, or especially, if you are only just starting your researches. In contrast, the national and county surname lists are probably not very useful until you have got back at least three generations. If you are thinking of starting your own one-name study, the site provides useful guidance.

Society of Genealogists

The SoG has three indexes for surnames and pedigrees:

- Surname Document Collection – a variety of documents and transcripts, including original certificates and wills, for around 10,000 surnames;
- Pedigrees Collection – 3,000 surnames;
- Members' birth briefs – 28,000 surnames from four-generation pedigrees submitted by SoG members.

All are linked from the 'Searching for surnames and families' page at <**www.sog.org.uk/library/surnames_and_families.shtml**>. For each of these, the site lists only the surname, with no indication of dates or location, and you will need to consult the original document. In some cases you can order copies by post – the Search & Copy Service is described at <**www.sog.org.uk/library/searches.shtml**> – but otherwise you will need to visit the Society's library.

RootsWeb

One of the most useful sites for surname interests is RootsWeb, which has a wide range of surname-related resources, all linked from <**resources. rootsweb.com/~clusters/surnames/**>. There is a separate page for each listed surname with:

- links to personal websites at RootsWeb which include the name;
- search forms for a number of databases hosted by RootsWeb;
- links to any mailing lists for the surname (see below).

The most general surname resource at RootsWeb is the Roots Surname List (RSL) at <**rsl.rootsweb.ancestry.com**>. This is connected with the ROOTS-L mailing list, the oldest genealogy mailing list on the internet, and contains well over a million entries submitted by around 200,000 individual genealogists. You can enter a geographical location to narrow your search, using Chapman county codes (see p. 260) and/or three-letter country codes – there is a list of standard codes at <**helpdesk.rootsweb.ancestry.com/ codes/**>. However, you may need to do a couple of searches to make sure you find all relevant entries as some people spell out English counties in full or use the two-letter country code UK instead of ENG, SCT, etc. If you check the list regularly, a useful feature is that you can restrict your results to those added or updated recently. Submitter details are not given on the search results page, but there is a link to them from the user ID of the submitter.

Discussion forums

The various types of discussion forum are described in detail in Chapter 18, but it is worth noting here that there are many groups devoted to individual surnames. Even if you do not participate in any of them – my impression is that they are not particularly useful as discussion forums – it will still be worth your while to look through the archives of past messages to see if anyone else is working on the same family or on the same geographical area.

John Fuller's list of mailing lists has information on those dedicated to individual surnames at <**www.rootsweb.ancestry.com/~jfuller/gen_ mail.html#SURNAMES**>, though many of the individual listing pages do not seem to have been updated since January 2010, so there will undoubtedly be some missing. However, many of these surname lists are hosted by RootsWeb and can also be found from the general list of mailing lists at <**lists.rootsweb.ancestry.com**> or via the individual surname pages mentioned above at <**resources.rootsweb.com/~clusters/ surnames/**>.

Alongside the surname mailing lists, there are web-based message boards or discussion forums for individual surnames. One of the largest sites hosting such discussion lists is GenForum at <**genforum.genealogy.com**>, which must have message boards for at least 10,000 surnames. Ancestry.com has a large set of surname message boards at <**boards. ancestry.com**> – follow the link to 'United Kingdom and Ireland', and then the link to the relevant part of the UK. You do not need to be an Ancestry subscriber to use these. In many cases, these boards relate to a surname mailing list hosted by RootsWeb. This means that you can contribute your own query via the web without having to subscribe to a mailing list. A particularly useful feature is that the individual boards can be searched, which makes it possible to find messages relating to particular places, something which is essential for common and widespread surnames.

Family history societies

Every family history society has a register of members' interests, and it will be worthwhile checking the societies which cover the areas where your ancestors lived. If you're lucky, the list will be available online. For example, the Suffolk Family History Society has a Members' Interest database at <**www.suffolkfhs.co.uk/interests/**>, which can be searched by non-members. The Sussex Family History Group has both a public members' interests area at <**www.sfhg.org.uk/extsw.html**> and a more extensive one for members only. Bear in mind that not all these members will be contactable by email and societies generally do not publish members' postal addresses online, so you may need to consult the society's journal for contact details. For a list of FHS websites consult the 'Family History and Genealogy Societies' page on Genuki at <**www.genuki.org.uk/Societies/**>.

Personal websites

Many genealogists have a personal website (see Chapter 20), and locating such sites can be a useful step in making contact with someone who shares your genealogical interests or even some of your ancestors. Cyndi's List has a 'Personal Home Pages Index' at <**www.cyndislist.com/personal/**> with sub-pages for each letter of the alphabet. Even though these pages include over 10,000 links, this will be only a fraction of the personal genealogical websites, and really you need to use a search engine to get more inclusive coverage. Unfortunately just typing a surname in a search engine will not be very helpful. You need to search for a surname and the word 'genealogy' and/or the phrase 'surname list' (see Chapter 19).

Pedigree databases

The surname interest resources do not provide genealogical information, they simply offer contact details for other genealogists who may share your interests. But there are several sites which allow genealogists to make their pedigrees available on the web. You can, of course, do this by creating your own website, as discussed in Chapter 20, particularly if you want to publish more comprehensive information. But if you just want to make your pedigree available online, these sites provide an easy way to do it. Even if you do not make your own pedigree available, many others have, and it is worth checking these sites for overlap with your own family tree.

There are two ways of getting your own pedigree into one of these databases. Some of them have facilities for you to create your pedigree entirely online, while the commoner method is to upload a GEDCOM file containing your pedigree. Information about GEDCOM files and how to create them will be found on p. 357, Chapter 20.

There is not space here to give more than a brief account of some of the most important sites, but for a comprehensive list of pedigree databases consult the 'Databases – Lineage-Linked' page on Cyndi's List at <**www.cyndislist.com/lineage-linked/databases/**>.

Several of the data services offer some sort of family tree facility, but since these are generally only accessible to subscribers, I have not listed them here.

Free databases

FamilySearch

FamilySearch at <**www.familysearch.org**> has been discussed as a source of record transcriptions in Chapter 7 (p. 41), but the site also includes two separate areas with pedigrees.

The search page at <**www.familysearch.org/#form=trees**> (click on 'Trees' on the FamilySearch home page) provides access to material from the old FamilySearch site, Ancestral File and the Pedigree Resource File, comprising pedigrees submitted by individual genealogists. For each record there is an id for the submitter, but this only serves to identify which entries belong to a particular submission and there are no contact details. The entries are therefore useful as a source of possible leads to follow up yourself, but not as a source of contacts.

A new development are the Community Trees, which have their own site at <**histfam.familysearch.org**>. Each tree represents a separate volunteer project carried out in partnership with FamilySearch and comes with detailed source information, making the material much more readily verifiable than most online pedigrees. Among the trees relevant to UK genealogists are:

- British Isles Families with Peerage, Gentry, and Colonial American Connections.
- The Knowles Collection (which includes Jewish families in the British Isles).
- Welsh Medieval Database Primarily of Nobility and Gentry (see p. 245).
- Local collections for Bedfordshire, Leicestershire, London, Surrey and Sussex.

A tree of the ancestors or descendants of any individual can be downloaded as a GEDCOM file (see p. 357) for viewing in your own family tree software. The article on the FamilySearch Wiki at <**www.familysearch.org/learn/ wiki/en/Community_Trees_Project**> provides further information.

At the time of writing there seems to be no way to submit new pedigrees, no doubt because the new site is a work in progress.

RootsWeb WorldConnect

Probably the largest collection of pedigrees is on RootsWeb, whose WorldConnect data has a home page at <**worldconnect.genealogy. rootsweb.ancestry.com**>. It currently contains over 640 million entries for over 5½ million surnames, submitted by over 400,000 users. Ancestry's World Tree provides access to the same database at <**www.ancestry.com/**

trees/awt/main.aspx> (this is freely accessible and does not require a subscription to Ancestry).

The initial search form provided on RootsWeb allows you to search on surname and given name, and the search results pages then list each matching entry with further details and offer a link either to the home page for the database in which the entry is found or to the specific person. If you get too many results to cope with, a more detailed search form provides options to narrow down your search with dates, places, names of parents, etc.

Figure 14-2 shows the results of an advanced search on WorldConnect for Elizabeth Collyer, with birth or christening in Surrey. Clicking on the name of the individual takes you to their data, while the link on the right takes you to details of the submitted database in which this individual is found, including the email address of the submitter. On the Ancestry site you need to register with your name and email address, free of charge, before you can search. However, the initial search form is more comprehensive.

Wikis

While most pedigree sites use searchable databases to store the material, the development of wikis has encouraged people to experiment with using the wiki technology to store and display articles on the individuals in a family tree. The first site to do this, WikiTree at **<wikitree.org>**, was launched in 2005 but at the time of writing it is closed for reconstruction.

RootsWeb's WorldConnect Project
Global Search

Names: 667,797,450 Surnames: 5,664,388 Databases: 434,852

Results 1-14 of 14

Name	Birth/Christening		Death/Burial		Database	Order record?	Other Matches
	Date	Place	Date	Place			
Collyer, Daisy Elizabeth	1886	Kingston, Surrey, England			greenpearson		Census Newspapers Histories
Father: William George Collyer Mother: Sarah Daisey Elizabeth Arnold Spouse: Matthew Allison							
Collyer, Elizabeth	1739	Horsell, Surrey	Dec 1819	Woking, Surrey	parr_cline		Census Newspapers Histories
Father: William Collyer Spouse: William Wigman							
Collyer, Elizabeth	1813	Bagshot Surrey, England	1886	Sandhurst Berks	jeb1904		Census Newspapers Histories
Spouse: Richard Bowdery							
Collyer, Elizabeth	1849	Bisley, Surrey, England			pabaggs		Census Newspapers Histories
Father: James Collyer Mother: Eliza Gosden							
Collyer, Elizabeth	1849	Bisley, Surrey. England			:615039		Census Newspapers Histories
Father: James Collyer Mother: Eliza Gosden							
Collyer, Elizabeth	1888	Normandy, Surrey, England			margoken		Census Newspapers Histories
Father: William Collyer Mother: Mary Bowler							

Figure 14-2 Search results on WorldConnect

WeRelate at <www.werelate.org> allows you to create wiki pages for individual ancestors, with links to the pages for their parents, spouses and children. Rather than a set of separate pedigrees, the aim of the site is to create a single unified family tree. You can search the site without registering, but to get full access to its material or to add individuals from your own pedigree (either by manual editing or by uploading a GEDCOM file), you need to create an account. This is free of charge and there is no subscription option, though you can make a donation if you choose.

Commercial services

Alongside the free pedigree databases, there are a number of commercial services. However, although commercial in nature, several of them offer basic pedigree service free of charge and you can often search the trees of users without yourself making a payment, though you will almost always need to complete some form of registration. In some cases you cannot do a blanket search but only look for matches to people in your own tree, which means you need to submit a pedigree yourself to get any benefit from a site. I should say that, with the exception of Genes Reunited and MyHeritage, I have not subscribed to these sites and the information is based on that published on the site itself and not on my own testing of the facilities.

Genes Reunited

By far the most important of the pedigree databases for British family historians is Genes Reunited at <**www.genesreunited.co.uk**>. The site, launched in November 2002, is an offshoot from the very successful Friends Reunited, and is one of the most popular UK genealogy sites. In fact it was launched as Genes Connected but the name was changed in 2004 to make the link more obvious.

Currently Genes Reunited claims to have over 11 million members. Although this is fewer than most of the other services mentioned here, the site's UK focus means that it must have the largest number of British and Irish ancestors of any pedigree database. Another consideration is the connection with Friends Reunited, which suggests Genes Reunited probably contains many submissions from people who do not regard themselves as serious family historians and who are unlikely to use any of the other resources discussed in this chapter. It may, therefore, be particularly good for contacting reasonably close cousins, especially if there are recent branches of your family you have lost touch with. On the other hand, there are also going to be entries from people who put up a tree in a moment of enthusiasm but have since lost interest and won't reply to contacts. But if my own experience is anything to go by, this is one of the most useful contact sites for British and Irish pedigrees – I have had dozens of useful contacts over the years.

Although it is essentially a commercial service, you do not have to subscribe in order to enter or upload your pedigree, nor to carry out searches on the database (Figure 14-3), and as a non-subscriber your tree will be visible to others, who can then contact you. But you *do* need to be a subscriber in order to initiate contact with the person who submitted an individual you find a possible match with. Genes Reunited does not give you the email address of a submitter; instead you type in a message on the site and Genes Reunited actually sends it. This offers some measure of privacy protection, since subscriber email addresses are not visible on the site and are never given out. The Standard subscription is £20 per year, though there tends to be a reduction on renewals. There is also a Platinum subscription which includes unlimited access to the site's data collections described on p. 54. The site provides several message boards and there are brief articles for the novice genealogist.

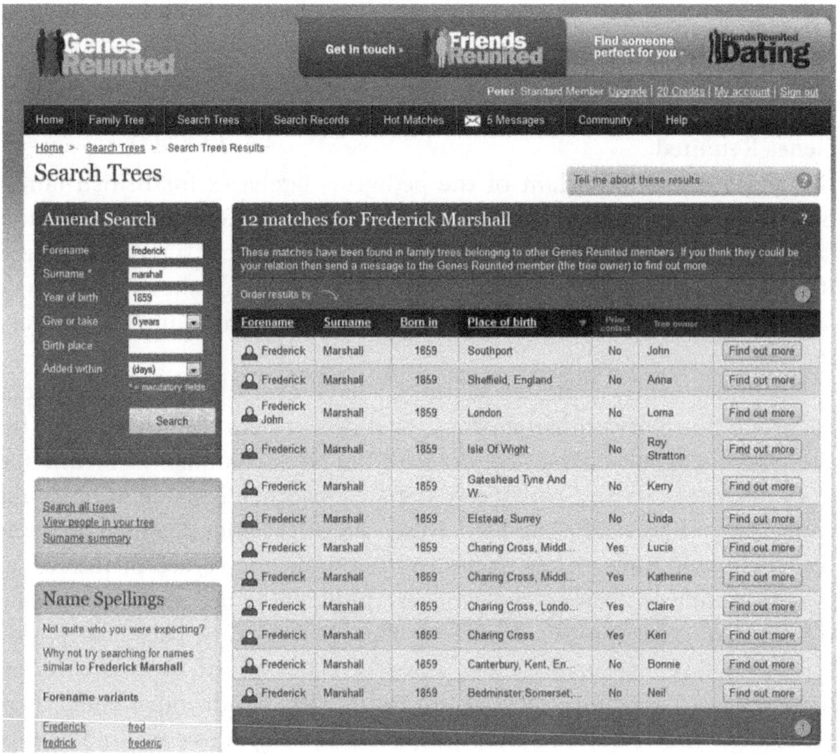

Figure 14-3 Search results in Genes Reunited

One irritating problem is that individuals are listed only with a birth year. Christening dates are not used, even in the absence of a birth date, so there will be no date given for that individual if there is only a christening date in the GEDCOM file.[1]

To help you find matches in the trees of others, the site has a 'Hot Matches' feature, which automatically compares people in your pedigree with all the others on the site. Some of its matching is very loose – you can find someone born in Cornwall matched with someone of the same name from Aberdeen – but it also shows you how many matches there are in another tree. Anything over 20 matches is likely to mean a genuine overlap with your own tree. In any case, you can contact the submitter to compare notes.

Other subscription services

The most popular of the commercial pedigree sites with an international scope is MyHeritage at <**www.myheritage.com**>. You can register and upload a tree of up to 250 individuals free of charge, while a monthly subscription of £4.50 or £7.95 allows you 2,500 or unlimited individuals respectively. If you are not already using any family tree software, the site's Family Tree Builder can be downloaded free of charge. There is no option to search other people's tree on the site, but the Smart Matches facility automatically lists possible matches to the individuals in your tree and gives you the possibility of contacting the submitter. Matching is not always exact – it matches my Tutt ancestors with some Tuttys, for example – but poor matches can be quickly rejected. Figure 14-4 shows the smart matches between my own tree and another, with potentially 71 individuals in common.

GeneaNet is a French-run site at <**www.geneanet.org**> which started in 1996. This allows you to upload a GEDCOM file, but it also has its own free software GeneWeb, which you can either use on the site or download. It has entries for almost 900 million individuals. You can use the site free of charge, but additional facilities are available as part of 'privileged membership' for €40 per year. These are listed at <**en.geneanet.org/privilege/**> and include some European civil registration records. For some entries you can only see the contact details, for others a pedigree is available. Its significant French user-base makes it a particularly useful if your family has connections with France.

---

1 A fudge to get round this, more or less, is to do a search and replace in your GEDCOM file before uploading it, substituting 1 BIRT for every occurrence of 1 CHR. This is preferable to entering a guessed-at birth year for everyone in your database, which is both bad practice *and* hard work.

Figure 14-4 MyHeritage Smart Matches

OneGreatFamily at <**www.onegreatfamily.com**> was launched in the summer of 2000 and now holds details of over 180 million ancestors. It has facilities for matching your own data with other trees on the site. Subscriptions are $9.95, $19.95 and $59.95 for one, three and twelve months respectively. There is also a seven-day free trial, though you have to give credit card information in order to sign up for this, and it automatically turns into a subscription if you do not cancel. To view pedigrees on the site you need to download the Genealogy Browser, which is a plug-in for your web browser. To find out more, it is worth reading Dick Eastman's very positive account of using the site at <**www.onegreatfamily.com/static-tpls/pr-eastman06-21-00.htm**>.

Among the other major services is Geni.com at <**www.geni.com**>, which has a limit of 100 people with its free account, while $5 and $7.95 per month allow 1000 and unlimited people in your tree respectively, as well as enhanced searching. Mytrees at <**www.mytrees.com**> offers a free account but this only allows you to share your tree with other family members, while the annual $120 subscription allows you to carry out more extensive searches and contact other users with matching records.

Record-based matching

Another approach to matching individuals is taken by LostCousins at <**www.lostcousins.com**> launched in September 2004. In this service, you don't submit general details of ancestors for matching, but the full reference to the record of an ancestor in census indexes. This approach means that matching will be very accurate and unambiguous, and unlike other types of pedigree database, you won't find vague or incomplete entries. The site started off matching entries just for the 1881 census index (see p. 87), but now includes the 1841 census for England and Wales, and the 1911 census for England, Wales and Ireland. You can also enter details from the 1880 US and 1881 Canadian censuses.

Because the site works by matching your entries to those of other users, you cannot use it without registering and submitting some entries of your own. Once you have entered details of an ancestor you will automatically receive an email when a match is found. You do not need to pay a subscription in order to register but, as with Genes Reunited, you cannot initiate contact unless you are a subscriber. Subscriptions cost £10 a year, with a joint subscription at £12.50.

Limitations

One point to bear in mind is that, with the exception of Genes Reunited and LostCousins, these databases are international in scope and only a minority of the individuals listed in them were born in the UK or Ireland. In fact, these collections feature predominantly ancestors born in the USA, so you should not be surprised if you do not find matches for your British and Irish ancestors in them, though it will be more likely if a branch of the family crossed the Atlantic.

The material on these sites consists entirely of submissions from individual genealogists. The completeness and accuracy of information is therefore highly variable, though some sites do basic checks in order to detect obvious errors, such as a death date earlier than a birth date. It is therefore best to regard these databases as a way of contacting people with similar interests, rather than as direct resources of data. It would be very unwise to incorporate such material directly into your own genealogy database without thorough checking. The obvious exception here is LostCousins, where matching is tied to a specific census record, and you don't have access to a pedigree as such.

In some cases checking will be simple; in others the information may be of little value, perhaps just a year and a country. In many of these databases there is no way to tell for certain which sources submitters have drawn their information from. But that does not lessen their advantage over the surname resources discussed earlier in this chapter, namely that they provide information about individuals and families, not just about surnames. This should make it fairly easy to establish whether the submitter is interested in the same family as you, something that may be particularly important for a common surname.

Rights

If you are intending to submit your own pedigree to one of these databases, there is one important issue you need to be aware of. On some sites, when you upload material to a database you grant the site unlimited rights to use the material as they see fit. This is not necessarily as unreasonable as it might sound. With free sites, for example, the site's administrators may have no way of contacting you if you change your email address and don't inform them. But it is perhaps understandable that some people baulk at allowing the fully commercial exploitation of their data without royalty by some sites, when they are already paying an annually renewable subscription attached to up-to-date contact details. For example, Genealogy.com's World Family Tree terms and conditions at <**www.genealogy.com/agreement.html**> assign to the company a 'royalty free, irrevocable, perpetual, non-exclusive, unrestricted, transferable, worldwide license' to exploit your material, which is not terminated if you cease to subscribe. On the other hand, it can be argued that since you yourself cannot exploit your pedigree commercially and you are gaining exposure of your pedigree to perhaps millions of potential contacts, you are not in practice suffering any disadvantage.

In any case, it is therefore important to check the terms and conditions of any pedigree database before you submit your own material.

Privacy

Another issue in placing your pedigree online is the privacy of living individuals. This is nothing to do with data protection, as is often thought – much of your information comes from public sources and there can be no legal bar in the UK to publishing it online, or indeed in any other medium, as long as it is accurate. The real issue is that people can be irritated or even distressed, understandably, if they find their family's personal details published online by someone else. Because of this, all the online pedigree databases have a policy on publishing information about living individuals. Here are some typical policies:

- RootsWeb has facilities which make it possible for you to remove living people entirely, or clean their entries of specific pieces of information, but it does not check your efforts.
- Genes Reunited has a condition that you do not include living individuals without their permission, but they do not check or modify the submitted data.

If you're going to submit to a site that doesn't have its own privacy protection mechanism, you will need to remove living individuals, or least their details. Most genealogy software programs have facilities for doing this: it may be an explicit option in the Export to GEDCOM process, or you may have to select those people who are to be included. If in doubt, excluding everyone born less than 100 years ago is a sensible policy. Ideally, exclude those born than less than 100 years ago only if they have no death or burial date.

There are a number of stand-alone tools for purging GEDCOM files of sensitive information – see the 'Privacy Issues' page on Cyndi's List at <www.cyndislist.com/software/privacy/>. Note that this is something that will also be necessary if you put a pedigree on a personal website (see Chapter 20). The issue of online privacy is discussed further on p. 403.

Genetics and DNA testing

With the advent of consumer genetic testing, there is now a scientific method of establishing kinship to add to the traditional historical methods. The ease and affordability of DNA testing has improved rapidly in recent years, giving rise to all sorts of expectations about what this can do for the genealogist. This is not the place to debate the merits and limitations of DNA testing in establishing or validating pedigrees, never mind the technicalities, but it clearly provides a method of confirming or establishing links between individuals.

The use of DNA testing in genealogy is not directly an internet development, but the web provides the mechanism by which the results of individual tests can be matched, and DNA projects for specific surnames rely on the internet for collaboration.

There is plenty of online information about DNA testing aimed at a genealogical audience. Useful introductory articles include:

- Genuki's 'DNA testing for Genealogy' page at <**www.genuki.org.uk/big/bigmisc/DNA.html**>;
- Megan Smolenyak's article on the BBC History site 'Genetic Genealogy – What Can It Offer?' at <**www.bbc.co.uk/history/familyhistory/next_steps/genetic_genealogy_01.shtml**>;
- Wikipedia's articles on 'Genetic genealogy' and 'Genealogical DNA test'.

Most of the companies offering DNA tests for genealogists have one or more FAQ pages with general information about DNA testing and genealogy. For example:

- Ancestry.com's DNA site has a comprehensive FAQ at <**dna.ancestry.com/faq.aspx**>.

- The World Families Network, which is linked to the commercial testing company Family Tree DNA, has useful set of FAQs at <www.worldfamilies.net/faq>, with explanations of Y-DNA and mtDNA at <www.worldfamilies.net/ydna> and <www.worldfamilies.net/about_mtDNA> respectively.

More in-depth coverage of the subject is provided by:

- The International Society of Genetic Genealogy (ISoGG) at <www.isogg.org>, a non-commercial organization whose mission is 'to advocate for and educate about the use of genetics as a tool for genealogical research, and promote a supportive network for genetic genealogists'. There is a section of the site for 'DNA-Newbies', which explains basic concepts and has a useful glossary at <www.isogg.org/course/glossary.htm>.
- Kerchner's DNA Testing & Genetic Genealogy Info and Resources Page at <www.kerchner.com/dna-info.htm>, which has a very thorough introduction to 'Genetics and Genealogy' at <www.kerchner.com/books/introg&g.htm> and a substantial glossary of DNA testing terminology at <www.kerchner.com/books/glossary.pdf>. It also has a very comprehensive set of links, including over a dozen testing companies.

The non-commercial sites mentioned generally have links to the websites of some of the many commercial DNA testing companies.

There are hundreds of DNA testing projects based on individuals with a shared surname, and many have a website and/or mailing list, which should give you the possibility of discussing whether there might be a connection, even if you're not involved in the project. The majority of these projects concentrate on Y-DNA, so are only relevant to the paternal line and only to male descendants. This does mean, however, that it is closely related to surname inheritance. MtDNA testing, which relates to the maternal line and is applicable to descendants of both sexes, is also available, though of course it cannot relate to a particular surname.

In a search engine, entering the phrase "surname DNA project" along with the surname of interest should be adequate to locate most of these. If you get no initial results, repeat the search but without the quote marks. There is a substantial list of projects at <www.worldfamilies.net/surnames/>. This site also provides free web pages for DNA projects.

If you have had a DNA test carried out, there are also sites where you can post the details of your own genetic markers in the hope of a match, or search for matches from the existing submissions, for example Mitosearch at <www.mitosearch.org>. This means that you do not need to be part of a surname project in order to make use of DNA testing. Ancestry.com's DNA site <**dna.ancestry.com**>, mentioned above, offers its own test kits and lets you upload test results from other services to try and find matches. FamilyTreeDNA hosts over 5,000 surname DNA projects, listed at <**www.familytreedna.com/projects.aspx**> and it also provides a free service Ysearch at <**www.ysearch.org**> which allows for the upload and comparison of test results from other testing services. SMGF (the Sorenson Molecular Genealogy Foundation) at <**www.smgf.org**> claims to be 'the foremost collection of genetic genealogy data in the world' and has a freely searchable genetic database with data from tens of thousands of participants, though you cannot actually upload results from companies other than their affiliate GeneTree.

There is a general mailing list devoted to this topic, GENEALOGY-DNA, details of which will be found at <**lists.rootsweb.ancestry.com/index/other/ DNA/GENEALOGY-DNA.html**>. RootsWeb also hosts mailing lists for a number of individual DNA projects, listed at <**lists.rootsweb.ancestry.com/ index/other/DNA/**>, including ISoGG's DNA-NEWBIE list.

Cyndi's List has a general page devoted to the subject under the heading 'Genetics, DNA & Family Health' at <**www.cyndislist.com/dna/**> and there are links to individual surname projects on the 'Surname DNA Studies and Projects' at <**www.cyndislist.com/surnames/dna/**>.

Royal, noble and notable families

The web has a wide range of resources relating to the genealogy of royal houses and the nobility, as well as to famous people and families. For initial orientation, Genuki's page on 'Kings and Queens of England and Scotland (and some of the people around them)' at <**www.genuki.org.uk/big/ royalty/**> provides a list of 'Monarchs since the Conquest, Kings of England, Kings of Scotland, Queens and a selection of the most notable Queens, Kings, Archbishops, Bishops, Dukes, Earls, Knights, Lords, Eminent Men, Popes and Princes'. There is also a detailed table of the Archbishops of Canterbury and York, and the Bishops of London, Durham, St David's and Armagh, from AD 200 to the present day at <**www.genuki.org.uk/big/eng/ History/Archbishops.html**>.

Cyndi's List has a page with over 200 links relating to Royalty and Nobility at <**www.cyndislist.com/royalty/**>.

The best place for genealogical information on English royalty is Brian Tompsett's Directory of Royal Genealogical Data at <**www3.dcs.hull.ac.uk/ public/genealogy/royal/catalog.html**>, which contains 'the genealogy of the British Royal family and those linked to it via blood or marriage relationships'. The site provides much information on other royal families, and includes details of all English peerages at <www3.dcs.hull.ac.uk/genealogy/royal/ **peerage.html**>. Another massive database devoted to European nobility will be found on the WW-Person site at <**www8.informatik.uni-erlangen.de/ html/ww-person.html**>. Family History UK has a family tree of the royal families of Europe at <**www.tree.familyhistory.uk.com/fproyal.php**>. Unlike most other examples, this data is stored in a database which can provide ancestor and descendant trees.

The official website of the royal family is at <**www.royal.gov.uk**>. The 'History of the Monarchy' section at <**www.royal.gov.uk/HistoryoftheMonarchy/ HistoryoftheMonarchy.aspx**> has pages devoted to each English, Scottish and UK monarch since the Dark Ages, though no actual pedigrees.

Burke's Peerage & Gentry at <**www.burkespeerage.com**> has a series of indented lineages of the rulers of England, Scotland and subsequently Great Britain among the free resources on its website at <**www.burkespeerage.com/ articles/roindex.aspx**> – see Figure 14-5. The main resources on the site are available via its subscription service, and comprise data from the published books, including:

- *Burke's Peerage & Baronetage*, 107th Edition, including Knights, Scottish Chiefs and Scottish Feudal Barons.
- *Burke's Landed Gentry*, 19th edition, The Kingdom in Scotland.
- *Burke's Landed Gentry*, 19th edition: The Ridings of York, The Principality of Wales, The North West, Irish Families, American families with British ancestry.

You can browse an index of Burke's Peerage and Gentry free of charge. This has links to brief entries for individuals and families, with full entries available only to subscribers. Subscriptions are £7.95 for 72 hours or £64.95 for a year, and you may find that your library has a subscription.

Darryl Lundy's thePeerage <**thepeerage.com**> is a very comprehensive site with details of the British peerage as well as many European royal families. Leigh Rayment's Peerage Page at <**www.leighrayment.com**> has comprehensive information on the peerages, baronetage, House of Commons, the orders of chivalry and the privy council. Genuki has part of *The English Peerage* (1790) online at <**www.genuki.org.uk/big/eng/History/ Barons/**>, with information on a number of barons and viscounts of the period.

Wikipedia has extensive coverage of royal and noble lineages of many countries. The easiest place to start from is the 'List of family trees' page. The Foundation for Medieval Genealogy's Medieval Lands project has 'narrative biographical genealogies of the major noble families which ruled

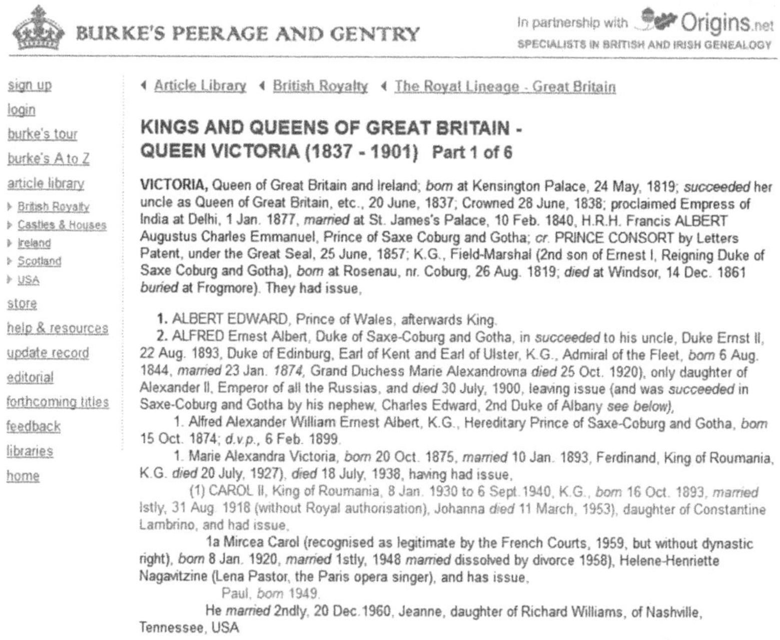

Figure 14-5 Burke's Peerage and Gentry: Descendants of Queen Victoria

Europe, North Africa and Western Asia between the 5th and 15th centuries' at <**fmg.ac/Projects/MedLands/**>.

Royal and noble titles for many languages and countries are explained in the 'Glossary of European Noble, Princely, Royal, and Imperial Titles' at <**www.heraldica.org/topics/odegard/titlefaq.htm**>.

You can also find information on the web on any other genealogically notable group of people. Thus, there are several sites devoted to the *Mayflower* pilgrims, including MayflowerHistory at <**www.mayflowerhistory.com/Passengers/passengers.php**>. Wikipedia has information on several generations of descendants of the *Bounty* mutineers in the 'Descendants of the Bounty Mutineers' article. The site also has an interesting article on 'Genealogical relationships of Prime Ministers of the United Kingdom'. The ancestry of the US presidents will be found on a number of sites, and <**www3.dcs.hull.ac.uk/genealogy/presidents/presidents.html**> provides a tree for each of them. The ancestry of Tim Berners-Lee, inventor of the World Wide Web, can be found at <**www.wargs.com/other/bernerslee.html**>. The Famous Family Trees Blog has links to many pedigrees of royalty and the famous at <**famousfamilytrees. blogspot.com**>. In March 2012, Roy Stockdill launched a 'Famous family trees' blog on Findmypast's blog site at <**blog.findmypast.co.uk/tag/roy-stockdill/**>. Mark Humphrys has a site devoted to the Royal Descents of

Famous People at <humphrysfamilytree.com/famous.descents.html>. There are, of course, countless sites devoted to biblical genealogies.

There are also plenty of pedigrees for fictional families online. For example, Wikipedia has family trees for the Simpsons, Harry Potter, the Sopranos and others, all linked from <en.wikipedia.org/wiki/Category:Fictional_family_trees>.

There are a number of relevant mailing lists including:

- GEN-ROYAL <lists.rootsweb.ancestry.com/index/other/Royalty-and-Nobility/GEN-ROYAL.html>
- BRITISH-NOBILITY <lists.rootsweb.ancestry.com/index/intl/UK/BRITISH-NOBILITY.html>
- PLANTAGENET <lists.rootsweb.ancestry.com/index/intl/UK/PLANTAGENET.html>
- SCT-ROYAL <lists.rootsweb.ancestry.com/index/intl/SCT/SCT-ROYAL.html>
- GEN-ANCIENT <lists.rootsweb.ancestry.com/index/other/Miscellaneous/GEN-ANCIENT.html>

Lists for further countries will be found at <www.rootsweb.ancestry.com/~jfuller/gen_mail_nobility.html>. Yahoo has over 200 discussion groups for royal and noble genealogy, listed at <dir.groups.yahoo.com/dir/Family___Home/Genealogy/Royal_Genealogies> (note the three underscores in the URL).

Clans

Some information on Scottish clans will be found among the surname resources discussed earlier in this chapter, but there is also more specific material online. The most comprehensive coverage of clans is provided by Wikipedia. It has a substantial 'Scottish clan' article, which links to a list of clans, and there are articles on many individual clans.

Another site with good coverage is Electric Scotland, which has a list of 'Official Scottish Clans and Families' at <www.electricscotland.com/webclans/clanmenu.htm> with links to information, albeit less copious than Wikipedia's, on the individual clans.

Both of these sites have clan maps, and there is a further map on the Scots Family site at <www.scotsfamily.com/clan-map.htm>. Of special interest because of its early date is Lizars' 1822 'Map of the Highlands of Scotland denoting the districts or counties inhabited by the Highland Clans' which is available on the National Library of Scotland site at <www.nls.uk/maps/scotland/thematic.html>.

A general mailing list is CLANS, details of which can be found at <lists.rootsweb.ancestry.com/index/intl/SCT/CLANS.html>, and RootsWeb has almost 200 mailing lists for individual clans, listed at <**lists.rootsweb. ancestry.com/index/intl/SCT/**>. However, even those for large and well-known clans seem to have few messages, so they are probably of less use than the lists devoted to the surnames. Rampant Scotland has a list of Scottish clan and family societies at <**www.rampantscotland.com/clans.htm**>.

You can expect to find copies of older books on the clans in the digital book archives discussed in Chapter 12. For example, *The Scottish Clans and their Tartans*, published by W. & A. K. Johnston around 1900, is available at the Internet Archive at <**www.archive.org**> and has colour plates of the tartans.

In 2009, the National Archives of Scotland launched the Scottish Register of Tartans at <**www.tartanregister.gov.uk**>. This is the official national repository of information on tartans, and the register includes the tartans of both clans and army regiments (see p. 149).

Wales

Recently, a large amount of information about the nobility of medieval Wales has appeared online thanks to two large, overlapping projects.

FamilySearch's new Community Tree site (see p. 231) has a 'Welsh Medieval Database Primarily of Nobility and Gentry', linked from <**histfam. familysearch.org/learnmore.php**>. The collection contains details of over a quarter of a million individuals and is largely based on digitizing the Welsh Genealogies compiled by the late Dr Peter Bartrum, covering the period 300–1500, along with a range of further sources. There is an article on this collection in the FamilySearch wiki at <**www.familysearch.org/learn/wiki/ en/Welsh_Families_Project**>.

Aberystwyth University has been running Project Bartrum to digitize Peter Bartrum's work. The home page for the project is at <**cadair. aber.ac.uk/dspace/handle/2160/4026**> and the online material includes scans of all the hand-drawn pedigrees and the typed index pages. At present the material is not easy to use if you are not already familiar with it. The 'Bartrum Collection' pages at <**cadair.aber.ac.uk/dspace/handle/2160/4691**> contain the pedigree images, each individually titled. To find which tree any individual is in, you need to use the 'Bartrum Indexes' at <**cadair. aber.ac.uk/dspace/handle/2160/6517**> and read through the images of the index pages. Unfortunately, there is no link directly from the indexes to the pedigrees.

Another site for medieval Welsh genealogy is the Center for the Study of Ancient Wales <**www.ancientwalesstudies.org**>.

Heraldry

Heraldry is intimately connected with royal and noble families, and there is quite a lot of material relating to it on the web. The authoritative source of information about heraldry in England and Wales is the website of the College of Arms at <**www.college-of-arms.gov.uk**>. Its FAQ page deals briefly with frequently asked questions about coats of arms. The SoG has a leaflet on 'The Right to Arms' at <**www.sog.org.uk/leaflets/arms.pdf**>.

For Scotland, the Lord Lyon King of Arms is the chief herald, with a website at <**www.lyon-court.com**>. The Public Register of All Arms and Bearings in Scotland has been digitized and is available on ScotlandsPeople (see p. 50), which gives information on these records at <**www.scotlandspeople.gov.uk/ content/help/index.aspx?r=554&1283**>.

Information on heraldry in Ireland will be found on the web pages for the Office of the Chief Herald on the National Library of Ireland's website at <**www.nli.ie/en/heraldry-introduction.aspx**>. There has been considerable uncertainty about the legal status of Irish arms granted after independence from Britain, and the issues are discussed in some detail in Sean J. Murphy's article 'An Irish Arms Crisis' at <**homepage.eircom.net/~seanjmurphy/ chiefs/armscrisis.htm**>.

Burke's Peerage and Gentry has its International Register of Arms online at <**www.armorial-register.com**>. This is not an official register and is not in any sense comprehensive – it contains only the arms of those who have paid to register them in the index. The site has a substantial list of heraldry societies.

The Heraldry on the Internet site at <**www.digiserve.com/heraldry/**> is a specialist site with a substantial collection of links to other online heraldry resources, and Cyndi's List has over 150 heraldry links at <**www.cyndislist.com/ heraldry/**>. The British Heraldry site at <**www.heraldica.org/topics/britain/**> has a number of articles on heraldry. The Heraldry Society will be found at <**www.theheraldrysociety.com**>, while the Heraldry Society of Scotland has a site at <**www.heraldry-scotland.co.uk**>.

For the meaning of terms used in heraldry, an online version of Pimbley's 1905 *Dictionary of Heraldry* is at <**www.digiserve.com/heraldry/ pimbley.htm**>, and there is an online version of James Parker 's *A Glossary of Terms used in Heraldry* (1894) at <**www.heraldsnet.org/saitou/parker/**>. Burke's Peerage has a 'Guide to Heraldic Terms' taken from the 106th edition of *Burkes's Peerage & Baronetage* at <**www.burkespeerage.com/articles/ heindex.aspx**>. Google Books at <**books.google.com**> (see p. 184) has the full text of a number of older works on heraldry, including William Berry's 1810 *An Introduction to Heraldry* and Hugh Clark's 1775 *A Short Introduction to Heraldry*. The Internet Archive at <**www.archive.org**> has G. Harvey Johnson's 1912

Scottish Heraldry Made Easy and Arthur Charles Fox-Davies's *A Complete Guide to Heraldry* from 1909.

Biography

The *Oxford Dictionary of National Biography* is the definitive national reference work for the lives of notable people, and information on access to the online edition is given on p. 186. Its website at <**www.oxforddnb.com**> has some freely accessible material, linked from <**www.oup.com/oxforddnb/ info/freeodnb/shelves/**>, including biographies for notable brewery founders and gardeners. There is a free index which provides the name and dates of all those in the dictionary. There are also some quite substantial articles on groups of people who played an important role in British history, such as the Women's Social and Political Union, the Chartists and the Pilgrim Fathers, though these do not generally provide any genealogical information.

The entire first edition of the DNB (1885–1900) is available in the Internet Archive. Given the haphazard cataloguing practices of the Archive, the easiest way to find the article you are interested in is to use the index of the individual volumes at <**onlinebooks.library.upenn.edu/webbin/ metabook?id=dnb**>.

Undiscovered Scotland has biographical articles on around 500 notable Scots at <**www.undiscoveredscotland.co.uk/usbiography**>

The *Dictionary of Ulster Biography* was published in 1993 and all articles are available online at <**www.ulsterbiography.co.uk**>.

Locating living people

The surname lists and databases already discussed will put you in touch with other genealogists who have made their researches – or at least their research interests – public, but you can also use the internet to locate long-lost relatives or their descendants, or simply people with a particular surname.

Phone numbers

BT provides an online directory enquiry service at <**www.thephonebook. bt.com**> and this will give you an address, postcode and phone number. You need to give a location – either a town or the first part of a postcode – so you cannot do a national search. Also, your search will fail if it gives too many results, so a search on surname only may not work if it is a common one and/or the location is too broad, e.g. a large city.

The internet is particularly useful for foreign phone numbers, since only a small number of major reference libraries in the UK have a full set of international directories. 192.com has links to many overseas telephone directories at <**world.192.com**>.

Historical telephone directories for the UK are available at Ancestry and are described on p. 192.

Electoral registers

The electoral registers are a traditional resource for establishing who lives at which address, and therefore for tracing living people. The problem with the printed registers is, of course, that they are not indexed, so without an approximate idea where someone lives, you need to have a great deal of time to spare to trace living people. However, the modern electronic register does not have this drawback. The registers are held by local authorities and can be inspected at various locations in the area, but are not made available online. However, an edited version can be searched online on a number of commercial websites, including:

- 192.com at <**www.192.com**> (6 credits for £11.94);
- TraceSmart at <**www.tracesmart.co.uk**> (5 credits valid for one month £3.49);
- The UK Electoral Roll at <**www.theukelectoralroll.co.uk**> (unlimited searches, 14-day subscription for £3.25);
- Ukroll.com at <**www.ukroll.com**> (unlimited searches for three days for £5.50).

The prices given here are those for the cheapest packages, but there are other schemes available for those with a need for heavier use, and these cost much less per search. TraceSmart has a 'peopletracer' service at <**www.peopletracer.co.uk**> from £7.99 for 25 credits which includes eight years of electoral rolls along with phone books and land registry information.

You can find other similar services by conducting a search on "UK electoral register" on any search engine.

Apart from the cost, the other limitation with these services is that individuals can request that their details are excluded from the commercially available data and obviously will not be findable by this method.

While the electoral rolls give more details than the phone book in that the full name is included, this will not necessarily be sufficient to identify a specific individual unless he or she has an uncommon name or you know the names of other family members who are likely to be living at the same address. But 192.com's free phone book search includes in its results full names of all the adults living in a particular household, which will often help you identify the individual you want.

Most of these sites also include civil registration searches, though since this data is freely available elsewhere (see Chapter 5) it is not worth subscribing just for this.

Two of the genealogy data services offer similar services, though in each case they are separate pay-per-view services and not included in any subscription. Findmypast (see p. 53) has a 'Living Relatives' section. The Electoral Roll search costs 10 units (less than 70p) and gives full details of all matching individuals. The advanced search includes an option to specify other people living in the same household. Ancestry UK's Living Relative Search at <www.livingrelativesearch.co.uk> draws on phone books, electoral rolls and property records. An initial search is free but to see full details requires payment, from £5.95 for a single search or £11.95 for 10 searches.

Social networking

Social networking sites such as Facebook at <www.facebook.com> can, in principle, be used for locating people, though you will generally need to be a member yourself in order to identify and contact people. But with just a name to go on, there's little chance of being sure you have the right person, though if you're lucky, there will be a photograph, which may help (though people do not always use a current photo of themselves). Also, checking the list of someone's friends will often reveal the names of other family members, which may be sufficient to identify the right person if you already have them in your family tree.

Probably the most useful site for the UK is Friends Reunited at <www.friendsreunited.com>, which is designed to put people in touch with former schoolmates or work colleagues. If you know where someone went to school or where they used to work, the problem of identifying the right person is greatly reduced.

There are so many people online with identical names that, apart from social networking sites, you are on the whole unlikely to be able to find an individual unless:

- they have a very unusual name;
- they have a personal website;
- they are listed on the website of a company, institution or organization they are employed by or otherwise connected with or
- you can identify them as the sender of a message to a mailing list or discussion forum.

Adoption and child migration

While the resources discussed so far can be useful for tracing people when you know their names, they may be of little use in the case of adoption or child migration, and you will need to go to sites specifically devoted to these issues.

Basic information about adoption in England and Wales will be found on the Directgov site at <**www.direct.gov.uk/en/Governmentcitizensandrights/Registeringlifeevents/Birthandadoptionrecords/Adoptionrecords/**>, while GROS has a page on 'Adoption in Scotland' at <**www.gro-scotland.gov.uk/regscot/adoption.html**>. For Ireland, a National Adoption Contact Preference Register was launched early in 2005 – details at <**aai.gov.ie/index.php/information-a-tracing/contact-preference-register.html**>. The Searching in Ireland site has a page for Irish-born adoptees at <**www.netreach.net/~steed/search.html**>.

Adoption Search Reunion is a site run by the British Association for Adoption and Fostering at <**www.adoptionsearchreunion.org.uk**>, with a range of useful resources. Probably the most important is the Locating Adoption Records database, which helps identity places where you may find relevant records. You can search by the name or location of a maternity or other home, by the organization or local authority which arranged the adoption, and even by the name of a staff member. The site also offers advice about making contact and links to other useful websites.

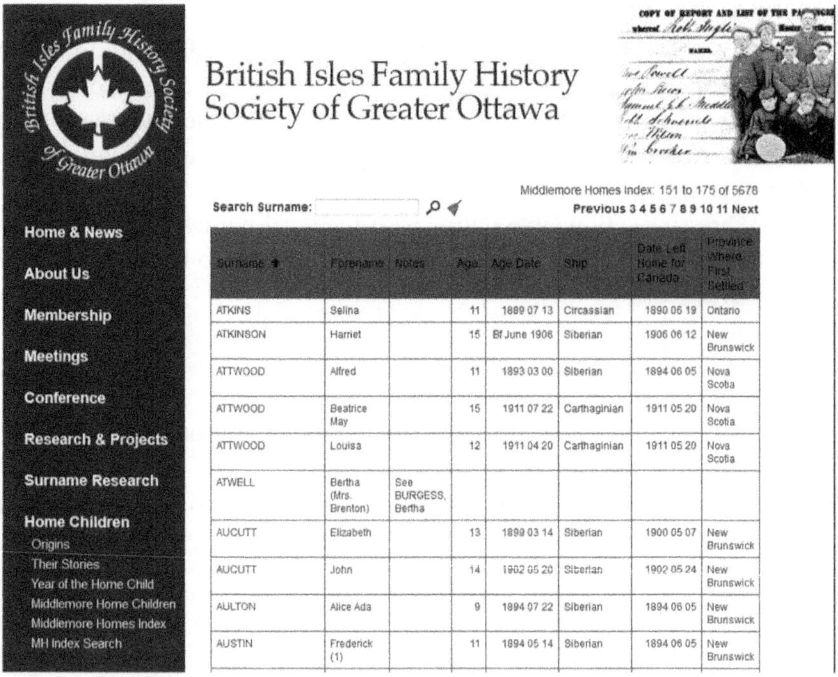

Surname	Forename	Notes	Age	Age Date	Ship	Date Left Home for Canada	Province Where First Settled
ATKINS	Selina		11	1889 07 13	Circassian	1890 06 19	Ontario
ATKINSON	Harriet		15	Bf June 1906	Siberian	1906 06 12	New Brunswick
ATTWOOD	Alfred		11	1893 03 00	Siberian	1894 06 05	Nova Scotia
ATTWOOD	Beatrice May		15	1911 07 22	Carthaginian	1911 05 20	Nova Scotia
ATTWOOD	Louisa		12	1911 04 20	Carthaginian	1911 05 20	Nova Scotia
ATWELL	Bertha (Mrs. Brenton)	See BURGESS, Bertha					
AUCUTT	Elizabeth		13	1899 03 14	Siberian	1900 05 07	New Brunswick
AUCUTT	John		14	1902 05 20	Siberian	1902 05 24	New Brunswick
AULTON	Alice Ada		9	1894 07 22	Siberian	1894 06 05	New Brunswick
AUSTIN	Frederick (1)		11	1894 05 14	Siberian	1894 06 05	New Brunswick

Figure 14-6 BIFHSGO index of Home Children

The Salvation Army offers a Family Tracing Service and their website has a section devoted to family tracing, with a home page at <**www1.salvationarmy.org.uk/familytracing**>, covering the whole of the British Isles.

The UK Birth Adoption Register at <**www.ukbirth-adoptionregister.com**> is a site for adoptees and birth parents to register their interest in making contact. A one-off registration fee of £10 is required to place your details in the database. The UK Adoption Tracing Service has an Adoption Contact Register at <**www.adoptiontrace.co.uk**> with a £3 registration fee.

Cyndi's List has a page devoted to Adoption resources worldwide at <**www.cyndislist.com/adoption/**>, and there is an extensive list of mailing lists relating to adoption at <**www.rootsweb.ancestry.com/~jfuller/gen_mail_adoption.html**>, though many of these are for specific localities.

For child migration, the Department of Health has a very comprehensive leaflet 'Information for former British child migrants'. This provides information on the various agencies involved in child migration from the UK (and the relevant dates), with contact details and links to websites. Unfortunately it has a 106-character URL, so start from the DoH home page at <**www.dh.gov.uk**> and search for 'child migrants'. A Select Committee report from 1998 on 'The Welfare of Former British Child Migrants' at <**www.parliament.the-stationery-office.co.uk/pa/cm199798/cmselect/cmhealth/755/75504.htm**> provides a historical perspective.

The National Archives' wiki has an article on the Children's Overseas Reception Board at <**yourarchives.nationalarchives.gov.uk/index.php?title=Children%27s_Overseas_Reception_Board**>, responsible for evacuating 2,664 children overseas in 1940.

Government sites in the receiving countries are also likely to have information relating to local records. For example, the National Archives of Australia has a fact-sheet on 'Child migration to Australia' at <**www.naa.gov.au/collection/fact-sheets/fs124.aspx**>. Library and Archives Canada has an online database of Home Children (1869–1930) at <**www.collectionscanada.gc.ca/databases/home-children/**>.

Genealogy World has some material relating to the Children's Friend Society, which sent children to the Cape of Good Hope in the 1830s at <**www.genealogyworld.net/immigration/children/children.html**> with details of many of the children.

The Child Migrants Trust is a charity which helps re-unite families of former child migrants. Its website at <**www.childmigrantstrust.com**> provides a history of child migration and links to websites of many organizations for former child migrants. BRITISHHOMECHILDREN is a mailing list for 'anyone who has a genealogical interest in the 100,000 British

Home Children who were emigrated to Canada by 50 child care organizations 1870–1948' – details at <**lists.rootsweb.ancestry.com/index/intl/CAN/ BRITISHHOMECHILDREN.html**>. The British Isles Family History Society of Greater Ottawa at <**www.bifhsgo.ca**> has general information about Home Children and a database of child migrants 1872–1932 (see Figure 14-6).

A more general resource which may be of use is Look4them at <**www.look4them.org.uk**>, an umbrella site run by nine organizations involved with tracing missing people. LookUpUK at <**www.lookupuk.com**> is a site for tracing both missing persons and those separated by adoption, with a number of message boards and other resources.

15

GEOGRAPHY

Maps and gazetteers are essential reference tools for family historians, and while the internet cannot offer the wealth of material available in reference libraries and record offices, let alone the British Library Map Library (see p. 274), there are nonetheless many useful resources online. Historical maps are quite rare, and the web has proved an ideal medium for making them much more readily accessible, with the result that family historians are now able to make more use of them.

Good starting points for online maps and gazetteers are the 'Maps & Geography' page on Cyndi's List <**www.cyndislist.com/maps/**> and the Genuki county pages.

Gazetteers

While your more recent ancestors perhaps all came from places you are familiar with, the more lines you follow the more likely you are to come across somewhere you've never heard of or don't know the location of. Although your local library will have some suitable gazetteers to help you locate them, you will almost certainly find that online sources offer a much wider range of information and are, of course, much more readily to hand. Historical gazetteers are useful sources of information about these places in previous centuries.

Modern

The Gazetteer of British Place Names at <**www.gazetteer.co.uk**> includes 50,000 names, and provides details about the present-day administrative divisions a place belongs in, but also gives the historical county. It includes 'commonly accepted spelling variations of place-names including an exhaustive coverage of Welsh and Gaelic spellings'. It gives OS grid references but, unlike many online gazetteers, does not link to online maps.

The National Gazetteer of Wales at <**homepage.ntlworld.com/geogdata/ ngw/**> is a similar site, covering around 6,000 Welsh places, with Welsh and English names.

Although created for a very different purpose, Archaeology UK's UK Placename Finder at <**www.digital-documents.co.uk/archi/ placename.htm**> may be useful. It includes around 160,000 places and provides a sophisticated search facility. Search results show counties and grid references with a link to two general mapping sites discussed below, Bing Maps and Streetmap.

The most comprehensive gazetteer of the UK is that of the Ordnance Survey, which claims to have 250,000 place-names. However, it is of limited usefulness – it will locate a place on the Ordnance Survey map, but provides no further information. There are no obvious links to it from the OS home page at <**www.ordnancesurvey.co.uk**>, but it will be found at <**www.ordnancesurvey.co.uk/oswebsite/freefun/didyouknow/**>. Its only real advantage is that it has a very broad concept of 'place' and covers not only towns and villages, but even many individual farms and named geographical features.

Wikipedia can also be used as a gazetteer, though it is impossible to tell how many places are covered. Any article on a UK place includes a grid reference which links to a Geohack page with links to online maps for the place in question on all the main mapping sites including Google Maps, the Ordnance Survey and A Vision of Britain (see below).

Historical

Of course, a significant problem for the family historian in using present-day gazetteers is that the information they give may not be appropriate for earlier historical periods. In particular, the county name given for a place will be its modern administrative county, and for places now in a unitary authority or a post-1974 county a modern gazetteer will not even indicate which county a place used to be in. For this reason historical gazetteers are an essential online resource. But more than that, many historical gazetteers provide contemporary descriptions, which can be helpful in understanding the places where your ancestors lived.

The most important historical gazetteer for England, Wales and Scotland is A Vision of Britain through Time at <**www.visionofbritain.org.uk**>, which describes itself as 'A vision of Britain between 1801 and 2001. Including maps, statistical trends and historical descriptions'. The site provides many different types of material – descriptive, statistical, graphical – and will take some time to explore, but the starting point is the 'Find a place' search. Figure 15-1 shows a typical page for a place (Tickhill, Yorkshire).

Gazetteer entries are drawn from three Victorian descriptive gazetteers:

- John Marius Wilson's *Imperial Gazetteer of England & Wales* (1872)
- Frances Groome's *The Ordnance Gazetteer of Scotland* (1885)
- John Bartholomew's *Gazetteer of the British Isles* (1887)

Figure 15-1 A Vision of Britain

The Bartholomew descriptions are fairly concise (particularly for smaller places), while Wilson's are more extensive. Note that the Bartholomew gazetteer includes the present-day Republic of Ireland. To access the entries from these, you need to go to the Descriptive gazetteer search at <www.visionofbritain.org.uk/descriptions/> (or via the 'Expert search' link on the home page). The 'Travel writing' area comprises the complete texts of many important works of travel literature, mainly from the eighteenth century, but including some earlier works.

The 'Units and statistics' link leads to a page listing the various administrative units the place has been part of and the available statistics for each of them. For an individual village, for example, it will tell you not only which county it is (or rather was) in, but the Poor Law or Registration District, any ancient hundred it was part of, and the like. This is useful for identifying which records may have information on a place. For the genealogist, the most useful of these units will probably be the 'civil parish and ancient parish' and information about it will be found by following the 'AP/CP' link on the 'Units and statistics' page. The parish pages have links to population and other statistics derived from the cenuses, a map showing the parish boundaries, historical descriptions and other information. The site's historical maps are discussed later in this chapter.

Genuki has a number of historical gazetteers which are useful for family history. The main Genuki Gazetteer at <**www.genuki.org.uk/big/Gazetteer/**> is intended in the first instance to make it easier to locate the appropriate page on Genuki for information about a particular place. It includes the locations of nearly all the civil parishes at the time of the start of civil registration in 1837 (which form the basis of Genuki's town and parish pages), but smaller places are gradually being added and for some counties coverage is *very* comprehensive, e.g. Cornwall with over 13,000 places. You can either view the locations of matching places on a Google map or as a list (see Figure 15-2). From the latter, you can go to a fuller gazetteer entry or the relevant Genuki parish or township page.

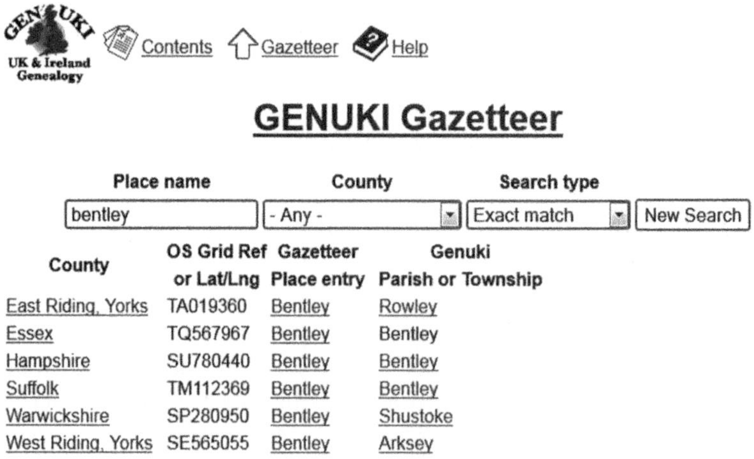

GENUKI Gazetteer

Place name	County	Search type	
bentley	- Any - ▾	Exact match ▾	New Search

County	OS Grid Ref or Lat/Lng	Gazetteer Place entry	Genuki Parish or Township
East Riding, Yorks	TA019360	Bentley	Rowley
Essex	TQ567967	Bentley	Bentley
Hampshire	SU780440	Bentley	Bentley
Suffolk	TM112369	Bentley	Bentley
Warwickshire	SP280950	Bentley	Shustoke
West Riding, Yorks	SE565055	Bentley	Arksey

Figure 15-2 The Genuki Gazetteer: results for 'Bentley'

The Genuki Church Database at <**www.genuki.org.uk/big/churchdb/**> (see Figure 15-3) provides the locations of all churches within a given distance of a particular place (the default is three miles). Results link to the Genuki parish page, if there is one.

Genuki also has a searchable database of places in the 1891 census at <**www.genuki.org.uk/big/census_place.html**> (covering England, Wales and the Isle of Man only). The results give the county, district and sub-district, as well as the piece number and the LDS microfilm number. There is a limited wildcard facility, in that you can truncate a name to as little as the first four letters. If you type in the name of a district or sub-district, you get a list of all the places it comprises, with their piece numbers.

Another useful tool is Darren Wheatley's Parish Finder at <**www.parishfinder.co.uk**>. This allows you not only to search for the county and grid reference for any parish, but you can also search for neighbouring parishes and discover the distances between parishes.

In addition to the descriptive gazetters at A Vision of Britain, the online book archives discussed in Chapter 12 have digitized copies of many similar works. The following are just some of those worth searching for:

- Steven Whatley, *England's Gazetteer* (1751)
- Robinson & Baldwin, *The Complete Gazetteer of England and Wales* (1775)
- *Crosby's Complete Pocket Gazetteer of England and Wales* (1815)
- James Bell, *A New and Comprehensive Gazetteer of England and Wales* (1835)
- A Fullarton, *The Parliamentary Gazetteer of England and Wales* (1851)
- *Leonard's Gazetteer of England and Wales* (1860)

Note that many of these works are in several volumes, digitized individually.

Figure 15-3 The Genuki Church Database: Bentley, Hampshire

Scotland

While Scotland is included in A Vision of Britain and Genuki, there is also a major project for a specifically Scottish gazetteer based at the University of Edinburgh and accessible at <**www.scottish-places.info**>, the Gazetteer for Scotland. This is described as 'vast geographical encyclopaedia, featuring details of towns, villages, bens and glens from the Scottish Borders to the Northern Isles'. Although there is a 'Places' search, this cannot actually be used to find towns and villages. Instead you need to use the 'Any Word' search at <**www.scottish-places.info/anyword.html**>, and select parishes and settlements. This takes you to a brief descriptive entry for the place with details of location, and a link to a very schematic county map. For a parish, it indicates all the settlements within the parish, each of which has its own description. Alternatively you can browse using the map by following the 'Maps and Places' link on the home page. The site includes many entries from Groome's *Ordnance Gazetteer of Scotland* (1882–85) – a 'quill and parchment' icon on a place entry indicates a link to an extract.

The second edition of Groome's six-volume *A Gazetteer of Scotland*, published in 1896, is also available in two digitizations, one at <**www.gazetteer ofscotland.org.uk**> with a place-name search to locate a particular entry, and another on Electric Scotland at <**www.electricscotland.com/history/ gazetteer/**> with a browsable index.

The *Statistical Accounts of Scotland*, which provide extensive descriptions of Scottish settlements are discussed on p. 279.

Ireland

For Ireland, there are a number of online sources to help you locate historical places. The National Archives of Ireland has an OS Parish List Index at <**www.nationalarchives.ie/search/index.php?category=17&subcategory =145**> (or go to the Finding Aids page at <**www.nationalarchives.ie/search/ databases.html**> and follow the Ordnance Survey link). *The Irish Times'* Irish Ancestors site has a place-name search at <**www.irishtimes.com/ ancestor/placenames/**>. The IreAtlas at <**www.seanruad.com**> is a database of all Irish townlands, with details of the county and civil parish.

The Public Record Office of Northern Ireland has a 'Geographical Index of Northern Ireland' at <**www.proni.gov.uk/index/local_history/ geographical_index.htm**>, which lists counties, baronies, poor law unions, dioceses, parishes and townlands in the six counties. The index is only browsable, not searchable, but there are several different routes through the material to help you find a specific place. However, I couldn't find any way of getting a single listing of all the places with a particular name, apart from an alphabetical list of parishes at <**applications.proni.gov.uk/geogindx/ parishes/**>.

The Placenames Database of Ireland <**www.logainm.ie**> gives both the Irish and English names of a place, along with the co-ordinates and the administrative units into which a place falls. For larger places, street names are included, and the database also covers topographical features such as islands and valleys. Co-ordinates use the the Irish National Grid, which is explained briefly on Wikipedia's 'Irish national grid reference system' article, and this page has links to more detailed information.

Library Ireland has a transcription of Samuel Lewis's 1837 *Topographical Dictionary of Ireland* at <**www.libraryireland.com/topog/**> and the full work is available free of charge as a PDF file from the Ordnance Survey of Ireland online shop at <**shop.osi.ie/Shop/pdf/LewisTopographicalDir.pdf**>. The Irish Place Names database at <**www.irish-place-names.com**> is based on the *Index to the Townlands, and Towns, Parishes and Baronies of Ireland* published in 1861 after the census of Ireland carried out in 1851. This database lists all of the villages, towns and townlands that were enumerated, as well as the Barony, Civil Parish and Poor Law Union that each was located in.

With the exception of the 'Geographical Index of Northern Ireland', all these resources cover the whole island of Ireland.

Counties and towns

As well as these national gazetteers, there are many resources for counties and larger towns. It is not possible here to give a comprehensive listing – the easiest way to find them is to go to the Genuki page for the relevant county at <**www.genuki.org.uk/big/**>. There are also many small-scale scans and transcriptions for individual places of material from historical gazetteers. The Genuki page for a county or for a particular town or village will normally start with a brief description taken from a nineteenth-century source. Trade directories, discussed on p. 189, will also give the location of a place and other information. For London, see p. 269.

Administrative geography

All towns and villages in the British Isles have a place in the administrative geography of the constituent counties, and this has not necessarily remained constant over the last few hundred years. A number of the gazetteers already mentioned include information on the administrative units to which towns and villages belong, most notably A Vision of Britain (p. 254). But there are also some resources specifically devoted to this issue, which is important for family historians because it has a bearing on where records are likely to be found.

Genuki provides a general overview of Administrative Regions and, as well as pages for the individual counties, has material on 'Local Government Changes in the United Kingdom' at <**www.genuki.org.uk/big/Regions/ UKchanges.html**> with detailed tables for England, Wales, Scotland and Northern Ireland. The situation in the Republic of Ireland is more straightforward as the pre-independence counties remain. The Gazetteer of British Place Names, mentioned above, has maps of the old counties as well as the new counties and unitary authorities at <**www.gazetteer.co.uk**>. It is also well worth looking at their 'Additional notes for historians and genealogists' at <**www.gazetteer.co.uk/section4.htm**>, which explains the difference between the historic counties, the 'registration counties' used by the GRO, and the nineteenth- and twentieth-century administrative counties and county boroughs.

If you are from outside the UK and are not familiar with the counties and other administrative divisions you will find Jim Fisher's page 'British Counties, Parishes, etc. for Genealogists' at <**www.jimella.me.uk/counties.cfm**> useful.

Where counties have changed their boundaries over the years, the individual Genuki county pages will provide relevant details. The complex set of changes which, in less than a hundred years, saw parts of the home counties, and indeed the whole of Middlesex, incorporated into the capital are dealt with on the Genuki London site at <**homepages.gold.ac.uk/genuki/LND/ parishes.html**>. Genealogists almost always refer to pre-1974 counties and any genealogical material on the internet is likely to reflect that. This is why there are no pages on Genuki for Tyne and Wear or the present-day divisions of Wales. But non-genealogical sites will tend to locate places in their current counties, even if the material is from the nineteenth century – a number of the sites with photographs discussed in Chapter 17 do this, for example.

The traditional pre-1974 counties are often referred to by three-letter abbreviations, usually referred to by genealogists as the Chapman County Codes, e.g. SFK for Suffolk. A list of these can be found on Genuki at <**www.genuki.org.uk/big/Regions/Codes.html**>. There is a brief account by Colin Chapman of the origin of the codes at <**www.lochinpublishing.org.uk/ chapman_cc.htm**>.

Overseas

Gazetteers may be even more important if you have ancestors who migrated. It is not possible here to cover individual countries outside the British Isles, but there are a number of places to look. As you would expect, Cyndi's List has links to many online gazetteers. They are included in the 'Maps & Geography » General Resources' page at <**www.cyndislist.com/maps/ general/**> under two distinct headings: 'Historical Maps, Atlases & Gazetteers' and 'National Gazetteers & Geographic Information', of which the latter has the most useful entries.

The most comprehensive world gazetteer is the Getty Thesaurus of Geographic Names Online at <**www.getty.edu/research/tools/vocabularies/ tgn/**>. Even for the UK this is useful, since it includes geographical, and some historical, information. However, it is not intended to be comprehensive, and concentrates on larger places. For example, it gives only one place in Ireland called Inch, while the Irish Ancestors site (see p. 258) lists a dozen.

The *Imperial Gazetteer of India* is discussed on p. 178.

If these resources fail to find your place, it is worth checking Wikipedia at <en.wikipedia.org>, which has many articles on individual places all over the world, and not just the major towns and cities. Otherwise, see whether there is a mailing list devoted to the country you are interested in – listed at <www.rootsweb.ancestry.com/~jfuller/gen_mail.html> – and post a query. There will almost certainly be people on the list with suitable reference works to hand or even local knowledge.

Modern maps

The OS website at <www.ordnancesurvey.co.uk> is the obvious starting point for any information about present-day mapping of the British Isles. This provides a facility called Get-a-map at <www.ordnancesurvey.co.uk/oswebsite/getamap/>, which allows you to call up a map centred on a particular place. You can search by place-name, postcode, or OS grid reference. Alternatively, you can just click on the map of the UK and gradually zoom in to your chosen area. The maps are free for personal use (including limited use on personal websites). The standard OS one-inch map is available, but there is also a 'ZoomMap' which shows more detail (individual houses), and is shown in Figure 15-4. Get-a-map requires you to install Microsoft Silverlight for your browser. You can print half-page maps free of charge but you cannot download maps as graphics except by doing a screenshot.

Figure 15-4 The National Archives in Get-a-map

A relatively unknown source of OS maps for England is the MAGIC (Multi-Agency Geographic Information for the Countryside) site at <**magic. defra.gov.uk**>, shown in Figure 15-5. The site is designed to provide information for countryside management, shown in a number of layers, over a base map, which is a monochrome modern OS map. MAGIC has a number of advantages over the Get-a-map service, though because this site is designed for specialist use, it is more complex to use than those designed for the general public. To access the maps, from the home page you need to choose Interactive Map, then choose Administrative Areas from the top field, and enter a place, postcode, or grid reference in the lower. There are many options once you are viewing a map. A Map Tools tab gives access to a range of tools, including the ability to identify an area, and to save a map as a GIF file. You can also bookmark the current view. Another useful feature of MAGIC is that it shows modern civil parish boundaries.

There are five main sites that provide free UK street maps. Streetmap at <**www.streetmap.co.uk**> allows searches by street, postcode, place-name, OS grid, Landranger grid, latitude/longitude or telephone code. Bing maps at <**www.bing.com/maps/**> offers similar facilities: the initial search option

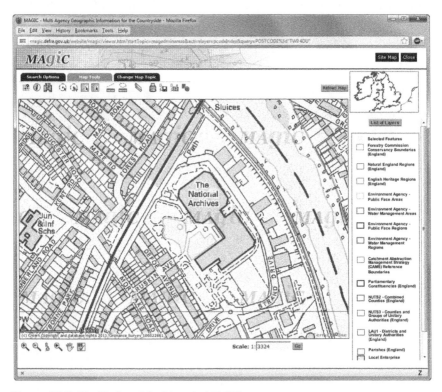

Figure 15-5 The National Archives in MAGIC

offers place or postcode, while the advanced search includes building and street. Google Maps at <**maps.google.co.uk**> shows only streets, and doesn't indicate even quite major landmarks (e.g. Canterbury Cathedral, Stonehenge). OpenStreetMap at <**www.openstreetmap.org**> is a non-commercial collaborative street mapping site, which includes not only street names, but also the names and locations of buildings like churches and pubs.

Genuki has instructions at <**www.genuki.org.uk/big/ModernLocations.html**> on 'How to find a present day house, street or place in the U.K. (or to find only the Post Code)' by using the Royal Mail site on Streetmap, Bing maps or Google Maps.

For aerial photographs, there are two main options. Bing provides photographs which, for the most populous parts of the country, are at a high level of detail. The site has an aerial view and a 'Bird's Eye' view (see Figure 15-6), which allows you to see the façades of individual buildings. Both are on the 'Bird's eye' menu. Google Maps has a satellite mapping option covering the whole country (and indeed the whole world), though resolution varies from area to area. There are various levels of zoom, options to rotate and tilt the images, and very quick panning. The same images can be viewed

Figure 15-6 Bing Maps: Bird's Eye view of Penny Lane, Liverpool

in Google Earth, a free downloadable viewer for satellite maps at <**earth. google.com**>. This has the advantage of an overlay showing roads and street names. It also offers a 'placemark' facility so that you can keep a permanent marker for places you want to view again. Because of the amount of data transferred, Google Earth requires a broadband connection and a fairly recent Windows PC. With an older machine you will need to check whether your graphics card is supported before downloading.

Historical Aerial Photography at <**www.oldaerialphotos.com**> is a commercial site offering aerial photographs for sale. Unfortunately, the site does not offer any preview – you have to select the location you want using the OS one-inch map. Photographs are supplied either as prints or as digital images on CD in TIFF format. A similar service is offered by UK Aerial Photos at <**www.ukaerialphotos.com**>, which includes aerial photos from the 1940s as well as from recent years. The photographs are JPEG images, which are sent by email. This site does offer a preview of the photo.

Historical maps

Ordnance Survey

The old Ordnance Survey maps are among the most useful for the family and local historian. Covering the whole country at a standard set of scales over a period of 170-odd years, with few exceptions they are the only maps which show, at the largest scale, every plot of land and every individual building.

A Vision of Britain is the best site for the old one-inch OS maps for England, Wales and Scotland. It has a full set of high quality scans covering the period up to 1948 from the Historical Maps page at <**www.visionofbritain.org.uk/ maps/**>. Unfortunately you cannot really download a whole map as the screen display is made up of numerous individual tiles, so the only way to have your own copy is to do a screenshot. The site also has two sets of Boundary Commision maps, based on the OS map, covering each county and the London metropolitan boroughs.

British History Online (p. 279) has one-inch maps for the whole of Great Britain and six-inch maps for around 20 major cities at <**www.british-history.ac.uk/map.aspx**>, which can be searched by place-name or postcode. Unfortunately the 25-inch OS maps of England and Wales do not seem to be publicly available online, though Higher Education users have access to them on the EDINA Digimap site at <**edina.ac.uk/digimap/**>.

But for Scotland, the National Library of Scotland has a comprehensive collection of OS maps online at <**maps.nls.uk/os/**>, including the 1st edition 25-inch maps, dating from 1855–1882. The site also has the Ordnance Survey town plans for 61 Scottish towns, made at the astonishing scales of 5 and 10 feet to the mile and dating from 1847–1895 with an extraordinary level of detail. Rather surprisingly, the site also has the one-inch maps for England and Wales, not linked from the OS map page mentioned, but accessible from <**maps.nls.uk/os/oneinch_new_popular_list.html**>.

Another site with nineteenth-century Ordnance Survey maps is the London Ancestor's collection of maps from the report of the 1885 Boundary Commission, which includes Ireland. There are maps for individual counties, and for the inner London boroughs. All are linked from the Old London Maps page at <**www.londonancestor.com/maps/maps.htm**> – the links for other areas are at the foot of the page. For Wales and Scotland, only a selection of counties and towns is included. For Ireland, it has these maps for 26 of the counties at <**www.londonancestor.com/maps/maps-ireland.htm**>. These are at a smaller scale of four inches to the mile but show barony and constituency boundaries.

Ordnance Survey Ireland at <**www.osi.ie**> has probably the most useful collection of Irish OS maps: alongside modern maps for the Republic, the nineteenth-century six-inch and 25-inch maps for the whole of Ireland are available at <**maps.osi.ie**> (the six-inch maps are provided in both greyscale and colour). You can only download maps via the online shop, though of course you can take a screenshot.

Ask About Ireland's Griffiths Valuation index at <**www.askaboutireland.ie/ griffith-valuation/**> (see p. 123) links index entries with contemporary OS map sheets. Unfortunately you can only see the map after entering a surname search, but if you enter a common Irish surname (Murphy, Kelly) and select a county, you can then navigate the map to find the right area. There is a slider at the top right of the map window which you can use to fade between the modern map and the historical map, making it fairly straightforward to find a place. You need to zoom in quite considerably to see any detail.

A long-standing commercial site for historical maps is Old-maps at <**www.old-maps.co.uk**>, which has scans of the First Series of six-inch OS maps of England, Wales and Scotland available for purchase, with a free preview. The initial place-name search brings up a modern map and you need to select a historical map from the scrolling list on the right of the window. This is too small to see any but the most obvious geographical detail, but clicking on 'Enhanced Zoom' brings a higher resolution image with a zoom button, which will allow you to blow up text and finer details.

Scotland

Scotland is particularly well served by historical map digitization projects. and there are two outstanding sites for maps of the country.

The National Library of Scotland, which has already been mentioned as a source of OS maps, has over 27,000 maps in its Digital Library at <**www.nls.uk/maps/**>. Among the others on the site are:

- Maps of the whole of Scotland from the mid 16th century on (around 1,300 maps)
- County maps of Scotland, 1580–1928
- 18th century military maps (see Figure 15-7)
- A number of estate maps, mainly for Edinburgh
- Aerial photographs from the 1940s

The quality of the scans is excellent.

The other major site is Charting the Nation at <**www.chartingthenation.lib. ed.ac.uk**>, which is run by the University of Edinburgh Library and has maps for the period 1550–1740. (In fact, there are some later maps, as the site includes The Board of Ordnance collection of military maps and architectural plans dating from around 1690 to about 1820.) While some of the maps are at too small a scale to be of any genealogical utility, there are others which are detailed enough to show individual streets and buildings. Unlike most map sites, rather than selecting a map and then having to load a map viewer, here you start the map viewer first and then select which map you want to look at. There are two different viewers, the second and more sophisticated of which requires the download and installation of a plug-in. The basic viewer can be slightly confusing at first, as it uses several different windows. It also requires your browser to have any pop-up blocker disabled – consult your browser's online help to find out how to do this.

Maps of the Scottish clans are discussed on p. 244.

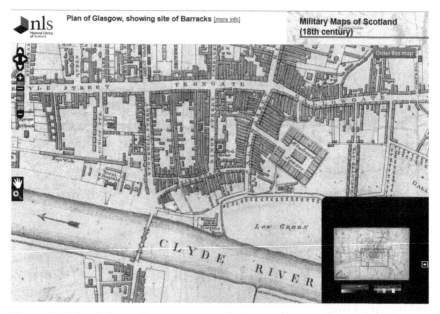

Figure 15-7 An eighteenth-century map of Glasgow (NLS)

Ireland

There are plenty of other maps of Ireland online, though the OS maps are probably by the most generally useful. Among the other offerings on the web, the University of Wisconsin-Madison has a Poor Law map, at <history.wisc.edu/archdeacon/famine/map.html>, University College, Cork has a collection of Irish county maps at <**www.ucc.ie/celt/ mapsireland.html**>, taken from an 1881 atlas, and the Perry-Castañeda Library has a 1610 town plan of Dublin at <**www.lib.utexas.edu/maps/ historical/dublin_1610_1896.jpg**>.

Irish Townland Maps at <**www.pasthomes.com**> is a commercial site offering maps of Irish townlands from the 1830s. An annual subscription costs $25, which allows you to browse the site, and you can then purchase maps at two different resolutions. Maps are provided in PDF format, and two sample maps show the size and resolution available.

Counties and towns

Many institutions and individuals have scanned classic historical maps and map editions. Those covering whole countries tend not to be very useful for genealogists because of their small scale, but this is not the case for maps of individual counties and towns.

The most extensive volunteer-run site is Genmaps at <**freepages. genealogy.rootsweb.ancestry.com/~genmaps/**>, which covers England, Wales and Scotland, with an enormous collection of maps for the counties, as well as many for individual towns and cities. The site doesn't give a figure for the total number of maps available, but it must be a couple of thousand – there are 200 just for Yorkshire, and even Rutland is represented by 40 maps. Genmaps also has an extensive collection of links to other historical map sites, including those of several dozen commercial map dealers, many of whom have low-resolution scans on their sites.

Other projects devoted to individual map collections include Tom Arnold's scans of Samuel Lewis' county maps of Wales and Ireland dating from around 1840. These are linked from <**homepage.ntlworld.com/ tomals/index2.htm**>. John Speed's early seventeenth-century maps of around 30 English towns and cities (plus Edinburgh) have been digitized by Professor Maryanne Horowitz of Occidental College, Los Angeles, and are available at <**faculty.oxy.edu/horowitz/home/johnspeed/**>. The proof versions of Speed's county maps have recently been digitized by Cambridge University Library and posted online at <**www.lib.cam.ac.uk/deptserv/ maps/speed.html**>. Maproom.org has maps from Cary's *Traveller's Companion* of 1790, showing main roads and distances, at very high resolution, at <**www.maproom.org/00/07/**>. There are also maps from some more modern printed works which are likely to be of interest. For example, Alan Gresley has scanned the town plans from the 1910 edition of Baedeker's *Great Britain Handbook for Travelers* at <**contueor.com/baedeker/great_britain/**>.

Mapseeker is a commercial site with a collection of historical maps under the heading 'Genealogy Map Resources' at <**www.mapseeker.co.uk/genealogy/**>. Particularly useful are the city maps for Birmingham, Edinburgh, Liverpool and Manchester. There are good-quality scans of a section of maps viewable free of charge, and many more are available for purchase.

There is no online map collection from the British Library, though the BL's Images Online website at <**www.imagesonline.bl.uk**> includes some digitized maps. These can be found by selecting the 'Maps and Landscapes' link from the Subject Index. The scans are only intended to enable you to make a purchase and are not high enough resolution to use in their own right. There is also an extensive range of supporting material on maps in the 'Help for researchers' area of the site at <**www.bl.uk/reshelp/findhelprestype/maps/**>, including articles on the various series of Ordnance Survey maps, useful background to some of the sites mentioned above.

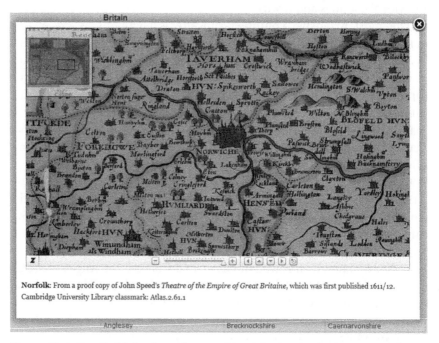

Norfolk: From a proof copy of John Speed's *Theatre of the Empire of Great Britaine*, which was first published 1611/12. Cambridge University Library classmark: Atlas.2.61.1

Figure 15-8 Detail of John Speed's map of Norfolk (Cambridge University Library)

The National Library of Wales's 'Digital Mirror' has maps from Thomas Taylor's 1718 work *The Principality of Wales exactly described*, the first atlas of Wales, at <**www.llgc.org.uk/index.php?id=132**>.

In addition to the sections for individual counties on Genmaps, there are many sites with map collections for individual counties and towns.

The University of Portsmouth's Geography department hosts two county collections, each with a very comprehensive range of historical county maps going back to the sixteenth century:

- Old Hampshire Mapped at <**www.geog.port.ac.uk/webmap/hantsmap/ hantsmap/hantsmap.htm**>
- Old Sussex Mapped at <**www.envf.port.ac.uk/geo/research/historical/ webmap/sussexmap/sussex.html**>

For County Durham, Pictures in Print at <**www.dur.ac.uk/ picturesinprint/**> is a collaborative project between the British Library and the various holders of map archives in Durham to produce an online catalogue for the maps of the county along with digital images. To view the images, you will need to download a plug-in (it downloads automatically for Internet Explorer, but may need to be manually installed for other browsers). There are several different search categories, of which the place search is likely to be the most useful. The subject search is also useful, though it is better to select from the list of subject index terms rather than try and guess the subject headings.

Lancashire has a wide selection of OS maps for the county at a variety of scales at <**www.lancashire.gov.uk/environment/oldmap/**>, covering the period from the First Series up to the 1950s, along with some older county maps.

A particularly good site is Cheshire's E-mapping Victorian Cheshire at <**maps.cheshire.gov.uk/tithemaps/TwinMaps.aspx**>, which allows you to compare a nineteenth-century map of an area (including the 1840s tithe maps) with a modern map. Figure 15-9 shows Tranmere in the tithe and modern maps. (Since tithe maps are primary sources for genealogists they are discussed in more detail in Chapter 8 on p. 120.)

London

There is an enormous wealth of online maps for London, many of which show the names of individual streets. Genmaps has scans of over 170 historical maps, plans and panoramas of London at <**freepages.genealogy. rootsweb.ancestry.com/~genmaps/genfiles/COU_Pages/ENG_pages/ lon.htm**> from the 1560s to 1920, including John Roque's detailed 24-sheet map of 1746 and many plans of City wards. The site also has many county maps for Middlesex, though these are mostly not at the same level of detail.

Another site with a range of important and useful maps is MOTCO, with historical maps and panoramas of London from 1705 onwards at <www.motco.com/map/>. Some maps have place indexes – for example Stanford's 1862 Library Map of London and its Suburbs has an index to around 5,000 streets, with a link to the relevant portion of the map. MAPCO has a number of the most detailed maps of the capital at <mapco.net/london.htm>, many at exceptionally high resolution.

The Collage site at <collage.cityoflondon.gov.uk> includes many maps and plans among its 20,000 or so images, mainly drawn from the Guildhall Library's Print Room. Particularly useful is the place search, which links to plans of individual City wards and parishes. There are also many views of individual streets, as well as insurance plans showing the locations of individual buildings. High resolution digital files of the images can be purchased online.

If you are trying to find a London street mentioned in a census but which no longer appears on the A–Z, the Lost London Streets site will be worth looking at. This gives an A–Z reference with details of what happened to the street. It covers over 3,500 streets that have undergone a name change or have disappeared altogether over the last 200 years. Unfortunately the original site was closed down a few years ago, but a copy of all the pages is available on the Wayback Machine: <members.aol.com/WHall95037/london.html> (11 August 2005).

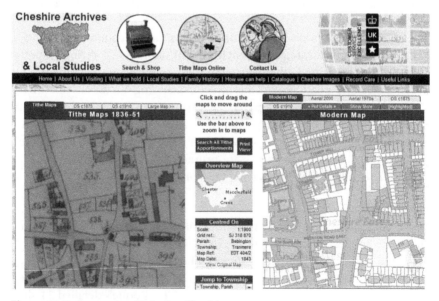

Figure 15-9 E-mapping Victorian Cheshire

GenDocs' Victorian London Street index will be found <**homepage. ntlworld.com/hitch/gendocs/lon-str.html**>. For over 61,000 streets this gives a postal district or locality and metropolitan borough, but no more precise location. For an earlier period, The London Ancestor has a street index to W. Stow's 1722 *Remarks on London: Being an Exact Survey of the Cities of London and Westminster...* at <**www.londonancestor.com/stow/ stow-strx-all.htm**>.

UCLA's Department of Epidemiology has an area of its website at <**www.ph.ucla.edu/epi/snow.html**> devoted to John Snow, one of the founders of the discipline, and this includes a number of London maps from the mid-nineteenth century. These have been scanned at very high resolution and are of exceptional quality.

One of the most famous London maps, Charles Booth's 1889 Map of London Poverty, is available on the LSE's Charles Booth site at <**booth. lse.ac.uk**>, which shows Booth's original map against a modern one (Figure 15-10).

For a more detailed survey of the most genealogically useful maps of London and the sites where they can be found, see my article 'London Maps Online' at <**www.spub.co.uk/articles/londonmaps.pdf**>.

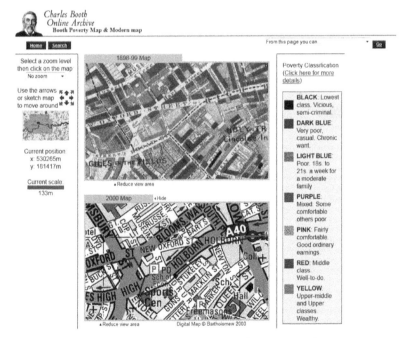

Figure 15-10 Charles Booth Online Archive, Booth Map & Modern Map

Parishes and administrative divisions

Maps of the ancient ecclesiastical parishes are among the most useful for the family historian.

FamilySearch has a dedicated map site at <**maps.familysearch.org**>, which currently has a single offering: English Jurisdictions 1851. Over a base map showing the counties of England, you can select one or more layers, each of which shows the boundaries for a particular type of administrative unit – Parish, County, Civil Registration District, Diocese, Rural Deanery, Poor Law Union, Hundred, Province, Division, and Probate. The ability to select more than one layer can be very useful: you can see which diocese a parish belongs to (see Figure 15-11) or which parishes are covered by a particular registration district. The 'Ordnance Survey' button at the top right of the window overlays the boundaties on a nineteenth-century OS map, so that you see the boundaries against the topography. Clicking on an individual parish produces a pop-up window with information about the parish or other unit.

For the civil parishes established in the nineteenth century, A Vision of Britain (p. 254) has a complete set of four-inch Ordnance Survey maps for England and Wales showing the Sanitary Districts and Civil Parishes. Larger-scale insets show the details of the much smaller parishes in cities

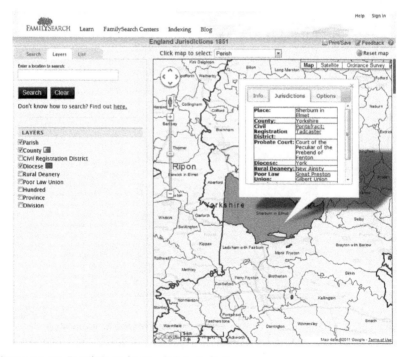

Figure 15-11 FamilySearch's English jurisdictions map

and large towns. From the maps page at <**www.visionofbritain.org.uk/ maps/**>, click on the 'Boundary maps' tab, then 'Ordnance Survey Sanitary Districts, showing Civil Parishes' and use the clickable map to zoom in on the county of interest. (See Figure 15-12.)

As mentioned in Chapter 7, the Church of England's A Church Near You site at <**www.achurchnearyou.com**> shows modern parish boundaries for each parish church, which for areas that are still rural should be a good guide to older boundaries (Figure 7-1, p. 99).

If you just need to see the location of a parish relative to the surrounding area, many Genuki county pages have a map showing the parishes within the county. Also, most family history societies have a map on their website showing the location of the parishes for their area. Look at Genuki's list of FHSs at <**www.genuki.org.uk/Societies/**>.

The Gazetteer of Scotland site (see p. 257) includes all the county maps – from the home page at <**www.gazetteerofscotland.org.uk/scotland/ctyindex. htm**> follow the link to 'Counties and County Maps'. These maps are quite hard to read, but they have been scanned at very high resolution and the six levels of zoom should allow you to see the details for smaller areas or you can download the image. The *New Statistical Accounts of Scotland* (see p. 257) has a number of parish maps but the most convenient way to access these is not via the Statistical Accounts website at <**edina.ac.uk/statacc/**>, but on Forrest Anderson's site at <**www.forrestdale.pwp.blueyonder.co.uk/ Parishes.html**>, where they are reproduced in good quality scans.

Figure 15-12 A Vision of Britain: Civil parish boundaries

Maps of Irish civil parishes, which match the Church of Ireland parishes, will be found on the Irish Ancestors site at <**www.irishtimes.com/ancestor/ browse/counties/civilmaps/**>, which has maps for the Roman Catholic parishes at <**www.irishtimes.com/ancestor/browse/counties/rcmaps/**>. For Counties Roscommon and Leitrim, there is a very comprehensive set of maps showing Roman Catholic and civil parishes, as well as Poor Law unions, at <**www.leitrim-roscommon.com/LR_maps.html**>.

Map collections

For guides to archival map collections, the British Cartographic Society's 'A Directory of UK Map Collections' at <**www.cartography.org.uk/ default.asp?contentID=705**> is a very comprehensive starting point. This is part of the site's 'Map Curators Toolbox' [*sic*], which contains much useful information about maps and mapping. The Toolbox home page is <**www.cartography.org.uk/default.asp?contentID=641**> (there seems to be no link to this from the BCS home page).

The catalogues of the archives and libraries mentioned in Chapter 13 include map holdings. The National Archives has a page on 'Looking for a map' at <**www.nationalarchives.gov.uk/records/looking-for-place/maps. htm**> and a research guide 'Maps for research' at <**www.nationalarchives. gov.uk/records/research-guides/maps-for-research.htm**>.

The national libraries all have significant map collections which are described on their websites:

- British Library: <**www.bl.uk/reshelp/bldept/maps/maplibover/ mapliboverview.html**>
- National Library of Scotland: <**www.nls.uk/collections/maps/**>
- National Library of Wales: <**www.llgc.org.uk/index.php? id=introduction3**>
- National Library of Ireland: <**www.nli.ie/en/printed-maps- introduction.aspx**>

Finding maps

Of course, there are many more maps online than it has been possible to mention here, particularly for local areas. Some of the larger sites mentioned have good collections of links, but there are two other obvious places to look for links to other online maps. First, the Genuki page for a county or parish (start from <**www.genuki.org.uk/big/**>) should have a range of links to relevant maps, and some of the parish pages have a map of the parish.

For older maps on a worldwide basis, probably the best starting point is the Map History gateway at <**www.maphistory.info/webimages.html**>, maintained by Tony Campbell, former Map Librarian of the British Library. The Europe page at <**www.maphistory.info/imagebi.html**> has links to over 60 sites with individual maps or map collections for the British Isles.

ABCgenealogy has a number of links to a number of maps and map collections for the UK and Ireland at <**www.abcgenealogy.com/Maps/ Europe/**>.

For map collections with local coverage it will always be worth checking the websites of the relevant record offices, whose online catalogues are also good places to start looking for details of the maps which aren't online.

Another source for historical maps online may be the sites of commercial map-dealers, many of whose websites have scans of the maps they have for sale. It is well worth using a search engine to locate sites which have the phrase "antique maps" and the town or county of your choice.

A new portal for locating historical maps on the web was launched in February 2012. Old Maps Online at <**www.oldmapsonline.org**> is a university-funded project to create a free website 'enabling users to search for online maps across many different digital libraries, based not on the titles of maps or who drew them, but on the places the user is interested in'. The site does not host maps itself, but links to the images on sites such the British Library, the National Library of Scotland, and A Vision of Britain. The scope of the project is worldwide, but initially the British Isles and North America have the fullest coverage. For the genealogist, the most useful materials are probably the huge range of Ordnance Survey maps. A date slider allows you to focus on the maps for a selected historical period.

Interactive mapping

One upshot of the increasing range of interactive facilities online is that it is now possible to have customized maps identifying places relevant to your family tree. Google, in particular, allows web designers to take a map from Google Maps and plot particular locations on it from a data source. You can see some of the possibilities from the Genuki gazetteer (p. 256), with its 'plot places on a map' option.

Obviously, setting this up on a website of your own requires considerable technical knowledge, but MapYourAncestors at <**www.mapyourancestors.com**> is a free service which enables you to plot the locations of your ancestors' dwellings or events in their lives on a Google map. Putting these locations in a sequence makes it possible to follow the travels or migrations revealed by records. The site is rather short on documentation, but there is an article about it by Dick Eastman at <**blog. eogn.com/eastmans_online_genealogy/2007/07/map-your-ancest.html**>

and About.com has an article by Kimberley Powell 'Map Adventures with Google' at <**genealogy.about.com/od/geography/a/google.htm**>. Further examples of the possible uses and a brief demonstration will be found in an article I wrote for *Ancestors* on the subject in 2009, which is available at <**www.spub.co.uk/articles/interactive-mapping.pdf**>.

16

HISTORY

While family history is concerned mainly with individual ancestors, their lives and the documents that record them cannot be understood without a broader historical appreciation of the times in which they lived. The aim of this chapter is to look at some of the general historical material on the internet that is likely to be of use to family historians.

General resources

There are, of course, many resources online relating to particular aspects of British and Irish history, but it is those covering local and social history which are most likely to be of use to the family historian. Even so, the material online is as nothing to the immense body of print publications on the subject.

The BBC History site provides a general introduction to British History at <**www.bbc.co.uk/history/british/**> and there is a separate area devoted to 'historic figures' at <**www.bbc.co.uk/history/historic_figures/**>.

Wikipedia has many articles on British and Irish historical topics, some of which are very comprehensive, and the best of them have good bibliographies and useful links to relevant online resources.

British History Online (BHOL) at <**www.british-history.ac.uk**>, run by the University of London's Institute of Historical Research and the History of Parliament Trust, is a 'digital library containing some of the core printed primary and secondary sources for the medieval and modern history of the British Isles'. Some of the parliamentary content requires a subscription but everything of interest to the genealogist is free. The material can be browsed by region, subject or period and includes many primary records mentioning named individuals (such as the *Fasti Ecclesiae Anglicanae* – see p. 143). The site has many older topographical works and modern *Victoria County History* volumes (see below).

Connected Histories at <**www.connectedhistories.org**> is a historical gateway which describes and links to a small number of major historical data projects. In fact all eleven projects currently on the site are significant

Figure 16-1 British History Online

enough to be discussed individually in this book, for example British History Online, mentioned above, and The Proceedings of the Old Bailey (see p. 124). However, the advantage of Connected Histories is that it provides a global search over all these projects, and the advanced search has fields for searching on given name and family name, which can therefore be used to search for references to individuals. In addition, the site has research guides to these resources under nine general headings such as 'Crime and justice' and 'Poverty and poor relief'.

Local history

For introductory material on local history the BBC's Local History page at <www.bbc.co.uk/history/trail/local_history/> is a good starting point. As well as describing what is involved in local history, it looks at how to approach the history of a factory, a landscape, and a village, by way of example. The National Archives site does not have a local history section as such, but its 'Looking for a place?' page at <**www.nationalarchives.gov.uk/ records/looking-for-place/**> has local history material, with links to pages on the records for towns and cities, villages and the countryside, maps, manors, and landed estates. There are also links for various types of institution. An earlier incarnation of TNA's website had a dedicated local history section, and this had useful material no longer on the current site. The UK Government Web Archive has a copy of the section at <**www.nationalarchives.gov.uk/localhistory/**> (2 October 2009).

If you want guidance on where to find information and sources, then the 'Getting Started' page on the *Local History Magazine* website at <**www.local-history.co.uk/gettingstarted.html**> will prove useful. Sites with information on repositories which hold sources for local history are covered in Chapter 9.

It would be unrealistic to expect much of the printed material on local history to be available online, but many volumes of the *Victoria County History* (VCH) are at BHOL. From the home page at <**www.british-history.ac.uk**> follow the 'Local History' link. Of the 225 or so published volumes, around 160 have been digitized, at least one for each county, with Middlesex, Oxfordshire and Wiltshire particularly well covered. In addition, the Internet Archive at <**www.archive.org/details/texts/**> has a number of VCH volumes which are not yet on the BHOL site. The VCH itself has a site at <**www.victoriacountyhistory.ac.uk**> with general information about the project and details of the progress with individual counties at <**www.victoriacountyhistory.ac.uk/counties**>. A useful feature is the parish index at <**www.victoriacountyhistory.ac.uk/counties/ parish-index**>, which can be used to identify the printed volume which covers the parish and links to BHOL if it has been digitized. Chris Phillips, who runs the very useful Medieval English Genealogy site at <**www.medievalgenealogy.org.uk**>, has compiled an index to place-names mentioned in the titles of topographical articles in the published volumes of the VCH. This can be found at <**www.medievalgenealogy.org.uk/vch/**>. His pages for the individual VCH counties link to online editions if available.

BHOL also has an increasing number of other local history sources. London is particularly well served with 45 volumes of the late-Victorian *Survey of London*, but there is also material for Cardiff, Glasgow, Newcastle-upon-Tyne, and several English counties.

For Scotland, the *Statistical Accounts of Scotland* at <**edina.ac.uk/ statacc/**> are a major source. These accounts are descriptive rather than financial and were published in two sets of volumes, one dating from the 1790s and the other from the 1830s. There is a chapter devoted to each parish, compiled by the local minister, and they offer 'a rich record of a wide variety of topics: wealth, class and poverty; climate, agriculture, fishing and wildlife; population, schools, and the moral health of the people'. Unfortunately, the full search facilities are accessible only to academic institutions and paid subscribers; other users can only browse the scanned pages. On the search page, there are drop-down lists to help you locate the pages for a particular parish, but any place that is not a parish can be very difficult to find. You may need to use a gazetteer (see p. 257) to identify which parish your place is located in.

There is an increasing amount of material online for individual cities, towns and villages. County record offices are among those exploiting the web to publish resources for local history, and there are a number of lottery-funded projects to put local history material online. Most larger cities have substantial historical resources on their websites, and there are plenty of smaller districts and individual parishes whose community sites have local historical material. Indeed, because of the smaller scale, parish sites can often aim at being very comprehensive.

Among the larger-scale projects for counties or regions are:

- PortCities <**www.portcities.org.uk**> (ports of Bristol, Hartlepool, Liverpool, London, Southampton)
- Tomorrow's History <**www.tomorrows-history.com**> (North East of England)
- Wiltshire Community History <**www.wiltshire.gov.uk/community/**>
- Gathering the Jewels <**www.gtj.org.uk**> (Wales)
- Powys Heritage Online <**history.powys.org.uk**>
- The Gaelic Village <**www.ambaile.org.uk/en/**> (Scottish Highlands and Islands)

Projects for individual places include:

- Digital Handsworth <**www.digitalhandsworth.org.uk**>
- Dursley Glos Web <**www.dursleyglos.org.uk**>
- TheGlasgowStory <**www.theglasgowstory.com**>
- The Kingston Local History project at <**fass.kingston.ac.uk/research/historical-record/projects/klhp/**> (Kingston-on-Thames)
- Knowsley (Lancs) Local History <**history.knowsley.gov.uk**>
- SilverCityVault <**www.silvercityvault.org.uk**> (Aberdeen)
- Soham On-Line <**www.soham.org.uk/history/**>
- Recording Uttlesford History <**www.recordinguttlesfordhistory.org.uk**>

Some of these have online data as well as general historical material. The photographic collections mentioned on p. 302 are also useful for local history.

Local authority websites will have details of any local studies or local history libraries in their area, though few of these seem to have historical material on the web.

It is also well worth checking the website of the Local Heritage Initiative at <**www.lhi.org.uk**>. This programme was launched in 2000 to 'help communities bring their local heritage to life', and the clickable map on the home page leads to a list of projects for the selected region.

There are many sites with small data extracts for local areas, often a single parish, examples of which will be found in Chapter 8. But a more comprehensive approach is represented by the Online Parish Clerk (OPC) schemes. Each county scheme has volunteers transcribing historical records for individual parishes. So far, there are schemes for Cornwall, Devon, Dorset, Essex, Hampshire, Kent, Lancashire, Somerset, Sussex, Warwickshire and Wiltshire. Links to the websites of these projects, which will link in turn to the pages for individual parishes, can be found on Genuki's OPC page at <**www.genuki.org.uk/indexes/OPC.html**>. Many Genuki county and parish pages themselves include descriptive extracts from historical directories and have links to other local transcriptions.

One-place studies aim to collect all historical, geographical and genealogical information about a single place as a background to the history of individual local families. A central index of these projects, arranged by county, is provided by the One Place Studies site at <**www.one-place-studies.org**>.

One often overlooked aspect of history which influenced our ancestors' lives is the climate. Climate History in the British Isles at <**www.booty.org.uk/booty.weather/climate/histclimat.htm**> allows you to see whether a particular year was affected by any severe meteorological events, national or local.

Societies

There are at least as many groups devoted to local history as there are family history societies, though of course not all of them have websites. A comprehensive listing for all parts of the UK and Ireland is provided by *Local History* magazine in the Local History Directory at <**www.local-history.co.uk/Groups/**>. This gives contact details including email addresses and websites where available. It also includes the many county-based record societies, whose print publications are such an important source for family historians. The British Association for Local History has a select list of links to local history society websites at <**www.balh.co.uk/directory.php**>.

Discussion forums

LOCAL-HISTORY is a general mailing list for the British Isles, which is hosted by JISCmail, the national academic mailing list service. You can see the archive of past messages for the list at <**www.jiscmail.ac.uk/cgi-bin/ webadmin?A0=local-history**>, and there are also instructions on how to subscribe.

There are two other places to look for genealogical discussion forums relating to local history. ONE-PLACE-STUDY is a mailing list for those involved in studying a single parish or group of parishes, details of which can be found at <**lists.rootsweb.ancestry.com/index/other/Miscellaneous/ ONE-PLACE-STUDY.html**>. British-Genealogy also hosts a discussion forum for one-place studies at <**www.british-genealogy.com/forums/ forumdisplay.php?f=177**>.

Curious Fox at <**www.curiousfox.com**> is a site which provides message boards for local history and genealogy. While most discussion forums are county-based, this site is different in that it is based on a gazetteer of over 50,000 towns and villages in the British Isles (including 3,000 in Ireland), each with its own page. You can search for the settlement name, generate lists of nearby villages and hamlets, and get links to the exact location on Streetmap and Old-maps. You can also search by family name. The site calls itself 'semi commercial': you can join and use the site free of charge, but a subscription of £5 provides additional facilities, including an automatic email when someone adds a message relating to a town or village you have stored as a place of interest. Without a subscription you can only contact subscribers.

Most of the genealogical mailing lists for counties, areas, and individual places are useful for local history queries, and there are some lists which specifically include local history in their remit. For example, the sussexpast group on Yahoo Groups at <**groups.yahoo.com/group/sussexpast/**> describes its interests as 'Discussions and questions/answers on archaeology, local history, museums and architecture in Sussex'. Lists which are more explicitly focused on the history of individual localities include:

- LANARK-HISTORY
- LONDON-LIFE
- WALES-LOCAL-HISTORY

Details of all three will be found in RootsWeb listings for Scotland, England and Wales, respectively, at <**lists.rootsweb.ancestry.com/index/**>.

Social history

Although the web provides material on any aspect of social history you care to name, from slavery to education, it is difficult to know what you can expect to find on a given topic in terms of quality and coverage. In view of the large number of possible subjects which come under 'social history', and the very general application of these headings (crime, poverty, etc.), using a search engine to locate them can be quite time-consuming. Also, of course, searching on these terms will bring up many sites that have nothing to do with the history of the UK. However, if you can think of any terms or phrases that refer only to British and Irish historical material ('1840 Education Act', 'Poor Law', etc.) this will make searching easier. Local history sites such as those discussed above are likely to include some material on social history and local museums, and may provide useful links to non-local material.

For more recent local and social history, local newspapers are an important source, and these are discussed on p. 193ff.

Where aspects of social history are bound up with the state, you can expect to find some guidance on official sites. The National Archives, for example, has research guides on Education, Enclosures, Lunacy and Lunatic Asylums, Outlawry, and the Poor Law, among other subjects – see <**www.nationalarchives.gov.uk/records/atoz**>. Records relating to crime and punishment are discussed on p. 124ff.

A comprehensive guide to social history sites is beyond the scope of this book, but the following examples may give a taste of some of the resources on the web.

Professor George P. Landow's Victorian Web includes an overview of Victorian Social History at <**www.victorianweb.org/history/sochistov.html**> with a considerable amount of contemporary documentation. This site, incidentally, was one of the first to use the web to make linked historical materials available.

There are a number of sites with material on institutions. The Workhouses site at <**www.workhouses.org.uk**> provides a comprehensive introduction to the workhouse and the laws relating to it, along with lists of workhouses in England, Wales and Scotland and a guide to workhouse records. The Rossbret Institutions site has information not only on workhouses but on a wide range of institutions, including Asylums, Almshouses, Prisons, Dispensaries, Hospitals, Reformatories, and Orphanages. Unfortunately, the site went offline in 2011 but is available at the Wayback Machine at <**www.institutions.org.uk**> (15 November 2010).

If you have an ancestor who was committed to a mental institution, the County Asylums site at <**www.countyasylums.com**>, though mainly about the buildings themselves, will also be of interest. GenDocs has a list of 'Workhouses, Hospitals, Lunatic Asylums, Prisons, Barracks, Orphan Asylums, Convents, and other Principal Charitable Institutions' in London in 1861 at <**homepage.ntlworld.com/hitch/gendocs/institute.html**>.

Hidden Lives at <www.hiddenlives.org.uk> is a site devoted to children in care between 1881 and 1918. It has details of around 170 care homes and many histories of individual children (not named). There are useful links to other online sources relating to children and poverty.

The Historic Hospital Admissions Records (HHARP) site at <hharp.org> is a collection of resources relating to four children's hospitals in London and Glasgow with admission records for various periods from the middle of the nineteenth century to 1914. The site provides historical background on each hospital, including articles on individual doctors and some patients, and a list of medical terms found in the records. Access to full search results and detailed case notes on individuals requires (free) registration.

Among the materials relating to Scotland are Origins' articles on aspects of Scottish social history at <www.origins.net/Help/resarticles.aspx>, which include the fishing and weaving industries, the Poor Law, and religion. Electric Scotland has a substantial account of the 'Social History of the Highlands' at <www.electricscotland.com/history/social/>, taken from a nineteenth-century work. The site has much other material on Scottish history. Radical Glasgow at <www.gcu.ac.uk/radicalglasgow/> covers the city's radical movements and their leading individuals from the Act of Union to the Upper Clyde Shipbuilders' work-in of the 1970s.

The Powys Heritage Online project mentioned above has sections devoted to crime and punishment, education and schools, religion in Wales, and care of the poor, at <history.powys.org.uk/history/intro/themes.html>, which make use of original documents and photographs.

Finally, the Spartacus Educational site at <www.spartacus.school net.co.uk> is a model of what can be done with historical material on the web. It has information on many topics in social history since the mid-eighteenth century, such as child labour, the railways, the textile industry and female emancipation. The site contains both general information and historical documents. The pages devoted to the textile industry, for example, at <www.spartacus.schoolnet.co.uk/Textiles.htm>, contain general information on the machinery, the various occupations within the industry and the nature of daily life in the textile factory, but also include biographical material on individual inventors, entrepreneurs and factory workers, the latter taken from interviews before a House of Commons Committee in 1832.

Names

Origins

A regular topic in discussion forums is the origin of surnames. When talking about surnames, though, the term 'origin' has two distinct meanings: how the name came about linguistically (its etymology); and where it originated geographically (its home). Unfortunately there is little reliable information on the web relating to the first of these. The authoritative sources for British surname etymologies are the modern printed surname dictionaries, which are not available online. If you are lucky you may find a surname site that quotes and gives references for the relevant dictionary entries for your particular surname, but in the absence of source references you should treat etymological information given on genealogy websites as unreliable. Even where sources are given, you should be cautious – some of the older surname dictionaries cited are the work of amateurs rather than scholars. Indeed, even the works of the latter may have been invalidated by subsequent research, particularly because we now have much more extensive information on surname distribution and variant forms than was available even 20 years ago.

Cyndi's List has a page devoted to surnames in general at <**www.cyndislist.com/surnames/general/**>, though many of the links are for surname *interests* (covered in Chapter 14) rather than surname origins.

Wikipedia has a number of articles on surnames, which seem to be quite sound. The most general one is 'Family name', and this has links to related articles. However, the Wikipedia pages for individual surname etymologies, which are generally unsourced and frequently unsound, are of little value.

In fact, there seems to be no very satisfactory site for surname etymologies. Nonetheless, you can find brief etymologies for the commoner surnames at Behind the Name's page on 'English Names' at <**surnames.behindthename.com**> and on About.com's 'Glossary of Last Name Meanings and Origins' page at <**genealogy.about.com/library/surnames/bl_meaning.htm**>.

However, many older printed works on British surnames are available online, usually at the digital book archives discussed on p. 184. For example, the following can all be found at Google Books and the Internet Archive:

- William Arthur, *An Etymological Dictionary of Family and Christian Names With an Essay on their Derivation and Import* (1857)
- Charles Bardsley, *Dictionary of English and Welsh Surnames* (1901)
- Henry Harrison, *Surnames of the United Kingdom: a concise etymological dictionary* (1912–1918) (the Internet Archive has only the second volume, M–Z)
- Mark Lower, *English Surnames. An Essay on Family Nomenclature, Historical, Etymological, and Humorous* (1849)
- Mark Lower, *Patronymica Britannica. A Dictionary of the Family Names of the United Kingdom* (1860)

None of these is a substitute for a modern surname dictionary, though William Arthur's 'Essay On The Origin And Import Of Family Names' at <www.searchforancestors.com/surnames/origin/essay.html> is still a useful brief introduction to the general sources of surnames. However, these older works may include sources for older usages of a name, which can be helpful.

SURNAME-ORIGINS-L is a US-based mailing list devoted to the etymology and distribution of surnames, and details can be found at <members.tripod.com/~Genealogy_Infocenter/surname-origins.html>.

Family Names of the United Kingdom (FaNUK) is a project based at the University of the West of England to create 'the largest ever database of the UK's family surnames' with information on the meaning, linguistic origin, geographical origin and distribution of each name. The project runs until 31 March 2014. There is no website for the project at the time of writing, but information about FaNUK will be found on the university's website at <www1.uwe.ac.uk/cahe/elc/research/researchcentresandgroups/fanuk.aspx> and there is a podcast interview with principal investigator Professor Richard Coates at <www.ahrc.ac.uk/News/Podcasts/Pages/familynames.aspx>, accompanied by a transcript.

Surname variants and systems for catching variants in online record searches are discussed on p. 39.

Distribution and frequency

Looking at the geographical distribution of a surname in a major database such as FamilySearch at <www.familysearch.org> can sometimes be helpful. However, you should be cautious about drawing etymological inferences from distributional information in this sort of database, not least because the various parts of the country are equally well represented.

The most important site for surname distribution is Great Britain Family Names (previously National Trust Names) at <gbnames.publicprofiler.org>, which draws on a project based at University College London. You can get distribution maps for the 1881 census or the 1998 electoral register, and the maps, even those for 1881, show the relative frequency for each postcode area, effectively the catchment area of each present-day post town (Figure 16-2). From the initial distribution map, you can get statistical information about frequency, though it does not give a breakdown for each area. The data covers England, Wales and Scotland.

GROS has various pages devoted to Scottish surnames and forenames, derived from birth registrations, linked from <www.gro-scotland.gov.uk/statistics/theme/vital-events/births/popular-names>, including 'Surnames in Scotland over the last 140 years'. Two linked PDF documents show the most common surnames in the Scottish counties in 1901 and 2001.

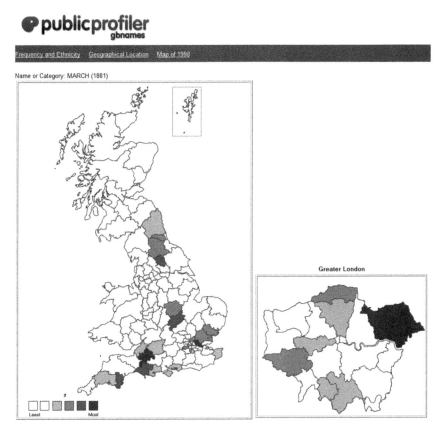

Figure 16-2 1881 distribution of the surname March at Great Britain Family Names

The classic Victorian work on the geographical origins of surnames is Henry Guppy's 1890 work *Homes of Family Names of Great Britain*, which is available at the Internet Archive (see p. 185).

For a list of the commonest surnames in various parts of the world, see Wikipedia's article 'List of most common surnames'. British Surnames and Surname Profiles at <**www.britishsurnames.co.uk**> has present-day and 1881 census frequencies, with separate information for surnames from various immigrant groups. Sofeminine, rather surprisingly, has present-day frequency lists for the UK as a whole at <**surname.sofeminine.co.uk/w/ surnames/uk.html**> and for individual local authority areas (follow the 'By county' link in the left-hand column). Only surnames with more than 1,300 occurrences are included.

Surname Studies at <**www.surnamestudies.org.uk**> preserves and develops the late Philip Dance's Modern British Surnames site, a guide to the resources for the study of surname frequency and distribution. The site includes discussion of the various approaches to surname origins, and has interesting statistical material. A site covering local names is Graham Thomas's Gloucestershire Names and their Occurrence at <**www.lroberts.co.uk/info/ gloucestershire%20names.htm**>.

Forenames

If you have access to Oxford Reference Online at <**www.oxfordreference.com**>, either via an educational institution or your local public library (see p. 180), you can consult Oxford University Press's *A Dictionary of First Names*. This has a searchable database of 6,000 forenames 'in common use in English', and this is the best place to start for the origins of any forename. Behind the Name at <**www.behindthename.com**> is a very comprehensive site devoted to the etymology and history of first names. In addition to English and Irish names it has details for a number of other countries and regions, as well as a listing of biblical names. What's In a Name at <**www.whatsinaname.net**> has well-sourced information about forenames and forename variants.

About.com has a page of links for 'Naming Patterns for Countries & Cultures' at <**genealogy.about.com/od/naming_patterns/Naming_ Practices_Patterns_for_Countries_Cultures.htm**>, which includes links for British and Irish names, as well as many others. A search for ["naming patterns"] in a search engine will reveal many other sites devoted to this topic. Anne Johnston has a useful list of diminutives for common Christian names at <**www.nireland.com/anne.johnston/Diminutives.htm**>. The website for the OLD-ENGLISH mailing list (see p. 290 below) has a listing of Latin equivalents of common forenames at <**homepages.rootsweb. ancestry.com/~oel/latingivennames.html**>, which will often be found in legal documents and early parish registers written in Latin.

For present-day forename frequencies, the authoritative sources are government sites. The National Statistics site at <**www.statistics.gov.uk**> has a number of reports on the current and historical frequency of first names. The material is not very helpfully organized, but a search for "baby names" from the home page will bring up a list of relevant publications and datasets.

GROS has a paper on 'Popular Forenames in Scotland, 1900–2000' at <**www.gro-scotland.gov.uk/statistics/theme/vital-events/births/popular- names/archive/forenames-1900-2000.html**>.

Image Partners has a forename thesaurus which attempts to match variant forename spellings at <**www.namethesaurus.com/Thesaurus/ Search.aspx**>, and Edgar's Name Page has 'A Brief Discussion of Nicknames and Diminutives' at <**webspace.webring.com/people/ge/edgarbook/ names/other/nicknames.html**>.

▌ Understanding old documents

One of the main things genealogists need help with is making sense of old documents, whether it is a census entry or a sixteenth-century will. In some cases it's just a matter of deciphering the handwriting, in others it is understanding the meaning of obsolete words. In older documents the two problems are often inseparable. While the internet hardly provides a substitute for the specialist books on these subjects, there are quite a few resources online to help with such problems.

Handwriting

As the mistakes in census transcriptions show, even fairly modern handwriting can often be problematic to read, and once you get back beyond the nineteenth century the difficulties become ever greater. Few genealogists bother to go on palaeography courses, but there are some outstanding online resources to help you.

The English Faculty at Cambridge University provides an online course on English Handwriting 1500–1700 at <**www.english.cam.ac.uk/ceres/ehoc/**> with high quality scans of original documents. There are extensive examples of every individual letter in a variety of hands, as well as examples of the many abbreviations found in documents of this period. A series of graded exercises gives you an opportunity to try your own skills at transcribing original manuscripts.

The National Archives also has an online palaeography tutorial at <**www.nationalarchives.gov.uk/palaeography/**> (Figure 16-3). The interactive part of the site offers 10 graded documents to try your hand at transcribing, with a pop-up alphabet for the hand, and there are another 30 example documents on the site. The 'Where to start' page offers tips for transcribing and covers some common abbreviations.

The Scottish Archive Network's dedicated palaeography website Scottish Handwriting at <**www.scottishhandwriting.com**> concentrates on the period 1500–1750. It includes a '1 Hour Basic Tutorial' and has detailed pages devoted to the forms of some of the more challenging individual letters. A problem solver suggests techniques for making sense of problem words and letters. There is also a dedicated tutorial for eighteenth-century testaments.

Dave Postles of the University of Leicester has materials relating to an MA in Palaeography online at <**paleo.anglo-norman.org**>. The site has two areas, one devoted to medieval and the other to early modern palaeography.

Dianne Tillotson has a site devoted to all aspects of Medieval Writing at <**medievalwriting.50megs.com/writing.htm**> with examples of all the main scripts up to the sixteenth century. There is useful material on abbreviations at <**medievalwriting.50megs.com/scripts/abbreviation/abbreviation1.htm**>.

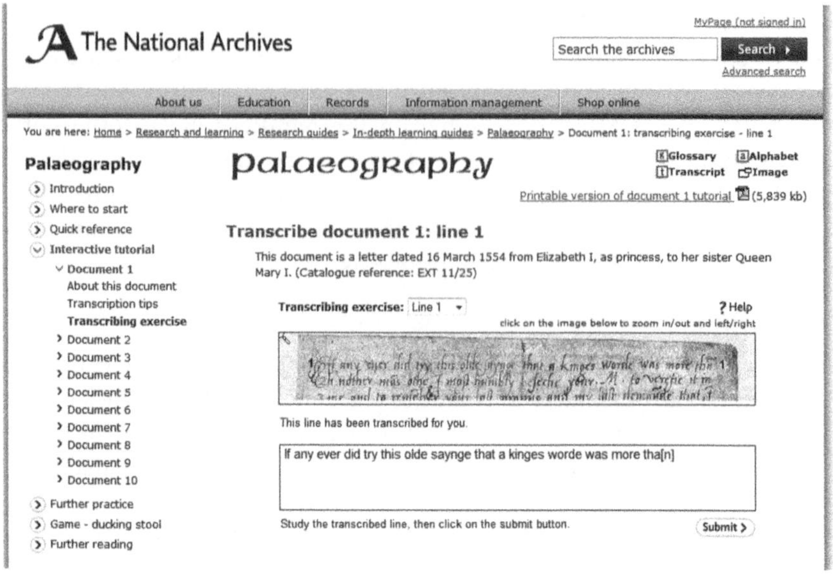

Figure 16-3 The National Archives' palaeography tutorial

The website for the OLD-ENGLISH mailing list at <**homepages. rootsweb.ancestry.com/~oel/**> includes pages on Old Law Hands and Court Hand with scans of plates from Andrew Wright's 1776 *Court Hand Restored* showing examples of all the common letter shapes of the period. Both are linked from <**homepages.rootsweb.ancestry.com/~oel/ contents.html**>.

While most palaeography sites deal with the early modern and medieval periods, there is also help for those struggling with Victorian hands. For example, the FreeBMD page on 'Reading the Writing' at <**www.freebmd.org.uk/handwriting.html**> shows how the shape of nineteenth-century pen nibs affects the thickness of the stroke, and also looks at how to deal with difficult scans.

If you have to deal with languages other than English, Brigham Young University's 'Script Tutorials' at <**script.byu.edu**> may be worth consulting, as it offers help with both manuscript and printed documents in English, German, Dutch, Italian, French, Spanish and Portuguese. It does not have additional original documents, but points to those on some of the other sites mentioned above.

Dates and calendars

There are a number of useful resources on the web to help you make sense of the dates and calendars used in older genealogical sources.

There are two particular types of dating which are generally unfamiliar to modern readers. The first is the dating of documents, particularly legal ones, by regnal years, i.e. the number of years since the accession of the reigning monarch (so *1 January 2012* is *1 January 59 Eliz. II*). The Regnal Year Calculator at <**people.albion.edu/imacinnes/calendar//Regnal_ Years.html**> will convert regnal years for the period from the Norman Conquest to George I. There is a useful table of regnal years up to Queen Victoria at <**www.amostcuriousmurder.com/kingdateFS.htm**>.

Second, particularly in early documents, Saints' days are a common method of identifying a date. Wikipedia has a useful article on the 'Calendar of Saints (Church of England)' and the 'On-line Calendar of Saints' Days at <**medievalist.net/calendar/home.htm**> gives the saints for every date in the year.

In September 1752 Britain switched from the old Julian calendar to the Gregorian. Wikipedia's 'Gregorian calendar' page has comprehensive information about the new calendar, but for more detailed information on the change of calendars in the UK see Mike Spathaky's article 'Old Style And New Style Dates And The Change To The Gregorian Calendar' on Genuki at <**www.cree.name/genuki/dates.htm**>. Calendars through the Ages has the text of the Calendar Act of 1751, which instituted this change, at <**www.webexhibits.org/calendars/year-text-British.html**>, with a calendar for 1752 showing the missing days. Steven Gibbs has a conversion routine for the Julian and Gregorian calendars at <**www.guernsey.net/~sgibbs/ roman.html**>, which may be useful if you are consulting records from countries which switched either earlier (most of Europe) or later (Russia) than the UK. Calendopaedia, the Encyclopaedia of Calendars, at <**calendopaedia.com**> has extensive information on calendars including the dates lost in the switch from the Julian to the Gregorian calendar for all the individual countries in Europe at <**calendopaedia.com/gregory.htm**>.

To find out what day a particular date fell on, consult Genuki's Perpetual Calendar at <**www.genuki.org.uk/big/easter/**>, which also gives the dates of Easter. The years 1550 to 2049 are covered.

Chris Phillips provides a comprehensive guide to chronology and dating at <**www.medievalgenealogy.org.uk/guide/chron.shtml**>, as part of a site devoted to medieval genealogy, while Cyndi's List has many links to online resources for all contemporary and historical calendars.

Translation
Latin
For medieval genealogy and for legal records up to 1733, you will often encounter texts written in Latin. Even in English texts, Latin phrases, or,

worse, abbreviations for them, are not uncommon. Latin has also, of course, been much used for inscriptions.

However, while there are very substantial online resources for help with Latin, most are intended for those reading classical Latin texts and may not include terms found in British legal documents. For that reason, it is best to start with materials specifically designed for genealogists. The National Archives' 'Beginner's Latin' tutorial at <**www.nationalarchives.gov.uk/ latin/beginners/**> is specifically aimed at those using British sources and offers a series of graded exercises, a grammar table covering the basics, and a wordlist.

If you just need to identify individual words rather than translate whole documents, then, in addition to TNA's wordlist, there is FamilySearch's 'Latin Genealogical Word List' at <**wiki.familysearch.org/en/Latin_ Genealogical_Word_List**>, which includes material on dates in Latin. Other genealogical glossaries for Latin include GenProxy's 'Simple Latin terms, words and phrases for genealogists reading old documents, wills, contracts, deeds, church and parish records' at <**www.genproxy.co.uk/ latin.htm**>, and Ancestry Solutions' 'Dictionary of Latin Words and Phrases' at <**www.ancestrysolutions.com/Defslatin.html**>. There is a list of 'Hard Little Words: Prepositions, Adverbs, Conjunctions (With Some Definitions of Medieval Usage)' at <**members.fortunecity.com/ kwhitefoot/HardLittleWords.html**>.

C. Russell Jensen's *Parish Register Latin* is an introduction based around exercises using authentic parish register entries and is available in the Internet Archive at <**www.archive.org/details/parishregisterla00crus**>. The Archive also has Charles Martin's 1892 book *Latin for genealogical research: a primer for record Latin*, which not only has an immense list of Latin abbreviations (including the much wider range of forms actually found in manuscripts rather than just those used in print) but also lists Latin equivalents of British forenames and place-names.

Latin abbreviations are often used, particularly in set phrases, and the FAQ for the soc.genealogy.medieval newsgroup has a list of some of those commonly found in genealogical documents at <**users.erols.com/wrei/faqs/ medieval.html#GN13**>.

Among the more general resources for help with Latin are the Latin Dictionary and Grammar Aid at <**archives.nd.edu/latgramm.htm**>, which provides a grammar and links to material on Latin. The Perseus Digital Library at Tufts University has the 1890 edition of Lewis's *An Elementary Latin Dictionary* at <**www.perseus.tufts.edu/hopper/text?doc=Perseus%3a text%3a1999.04.0060**> and the digital book archives discussed in Chapter 12 have scans of other older Latin dictionaries.

There is a LATIN-WORDS mailing list which is for 'anyone with a genealogical or historical interest in deciphering and interpreting written documents in Latin from earliest to most recent twentieth century times, and discussing old Latin words, phrases, names, abbreviations and antique jargon'. Subscription details will be found at <**lists.rootsweb.ancestry.com/ index/other/Translations_and_Word_Origins/LATIN-WORDS.html**> and the list archive is at <**archiver.rootsweb.ancestry.com/th/index/ LATIN-WORDS**>.

Other languages

The Dictionary of the Scots Language site at <**www.dsl.ac.uk/dsl/**> provides electronic editions of two key works of Scottish lexicography, the *Dictionary of the Older Scottish Tongue* (DOST) and the *Scottish National Dictionary* (SND). Between them, these two dictionaries cover the use of Scots words from the twelfth century to the present day. A search can be conducted in either or both works. Quite apart from their general interest, an obvious use for genealogists is to help with understanding Scottish wills and other legal documents. A wide-ranging glossary of Scottish terms will be found on The Wedderburn Pages at <**euroleader.pagespro-orange.fr/wedderburn/ glossary.htm**>, including both archaic and modern terms. General information about the Scots language will be found in the Wikipedia 'Scots language' article.

With the release of the 1911 census, which allowed non-Anglophone families to record their household using Welsh or Irish, you may need recourse to a dictionary to translate the family relationships and the occupations. For Welsh, consult the Welsh–English/English–Welsh On-line Dictionary provided by the Department of Welsh, Lampeter at <**www.geiriadur.net**>.

There is an online Irish dictionary with basic vocabulary at <**www.irishdictionary.org**>, and a list of the Irish words for family relationships at <**www.irishgaelictranslator.com/articles/?p=30**>. Detailed help in dealing with the Irish language entries in the 1911 census is given in Chapter 15 of *Census: The Expert Guide*.

The general census reports for 1911, available at Histpop <**www.histpop.org**>, include general information about the linguistic situation in Wales and Ireland. For the Irish report, search for [general report Ireland 1911] and select the 65-page document. Helpfully, the Welsh Language Board has extracted the section on 'Language Spoken in Wales and Monmouthshire' from the England & Wales report at <**www.byig-wlb.org.uk/English/publications/Publications/638.pdf**>.

The FamilySearch Wiki has pages for both Irish and Welsh language at <**wiki.familysearch.org/en/Ireland_Language_and_Languages**> and

<wiki.familysearch.org/en/Wales_Language_and_Languages> respectively. At the time of writing, the Irish page has little of use, but the Welsh page offers some basic help and links.

Technical terms

Genealogists encounter technical terms from many specialist areas, and have the additional difficulty that it may not be apparent whether a term is just specialized or in fact obsolete. The definitive resource for such questions remains the *Oxford English Dictionary* – see p. 186 for details of online access, and Figure 9-1 for a sample entry. The particular merit of the OED is that the various senses of a word are dated, which makes it easier to identify which meanings are possible for a document from a particular period. Some terms may be important enough to deserve their own entry in an encyclopedia, in which case consult Wikipedia at <**en.wikipedia.org**> or, if you have access, the online edition of *Encyclopædia Britannica* (again, see p. 186).

Other places to turn when you encounter this sort of problem include the rather inappropriately named OLD-ENGLISH mailing list, which is for 'anyone who is deciphering old English documents to discuss interpretations of handwriting and word meanings', or the OLD-WORDS mailing list 'for the discussion of old words, phrases, names, abbreviations, and antique jargon useful to genealogy'. OLD-ENGLISH has its own website at <**virts.rootsweb. ancestry.com/~oel/**>, which has an excellent collection of material, as well as some useful links. Details of how to subscribe to OLD-WORDS are at <**lists. rootsweb.ancestry.com/index/other/Translations_and_Word_Origins/ OLD-WORDS.html**>. You can also browse or search the archives for them at <**archiver.rootsweb.ancestry.com/th/index/OLD-ENGLISH**> and <**archiver. rootsweb.ancestry.com/th/index/OLD-WORDS**> respectively. Bear in mind that the contributors to the lists have widely varying expertise, and you will need to evaluate carefully any advice you receive.

Guy Etchells has a list of 'Leicestershire Agricultural Terms' taken from a work of 1809 at <**freepages.genealogy.rootsweb.ancestry.com/~framland/ framland/agterm.htm**>. Old terms for occupations are discussed on p. 129.

Sources for specifically genealogical terms are discussed on p 15.

Legal

Even where they are not written in Latin, many early modern texts, particularly those relating to property, contain technical legal terms that are likely to mean little to the non-specialist, but which may be crucial to the understanding of an ancestor's property holdings or legal transactions. A useful list of 'Legal Terms in Land Records' will be found at <**www.directlinesoftware.com/legal.htm**>, while the equivalent but distinct terminology for Scotland is explained in the Customs & Excise notice 'Scottish Land Law Terms' (the URL is the 187-character address given on p. xiii, so instead follow the link from the website for this book). These are both guides to present-day usage, but in view of the archaic nature of landholding vocabulary this should not be a hindrance. A more specifically historical glossary is provided on the Scottish Archive Network site at <**www.scan.org.uk/researchrtools/glossary.htm**> (again note the 'r' after 'research'), and legal terms are included in The Wedderburn Pages mentioned above. The Manorial Society of Great Britain has a glossary of manorial terms at <**www.msgb.co.uk/glossary. html**>.

Wikipedia has an article on 'Legal English' which discusses some general features of legal language.

Among the many more general online resources for legal terms, the Free Dictionary has a dictionary of legal English at <**legal-dictionary. thefreedictionary.com**>, though this seems to be based largely on US sources and may not contain some UK terms that have now fallen out of use.

Medical

Death certificates of the last century, and earlier references to cause of death, often include medical terms that are unfamiliar. Some can be found in one of the online dictionaries of contemporary medicine, such as MedTerms at <**www.medterms.com**> or the Medical Dictionary Online at <**www.online-medical-dictionary.org**>. But for comprehensive coverage of archaic medical terms, refer to Antiquus Morbus at <**www.antiquusmorbus.com**>, which has old medical terms in English, Latin, German, French and many other European languages. Each entry comes with a bibliographical reference, and there are links to around 20 further online sources for the medical terms. Within the English section, there are individual lists for occupational diseases, poisons and alcoholism; there is also a separate list of Scots terms. Cyndi's List has a 'Medical & Medicine' page with a section for 'Diseases and Medical Terms' at <**www.cyndislist.com/medical/diseases/**>.

Incidentally, the Our Ward Family Website has a list of major disease outbreaks in the UK from the Black Death onwards at <**www.ourwardfamily.com/pages/history_of_diseases.htm**>.

Measurements

Old terms for measurements are encountered in records of trade and in descriptions of landholdings, in tax records and property deeds. Leicester University's palaeography course materials, mentioned on p. 289, include a number of useful lists covering terms likely to be found in old legal documents: land measurement terms, the Latin equivalents of English coinage, and Roman numerals. See the Medieval palaeography pages at <paleo.anglo-norman.org/medfram.html>.

Steven Gibbs's site, mentioned on p. 291, has facilities for converting to and from Roman numerals at <www.guernsey.net/~sgibbs/roman.html>.

Details of old units of measurement (though not areal measurements) can be found at <www.fergusoncreations.co.uk/home/shaun/metrology/english.html>, while both linear and areal measures are covered by <www.johnowensmith.co.uk/histdate/measures.htm>. There is a comprehensive Dictionary of Measures at <www.unc.edu/~rowlett/units/> which includes a useful article on 'English Customary Weights and Measures' at <www.unc.edu/~rowlett/units/custom.html>. Cyndi's List has a page devoted to 'Weights and Measures' at <www.cyndislist.com/weights>. Many individual terms have their own articles in Wikipedia at <en.wikipedia.org>.

Medieval

There are a number of general guides to medieval terms, including NetSERF's Hypertext Medieval Glossary at <netserf.cua.edu/glossary/home.htm>. The useful Glossary Of Medieval Terms has been defunct for some years now but is still available in the Wayback Machine with the URL <cal.bemidji.msus.edu/History/mcmanus/ma_gloss.html> (8 March 2005). Resources for the terminology of heraldry are discussed on p. 246.

Value of money

An obvious question when reading wills, tax records and the like is the present-day equivalent of the sums of money quoted. While there can be no definitive answer – goods are now cheaper than ever, while labour is much more expensive – there is plenty of material online to give you an idea of what things were worth.

There is a very detailed analysis of the historical value of sterling in a House of Commons Research Paper 'Inflation: the Value of the Pound 1750–1998', which is available online in PDF format at <www.parliament.uk/commons/lib/research/rp99/rp99-020.pdf>. For a longer time-span, there are two tables covering the period from the thirteenth century to the present day at <www.johnowensmith.co.uk/histdate/moneyval.htm>.

Measuring Worth is a site with a great deal of information on this topic. Its page on the 'Purchasing Power of British Pounds from 1264 to 2007' at <www.measuringworth.com/calculators/ppoweruk/> enables you to find the modern equivalent of an amount in pounds, shillings and pence in a particular year. There is also a useful page on 'Five Ways to

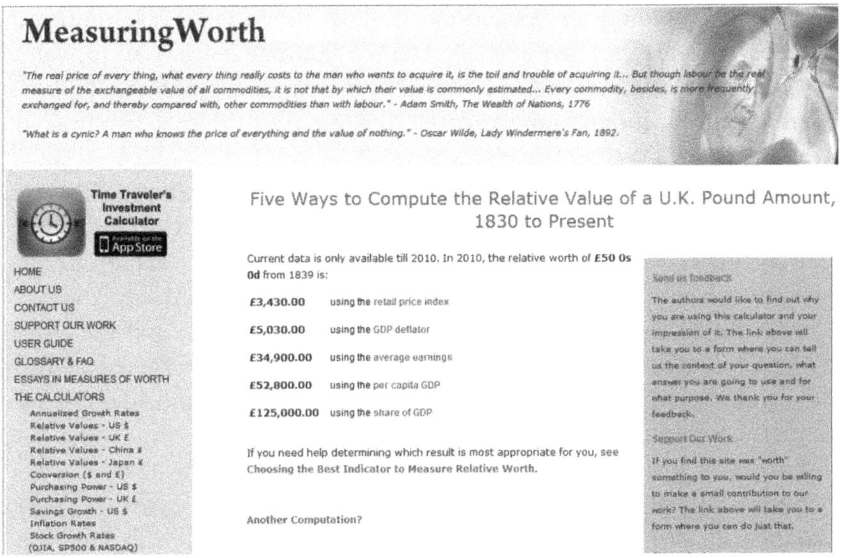

Figure 16-4 Measuring Worth

Compute the Relative Value of a UK Pound Amount, 1830 to Present' at <**www.measuringworth.com/ukcompare/**> (Figure 16-4). This page clearly makes the point that there is no simple way to equate historical sums of money with a modern equivalent. Other pages on this site, all linked from the left-hand navigation panel, have information on things like the UK and US inflation rates since the 1660s and the pound–dollar conversion rate for the last 200 years.

Alan Stanier's 'Relative Value of Sums of Money' page at <**privatewww. essex.ac.uk/~alan/family/N-Money.html**> has statistics for the wages of various types of worker, mainly craftsmen and labourers, but also domestic servants and professionals.

Details of inflation since the eighteenth century will be found in a 2004 paper 'Consumer Price Inflation Since 1750' from the Office of National Statistics at <**www.ons.gov.uk/ons/rel/elmr/economic-trends-- discontinued-/no--604--march-2004/consumer-price-inflation- since-1750.pdf**>. The basic figures are more easily consulted on the 'Historical UK Inflation And Price Conversion' page at <**safalra.com/other/ historical-uk-inflation-price-conversion/**>, which also has a historical price converter.

The National Archives website offers a 'Currency converter' at <**www.nationalarchives.gov.uk/currency/**> with information both on relative value and on buying power. (Incidentally, TNA has also worked with a commercial developer to produce a smartphone app, Old Money, to convert past sums of money to present-day values – see <**www.revelmob.com/ currency-converter**>.) The Scottish Archive Network (see p. 206) provides a Scots Currency Converter at <**www.scan.org.uk/researchrtools/scots_ currency.htm**>, though unfortunately this requires Internet Explorer and Microsoft Office Web Components to work.

An excellent collection of links to sites with information on the historical value of the pound and other currencies is Roy Davies's 'Current value of Old Money' page at <**projects.exeter.ac.uk/RDavies/arian/current/ howmuch.html**>, which includes an extensive list of printed sources.

There is an Excel spreadsheet with data on the 'Wages and the cost of living in Southern England 1450–1700' linked from <**www.iisg.nl/hpw/ dover.php**>, with individual figures for Oxford, Cambridge, Dover, Canterbury and London.

Finally, if you are too young to remember the pre-decimal system of pounds, shillings and pence, then 'What's A Guinea?' at <**www.web40571. clarahost.co.uk/currency/PreDecimal/predecimal.htm**> will enlighten you.

17

PHOTOGRAPHS

Among the many reasons for the success of the web is the ease with which it can be used to make images available to a wide audience. The questions of cost and commercial viability that face the printed photograph do not really apply on the web – apart from the labour involved, it costs effectively nothing to publish a photograph online. The widespread availability of inexpensive scanners and the popularity of the digital camera mean that more and more people have the equipment to create digital images. While few archives are in a position to publish a significant fraction of their photographic holdings in print, online image archives are mushrooming, and some offer very substantial collections.

Photographs are, of course, primary historical sources. But most historical photographs online are of towns, villages, buildings, and unnamed individuals, so the chances of coming across a picture of your great-great-grandmother on the web (unless she was, say, Queen Victoria) are quite small. So, for the genealogist, online photographs mainly provide historical and geographical background to a family history, rather than primary source material. But you may be lucky, and there are certainly some significant collections with photographs of named individuals, some of which are highlighted here.

The web is also a good source of information for understanding and managing your own family photographs, and there are sites devoted to dating, preservation, restoration, and scanning.

Cyndi's List has a page with links for 'Photographs and Memories' at <www.cyndislist.com/photos/>, covering all aspects of photography and family history. Information on using search engines to locate images online is covered in Chapter 19 on p. 343. Present-day aerial photographs tend to be provided by mapping sites and are covered in Chapter 15, p. 263.

National collections

For photographs of historic buildings, there are two national sites for England. The National Monuments Record's (NMR) Images of England site at <www.imagesofengland.org.uk> is intended to be 'an internet home for England's listed buildings' with good-quality photographs and descriptions of every listed building in the country. There are over 300,000 listed properties included on the site. You can do a quick search without further ado, while the free registration gives you access to more sophisticated standard and advanced searches. Search facilities include search by county or town, building type, period, or person (an architect or other individual associated with a building). Thumbnail images link to full size images with a description.

ViewFinder is run by English Heritage at <viewfinder.english-heritage. org.uk>. This aims to make part of the NMR's image archive available online. Whereas Images of England contains contemporary photographs, the ViewFinder images are older. The site has around 25,000 images in a number of collections drawn from individual photographers. The largest collection, with over 13,000 photographs, represents the work of Henry W. Taunt, an important Oxford photographer of the late nineteenth and early

Figure 17-1 ViewFinder: Images of Hastings

twentieth century. London is well served by these collections, with many street views and material relating to the Port of London. There is also a project relating to 'England at Work', with 5,000 images illustrating England's industrial heritage (click on 'Photo Essays' on the home page, and then select 'England at Work' from the subject drop-down list). The photographs come in three sizes: a small thumbnail, a basic view of about 450 × 300 pixels, which you can save, and an enlarged view of around 700 × 480 pixels which your browser won't let you save. Even though the images are historical, the search is based on present-day counties, not the pre-1974 counties. Another English Heritage image collection, though more of interest to historians and archaeologists, is PastScape at <**www.pastscape.org.uk**>.

A similar collection for Scotland is Historic Scotland Images at <**www.historicscotlandimages.gov.uk**>, which, like Images of England, has contemporary photographs. These are displayed both as thumbnails and very high quality images, though unfortunately the thumbnails do not identify the location. There is a keyword search, or you can browse by category. The Royal Commission on the Ancient and Historical Monuments of Scotland's 'Old Scotland' pages at <**www.rcahms.gov.uk/ old-scotland.html**> also have modern photos of old buildings. The search facility covers all items in the catalogue, not just the photographs, so it may be easier to browse the available photographs via the thumbnail pages for each region. The National Galleries of Scotland has a small collection of nineteenth-century photographs from their collections on Flickr at <**www.flickr.com/photos/nationalgalleries**>.

The National Library of Wales's Digital Mirror (Figure 17-2) offers seven online collections relating to Wales and Welsh photography at <**www.llgc.org.uk/index.php?id=133**> and has information about the National Collection of Welsh Photographs at <**www.llgc.org.uk/index.php? id=introduction2**>. The Library has over 700 items from the P. B. Abery Collection available on Flickr at <**www.flickr.com/photos/37199428@N06**>.

The Public Record Office of Northern Ireland has used Flickr to publish photographs from its collection. Around 1,300 photographs from the Allison Collection are available at <**www.flickr.com/photos/proni**>. These are of particular interest to family historians because they include over 1,000 wedding photographs, taken between 1900 and 1950, with the name of the family and the date of the wedding making identification easy.

The National Library of Ireland's Digital Photographs collection at <**www.nli.ie/digital-photographs.aspx**> comprises eight individual collections, mostly covering the period before independence. While most are of buildings and places, there are many of groups and individuals, often with the name of the family.

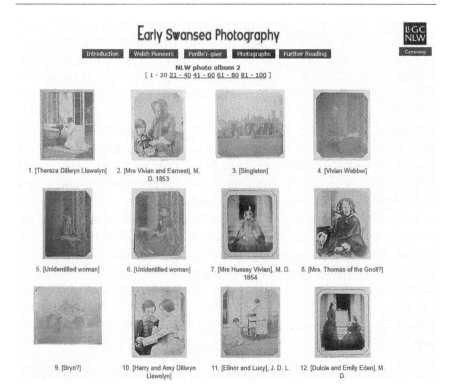

Figure 17-2 The National Library of Wales's Digital Mirror

Regional and local collections

Record offices and libraries have substantial collections of photographic material, and this is increasingly being made available online, in many cases with lottery funding. Some of these collections are purely photographic, while others include scanned prints, drawings and even paintings. The following will give you some idea of the sort of material available.

Collage at <**collage.cityoflondon.gov.uk**> is the Guildhall Library's image database. Its 20,000 or so images of the capital include maps, plans, engravings and photographs of places, with a large collection relating to trades and industries, including the City Livery Companies.

For suburban London, the Ideal Homes site at <**www.ideal-homes.org.uk**> (see Figure 17-3) includes historical photographs for the six South-East London Boroughs. The images are not accessible from the home page, but from the home page for each borough there are links from the right-hand navigation bar. Thumbnails link, in turn, to larger images with a description.

Glasgow's Mitchell Library, which houses the City Archives, offers the 'Virtual Mitchell Collection' at <**www.mitchelllibrary.org/virtualmitchell/**>

Figure 17-3 Ideal Homes: Double's Butchers, Chislehurst

– note the three consecutive l's in the URL – which is a selection from the images in the collection covering 'street scenes and buildings, but also scenes of past working lives and of social life in the city'. Searches can be made by street name or subject.

West Sussex Record Office has an online database, West Sussex Past Pictures, at <**www.westsussexpast.org.uk/pictures/**>, with details of 31,000 photographs held in the record office, of which over 12,000 are available online. The online database provides record office references so that scans of photographs can be requested if the image is not already online.

The North of England seems to be particularly well served by online image libraries. Probably the largest is Picture the Past at <**www.picturethepast.org.uk**>. This is the website for the North East Midland Photographic Record, a project run by the local authorities of Derby, Derbyshire, Nottingham, and Nottinghamshire, and intended to 'conserve and make publicly accessible the photographic heritage of the North East Midlands'. The site holds around 90,000 images, including many of individual streets and houses. There is a comprehensive search facility – you can specify a county or a place, and enter individual keywords (though the site does not indicate what keywords are used in the database). Individual images are presented on-screen at around 250 × 190 pixels, and you can order high quality prints online. A useful feature of the database is that each image has a link to a present-day map showing its approximate location.

Many pictures are accompanied by historical notes (see Figure 17-4) and there is also a facility for those with local historical knowledge to contribute additional information.

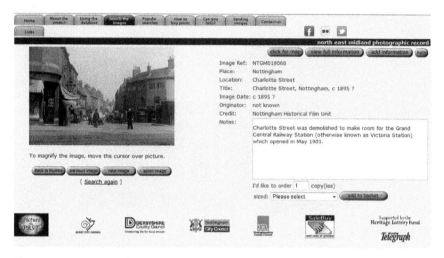

Figure 17-4 A Nottingham street scene from Picture the Past

Picturesheffield.com at <**www.picturesheffield.com**> is an online version of Sheffield Local Studies Library's computerized image system. Funded from the Heritage Lottery Fund, the site contains around 35,000 photographs, about two-thirds of the Library's collection. Low resolution images (typically around 350 × 200 pixels at 72 dots per inch) can be downloaded from the site free of charge, and high-resolution photographic prints can be purchased.

Leeds Library & Information Service has a photographic archive of the city, Leodis, at <**www.leodis.net**> with almost 60,000 images. The search results give only the title and description (often quite extensive) and you need to follow the link to see the image. As with Picture the Past, there is a facility to add comments, which often include information from local people about the history and inhabitants of a place.

Bury Image Bank at <**www.buryimagebank.org.uk**> is an online database of over 18,000 images of streets and buildings from the mid-nineteenth century onwards.

Chester Image Bank at <**chesterimagebank.org.uk**>, maintained by the Cheshire & Chester Joint Archive Service has 'several thousand photographs'.

Alongside these official sites, there is the occasional personal site, such as the Old Scottish Borders Photo Archive at <**www.ettrickgraphics.com/ bordersindex.htm**>, which has views of border towns, and Kevin Quick's photographs of Bedfordshire and Buckinghamshire towns and villages at <www.countyviews.com>.

It is always worth checking a relevant record office website for photographic collections. Even if there is little or no material on the web, you can expect to find information about their holdings. For example, Greater Manchester CRO has details of its Documentary Photography Archive at <**www.manchester.gov.uk/info/448/archives_and_local_ studies/4689/documentary_photography_archive**>, which is an important collection for family historians because it includes many family photographs up to the 1950s. Photographs are usually an important part of official local history sites for specific places (see p. 278).

Specialist collections

Alongside these geographically-based collections, there are countless sites devoted to photographs of particular subjects. The websites of specialist museums are an obvious place to look. For example, the London Transport Museum has an online photographic collection at <**www.ltmcollection.org/ photos/**>, which includes over a hundred photographs of named London bus conductors (Figure 17-5). The British Empire and Commonwealth Museum's Images of Empire site at <**www.imagesofempire.com**> is 'the largest dedicated online resource of still and moving images on the British colonial period', and includes material from nearly 150 photographic collections, which can be viewed either by searching or by browsing the collections individually. A selection of material can be viewed under 10 thematic headings (e.g. domestic life, transport).

Several of the military sites mentioned in Chapter 10 include photographs. Fred Larimore's site devoted to Nineteenth Century British And Indian Armies And Their Soldiers at <**www.members.dca.net/fbl/**> has a collection of photographs for the period 1840 to 1920, in some cases with information about the individual shown and commentary on uniform details. And several of the sites devoted to individual occupations (see Chapter 9) have photographs.

The International Mission Photography Archive at <**digitallibrary.usc.edu/ impa/controller/index.htm**> has historical photographs relating to the work of missionaries in Africa, Asia and the Caribbean.

County Record Office sites, too, may offer specialist collections. Buckinghamshire, for example, has an online database of Victorian prisoners in Aylesbury Gaol at <**www.buckscc.gov.uk/sites/bcc/archives/ea_ libprisoners.page**>, around a quarter of which have photographs.

The website of the Roger Vaughan Picture Library at <**www.rogerco. freeserve.co.uk**> has around 3,000 Victorian and Edwardian studio photographs, with links to other sites with many more. Most of the subjects

Figure 17-5 The London Transport Museum Photographic Collection

aren't named, so this is more useful for help with dating and information on professional photographers.

The Scottish Highlander Photo Archive at <**www.scottishhighlander photoarchive.co.uk**> is a commercial site with almost 3,000 named portraits.

Churches

Of particular interest to genealogists are pictures of the churches in which ancestors worshipped and married, and while the national and regional collections mentioned above naturally include some photographs of church buildings, there are several volunteer-run sites devoted specifically to church photographs, often accompanied by historical information:

- Genuki's Church Database at <**www.genuki.org.uk/big/churchdb/**> (see p. 256), which aims to list all the churches in the British Isles, has photos of some 8,000 churches in England, with significant coverage for Cheshire, Cornwall, Hampshire, Lancashire, Norfolk and Yorkshire.

- Steve Bulman's The Churches of Britain and Ireland at <**www.churches-uk-ireland.org**> has collected over 21,000 photographs.
- Churches of the World is an ambitious site at <**www.photosof churches.com**>, which is particularly strong on Welsh churches.
- Essex Churches at <**www.essexchurches.info**> has photos of over 400 of Essex's churches to date.
- Michael Day's Dorset Churches has photographs and detailed histories of a large number of the county's churches at <**people.bath.ac.uk/lismd/ dorset/churches/**>.
- ChurchCrawler at <**www.churchcrawler.co.uk**> has church photographs for a range of counties and areas, with particular concentration on Bristol.
- The website of Scottish Church Heritage Research at <**www.scottish churches.org.uk**> has a database of Scottish churches and many of the entries include photographs.
- Jo Mitchell's Irish Church site at <**freepages.genealogy.rootsweb. ancestry.com/~irishchurches/Irish%20churches.html**> covers churches of all the main denominations found in Ireland.

There are, of course, many pictures of churches on photo-sharing sites such as Flickr (see p. 313), and image search engines can be used to find images of an individual building.

Schools

Many school photographs will be found online. For a simple example, see Kennethmont School's page at <**www.kinnethmont.co.uk/k-school.htm**>, which offers a selection of group photos from 1912 onwards with many pupils and teachers identified by name (Figure 17-6). (Yes, the site and the school differ in spelling!) Jeff Maynard has a more extensive collection for Harrow County School with form and sports team photos going back to the 1920s at <**www.jeffreymaynard.com/Harrow_County/photographs.htm**>, with something for almost every year.

A good way to find photographs for particular schools is to check the website of the school itself, if it still exists. Where a school is under local authority control, the school website will often have the format <**www.*name-of-school.name-of-localauthority*.sch.uk**>, e.g. <**www.longlands. bexley.sch.uk**>. But many schools, and of course all independent schools, will have their own internet domain, in which case a general search on the school name in a search engine will quickly find the site. A local history site may include school photographs, too.

Kennethmont School 1937

Mr Fowlie, Headmaster, Andy Munro, Billy McDonald, Jas Greig, Jim Andrew, Sandy Andrew, Bill Pirie, Jim Dey, Gordon Watt

Margt Stewart, Winifred Beattie, Mary Cruickshank, Daisy Morgan, Harriet Simpson, Jean Lawson, Annie Fraser, Helen Borthwick, Isobel Dey

Margt Innes, Twin Rennie, Clare McRobbie, Annie Souter, Annabella Mackie, Janet Mackie, Helen Skinner, Twin Rennie, Williamina McDonald

Alexander Simpson

Figure 17-6 Kennethmont School photograph from 1937

Friends Reunited at <**www.friendsreunited.co.uk**>, which aims to put users in touch with old schoolfriends, has a page for every school in the country and these often have photos submitted by former pupils. You will need to register in order to see the material.

Incidentally, if you come across a site called World School Photographs, ignore it – it seems to be solely designed to collect personal information, and has *no* school photographs.

Commercial photographers

The commercial picture libraries have not been slow to exploit the web as a means of providing a catalogue for prospective purchasers of their material or services. These resources are also useful to non-professional users because access to the online catalogues and databases is usually free, though the image size and quality is likely to be reduced, and the scans may have some overprinting to prevent them being used commercially.

Perhaps the most important commercial site with old photographs for the UK is the Francis Frith Collection at <**www.francisfrith.com**>. Frith was a Victorian photographer whose company photographed over 7,000 towns and villages in all parts of the British Isles, from 1860 until it closed in 1969. The entire stock was bought by a new company, which now sells prints. While the aim of the website is to act as a sales medium, it has reasonable size thumbnails (under 400 × 274 pixels) of all 120,000-odd pictures in the collection, which can be located by search or via a listing for each (present-day) county without the need to make a purchase. There are also some historic aerial photographs. The site allows you set up an 'album' to store the pictures you want to view again.

Frith's photographs and many other commercial photographs of towns and villages were issued as postcards, which means that postcard sites may have material of interest. For example, there is a collection of Isle of Wight postcards at <**members.multimania.co.uk/bartie**>; Eddie Prowse has an online collection of postcards of Weymouth and Portland at <**www.eprowse. fsnet.co.uk**>; Postcardworld at <**www.postcardworld.co.uk**> is a commercial site with postcards of all parts of the UK, with 300 × 200 pixel scans on the site. Old UK Photos at <**www.oldukphotos.com**> has a growing collection of old photos of places, which are mainly taken from old postcards.

Professional photographers

In one sense, professional photographers are just another occupational group (see Chapter 9). But their role in creating a unique part of the recent historical record makes them of interest not just to their descendants. Information about their working lives can be important in dating and locating family photographs.

A useful site for information on UK photographers is the New Index of Victorian, Edwardian & Early 20th Century UK Photographers at <**www.thornburypump.myby.co.uk/PI/**>. This has a database of photographers (which, however, can only be searched by county) and links to many other sites. Roger Vaughan has a list of several hundred Victorian photographers at <**freepages.family.rootsweb.ancestry.com/ ~victorianphotographs/pixs/carte.htm**>, while PhotoLondon has a 'Database of 19th Century Photographers and Allied Trades in London: 1841–1901' at <**www.photolondon.org.uk**>. Another useful site is Christine Hibbert's Victorian Photographers of Britain 1855–1901, which lists photographers, with towns and dates. Unfortunately, the site itself closed down at the beginning of 2008, but the content is still available on the Wayback Machine with the URL <**mywebpage.netscape.com/ hibchris/instant/aboutme.html**> (18 September 2008).

EdinPhoto at <**www.edinphoto.org.uk**> is a comprehensive site devoted to the history of photography in Edinburgh. The pages on the city's professional photographers at <**www.edinphoto.org.uk/2/2__ professional_photographers.htm**> (note the *two* underscores before *professional*) provide details of around 250 individuals and hundreds of studios, in many cases with examples of their work. There are also family trees for a few of the city's photographic dynasties. Details of almost 150 'Jersey Photographers and Studios' will be found on the Jerseyfamilyhistory site at <**jerseyfamilyhistory.co.uk/?page_id=11**>. Sussex PhotoHistory at

<www.photohistory-sussex.co.uk> has details of photographers and studios active in the county between 1841 and 1910, with detailed histories and in many cases sample photographs.

The 'Identifying Photographers' page on Cyndi's List at <**www.cyndislist.com/ photos/identifying/**> lists a number of other sites giving dates and places for British professional photographers, often for specific towns or counties (including Ayrshire, Birmingham, Bristol, Liverpool, and the Isle of Man).

UK-PHOTOGRAPHERS is a mailing list for the discussion and sharing of information regarding photographic studios and the dating of photographs produced by professional photographers in England and Wales between 1850 and 1950. Information on subscribing will be found at <**lists.rootsweb. ancestry.com/index/other/Occupations/UK-PHOTOGRAPHERS.html**>, which has a link to the archive of past messages.

Film and video

Most digital video available online is of fairly recent origin. Of course your wedding video *is* of genealogical interest, but not to anyone outside your family. Video sharing sites like YouTube at <**www.youtube.com**> nonetheless do have some older material digitized from film, but the problem is that there's no reliable way to find this among the millions of pieces of recent home video, since the only text you can search on is the title given to each clip by the uploader. Unless you are looking for something very specific – finding clips of, say, Glasgow's last tram or of a particular football club is simple enough – probably the best you will be able to do is find historical material of local interest by searching on a place-name and a year. However, there are a few sites with professionally catalogued clips of archive film.

The Scottish Screen Archive, part of the National Library of Scotland, is Scotland's national moving images collection. The catalogue on its website at <**ssa.nls.uk**> lists all items in the archive, indicating whether a clip or full-length video is available online. Each item is accompanied by a detailed description of the shots in the film (see Figure 17-7).

The British Universities Film & Video Council (BUFVC) has an online catalogue with details of some 13 million items at <**beta.bufvc.ac.uk**>. Most of the entries relate to TV transmissions from the last 60 years, not especially relevant for genealogists, but it has details of newsreel material, which may be useful for old items of local news. The site does not host the newsreels itself, but links to the two major film company sites for newsreel footage: British Pathé at <**www.britishpathe.com**>, which offers 90,000 items of newsreel from 1896 to 1976, and Movietone at <**www.movietone.com**> with presumably similar coverage. The Movietone site requires (free) registration.

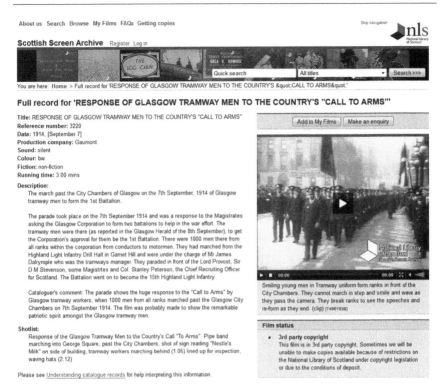

Figure 17-7 A record from the Scottish Screen Archive

Dating, preservation, restoration

The web can be useful in connection with your own photographs, if you need to date them or if you need advice on preservation or restoration.

For help with the dating of old photographs, Andrew J. Morris's site 19th Century Photography at <**ajmorris.com/roots/photo/**> provides a detailed account of the various types of photographic process and technique. The Roger Vaughan Picture Library has a section devoted to dating portraits at <**www.cartes.freeuk.com/time/date.htm**> with examples of (approximately) dated photographs for years between 1860 and 1952.

The Open University has a unit 'Picturing the family' at <**openlearn. open.ac.uk/course/view.php?id=2688**>, an online tutorial (designed to take 12 hours) which 'looks at some of the ways photographs can reveal, and sometimes conceal, important information about the past', with around a hundred photographs for analysis and interpretation.

If you are interested in preserving and restoring old photographs, Colin Robinson has information about their care and conservation at <**www.colinrobinson.com/care.html**>, while David L. Mishkin's article on 'Restoring Damaged Photographs' at <**www.genealogy.com/10_restr. html**> covers the various approaches to restoration. (If you access this site via a UK ISP, you will get an irritating page which asks if you want to go to the UK Ancestry site – you need to click on the 'Remain on Genealogy.com' link.)

The US National Archives website has a useful section on 'Caring for Your Family Archives' at <**www.archives.gov/preservation/family-archives/**>, which covers all aspects of caring for photographic prints.

If you want to scan photographs and restore them digitally, it is worth looking at Scantips <**www.scantips.com**>, which not only has extensive advice about scanning in general but also includes a page on 'Restoration of genealogical photos' at <**www.scantips.com/restore.html**>. About.com has a series of articles by Kimberley Powell on 'creating and editing digital photos' at <**genealogy.about.com/cs/digitalphoto/a/digital_photos.htm**>.

These sites offer advice not just on the obvious topic of repairing the signs of physical damage but also on correcting tonal problems with faded originals. Sites devoted to digital restoration generally assume you are using Adobe Photoshop, but the principles transfer to other graphics editing packages, though there may be some differences in terminology.

A general source of help with old photographs is the RootsWeb mailing list VINTAGE-PHOTOS, which is devoted to 'the discussion and sharing of information regarding vintage photos including, but not restricted to, proper storage, preservation, restoration, ageing and dating, restoration software, photo types and materials used, restoration assistance, and scanning options'. Information on how to join the list will be found at <**lists.rootsweb. ancestry.com/index/other/Miscellaneous/VINTAGE-PHOTOS.html**>, which also provides links to the list's archives. The GenPhoto list at Yahoo Groups is a mailing list about photography specifically for family historians. Its coverage includes identifying old photographs, and using digital photography and scanning to share and preserve family photos. You can read archived messages and join the group at <**groups.yahoo.com/group/ genphoto/**>. The Photo Identification Discussion Group is also on Yahoo Groups, at <**groups.yahoo.com/group/photoid**>, and is devoted to 'techniques for identifying the date and subjects of old photographs'. Archived messages can be read only once you have joined the group.

Digital archiving

While modern digital photographs don't need 'preservation' as such, appropriate archiving is essential if future generations are to see them. Digital photographs may not get torn or faded, but image files can easily become corrupted or destroyed, as can the physical media on which they are stored. Also, it's a lot easier to write a name and a date on the back of a photographic print than to attach the same information securely to a file. Good starting points for exploring this issue are the following articles:

- Christopher Auman, 'Archiving & Preserving Digital Photography' at <**blogcritics.org/culture/article/archiving-digital-photography-part-1/**>
- Howard Miller, 'Digital Life Preservers; How To Organize, Archive, And Protect Your Valuable Photos' at <**shutterbug.com/techniques/digital_ darkroom/0905digitallife/**>
- Ken Watson, 'All About Digital Photos – Storing and Archiving Digital Photos' at <**www.rideau-info.com/photos/**>

If you're serious about digital preservation, then an important consideration is the long-term stability of the storage media. Authoritative guidance on the life of optical media (CD, DVD) is available in a report from the US National Institute of Standards and Technology at <**www.creativetechs.com/tips/SVC-backup/StabilityStudy.pdf**>. The body of the article is very technical, but the conclusions are probably all you need.

Photo sharing

In the last few years we have seen increasing possibilities for collaboration on the web, and an example of this are photo sharing sites, which provide a platform for individuals to share their photos online without going to the trouble of setting up a personal website.

The best known of these is undoubtedly Flickr at <**www.flickr.com**>, which allows users to maintain collections of online photos free of charge. Photos can either be entirely public or you can restrict access to selected family members and friends, making it an easy way to share new digital photos of family events or scans of historical photos. Where photos are public, they can be located via the search facility, so sites like Flickr can be used as a way of finding contemporary photos of places in addition to the official geographical collections mentioned at the beginning of this chapter. Even the smallest village is likely to be represented by a dozen or more photographs showing the major buildings and the surrounding landscape. Figure 17-8 shows some of the 600 or so images for the village of Sproughton in Suffolk. (And you can see photos of the author in his earliest youth at <**www.flickr.com/ photos/petex/sets/72157603870404149/**>.)

You can get a list of similar sites from the Wikipedia article on 'Photo sharing' which also provides an overview of the various types of photo sharing site.

Figure 17-8 Flickr images for Sproughton, Suffolk

Mapping sites provide an ideal framework for organizing photographs of places and Google Maps at <**maps.google.co.uk**> (see p. 263) includes a facility for people to attach a photo to a particular location. To see which locations have photos, you need to move the mouse over the 'Traffic' drop-down list at the top right of the map display and then tick the Photos option (see Figure 17-9). Geograph at <**www.geograph.org.uk**> takes a similar but more methodical approach: it invites people to submit photographs of the main geographical features for every 1km grid square of the British Isles.

Wikimedia Commons at <**commons.wikimedia.org**> also has many user-submitted photographs of places – just search on the place-name in the search box on the home page. Many of these, incidentally, are uploaded under a Creative Commons licence (see <**creativecommons.org**>), which means you could use them for your own website or printed family history without seeking permission.

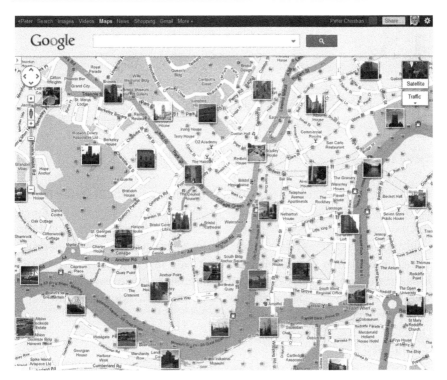

Figure 17-9 Google Maps: photo locations in Bristol

18

DISCUSSION FORUMS

One of the most useful aspects of the internet for anyone researching their family history is that it is very easy to 'meet' other genealogists online to discuss matters of common interest, to exchange information, and to find help and advice. The specific issues of locating other people with interests in the same surnames and families are dealt with in Chapter 14. This chapter looks at the two main types of online discussion group – mailing lists and web-based forums – and at the use of social networking services such as Facebook for genealogy.

Mailing lists

Electronic mailing lists provide a way for groups of people to conduct online discussions via email. They are simply a logical extension of your electronic address book – instead of each member of a group having to keep track of the email addresses of everyone else, this list of email addresses is managed by a computer called a 'list server'. This arrangement allows people to add themselves to the list, or remove themselves from it, without having to contact all the other members.

You join a list by sending an email message to the list server. Thereafter you receive a copy of every message sent to the list by other list members; likewise, any message you send to the list gets circulated to all the other subscribers.

Finding lists

The first genealogical mailing list, ROOTS-L, goes back to a period long before the internet was available to the general public – its first message was posted in December 1987. There must now be well over 50,000 English-language mailing lists devoted to genealogy.

Every mailing list is hosted on a specific server, which is responsible for dealing with all the messages, and a large proportion of the genealogy lists (over 32,000) are hosted by RootsWeb, whose main mailing lists page will be found at <lists.rootsweb.ancestry.com>. The 'browse mailing lists' link on this page takes you to a list of subject categories, which is useful for finding lists devoted to a particular topic. General lists for the UK (which includes those for occupations, for example) are linked from <**lists.rootsweb. ancestry.com/index/intl/UK/**>, while the linked individual pages for England, Ireland, Scotland and Wales cover lists for regional and local interests. There is no master listing of all RootsWeb lists, so it can be hard to find those which do not fall into obvious categories. The keyword search on the home page will help, though it only searches for the exact words in the names and descriptions of lists, with the result that, for example, searches on 'navy' and 'navies' produce quite different results. However, if you know the name of the list, this limitation is not a problem.

A general mailing list site that hosts around 15,000 genealogy lists is Yahoo Groups at <**groups.yahoo.com**>. Most of the genealogy groups hosted here are listed under the **Family & Home** category on the home page, though there are many others for particular countries and areas, which can be found by using the search facility.

In spite of the large number of lists, it is a simple matter to find those which might be of interest to you, as there are two sites which compile this information. The more definitive is the late John Fuller's Genealogy Resources on the Internet site at <**www.rootsweb.ancestry.com/~jfuller/ gen_mail.html**>, now maintained by Linda Lambert and Megan Zurawicz. This has a comprehensive listing of genealogy mailing lists, subdivided into the following categories:

Countries Other Than USA	Jewish
USA	LDS
Surnames	Native American
Adoption	Newspapers
African-Ancestored	Nobility/Heads of State/Heraldry
Cemeteries/Monuments/Obituaries	Occupations
Computing/Internet Resources	Religions/Churches
DNA Studies/Testing	Societies
Emigration/Migration Ships and Trails	Software
Family History, Folklore, and Artifacts	Translations and Word Origins
Freedmen	Vital Records (census, BDM)
Genealogical Material	Wars/Military
General Information/Discussion	Uncategorized

The 'uncategorized' lists include a number devoted to topics of general interest, such as the GEN-MEDIEVAL and SHIPWRECK lists.

However, more useful for those with UK interests is Genuki's Mailing Lists page at <**www.genuki.org.uk/indexes/MailingLists.html**>. This has the advantage of listing only those relevant to British and Irish genealogy. It also includes lists which, although of interest to UK genealogists, are not categorized under the UK by John Fuller or RootsWeb, notably war-related lists such as AMERICAN-REVOLUTION, BOER-WAR or WARBRIDES. The organization of the Genuki listing makes it easier to find lists of interest: at the top of the page are those devoted to general topics, but the main body of the page gives all the lists for each county in the British Isles. Another advantage over John Fuller's pages, which give only subscription information, is that the Genuki listing has links to the web page for each list, so you can easily find further information or access the list archives if they are publicly accessible.

In general, the most useful mailing lists are probably those for individual counties. RootsWeb has lists for every county in the British Isles and these are good places to find discussion of or ask questions about the areas where your ancestors lived and about local records.

As well as the lists for each county as a whole, there are many devoted to areas within a county, and to particular towns and villages. Staffordshire, for example, is covered not only by a general list, STAFFORDSHIRE, but also by lists for local areas such as the Black Country and the Potteries, as well as a number of individual towns such as Walsall and Sedgley. Staffordshire interests are also covered by the broader MIDMARCH and SHROPSHIRE-PLUS lists.

RootsWeb has at least one list for over 150 other countries, with messages generally in English, which makes these potentially good starting points if you need help researching an overseas ancestor. However, there is wide variation in the level of activity on these lists, and often the lists for individual regions within a country look more useful than the general country-wide lists.

Alongside such geographically based lists, there are general lists covering particular topics in relation either to the entirety of the British Isles, or to some constituent of it. Examples of these are lists like AUS-CONVICTS, BRITREGIMENTS, RAILWAY-UK and UK-1901-CENSUS. Other lists are mentioned in Chapters 8, 9, 10, 14 and 15.

There are also many mailing lists for individual surnames. These are discussed in detail on p. 229.

Of course Genuki and Genealogy Resources on the Internet only have details of lists aimed at the genealogist, and there may be useful contacts in lists for related topics, such as local history. If you want to find mailing lists on other topics, there is unfortunately no definitive catalogue – in fact such a thing would be impossible to compile and maintain. However, since most mailing lists have either a website of their own or at least a listing somewhere on the web, a search engine can be used to locate them.

SUSSEX-PLUS Mailing List

SUSSEX-PLUS-L
lists2

Topic: A mailing list for anyone with a genealogical or historical interest in the county of Sussex, England and the adjacent counties of Surrey, Kent and Hampshire. Additional information can be found on the Sussex Plus Mailing List Web Site below:

There is a Web page for the **SUSSEX-PLUS** mailing list at http://www.users.globalnet.co.uk/~juliec/sxplus/index.htm.

For questions about this list, contact the list administrator at SUSSEX-PLUS-admin@rootsweb.com.

- **Subscribing.** Clicking on one of the shortcut links below should work, but if your browser doesn't understand them, try these manual instructions: to join **SUSSEX-PLUS-L**, send mail to SUSSEX-PLUS-L-request@rootsweb.com with the single word *subscribe* in the message subject and body. To join **SUSSEX-PLUS-D**, do the same thing with SUSSEX-PLUS-D-request@rootsweb.com.
    - Subscribe to SUSSEX-PLUS-L
    - Subscribe to SUSSEX-PLUS-D (digest)
- **Unsubscribing.** To leave **SUSSEX-PLUS-L**, send mail to SUSSEX-PLUS-L-request@rootsweb.com with the single word *unsubscribe* in the message subject and body. To leave **SUSSEX-PLUS-D**, do the same thing with SUSSEX-PLUS-D-request@rootsweb.com.
    - Unsubscribe from SUSSEX-PLUS-L
    - Unsubscribe from SUSSEX-PLUS-D (digest)
- **Archives.** You can search the archives for a specific message or browse them, going from one message to another. Some list archives are not available; if there is a link here to an archive but the link doesn't work, it probably just means that no messages have been posted to that list yet.
    - Search the SUSSEX-PLUS archives
    - Browse the SUSSEX-PLUS archives

Figure 18-1 The home page for a typical RootsWeb list

List archives

Many genealogy mailing lists, including almost all those hosted by RootsWeb, have an archive of past messages. The RootsWeb list archives can be found at <**archiver.rootsweb.ancestry.com**>. There are also links to the archives for each list from its home page (see Figure 18-1). Not all list archives are open to non-members of the relevant list, but where a RootsWeb list has open membership it is not very common to find that the archive is closed. On Yahoo Groups the home page for each list has a link to 'Messages', which contains all past messages in reverse order of date. For many Yahoo groups, however, you do have to join a list to see its messages.

List archives have several uses. First, they allow you to get an idea of the discussion topics that come up on the list and judge whether it would be worth your while joining. Also, an archive will give you some idea of the level of traffic on the list, i.e. how many messages a day are posted – there is seldom any point in joining a list that has only half a dozen messages a year. Finally, the archives provide a basis for searching, whether by the list server's own search facility, or by a general search engine such as those discussed in Chapter 19. This means that you can take advantage of information posted to a mailing list without even joining it, though of course you will need to join to post your own messages.

Joining a list

In order to join a list you need to send an email message to the list server, the computer that manages the list, instructing it to add you to the list of subscribers. Genealogy Resources on the Internet provides subscription instructions for every list, and the web page for any list will obviously do likewise. On Rootsweb, clicking on the 'subscribe to...' link (see Figure 18-1) will automatically start an email message ready for you to send. (Incidentally, do not be worried by the word 'subscribe'. It does not mean you are committing yourself to paying for anything, it just means that your name is being added to the list of members.)

One thing to note is that a list will normally have three distinct email addresses for different purposes. There is one address for sending requests to subscribe or unsubscribe – that's all it is used for, and in fact such messages are dealt with automatically by the mailing list system. Then there is the address of the list itself – this is the address to which you send messages to go out to all the other members. Finally, there is an address for the list administrator(s) – messages sent to this address are dealt with personally by whoever is in charge of the list. Normally, this should only be necessary if there is some problem: perhaps messages from the list have stopped being delivered, or another list member is sending abusive messages.

If you have more than one email address you need to make sure that you send your joining message from the one you want to use to send and receive messages. Mailing lists will reject an email message from an address it does not have in its subscriber list. If you want to be able to use more than one email address to post messages to a list, you will need to ask the list administrator to add further addresses for you.

There are some circumstances in which you will not be able to join a list just by sending a message or clicking on a link: some lists are 'closed', i.e. they are not open to all comers. This is typically the case for mailing lists run by societies for their own members. In this case, instead of sending an email to the list server you will probably need to contact the person who manages the list, providing your society membership number, so that he or she can check that you are entitled to join the list and then add you.

Digests

Many mailing lists have two ways in which you can receive messages. The standard way is what is called 'mail mode', where every individual message to the list is forwarded to you as soon as it is received. However, some older email systems were not able to cope with the potentially very large number of incoming messages, so lists also offered a 'digest mode'. In this, a bunch of messages to the list are combined into a single larger message, so reducing the number of messages arriving in the subscriber's mailbox. Even though few of us nowadays are likely to be affected by this sort of technical limitation, some people do not like to receive the dozens of mail messages per day that can come from a busy list, and prefer to receive the messages as a digest.

However, there are also disadvantages to this. For a start, you will need to look through each digest to see the subjects of the messages it contains, whereas individual messages with subject lines of no interest to you can quickly be deleted unread. Also, if you want to reply to a message contained within a digest your email software will automatically include the subject line of the *digest*, not just the subject of the individual message within the digest you are replying to. The result is that other list members will not be able to tell from this subject line which earlier message you are responding to. If your email software automatically quotes the original message in reply, then you will need to delete almost all of the quoted digest if you are not to irritate other list members with an unnecessarily long message, most of which will be irrelevant (see Netiquette, p. 327). Unless you have only a slow internet connection and your email software does not offer a filtering facility (see below), there is no good reason to subscribe in digest mode. If you do decide it is more suitable for your way of working, the home page of the list should tell you how to switch to that option.

Text formatting

Email software generally allows you to send messages in a number of different formats, and normally you do not need to worry about exactly how your mail software is formatting them. When you start sending messages to mailing lists, however, you may find that this is an issue you need to consider. The reason for this is that some mailing lists will not accept certain types of formatting, and even if they do, some recipients of your formatted messages may have difficulties.

The standard format for an email message is plain text. This can be handled by any list server and any email software. However, most modern email software will let you send formatted text with particular fonts and font sizes, colour, italics and so on, i.e. something much more like what you produce with your word processor, and some software even uses this as the default. The way it does this is, typically, to include an email attachment containing the message in RTF format (created and used by word processors) or HTML format (used for web pages).

You may feel that this is exactly how you want your email messages to look. But if someone is using email software that can't make sense of this format they may have trouble with your message. Different lists and list systems deal with this problem in a variety of ways. Yahoo Groups allows you to choose whether you receive messages from the list as HMTL or as plain text. RootsWeb does not permit the use of HTML or RTF formatting at all, and will not allow messages with formatted text to get through.

If you need to find out how to turn off the formatting features of your email software, RootsWeb has a useful page on 'Sending Messages in Plain Text' at <**helpdesk.rootsweb.ancestry.com/listadmins/plaintext.html**>. The page shows you how to do this for over 20 of the widely used email packages. The page does not seem to be very up-to-date, so the email software you use may not be included or the instructions may be for an older version, but even so it should give you an idea of what to look for in your own email software. The online help for your email software should also tell you how to do this.

The only formatting feature that can be really useful in an email message is the ability to highlight words to be stressed, and the traditional way of doing this in a plain text message is to put *asterisks* round the relevant word. One thing *not* to do, in genealogy mailing lists anyway, is put words in upper case – this is traditionally reserved for indicating surnames.

Filtering

If you do not want to subscribe to mailing lists in digest mode, you can still avoid cluttering up your inbox with incoming messages from mailing lists. Most email software has a facility for *filtering* messages, i.e. for moving them automatically from your incoming mailbox to another mailbox when it spots certain pieces of text in the header of the message. You will need to consult the online help for your email software in order to see exactly how to do it, but Figure 18-2 shows a 'rule' in Microsoft Outlook which will filter all mail received from the GENBRIT mailing list into a dedicated mailbox called *genbrit*. This does not reduce the number of messages you receive, but it keeps your list mail separate from your personal mail and you can look at it when it suits you. Since GENBRIT can give rise to as many as 30 messages a day, this is the only practicable way to deal with the volume.

If your ISP allows you multiple email addresses (or if you have registered your own internet domain and use this for your email), it can be worth setting aside an address which you just use for list mail.

News feeds

For RootsWeb mailing lists, another method of automating the receipt and sorting of messages is to use the 'news feed' facility. News feeds and how to use them are described in more detail on p. 385, but essentially, if you subscribe to the news feed for a mailing list, details of newly posted messages

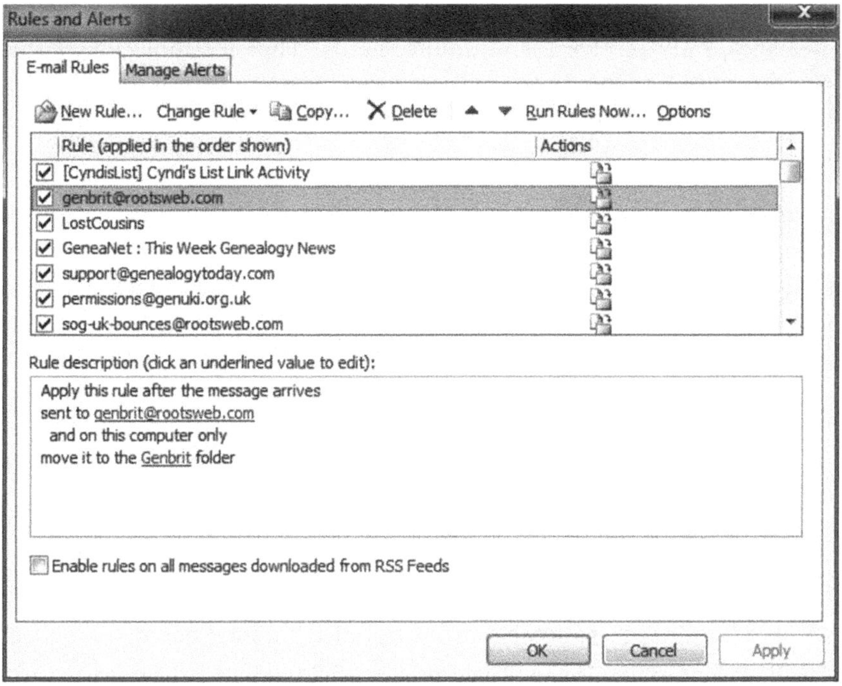

Figure 18-2 This Microsoft Outlook filter will transfer any incoming mail from 'genbrit@rootsweb.ancestry.com' to a dedicated mail folder

will automatically appear in an appropriate folder in your email program or be accessible via a bookmark in your browser, depending on the method you have chosen.

To start receiving a mailing list news feed, go to the web page for any RootsWeb mailing list and follow the link to the 'Browse the archives' page. At the foot of the Archives page you will find an orange RSS button – clicking on this will allow you to add the feed to your email program or browser, as you prefer.

However, there is one important limitation: since you are not actually subscribing to the list, you won't be able to send messages to it, you will just be 'lurking', i.e. reading the messages but not taking part in the discussions.

Other uses of mailing lists

Although, in general, mailing lists allow all members to send messages, and messages are forwarded to all members, there are two types of list that work differently.

Some lists are not used for discussion at all, but only for announcements. Typically, this sort of list is used by an organization to publish an email newsletter. It differs from a normal list in that you will not be able to send messages, only receive the announcements. The electronic newsletters mentioned in Chapter 21 (p. 382) are in fact mailing lists of this type, and from the receiver's point of view these are indistinguishable from news feeds.

Newsgroups

Before the internet was dominated by the World Wide Web, the other main type of discussion technology was the newsgroup, which required special software, a 'newsreader'. But nowadays, apart from a few internet old-timers, almost no-one uses newsgroups. Certainly, for genealogists, there is no need to: for each one of the 20 genealogy newsgroups, RootsWeb provides a parallel mailing list, which carries all the same messages. Indeed the GENBRIT mailing list, mentioned above, actually started life as the newsgroup soc.genealogy.britain.

Web forums

The other main type of discussion group is the web-based forum. There is no single term for these but they are often called 'message boards' or 'bulletin boards' – a website acts as a place where people can post messages for others to read. While using a web-based system is in some ways easier than using mailing lists, these forums have a significant disadvantage: as there is no way to select a whole group of messages for reading, you have to look separately at every single message of interest, each of which is delivered to you as a separate web page. If you want to read every message in a forum, this will be *very* tedious.

Unfortunately, there is no comprehensive list of such discussion forums, but there are popular sites like Yahoo Groups (see p. 317) or Google Groups at <**groups.google.com**>, which provide such facilities for all comers. In fact the distinction between mailing lists and web-based discussion is not absolutely clear-cut. Yahoo Groups, for example, allows you either to read messages on the web or to receive them by email.

The main UK site for genealogy discussion forums is British-Genealogy at <**www.british-genealogy.com/forums**>. This has a forum devoted to each county, and in some cases there are forums for individual places within the county. There are also topic-based forums, covering subjects such as the census, emigration, and a number of occupations, though quite a few of these do not seem to be very active. The site also provides a news feed (see above, and p. 385) for each forum.

Another site for UK and Irish interests is RootsChat at <**www.rootschat.com**>. This has discussion forums for all parts of the British Isles, including every individual county. Within the counties, there are separate forums for lookup

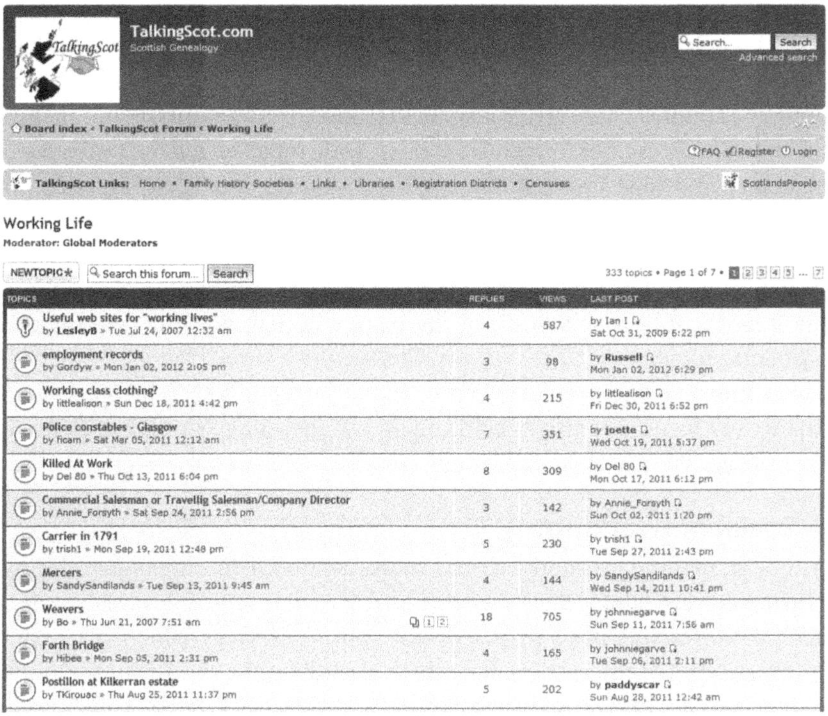

Figure 18-3 The Working Life forum on TalkingScot

offers and requests, and details of online resources. There are also forums for the English-speaking former colonies, and a few general topics such as the armed forces and photo restoration.

TalkingScot provides forums for those with Scottish ancestry at <**www.talkingscot.com**>. It has separate discussion groups for the various types of genealogical record as well as individual groups for Scottish emigration to particular countries or regions. Unlike most other genealogy forum services, it does not have boards for individual counties or regions. Figure 18-3 shows some of the messages in the Working Life forum.

One of the major sites providing discussion forum facilities for genealogy is Genealogy.com's GenForum at <**genforum.genealogy.com**>. There are forums for over 100 countries, including all parts of the British Isles. On the page for each country there is also a link to 'Regions for this Country' which leads to forums for individual counties or major towns, though not every county has its own forum. There is a forum for each US state, and around 80 devoted to general topics (e.g. emigration, Jewish genealogy, marriage records), including 20 or so devoted to computers and genealogy software. There are thousands of forums relating to individual surnames.

Ancestry/RootsWeb also offers message boards at <**boards.ancestry.com**> and <**boards.rootsweb.com**>, covering over 160,000 topics and surnames. There are boards for all parts of the UK and Ireland, with at least one for every pre-1974 county. There are also boards for most other countries and many of the individual counties in each US state. A wide range of general topics have a dedicated message board and these are listed at <**boards.rootsweb.com/ topics/mb.ashx**>.

You can browse or search the many boards dedicated to individual surnames from the 'Find a Board' option on the main page, and the 'Search the Boards' option at the top of the page will help you find messages on particular topics.

Forums on other providers can be found by using a search engine, and a link to any forum relating specifically to UK genealogy should be found on the relevant county page on Genuki.

Social networking

Although mailing lists and web-based discussion forums are older examples of what is now called 'social networking', based around messages, the term itself is nowadays used primarily for online services which offer more complex types of interaction, but which also allow the sharing of messages.

By far the best-known social networking service is Facebook at <**www.facebook.com**>, which claims a sizeable proportion of the world's population as members. MySpace at <**www.myspace.com**> is a similar service, though its membership has been declining and at the time of writing is less than 10 per cent of Facebook's.

Facebook's Groups feature allows you to set up a page for messages relating to a particular topic. There is no central listing of groups on the site, and no way of telling accurately how many of these are devoted to family history. The only way to find whether there is a group for a particular topic is to use the search box at the top of the Facebook page. Probably the most useful search terms are [genealogy] or [family history] along with the name of a region or county, which in most cases should turn up at least one group. There seem to be quite a few groups for individual families or surnames, too, so you might be lucky and find one for a surname of interest to you. It's a good idea to include the word [group] in your search terms, otherwise your search will find all sorts of Facebook pages which are *not* groups. For example, many family history companies and organizations (see Chapter 21) have information pages on Facebook which are not meant for discussions. Likewise, if you search on a surname alone, you will turn up thousands of non-group pages for individuals with that surname (though, of course, for a one-name study that might itself be quite useful).

Figure 18-4 shows the initial results of a search on Facebook for [genealogy Ireland group]. Clicking on the name or icon will take you to the group's information page. In the case of an open group you will also be able to see all the messages that have been posted to the group's 'wall', and if you have already registered as a Facebook user you can join such a group simply by clicking on the 'Join' button on the group's main page or, for closed groups, the 'Ask to join group' button in the listing. Once you have joined a group, it is not much different from using a web-based discussion forum. In 2011, Google launched its Google+ social networking service at <**plus.google.com**>. Given Google's high profile, it has the potential to become a significant rival to Facebook. But at the time of writing, it is too early to identify specific benefits of Google+'s features to family historians.

In spite of the huge membership of Facebook, only a handful of the genealogy groups seem to be very active, and I doubt whether it is worth joining Facebook just to take advantage of the groups. If you are already a Facebook user, on the other hand, it may well be worth your while to check for suitable groups. All the same, in terms of topic coverage and usefulness Facebook has a long way to go before it can compete with the well-established mailing lists and forums discussed above.

Netiquette

Electronic discussion forums are social institutions and, like face-to-face social institutions, they have a set of largely unwritten rules about what

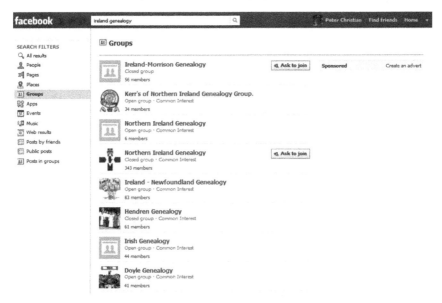

Figure 18-4 Irish Genealogy groups on Facebook

counts as acceptable or unacceptable behaviour. While individual groups may spell some of these out in an FAQ or a welcome message, the core rules are common to all online discussion groups and are often referred to collectively as 'netiquette', short for 'internet etiquette'. Many systems make some of these rules explicit conditions for their use, and list/forum administrators usually exclude members who persistently ignore them.

The 'official' Netiquette Guidelines are at <**tools.ietf.org/html/rfc1855**> – section 2.1.1 covers email. Virginia Shea's book *Netiquette*, the complete text of which is online at <**www.albion.com/netiquette/book/**>, offers more extensive advice. Malcolm Austen has some brief but useful 'Notes on List Etiquette' at <**mno.org.uk/email-list-etiquette/**>.

Frequently Asked Questions (FAQ)

Once you have been reading a particular discussion forum for some time, you will realize that certain questions come up again and again. Needless to say, regular members of a discussion forum don't relish the thought of repeatedly taking the time to answer these basic questions, so many major mailing lists and forums have what is called an FAQ, a file of 'frequently asked questions'. The FAQ for a mailing list is normally posted to the list periodically, but the actual frequency varies from list to list.

If you are thinking of asking a question on a particular list for the first time, and especially if you are just starting to research your family tree, it's a good idea to consult the FAQ. This will give you a guide as to what are considered appropriate or inappropriate issues to discuss and above all provide answers to some of the most obvious questions asked by beginners.

The easiest way to find the FAQ for a mailing list is to search the list archive. On a web-based system, there may be a link from the home page or a 'sticky' message, which remains permanently at the top of the list of messages.

There is a long-standing FAQ for the GENBRIT mailing list at <**www.woodgate.org/FAQs/socgbrit.html**> and a relatively new replacement for it, still under development, at <**www.genealogy-britain.org.uk**>. Because of their general coverage, these are well worth looking at even if you don't intend to post messages to GENBRIT.

Query etiquette

Here are some of the main dos and don'ts relevant to genealogical forums:

- Make sure that any messages you send are relevant to the forum topic, as
  - a Welsh genealogy query in a Hampshire forum is a waste of everyone's time;
  - discussion of politics and religion, unless strictly relevant to a genealogical issue, is likely to cause friction.

- Give an explicit subject line so people can see what topic your question relates to – avoid one-word subjects, especially if that word is 'help' or 'problem'.
- Read the FAQ if there is one.
- Don't ask factual questions you can easily find the answer to online for yourself.
- Don't post the same query in several different places. If you're not sure which is the right place, ask.
- Always be polite and considerate in responding to others. It's perfectly possible to be critical, should the need arise, without being rude.
- Don't quote the entirety of a previous message in a reply, particularly if your reply comes right at the bottom – just quote the relevant part.[1]
- Don't post a reply to the list or group if your answer is going to be of interest only to the sender of the original message – email that person directly.
- Don't advertise goods or services – there are other places designed for this.
- Don't expect other people to look up records for you unless the forum explicitly permits lookup requests.
- Don't post messages containing other people's data or data from CD-ROMs. This is more than bad manners; it's copyright infringement. (See p. 402f.)

Starting your own discussion group

There are many websites that allow you to start your own discussion group. The advantage of using well-known services like Yahoo Groups at <**groups. yahoo.com**> or Google Groups at <**groups.google.com**> is that people will be much more likely to come across your group. RootsWeb hosts an enormous number of genealogical mailing lists and is a good place to create a new one. Details of how to request a new mailing list will be found at <**resources.rootsweb.ancestry.com/adopt/**>. There is detailed coverage of mailing list administration at <**helpdesk.rootsweb.ancestry.com/ listadmins/**>.

Bear in mind that maintaining a mailing list or discussion group could end up requiring a significant amount of your time if it becomes popular. Unless a list is small, it is certainly much better for it to be maintained by more than one person so that responsibilities can be shared. On the other

---

1 One of the great religious schisms on the internet is between the 'top-posters' and the 'bottom-posters', who have different views on where in the message one should add one's own remarks when replying. For discussion of the relative merits of differing posting styles, see the Wikipedia article on 'Posting styles'.

hand, a mailing list for a particular surname is not likely to generate nearly as much mail as one on a general topic. RootsWeb provides detailed information about the responsibilities of list owners on their system at <helpdesk.rootsweb.ancestry.com/listadmins/duties.html>, and other sites that provide discussion forums will provide something similar.

Which discussion group?

Which mailing lists or forums you read will, of course, depend on your genealogical interests. The main general mailing list for British genealogy is GENBRIT. However, if you are not already familiar with mailing lists, you may not want this to be the first one you join – you could be a bit overwhelmed with the 20-plus messages per day arriving in your mailbox. Also, it can be a rather boisterous group. There is no web-based forum with the status of GENBRIT.

If you know where your ancestors came from, it may be more useful to join the appropriate county mailing lists (see <**www.genuki.org.uk/indexes/ MailingLists.html**>). There are fewer messages, and more of the postings are likely to be relevant. You will certainly have a better chance of encountering people with whom you share surname interests, not to mention common ancestors. Other useful lists are those for special interests, such as coalminers or the Boer War.

You might think that the best thing to do is join the lists for all your surnames of interest, and there are thousands of lists and web-based forums devoted to individual surnames. However, they differ widely in their level of usefulness. Some have very few subscribers and very few messages, while, particularly in the case of reasonably common English surnames, you may well find lists dominated by US subscribers with mainly post-colonial interests. But with a reasonably rare surname in your family tree, particularly if it is also geographically limited, it is very likely that some other subscribers on a surname list will share your interests. Whereas the relevant county mailing list is certain to be useful, with surname lists it's more a matter of luck.

The simplest way to see whether any discussion forum is going to be worth joining is to look at the archives for the list to see the kind of topics that are discussed. This also has the advantage that you can get a rough idea of how many messages a month you would be letting yourself in for. You could also simply join a group and 'lurk', i.e. receive and read the messages without contributing yourself.

19

SEARCH ENGINES

One of the most obvious features of the internet that makes it good for genealogical or indeed any research is that it is very large, and the amount of material available is continually increasing. It is impossible to get an accurate idea of the size of the web, but it is reasonable to assume that it is at least tens of billions of pages, and that figure does not include any data held in online databases.[1] But the usefulness, or at least accessibility, of this material is mitigated by the difficulty of locating specific pages. Of course, it is not difficult to find the websites of major institutions, but much of the genealogical material on the web is published by individuals or small groups and organizations, which can be much harder to find. For more extensive websites, there's the problem that the wealth of material on a particular topic may not be evident from the home page. Also, since there is no foolproof way to locate material, a failed search does not even tell you that the material is not online.

The standard tool for locating information on the web is a search engine. This is a website that combines an index to the web and a facility to search the index. Although many people do not recognize any difference between directories, gateways and portals on the one hand, and search engines on the other, they are in fact very different beasts (which is why they are treated separately in this book) and have quite different strengths and weaknesses, summarized in Table 19-1.

---

1 Pandia's February 2007 article 'The size of the World Wide Web' at <www.pandia.com/sew/383-web-size.html>, which gathers together a number of estimates, concludes that 'the number of web pages must be somewhere between 15 and 30 billion – and probably closer to the latter'. In July 2008 Google claimed to have indexed one trillion unique URLs – see <googleblog.blogspot.com/2008/07/we-knew-web-was-big.html>. They also claim that 'the number of individual web pages out there is growing by several billion pages per day'. To put this in perspective: the British Library's integrated catalogue includes a mere 13 million printed items, with at best probably five billion pages between them.

Table 19-1 Comparison of directories, etc., with search engines

Directories, gateways and portals	Search engines
Directories and gateways list web*sites* according to general subject matter.	Search engines list individual web *pages* according to the words on the page.
Directories are constructed and maintained by humans. In the case of genealogy gateways you can assume the compilers actually have some expertise in genealogy.	Search engines rely on indexes created automatically by 'robots', software programs which roam the internet looking for new or changed web pages.
Directories and particularly specialist gateways for genealogy categorize genealogy websites intelligently.	While some search engines know about related terms, they work at the level of individual words.
Directories are selective (even a comprehensive gateway like Genuki only links to sites it regards as useful).	Search engines index everything they come across.
Directories, offering a ready-made selection, require no skill on the part of the user.	The number of results returned by a search engine can easily run into six or seven figures, and success is highly dependent on the searcher's ability to formulate the search in appropriate terms.
Gateways often annotate links to give some idea of the scope or importance of a site.	A search engine may be able to rank search results in order of relevance to the search terms, but will generally attach no more importance to the website of an individual genealogist than to that of a major national institution.

These differences mean that directories, and particularly gateways and portals, are likely to be good for finding the home pages of organizations and projects, but much less well suited to discovering sub-pages with information on individual topics. Even genealogy directories with substantial links to personal websites and surname resources probably don't include more than a fraction of those discoverable via a search engine. A directory or gateway might give you a link to the home page of a body like the Society of Genealogists, but only a search engine will take you straight to the page for the opening times. And if you are looking for pages which mention the name of one of your ancestors, there is little point in using a directory or gateway. You have to use a search engine.

There are dozens of different search engines, but the most widely used general-purpose search engines are four in number:

Google	<www.google.com>[2]
Yahoo Search	<search.yahoo.com>
Bing[3]	<www.bing.com>
Ask	<www.ask.com>

In fact Yahoo Search uses the same web index as Bing, so their search results will be very similar (but, oddly, not always identical).

For a comprehensive list of search engines, see Wikipedia's page 'List of search engines', which links to individual articles.

Using a search engine

In spite of the more or less subtle differences between them, all search engines work in basically the same way. They offer you a box to type in the 'search terms' or 'keywords' you want to search for, and a button to click on to start the search. The example from Yahoo Search shown in Figure 19-1 is typical. Once you've clicked on the 'Search' button, the search engine will come back with a page containing a list of matching web pages (see Figure 19-2), each with a brief description culled from the page itself, and you can click on any of the items listed to go to the relevant web page. Search engines differ in exactly how they expect you to formulate your search, how they rank the results, how much you can customize display of the results and so on, but these basics are common to all.

Search engines generally report the total number of matching web pages found, called 'hits', and if there is more than a page (typically 10 or 20), it will provide links to subsequent pages of hits. (In Figure 19-2, you can see

2 If you access Google from a UK ISP, you will be redirected automatically to <www.google.co.uk>.
3 This is Microsoft's search egine, previously called Windows Live Search and, before that, MSN Search.

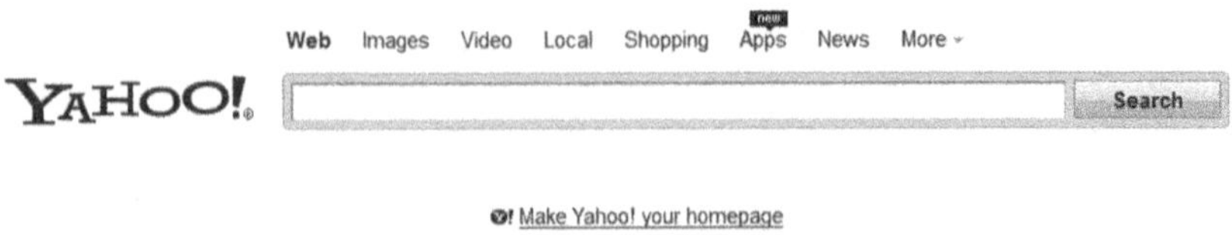

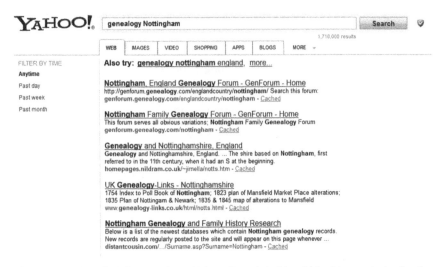

Figure 19-1 The Yahoo Search home page at <search.yahoo.com>

Figure 19-2 Results of a search on Yahoo Search (with ad blocking switched on)

this information in a very small font just beneath the search box.) Usually the words you have searched on will be highlighted in some way.

On some search engines, at the top of the search results or alongside the first results, there may be adverts from websites with material more or less relevant to your search terms. For any search on the word [genealogy] or genealogical records like [parish registers], for example, these are most likely to be for some of the commercial data services described in Chapter 4. You will not see these if you have an ad blocking tool enabled in your browser.

Formulating your search

Your success in searching depends in part on your choice of search engine, which is discussed on p. 347, but is also greatly dependent on your skill in choosing appropriate search terms and formulating your search.

In this chapter I have put search terms between square brackets. To run the search in a search engine type in the text between the brackets *exactly*, but don't include the square brackets themselves. Note that the figures given for the number of hits have indicative status only – they were correct when I tried out these searches, but the indexes used by search engines grow daily, so you will not get identical results. Also, there is no way to verify the accuracy of the figures except where they are under a thousand or so. But the differences between the various *types* of search and formulation should be of the same order.

Basic searching

There are actually several different types of search offered by search engines. In the basic search – the one you get if you don't select any options and just type in words to be searched for – the results will include all web pages found that contain *all* the words you have typed in the search field. This means that the more words you type in, the fewer results you will get. If you type in any surname or place-name on its own, unless it's a fairly unusual one, you will get thousands of hits. So it's always better to narrow down your search by entering more words if possible. This type of search is called an AND search. AND and OR are just the most commonly used parts of a general technique for formulating searches called Boolean logic.[4]

Looking for alternatives

Search engines automatically include some alternatives when looking for common words, as they have information about related word forms and common misspellings. If you search on [ships] or [shipp] the result will include pages with the word 'ship'; searching on [walk] will find pages with 'walking'. Search engines call this technique 'stemming' and it is used by default in all searches. If you don't want the variant forms included in search results, prefix your search term with what is called an 'inclusion operator'. In most search engines the + sign is the inclusion operator, and it effectively means 'this word must be in the results and in this exact spelling only'. Irritatingly, in October 2011, Google stopped using the + in this standard way – to achieve the same effect in Google you now have to put each individual word between inverted commas.

Among other things, inclusion is a useful way of excluding variant spellings if you have a surname that is also a common noun or similar to another word: a search for [+Bridges] will not find pages which only have the singular form 'bridge'; a search for my ancestor [Edward Weimark] on

---

4 This topic can be handled only briefly here. For more information on using Boolean expressions for searching, look at the help pages of the search engines or Part 3 of BrightPlanet's 'Guide to Effective Searching of the Internet' at <**brightplanet.com/images/ uploads/SearchEngineTutorialFormatted041218.pdf**>.

Bing brings up pages on Edward of Saxe-Weimar, which can be got rid of with [Edward +Weimark].

But if you want to carry out a search which includes other alternatives, you cannot do it just by including all the forms you can think of. For example, if you were looking for the baptisms for a particular family, you might be tempted to search on both 'baptism' and 'baptized' along with the surname, perhaps throwing in 'christened' and 'christening' for good measure. But each extra word reduces the number of matching pages found. On Bing, therefore, [Hollebone baptism] produces 30 hits, [Hollebone baptized] 11 hits, while the combination [Hollebone baptism baptized] produces not more than 30, as you might have hoped, but many fewer – only seven. And [Hollebone baptism baptized christened] gives only two, both from the full texts of surname dictionaries.

The same will happen if you give alternative surname spellings: for example Google gives around 4.3 million hits for [Waymark] and 586,000 for [Wymark], and 1.2 million for [Whymark] and 90,000 for [Weymark], but [Waymark Wymark Whymark Weymark] produces just 81, a tiny number of pages which have all four variants. Adding a fifth variant, [Weimark] reduces this to just seven hits. Of course, if you are searching for pages which actually discuss the variants of this particular name, you might be happy with a small number of results, but if you are looking for all pages that might mention someone with any variant of this surname, you will not want to miss pages which have only a single spelling.

The AND search is not suitable for looking for alternatives, unless you really do require pages that have all of them. What you need instead is an OR search, which will retrieve all pages containing at least one of the search words.

All the main search engines offer the option of doing an OR search. There are normally two ways to do this. First, all search engines have an Advanced Search page: there will be a link to this somewhere near the search box on the main page, often to the right, though in Yahoo Search (Figure 19-1) you need to click on the 'More' link, and on Bing you can only get to the advanced search from a page of search results, not from the home page.

The advanced search will offer you a wide variety of things to specify about what you are looking for but near the top should be options to 'look for all of the words' and 'look for any of the words'. The first of these is for words which *must* be included, the latter where any *one* of the alternatives you give will do. Figure 19-3 shows how to do this on Google's Advanced Search page at <**www.google.com/advanced_search**> and that at Yahoo is very similar.

Bing does not use a comprehensive form like Google and Yahoo, which show all the options at once. Instead, you enter each group of search terms and select whether you want:

- all of these terms
- any of these terms
- this exact phrase
- none of these terms

Figure 19-4 shows how to enter the terms for an OR search. When you click on the 'Add to search' button your search terms are translated into the correct syntax in the search field.

The other way to create an OR search – and one which is much quicker once you know what you're doing – is simply to type in the correct formulation directly in the search field. Strictly, the correct way to do this is shown in the following example:

[Hollebone AND (baptism OR baptized)]

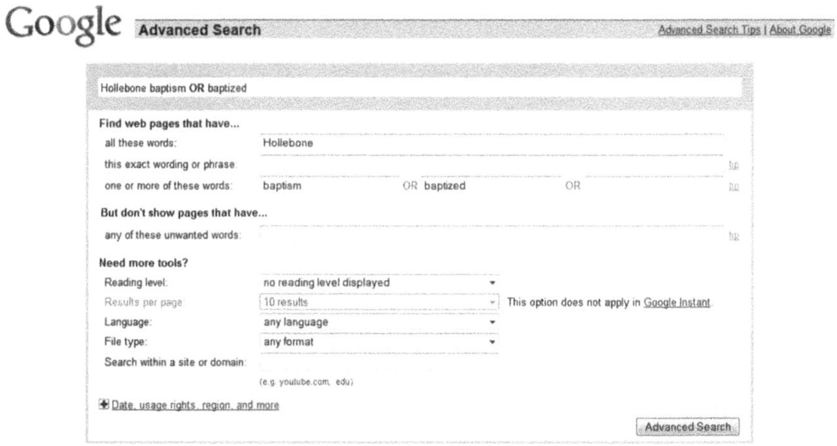

Figure 19-3 An OR search on Google's Advanced Search page

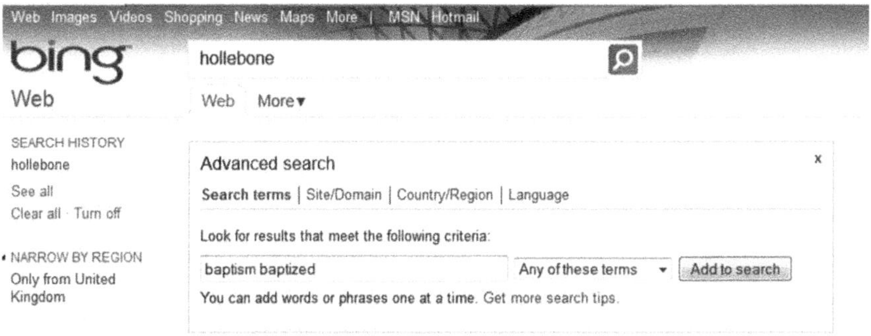

Figure 19-4 Creating an OR search with Bing

But given that the default search is an AND search, this is equivalent to

[Hollebone (baptism OR baptized)]

which is what Bing search requires. Bing also permits the use of the 'pipe' symbol | instead of OR.

However, many search engines are more relaxed. For example, Yahoo and Google only require the OR, not the AND or the parentheses:

[Hollebone baptism OR baptized]

All of them also seem to accept the strict syntax, so that will be the best approach if you can't find specific information about this topic on their help pages.

You can use the same principles to construct more complex searches:

[Robinson AND (genealogy OR "family history") AND (Nottingham OR Notts) AND (cobbler OR cordwainer)]

which Google would allow you to enter as

[Robinson genealogy OR "family history" Nottingham OR Notts cobbler OR cordwainer].

Exclusion

Often you will find yourself searching on a word that has several meanings or distinct uses, in which case it can be useful to find a way of excluding some pages. The way to do this is to choose a word which occurs only on pages you don't want, and mark it for exclusion, which most search engines do by prefixing with a hyphen. For example [Bath Somerset -tub -tap] would be a way to ensure that your enquiry about a city in Somerset was not swamped by results for plumbing suppliers.[5]

There is one very common problem when searching for geographical information which this technique can help to alleviate: names of cities and counties are used as names for ships, regiments, families and the like; also, when British emigrants settled in the colonies they frequently reused British place-names. This means that many searches which include a UK place-name will retrieve a high proportion of irrelevant pages.

---

5   This hyphen is to be regarded as a substitute for the typographically correct minus sign, which your browser would almost certainly ignore and therefore not submit as part of your search.

If you do a search on [Gloucester], for example, you will soon discover that there is a Gloucester County in Virginia and in New Brunswick, a town of Gloucester in New South Wales and in Massachusetts (not far from the town of Essex), and you probably do not want all of these included in your results if you are looking for ancestors who lived along the Severn. Then there is HMS Gloucester, the Duke of Gloucester, pubs called the Gloucester Arms, towns with a Gloucester Road, and so on. Likewise, if you're searching on [York], you certainly do not want to retrieve all the pages that mention New York.

Obviously it would be rather tedious to do this for every possibility, but you could easily exclude those which an initial search shows are the most common, e.g. [Gloucester -Virginia] or [York -"New York"]. (Another way to cut down on these irrelevant results would be to search for [Gloucester England], though this will miss many personal genealogy sites, where the country tends to be taken for granted.)

Another case where this technique would be useful is if you are searching for a surname which also happens to be that of a well-known person: a search such as [Woolf -Virginia] will reduce the number of unwanted results you will get if you are searching for the surname Woolf, and do not want to be overwhelmed with hundreds if not thousands of hits relating to the most high-profile bearer of the name, who is likely to dominate the first few pages of results.

Unfortunately, if you are searching for a surname which is also a place-name, e.g. Kent or York, there is no simple way to exclude web pages with the place-name, though on p. 349 I suggest a technique for restricting your hits to personal genealogy websites.

A further problem arises from the attempts of the search engines to spot mistakes in your search terms, discussed above. If you enter something that seems on the face of it to be an error, Google may give you the results for the *corrected* form and offer your original as an alternative (try [Hodgeson]), or, worse, the results may mix the corrected and uncorrected forms (try [Childs]). Some of their efforts are rather surprising: if you search on Bing for [Dallaway], 99 per cent of the results are for [Callaway]! As mentioned above, the way to prevent this is to use the inclusion operator.

Stop words

The reason for putting the Boolean operators AND/OR in upper case, incidentally, is that these are small words which search engines normally ignore, so-called 'stop words': [Waymark OR Wymark] finds 4.8 million hits on Google, [Waymark or Wymark] finds only 6,570 – the 'or' has been ignored and the alternative spellings treated as an AND search.

Other stop words include 'the' and 'of': if you search for [Alfred the Great] or [Isle of Man], you should find that the number of search results is very similar to those for [Alfred Great] or [Isle Man].

You can enforce the inclusion of a stop word by using the plus sign, but for searching on names, places and occupations, this is not likely to be very useful – if you have a stop word in a name, e.g. John of Gaunt, Robert the Bruce, Isle of Man, it is better to treat the entire name as a phrase, as explained in the next section, in which case any stop word is not ignored.

Phrases and names

Another important issue when using a search engine is how to group words together into a phrase. If you just type in a forename and surname, for example, search engines will treat this as an AND search on the two components.

This *may* not matter, especially if you are looking for a site by name, as search engines tend to put near the top of their listings those hits which include all search terms in the page title. This is particularly the case with organizations and projects, so, for example, a Windows Live search on [Manorial Documents Register] produces around 113,000 hits, but the MDR area on The National Archives' site, which is the official home of the MDR, is at the top of the list (see Figure 19-5).

This will also work for many two-word terms used in genealogy: you should expect all the top results for [poor law], [window tax] and [parish register] to be relevant. Even with relatively obscure occupational terms such as [fellowship porter] or [boot sprigger], you should find that most of the top results are not just pages where the two words happen to occur separately.

However, you can't count on this, and even with two-part place-names, which you might expect a search engine to recognize, your results may include many irrelevant hits. On Bing, for example:

- in a search for [genealogy Long Ditton] the first hit is the Genuki page for Ditton in Lancashire, which includes the phrase 'a very long time';
- in a search for [genealogy South Norwood] the first hit is for a Norwood family forum which mentions South Carolina.

(Google, incidentally, is better at recognizing these two place-names.)

But if you want to be sure that your words are treated as a complete phrase, you need to place them between inverted commas, e.g. ["South Norwood"] or ["John Smith"] or ["National Register of Archives"].

However, there is a downside: although you are getting more manageable and correct results, the phrase search will miss pages with "Smith, John" or

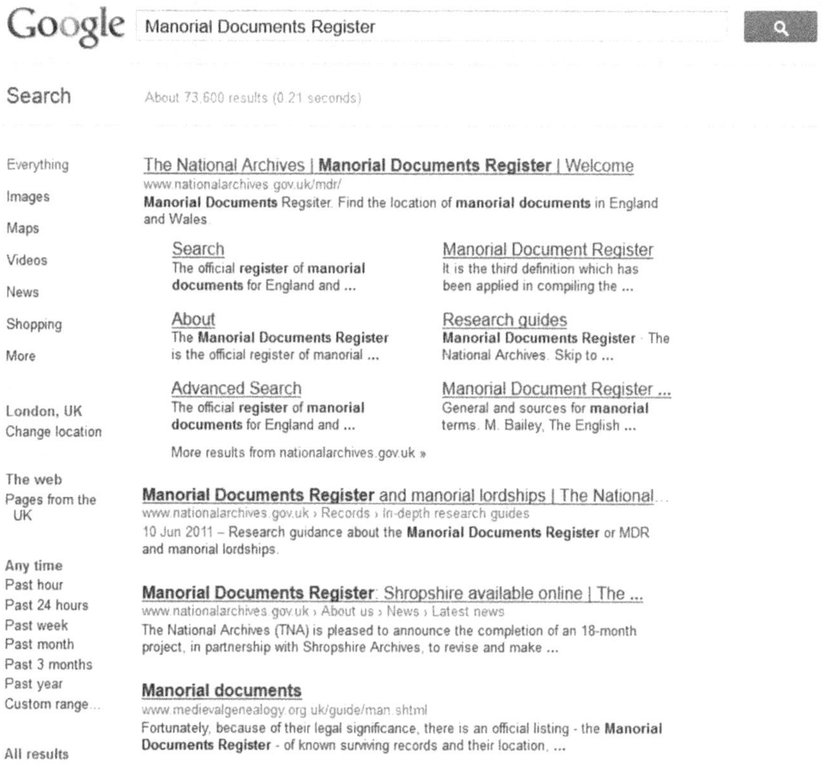

Figure 19-5 A search for [Manorial Documents Register] on Google

"John Richard Smith", so it is not an unmixed blessing. It will also inevitably miss "John, son of Richard and Mary Smith", though with present technology this is simply beyond the capabilities of search engines. Even so, with a reasonably unusual name, the phrase search can produce a list of hits short enough for each one to be checked – for example, a search for ["Cornelius McBride"] on Google produces only 1,240 hits, compared to 11 million for [Cornelius McBride]. As soon as you add a place-name, this becomes a manageable set of results.

Refining your search

If you're looking for something very specific, you may find it immediately, as with the search in Figure 19-5. This is particularly the case if you are searching on the name of a high-profile site. Otherwise, however, you shouldn't assume that your initial search will find what you want and produce a manageable list of results. If, for example, you are looking for individuals or families, or trying to find information on a particular genealogical topic, it is likely that you will have to look at quite a lot of the hits a search engine retrieves before finding what you are looking for. This makes it important to refine your search as much as possible.

The previous pages offer some advice on formulating your search, but however well you formulate it for the first run, you will often be able to refine it once you have looked at the initial results. Search engines provide a search box with your search terms at the top of each page of hits, so it is very straightforward to edit this and re-run the search.

Some search engines offer facilities to refine your search within the results you have already retrieved. In Google, clicking on the 'Search within results' link at the bottom of a results page takes you to another search page where you can specify a narrower search with additional words. However, this does not actually do anything clever – it just adds the new terms and re-runs your original search. If you know how to formulate searches, these facilities don't offer anything extra.

Search tips

Apart from taking care in formulating your query, there are a number of other things to bear in mind if your searching is going to be successful and not too time-consuming.

First, the better you know the particular search engine you are using, the better the results you will get. Look at the options it offers, and look at the Help or Tips pages. Although I have highlighted the main features of search engines, each has its idiosyncrasies. And while it is quite easy to find what a search engine will do, sometimes the only way to find out what it *will not* do is to see what is missing from the Help pages. It is also worth trying out some different types of query, just so you get a feel for how many results to expect and how they are sorted.

If you carry out searches on your particular surnames on a regular basis, it can be worth adding the URL of the results pages to your bookmarks (Firefox) or favorites (Internet Explorer), making it easy to run the same query repeatedly. This works because in most search engines the browser submits the search terms as an appendage to the URL, which is then shown as the web address of the first page of results. Bookmarking this page will allow you to retrieve the entire URL and then re-run the search.

There is one simple browser technique which will save you time when searching. Once you have got a list of search results that you want to look at, open each link you follow in a new window or tab so that the original list of search results remains open. (On Windows browsers a right mouse click over the link will bring up a menu with this option; on the Macintosh shift+click). Otherwise, each time you want to go back to your results the search engine will run the search all over again. Another useful trick for a long page of results is to save the page to your hard disk so that you can explore the hits at your leisure later.

Searching for files

Search engines can be used for finding other types of material online in addition to web pages. This material falls into two broad categories, which are generally dealt with in distinct ways.

First, there are files with textual material but which are in a proprietary document format rather than the public HTML format used for web pages. All the main search engines index such material for a number of file formats, notably Adobe Acrobat (PDF) files, described in more detail on page 60, and Microsoft Word files. This is important because many bodies put longer-term official information online in PDF format.

The content of such files is usually included automatically in the search engine's index, so you do not need to specify a particular file type when searching. However you will be able to choose 'file type' on the advanced search page of most search engines.

Multimedia files are generally handled differently, and the tendency is to have a separate search facility for each format. As you can see in Figure 19-1, Yahoo Search has separate tabs for images and video (audio is available from the 'more' link), while Google offers the images, groups (i.e. newsgroups, see p. 324), news, and maps tabs at the top of the home page.

Searching for photographs

Of the various multimedia file types, those of most interest to genealogists will be the graphics files of scanned or digital photographs. An overview of the sorts of photographs you can expect to find online is given in Chapter 17.

When searching for images, you can't simply use the standard facilities of the search engines, since these look for text. Although any search results *will* include pages with images on them, particularly where there are relevant captions, this may not be obvious from the list of search engine results. This might be a way to find sites or pages that are devoted to photographs or postcards, but it will be a time-consuming way to find individual photographs.

Google has an excellent image search facility at <**images.google.com**>. The search results pages show thumbnail versions of the images which match your search criteria – moving the mouse over an image produces a slightly larger version with some text from the source page, while clicking on an image takes you to the original page from which the image comes – Figure 19-6 shows the results of a search for [Deptford dockyard].

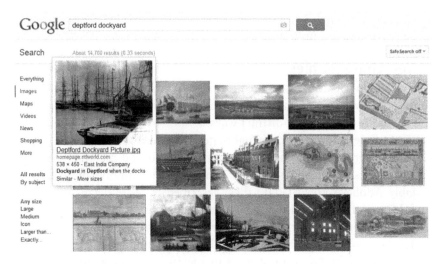

Figure 19-6 Search results in Google Images

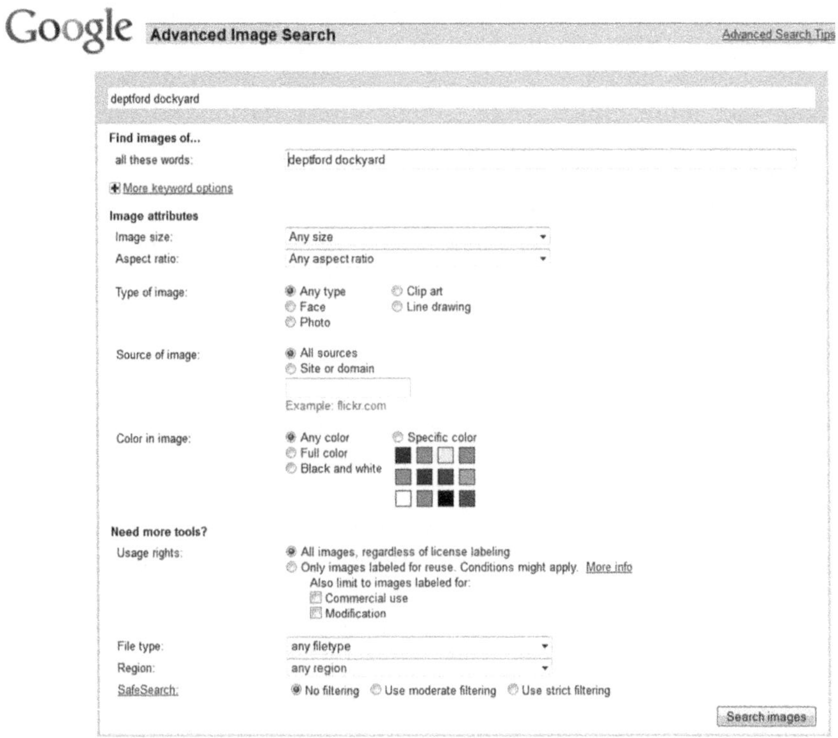

Figure 19-7 Google's Advanced Image Search

Mostly you will just get a normal search box, but if there is an advanced image search this should allow you to be more precise about the sorts of image you want, such as that from Google shown in Figure 19-7.

The Technical Advisory Services for Images has a very comprehensive review of image search facilities, including both general and specialist search engines, at **<www.jiscdigitalmedia.ac.uk/stillimages/advice/review-of-image-search-engines/>**. Although it is now a few years old, and some details will be out of date, it remains a useful introduction to the topic.

Other resources for finding images are discussed in Chapter 17.

Sites and domains

Although search engines are mainly used for searching the whole web, they can also be used to search individual websites. Since most major sites have their own search engine, the value of this may not be immediately obvious. But there are two advantages: you don't have to get to grips with a new search engine every time you visit a new site, and the big search engines often have much more sophisticated search facilities than those on individual sites, particularly the smaller ones. Using a general search engine, you can use the advanced search options to do more complex searches, specify a date range for pages retrieved, look for particular filetypes, etc. However, the external search results may not be as complete or as up-to-date as those from the internal search engine of a well-managed site.

Most search engines allow you to specify a particular site as one of the advanced search options – look on the advanced search page for a field labelled with the words 'site' or 'domain'. Just as with the OR search, you will see that if you know how to formulate it, you can carry out this type of search without going via the advanced search page, by using a special keyword in the basic search. The keyword varies from one search engine to another: in most it's the keyword **site** followed by a colon, and then the site to be searched, e.g.

["tithe maps" site:www.nationalarchives.gov.uk]

In fact, you do not need to specify a complete site, but can restrict your search to a 'domain'. For example, a search with [site:nationalarchives.gov.uk] will include all National Archives sites, not just the main one. You can specify even less: [site:gov.uk] will conduct a search on pages from *any* UK government website, including those of local authorities. So the following search would be a good way of finding out which local record offices have projects to digitize tithe maps:

["tithe maps" project site:gov.uk]

Even if you want a specific county, it will often be quicker to type, say,

["tithe maps" project Staffordshire site:gov.uk]

than to find the site for Staffordshire's local authority or CRO, visit it, and then use its own search facility to find the tithe maps project.

However, there are some sites which can't be searched in this way: Genuki and WorldGenWeb, for example, are *distributed* services, which means that material is spread among many different servers. A search on [site:genuki.org.uk] will find only material which is on Genuki's main server and miss much of the county material which is in fact held elsewhere. Genuki, has its own search (see p. 352), which is not affected by this problem (since, naturally, Genuki's search engine has a list of all the Genuki servers).

Limitations

It is important to bear in mind some of the limitations of search engines. The most significant is that no search engine indexes anything like the whole of the web. A 1999 study found that no search engine covered more than 16 per cent of the web.[6] This study may be a decade old, but there has not been any revolution in search engine technology to suggest the results are no longer broadly valid. For this reason, when you cannot find something with a search engine, it does not mean it is not there.

Also, do not expect all results to be relevant. Even a fairly precisely formulated query may get some irrelevant results. A particular problem will be pages with long lists of names and places – these will inevitably produce some unwanted matches. For example, a surname interest list which contains an Atkinson from Lancashire and a Chapman from Devon would be listed among the results for a search on [Chapman Lancashire]. Particularly if you do not include terms like [genealogy] or ["family history"], or something that occurs more frequently on genealogy sites than elsewhere – ["monumental inscriptions"] or ["parish register"], for example – you will get many irrelevant results. And, of course, searching for a fairly common surname may retrieve numerous genealogical pages that are nothing to do with your own line.

There are ways to cut down on irrelevant results if you are looking for a particular family. The more precise your geographical information the better: if you know your Chapman family came from Exeter, search not for [Chapman Devon] but for [Chapman Exeter Devon]. (Keep [Devon]

6   Steve Lawrence & C. Lee Giles, 'Accessibility of information on the web', *Nature,* 8 July 1999, pp. 107–109 (online at <**www.ist.psu.edu/faculty_pages/giles/publications/ Nature-99.pdf**>).

in – you do not want Exeter College, HMS Exeter, Exeter in New Hampshire, etc.) If you search on both surnames of a married couple, even if they are individually quite common, you are much more likely to get relevant results, for example [Chapman Atkinson Exeter Devon genealogy]. If you use full names, all the better – even ["John Smith" "Ann Williams"] finds only 208,000 pages on Google; if you add [Yorkshire], it comes down to around 6,000! A village name will cut it down even more. You will still tend to retrieve a few surname listing pages, but there is little that can be done about that.

Finally, the web is full of spelling errors. For example, Google finds over a quarter of a million pages which mention a supposed county of 'Yorskhire'. In this sort of case, most search engines will spot that you probably meant Yorkshire and give you the results for the correct spelling, though of course this means you may miss pages put up by distant cousins who don't use a spelling checker. The search engines often seem able to spot obvious misspellings for even quite small places, but you can't assume they will be as successful with surnames.

The 'invisible web'

Another problem in finding material on the internet, particularly records relating to individuals, is that much of it is simply not available in permanent web pages, which are readily accessible and can be indexed by search engines. This is what is called the 'invisible web', 'hidden web' or 'deep web', and it includes:

- data held in databases, which can only be retrieved by completing a search form;
- pages which cannot be seen without some sort of registration or login;
- sites which deliberately exclude search engines.

The only way to find the information is to go to the site and complete the registration procedure or fill in the search fields. Such material, which will include that provided by the commercial data services and other records covered in Chapters 4 to 6, cannot normally be retrieved by search engines. The same is true for much of the material covered in Chapter 14.

Choosing a search engine

Which is the best search engine depends on a number of factors. The overriding question is: what are you looking for? There are several different aims you might have when using search engines. You might be trying to locate a particular site that you know must exist – you only need one result and you will recognize it when you see it. This is usually a search for a particular organization's website, or some particular resource that you've heard of but can't remember the location of.

Alternatively, you may be trying to find a good site on a particular topic or any site which might have information on a particular surname, or even a particular ancestor. The difference between this and the previous search is that there is no way of telling in advance what your search will turn up, and probably the search results will include a certain number, perhaps even a lot, of irrelevant sites. Another difference is that in the first case, you almost certainly have some idea of what the site might be called.

With this in mind, there are three main criteria to consider when deciding which search engine to use:

- the size of the index;
- the way in which results are ranked;
- the range of search options available.

Size

The first of these is the most fundamental. Other things being equal, the search engine with the larger index is more likely to have what you are looking for. However, while this will be very important in looking for pedigree-related information, it will be largely irrelevant if you are looking for something like the Society of Genealogists' website, which you would expect *all* search engines to have in their indexes.

Since search engines are constantly striving to improve their performance and coverage, there can be no complete guarantee that what is the most comprehensive search engine at the time of writing will still hold that position when you are reading this. However, Google has been dominant for many years and the difference between it and its nearest rival can be seen from the graphs at <**www.worldwidewebsize.com**>.

Table 19-2 Hits for [genealogy] on the main search engines (October 2011)

	[+genealogy]	[+genealogy +Gloucestershire]	[+genealogy +Gloucestershire +Fairford]	[+genealogy +Gloucestershire +Fairford +Farmor]
Google	240m	7m	over 1,000	91
Yahoo	63m	2m	389	7
Bing	59m	1.6m	367	7
Ask			829	6

To get an idea of what the differences mean for the family historian, Table 19-2 shows the number of hits for some typical genealogical searches on the four main search engines in October 2011. The figures in the first two columns should be treated with considerable caution (not to mention scepticism) as there is no way to verify their accuracy, and Ask does not give figures for its search results. The figures for the two narrowest searches, however, are based on my manual count of the results, (though Google won't display more than 100 pages). Overall, there is no reason to doubt the claim that Google is quite significantly ahead of its rivals in terms of coverage.

Ranking

Unless you get only a handful of hits, one of the issues which will determine the usefulness of search results will be whether the most relevant ones are listed first. In fact, poor ranking effectively invalidates the virtues of a large index – a page which is ranked 5,000 out of 700,000 might as well not be included in the results at all because you're never going to look at it.

It's difficult to be specific about how search engines rank their results (since these are valuable commercial secrets) but broadly speaking they assess relevance based on:

- the frequency of your search terms in the pages retrieved;
- the presence of these words in high-profile positions such as the page title, headings, etc.

Google explicitly uses a popularity rating, giving higher priority to pages which many others are linked to, though probably other search engines do this, too. This is good if what you want are recommendations – which is the best site on military genealogy, say. But if you are searching for surnames and pedigrees, which are probably on personal websites, it may be positively unhelpful, as these will automatically rank lower than well-connected commercial sites which happen to have the same surname on them. Almost any surname search will tend to list the major genealogy sites high up, especially those with pages for individual surnames or surname message boards. Unfortunately, in spite of past experiments in this area, none of the major search engines currently offers any way of controlling how results are ranked.

For personal genealogy pages, the only way I have found of doing this is to include the phrase ["surname list"] in the search terms. The basis for this is that many of the software packages used to create a website from a genealogy database (see Chapter 20) will create a page with this as a title or heading. The results will also include, of course, some non-personal sites such as the county surname lists mentioned on p. 225, but the phrase does not seem to be common on non-genealogy sites, and is less likely to be encountered on commercial genealogy sites.

However, there is an argument that choosing the 'best' search engine is not enough. It's not just that no individual search engine indexes more than half the web. The fact is that each search engine includes in its index some pages which may not be in another search engine's index at all. And there is a very useful tool which illustrates the size of the problem, the Ranking utility at <**ranking.thumbshots.com**>. This allows you to compare the top 60 hits for a search on any two search engines, and if you try it with something reasonably rare you get a clear indication of the limited coverage.

Overlap

Figure 19-8 shows the results for the phrase ["bounty migrants"] in Google and Yahoo: of the top 60 hits (the first six pages of results), only 20 per cent of the sites found are common to both search engines. Of course, there are cases where this won't matter: if you're looking for a particular site such as that of a genealogy organization, for example. But if you're searching, as here, for historical information, or for a particular ancestor by name, you could be missing useful material if you only use one search engine.

The moral is obvious: in a comprehensive web search for individual ancestors and matching surname interests, you cannot afford to use only one search engine, no matter how large its index may be.

Figure 19-8 Thumbshots: searches for ["bounty migrants"]

One technique for overcoming the fact that no search engine indexes the whole of the web is to carry out the same search on several different search engines. The easiest way to do this is to add a range of other search engines to your browser's built-in search facility: in Internet Explorer, click on the down arrow to the right of the search box and select 'Find More Providers'; in Firefox, click on the down arrow to the left of the search box and select 'Manage Search Engines'. Once you have done this you can quickly carry out a search on several different search engines in sequence.

Genealogy search tools

The search engines discussed so far have been general-purpose tools, but there are also many special-purpose tools. Some of these are discussed elsewhere in the text. Image search tools are discussed earlier in this chapter. Online gazetteers are dedicated tools for locating places (see p. 253). Chapter 12 covers online catalogues to material which is itself not online. All of these are going to be better for their particular purpose than the general search engines.

Over the years, there have been a number of attempts to create a comprehensive search engine specializing in genealogy. These have generally been short-lived, in part, no doubt, because of the difficulty of compiling a well-defined list of genealogy sites to index. Cyndi's List has a 'Search Engines' page at <**www.cyndislist.com/search.htm#Genealogy**>, but many of the sites listed are in fact directories and others are limited to searching online pedigrees (these are covered in Chapter 14).

The most recent attempt at a genealogy search engine is Mocavo at <**www.mocavo.com**>, which was launched in March 2011. In November 2011 a UK version was launched at <**www.mocavo.co.uk**>. The basic search is free, but an annual subscription of $119.40 gives access to more advanced search options. There is no detailed information on the site about its site selection criteria but it includes many genealogy message boards and blogs as well as more general genealogy sites. Also, there is the option to upload your own family tree in GEDCOM format (see p. 357).

Initially, the site has concentrated mainly on US material and this is the case even for the UK service, so it is not yet very useful for British and Irish genealogy beyond the coverage of message boards, and even here, specifically British services like TalkingScot and British-Genealogy are absent. It includes the main Genuki server at <**www.genuki.org.uk**> but not Genuki pages hosted elsewhere, and the websites of family history societies and record offices do not seem to have been captured at all. Searching on [Gloucestershire Fairford Farmor], as above, found only six results, all from the Internet Archive.

However, at the time of writing the site is still very new, and no doubt more UK sites will be included. In any case, even with these limitations it is useful to have a search whose results are exclusively genealogical. It should certainly be a more effective tool for finding material on genealogy blogs and the larger message boards than a general-purpose search engine.

The Genuki Search at <**www.genuki.org.uk/search/**> is probably the most useful dedicated search engine for British and Irish family history. Although it confines itself to 'institutional' websites with material relevant to the British Isles, its index in fact includes many of the most important non-commercial genealogy sites:

- Genuki itself
- The National Archives
- the Society of Genealogists
- the Federation of Family History Societies
- the Guild of One-Name Studies
- the family history societies listed by Genuki (see p. 20)
- most county surname interest lists (see p. 225)

Further information

Because of the importance of searching to serious use of the internet and for professional researchers in *any* field, there are many sites with guides to search engines and search techniques.

Among the many online tutorials, the University of California at Berkeley's 'Finding Information on the Internet' at <**www.lib.berkeley.edu/TeachingLib/ Guides/Internet/FindInfo.html**>, and BrightPlanet's very comprehensive 'Guide to Effective Searching of the Internet' at <**brightplanet.com/images/ uploads/SearchEngineTutorialFormatted041218.pdf**> are particularly recommended. Rice University has a concise guide to 'Internet Searching Strategies' at <**library.rice.edu/services/dmc/guides/e-resources**>, which, though severely out of date in terms of the search engines mentioned, nonetheless has good advice about general techniques.

Kimberley Powell has a guide to searching specifically for genealogy sites and pages in 'Finding your ancestors on the Internet: A Guide to Internet Search Techniques for the Surnames in Your Family Tree' at <**genealogy. about.com/library/weekly/aa041700a.htm**>.

While there are any number of books about searching the web, there is, so far as I am aware, only one current book on the subject specifically for genealogists: Daniel M. Lynch's *Google Your Family Tree* (FamilyLink.com, 2008) covers the whole range of Google's facilities and services from a family history perspective, and three of its 14 chapters are devoted to getting the best out of the search engines.

20

PUBLISHING YOUR FAMILY HISTORY ONLINE

So far we have been concentrating on using the internet to retrieve information and contact others who share your interests. But you can also take a more active role in publicizing your own interests and publishing the results of your research for others to find.

Two ways of doing this have already been touched upon. You can post a message with details of your surname interests to a suitable mailing list (see Chapter 18). Although your message may be read by only a relatively small number of readers (compared to the total number of people online, at least), it will be archived, providing a permanent record. Also, you can submit your surname interests to the surname lists for the counties your ancestors lived in (Chapter 14). This will be easier for others to find than material in mailing list archives, since many people with ancestors from a county are likely to check the surname list.

Both of these methods are quick and easy, but they have the limitation that they offer quite basic information, which may not be enough for someone else to spot a link with your family, particularly with more common surnames. The alternative is to publish your family history on the web.

Publishing options

There are two main ways of putting your family history online: you can submit your family tree to a pedigree database such as those discussed in Chapter 14, or you can create your own website. In fact, these are not mutually exclusive, and there are good reasons for doing both, as each approach has its merits.

Pedigree databases

There are obvious advantages in submitting your family tree to one of the pedigree databases:

- It is a very quick way of getting your tree online.

- The fact that these sites have many visitors and are obvious places to search for contacts means that you are getting your material to a large audience.

But there are some disadvantages to note:

- The material is held in a database, which means it can only be found by going to the site and using the built-in search facilities. It will not be found by anyone using a general web search engine such as those discussed in Chapter 19.
- You can only submit material that is actually held in your genealogy database, and you will not be able to include any other documentary material relating to your family history (though you may be able to include a photograph of each individual).
- Depending on which pedigree database you use, you may be giving up some rights, and your control over the material may be limited (see p. 238).

As long as you check the terms and conditions of any site you use for this purpose, these disadvantages shouldn't discourage you from submitting your pedigree to a database. They simply mean that you might want to consider having your own website as well.

The main pedigree databases are discussed on p. 230ff.

A personal website

Creating your own website will, of course, be more work, but there are a number of reasons why it can be better than simply uploading your family tree to a database:

- You can put a family tree on your own site almost as easily as you can submit it to a database.
- You can include any other textual material you have collected which may be of interest: transcriptions of original documents, extracts from parish registers or General Register Office indexes for your chosen names.
- You can include images, whether they are scanned from old photographs in your collection or pictures you have taken of places where your ancestors lived.
- Once search engines become aware of your site, all the information on your site will be indexed by them, so they can be found by the techniques discussed in Chapter 19. People will not need to visit or even know about a particular pedigree database site.

- There will be no issues of rights or the ability to edit or remove material – it will be entirely under your control.

The great thing about a personal website is that it is not like publishing your family history in book form: you do not have to do all these things at once. You can start with a small amount of material – a family tree, or even just a single page with your surname interests, perhaps – and add to it as and when you like.

But there are a couple of issues to be aware of if you are going to create your own site:

- If you set it up in free web space provided by your ISP you will have to move the whole site if you subsequently switch to another provider. Search engines entries and links to your site will not work for a while.
- If your site is going to provide more than a basic family tree, you will need to learn how to create web pages.

Both of these issues are tackled later in this chapter.

It is worth pointing out that apart from the major online databases, much of the genealogical material on the web is the result of the efforts of individuals making it available on personal sites. If you have any genealogical information that may be of interest to others, in addition to your personal pedigree, you should consider making it available online.

Document sharing

Both a pedigree database and a personal website enable you to put a navigable family tree online, but if you can do without that facility, there is another possibility: document sharing. There are number of ways, short of setting up your own website, to make electronic documents publicly available online.

Scribd is a document-sharing site at <**www.scribd.com**>. It allows you to upload documents in a wide range of formats and converts them so that they can be viewed on the web. You can choose to make documents completely public or they can be hidden from public view but accessible to individuals to whom you give a special private URL. Scribd has no limit on the amount of material you can upload, though no individual file can be larger than 100MB. A particular benefit of Scribd is that uploaded files are automatically submitted to search engines once the upload is complete.

Figure 20-1 shows an Ancestor Report saved from Family Historian (as an RTF file) and uploaded to Scribd as <**www.scribd.com/doc/ 72684284/wim**>.

Figure 20-1 A report from a family history program uploaded to Scribd

A different approach is to use Dropbox at <**dropbox.com**>. This is a web-based file hosting service, mainly designed as a way of backing up the files on your own computer and making chosen files available to individuals you wish to share them with. However, since you can upload any type of file and you can choose to make any file public, you can use it in just the same way as Scribd. Unlike Scribd, though, Dropbox does not pay any attention to the format of the file you upload and does not do any conversion, so your files will already need to be in a format which can be handled by a web browser. The file shown in Figure 20-1, converted to Adobe Acrobat format, can also be viewed in my Dropbox public folder at <**dl.dropbox.com/ u/18534793/wim.pdf**>. In fact, if you upload all the files for a complete website, it will function as such, and not just as a collection of individually downloadable files. Dropbox offers 2GB of storage space free of charge, more than enough space for even the largest personal website.

For further information, including basic instructions, see Dick Eastman's article 'Publish Your Genealogy Database on the Web with Dropbox' at <**blog.eogn.com/eastmans_online_genealogy/2011/07/publish-your-genealogy-database-on-the-web-with-dropbox.html**>.

Family trees for the web

Probably the most important thing to put on the web is your family tree. This will make it possible for other genealogists to discover shared interests and ancestors, and get in touch with you.

Whether you are going to submit your family tree to a pedigree database or create your own site, you will need to extract the data from your genealogy database software in a format ready for the web. (If you are not yet using a genealogy database to keep a record of your ancestors and what you have discovered about them, look at 'Software' on p. 387.) The alternative would be to type up the data from scratch, which would be both time-consuming and prone to error.

GEDCOM

GEDCOM, which stands for GEnealogical Data COMmunication, is a standard file format for exchanging family trees between one computer and another, or one computer program and another. It was developed in the 1980s by the LDS Church as a format for church members submitting their pedigrees. It has subsequently been adopted and supported by all major genealogy software producers to enable users to transfer data into or out of their programs, with the result that it has become the *de facto* standard for exchanging genealogical data electronically.

The reason you need to know about GEDCOM is that all the pedigree databases expect you to submit your family tree in the form of a GEDCOM file. Also, provided your genealogy software can save your pedigree information in GEDCOM format, there are many programs which can automatically create a set of web pages from that file. On a PC running Windows, GEDCOM files have the file extension *.ged*.

You do not need to know the technical details of GEDCOM in order to publish your family tree on the web, but Dick Eastman has a straight-forward explanation of what GEDCOM is at <**www.eogn.com/archives/news0219.htm**>. For the technically inclined, the GEDCOM specification is at <**homepages.rootsweb.ancestry.com/~pmcbride/gedcom/55gctoc.htm**>. Cyndi's List has a page devoted to GEDCOM resources at <**www.cyndislist.com/gedcom/**> with links to explanatory material and GEDCOM software.

Whatever genealogy software you are using for your family tree, you should be able to find an option to export data to a GEDCOM file. Typically, this option will be found under **Export** on the **File** menu but, if not, the manual or the online help for your program should contain information on GEDCOM export. Unfortunately, there are slight differences in the way that the various programs handle GEDCOM files, so occasionally some of the data does not transfer correctly, but this should not affect the basic pedigree details.

There are also a number of programs which simply convert a GEDCOM file into a set of web pages. These are useful if your genealogy database does not have website creation facilities. The GEDCOM page on Cyndi's List includes a number of these.

Genealogy databases

Almost all the main genealogy database programs have facilities to create a set of web pages from your family tree data. A notable exception is Family Tree Maker, which has facilities for uploading a tree to Ancestry.com but cannot create standalone web pages. If your genealogy database cannot create a website, then you can either use one of the standalone GEDCOM converters or import your data into another genealogy database program which can: the free Standard Edition of Legacy is ideal for this purpose (details on p. 388).

Genealogy databases vary in what they actually produce for a website, but at the very least they will give you:

- a surname index;
- an index of individuals;
- a series of linked pages with family groups or details of individuals.

You should have a choice between an ancestor tree, a descendant tree, or a full pedigree, and there are many options as to which individuals, and what information about them, to include.

By way of example, Figure 20-2 shows a page created by Legacy 7.4. This is a web version of a standard descendancy report. Whereas in a printed

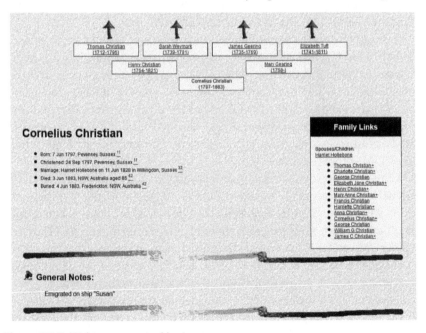

Figure 20-2 Web page created by Legacy

pedigree you have to turn manually to other pages, here the highlighted names are links which will take you straight to the entries for or parents, grandparents or children. The small superscript numbers link to descriptions of the sources.

Family websites

Another possibility, halfway between a pedigree database and creating your own website, is to use one of the subscription services which act as online genealogy databases. These differ from the pedigree databases in that they provide more sophisticated facilities, such as sharing material with your family while excluding it from general view. They may also have a facility to enter data directly rather than submitting a GEDCOM file, though it's unlikely this would be a useful facility for anyone but the casual family historian. Among the sites which provide this sort of facility are:

- TribalPages at <**www.tribalpages.com**>, which allows you to set up a free website with certain limitations (no more than 50 photos), or you can subscribe for between $24 and $48 a year for a site with greater facilities. With TribalPages you can choose to have your site password protected, which means you can restrict access to chosen members of your family.
- MyTrees.com at <**www.mytrees.com**>, which offers a basic service free of charge and a subscription service at $20 for one month and $120 for a year. Details of living people are normally hidden but can be made accessible to family members.

If you just want to share your family tree with your immediate (known) family, these may provide a better solution than trying to password protect an individual website. But they involve considerable ongoing expense and are less well suited to disseminating your pedigree to the wider world than a pedigree database.

Web publishing basics

If you are just going to upload a GEDCOM file to a pedigree database, you do not need to know anything else about web publishing. But if you are going to create your own website you will need to familiarize yourself with what is involved in the process. While it is increasingly possible to create a website without in-depth technical knowledge, it is still essential to have *some* understanding of what is involved. There is not space here to deal with the topic in detail, but this and the following sections cover the basics and there are suggested sources of further information at the end of this chapter.

What is a website?

A website is simply a collection of individual files stored on a web server, which is a computer with a permanent, fast connection to the internet and the capacity to deal with lots of requests for web pages from all over the internet. While larger companies have their own dedicated computers to act as web servers, smaller organizations and home users simply get a portion of the file space on the server belonging to their Internet Service Provider or a commercial web hosting company.

When you create a website, you first create all the pages on your own computer, then you upload the files to your space on the web server.

Assuming you already have internet access, what you need in order to create a website is:

- web space;
- software for creating web pages;
- software for uploading the pages to your web space.

If you are going to have photographs or scanned images of documents on your site, you will also need graphics editing software.

One important aspect of web publishing is that it can be done with any computer and a wide range of software. You do not need an especially powerful computer, and you almost certainly have web publishing software on your computer already even if you don't realize it (see p. 364). You will probably be able to use your browser for uploading pages, though there is dedicated free software which will make the process easier.

The other thing you need for a website is time. Even though basic web publishing is not difficult, you will need to learn how it works and you will want to experiment before unleashing your site on the public. You will also need to give some thought to exactly what material you are going to publish, and how best to organize it so that your visitors can find the information they are looking for – just as you would for a book, in fact. Also, getting a basic set of web pages up and running may be straightforward, but giving your site a more polished look and additional features, if that is your ambition, will require significantly more time and effort.

Web space

In order to have a website, you need to have space on a web server for the files which make up your website. If you have your own internet connection at home, you will almost certainly find that your Internet Service Provider offers this facility at no extra cost. There may, in principle be a limit on space (50MB is typical) but a personal genealogy site is unlikely to be anywhere near as large. It is even quite a respectable amount for a family history society.

If you do not have your own internet connection, or if your ISP does not provide free web space, you have two options. First, you could use a commercial web hosting company. This will require a subscription, but web hosting prices are not very great and you may well not need to pay more than £2 a month. Although you can find extensive lists of web hosting companies (see, for example, the Open Directory's UK page at <**www.dmoz.org/ Regional/Europe/United_Kingdom/Business_and_Economy/Computers_ and_Internet/Internet/Web_Hosting/**>, it is probably best to rely on recommendations such as those on Hostratings at <**www.hostratings.co.uk**>, Hostfinder at <**www.hostratings.co.uk**>, or in computer magazines.

Alternatively, you could use a site which offers free web space. The best known of these is Google Sites at <**sites.google.com**>. This service has the particular merits that new material and changes will immediately be picked up by Google's search engine, and you can easily integrate other resources provided by Google, such as maps from Google Maps, into your site.

A good home for genealogy sites is RootsWeb with its 'Freepages', free unlimited web space. Details will be found at <**accounts.rootsweb. ancestry.com**>. The only significant limitation is that RootsWeb does not let you upload GEDCOM files – they insist you submit them to their WorldConnect site instead (see p. 231). An interesting provider is AncestryHost at <**www.ancestryhost.org**>, which offers free web hosting as long as your site is genealogy-related and you already have your own domain name (see below).

Other companies can be found by searching Yahoo for the phrase 'free web space', or consult the Free Webspace directory at <**www.free-webhosts.com**>. Wikipedia's 'Comparison of free web hosting services' article covers a dozen of the main services.

The web address of your site will depend on who is providing your web space and what sort of account you have with them. If you are planning a substantial website with material of general interest rather than simply your own pedigree, or if you are going to set up a site for an organization or genealogy project, it is useful to have a permanent address rather than one that is dependent on your current ISP or web space provider. One possibility is to use 'redirection service' such as Go.to at <**www.go.to**>. This allocates a permanent free web address of the format <**go.to/user-id/**>, which redirects people to your actual web space, wherever it currently may be.

But the ideal solution is to register your own domain name, which can then simply point to your website, wherever it happens to be. All commercial and some of the free hosting services allow you use your own domain name.

The annual registration will require some modest expenditure, but you should be able to secure a .uk domain name for as little as £3 a year. You will also need to master one or two technical issues, as it will be up to you to ensure that your domain name is correctly set up to point to your current web space, though your web hosting company will be able to supply the necessary information. The process will be easier, though, if you use the same company for both name registration and hosting, and, indeed, you may well get a discount for combining the two.

Nominet is the registration authority for UK domains, and the 'New to domain names?' box on the home page at <**www.nic.uk**> has links to basic information. You can't actually register a domain name directly with Nominet, but need to use a commercial registrar – most web hosting companies also act as domain name registrars.

There are plenty of articles online about setting up a domain, such as Matt Doyle's 'How to Set Up Your Own Domain Name' at <**www.elated.com/articles/set-up-your-own-domain-name/**>. There are two articles by Dick Eastman in his newsletters for 25 September and 2 October 2002, archived at <**www.eogn.com/archives/news0238.htm**> and <**www.eogn.com/archives/news0239.htm**> (though note that some specific company recommendations will be out of date).

What is a web page?

When viewed on a web browser, web pages look like a form of desktop publishing and you might think that you need very complex and expensive software to produce a website. In fact the opposite is true: web pages are in principle very simple. Each page is simply a text file with the text that is to appear on the page along with instructions to the browser on how to display the text. The images that appear on a page are not strictly part of it; they are separate files. The page contains instructions telling the browser where to download them from. (This is why you will sometimes see the individual images being downloaded after the text of a page has already appeared in the browser window.) In a similar way, all the links on a web page are created by including instructions to the browser on what page to load when the user clicks on the links. (You can easily get a general idea of how this all works if you load a web page, ideally a fairly simple one, into your browser and use the **View Source** option in Firefox or Internet Explorer, on the **View** menu in both browsers.)

This means that a web page is not a completed and fixed design like the final output of a desktop publishing program on the printed page. It is a set of instructions which the browser carries out. And the reader has a certain amount of control over how the browser does this, telling it whether to load images, what font or colour scheme to use, what size the text should be and, most obviously, controlling the size and shape of the browser window it all has to fit into. The reason for this flexibility is that those who view a web page will be using a wide variety of different computer equipment, with a range of screen sizes and resolutions and no guarantee that particular fonts will be available. Also, readers will be using a range of different web browsers. The web page designer has to create a page that will look good, or at least be readable for all these users.

Figure 20-3 shows the text for a very simple web page. Figure 20-4 shows what this page looks like when displayed in a browser.

In Figure 20-3, the angled brackets mark the 'tags' which act as instructions to the browser, so the tag <img...> tells the browser to insert an image at this point. The tags are collectively referred to as 'markup', because they instruct the browser what to do with the text in the same way that in traditional publishing an editor marks up a manuscript for typesetting. All the text that is not inside angled brackets appears on the page, but the tags themselves do not. Many of the tags work in pairs, for example the tags ... tell the browser to find a way to emphasize the enclosed text, which is usually done with italics. Links to other websites and other pages on your own site are created by putting the tag <a href="site-or-file-name">...</a> round the hotspot, i.e. the text you want the reader to click on, with the web address or file name between the inverted commas ('a' stands for 'Anchor').

You can get a good idea of how this works by saving a copy of the page shown in Figure 20-4 from <**www.spub.co.uk/tgi5/dummypage.html**> and then editing it in Notepad or another text editor to see what happens if you move or delete tags. (Do not try it with a word processor!)

The set of tags that can be used to create web pages is specified in a standard called Hypertext Markup Language (HTML). The standard is controlled by the World Wide Web Consortium (W3C) <**www.w3.org**> on the basis of extensive consultation with those who have an interest in the technology of the web. HTML has been through several versions since its inception in 1991, and the latest is version 4, which came into use at the beginning of 1998, though a new HTML 5 is nearing final approval and is increasingly supported by browsers.

```
<html>
<head>
<title>This appears at the top of the browser window</title>
</head>
<body>
<h1>Here's the main heading</h1>
<p>Here's a very brief paragraph of text with <strong>bold</strong> and <em>
italics</em>.</p>
<p><img src="tree.gif">Here's another paragraph, with an image at the start</p>
<p>Here's a link to the
<a href="http://www.nationalarchives.gov.uk/">National Archives</a> web site.</p>
</body>
</html>
```

Figure 20-3 The text file for a simple web page

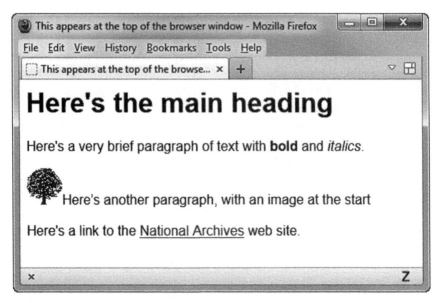

Figure 20-4 The page in Figure 20-3 viewed in a browser

Software

In order to create your website you will need suitable software, and there is quite a range of possibilities. Which is best depends on what software you have already got, what your website is to contain, and how serious you are about your site. One thing to remember is that no matter what software you use, the output is always a plain text file. It is not a file in a proprietary format belonging to a single manufacturer, which is what makes exchanging files between different word processors so problematic. This means you can use a variety of software programs to edit a single page, or you can collaborate with another family member without worrying whether you both have the same software.

Another important point is that you do not need to buy additional software – you will almost certainly have some web publishing tools installed on your computer already, and if not there are free programs which will provide all the facilities you need.

There are three basic approaches to creating web pages:

- You can create them 'by hand', i.e. by typing in the tags yourself using a text editor.
- You can use a program which works like a word processor but automatically converts the page layout into the appropriate text and tags.
- You can use a program which automatically generates pages from a set of data.

The following sections look at the sorts of software that can be used to create web pages.

Editors

In the early days of the web there was no special-purpose software designed for creating sites, and commercial software had no facilities for turning material into web pages. The only way to create a site was with a text editor, typing in both the text of a page and the HTML tags. The surprising thing is that, in spite of the many pieces of software that are now able to create web pages, text editors are still in use among professional web authors. The reason is that these give you complete control and do not make decisions for you. The disadvantage, of course, is that you will need to know what the relevant tags are and how to use them. But even if you mainly use another program to create your web pages, a text editor can still be useful. This is particularly the case where you have been using a program that is not designed specifically for web authoring, but has the facility to save files in HTML format as an add-on. All such programs have *some* failings in their web page output. If you need to correct these, it is easiest to use a text editor.

Although you can use a very basic text editor like the Windows Notepad, you will find it is hard work to create web pages with something so primitive, and it is better to use a more sophisticated editor. Some, like TextPad or NoteTab (downloadable from <www.textpad.com> and <www.notetab.com> respectively), even though designed as general-purpose text editors, offer a number of features to make web authoring easier. TextPad, for example, allows you to have many documents open at once, and has a comprehensive search and replace function covering all open documents. It has a 'clip library' of the main HTML tags – just clicking on an entry in the library adds the tags to your page.

Word processors

All the main word processors have the ability to create web pages. This is particularly useful if you already have material typed up, because you will be able to turn it into web pages very easily – there should be a **Save as HTML** or **Save as Web Pages** option on the **File** menu. But note that this will not create a web page for each *page* of your word-processed document; it will turn each *document* into a single web page. Once you have saved a page (and thereby given it a file name) you will be able to make links to it from other pages.

You might think that with this sort of facility there is no real need for other web authoring software but, unfortunately, word processors are not always particularly good at producing web pages that will read well on the wide variety of set-ups internet users have. In particular, they often try to reproduce precisely every nuance of the word-processed document, particularly the page layout, which may have no relevance for a web browser. This can lead to very cumbersome web pages that may display poorly. However, for text-only pages with a straightforward layout, this is a very quick way to get material on to the web.

LibreOffice is a freeware office suite (with word processing, spreadsheet, etc.) available for Windows, Macintosh OS-X and Linux. The word-processing component, Writer, can be used as a web editor with WYSIWYG ('what you see is what you get') and text-editing views. If you create a new HTML document from scratch, it produces good web pages, but pages created from existing word-processed documents are less good. Unfortunately, the LibreOffice Writer cannot be downloaded separately, you have to download the whole suite (from <**libreoffice.org**>), which is almost 200MB in size. OpenOffice.org at <**www.openoffice.org**> is more or less the same product.

Dedicated web authoring software

A better all-round option is a piece of dedicated web authoring software. This will provide *only* the layout facilities that are available in HTML. Many such packages offer both a design/layout mode, which looks like a word processor, and a text editing mode which allows you to work directly with tags. For the last few years, the most highly regarded commercial program has consistently been Adobe Dreamweaver (see Figure 20-5). Microsoft's Expression Web is also well regarded. Unfortunately, both of these are priced for professional web authors, and it would be difficult to justify the expense for a small personal website, though there are very substantial discounts for educational users.

If you are only going to create a fairly simple site, you do not need to pay for a commercial web authoring package, as there are a number of programs which are available for free download, including:

- **EvrSoft's FirstPage** at <**www.evrsoft.com**>
- **Nvu** at <**www.nvu.com**>
- the recently released **BlueGriffon** at <**www.bluegriffon.org**> (Figure 20-6)

FirstPage is available only for Windows; the other two will also run on Macintosh OS-X and Linux machines.

Trial versions of web authoring packages are frequently to be found on the cover CD-ROMs of computer magazines, and dozens of other shareware packages are available for free downloading. A good place to look is Tucows, which has a wide selection of web authoring software for Windows and Macintosh under 'HTML editors' and 'Visual and WYSIWYG editors' on

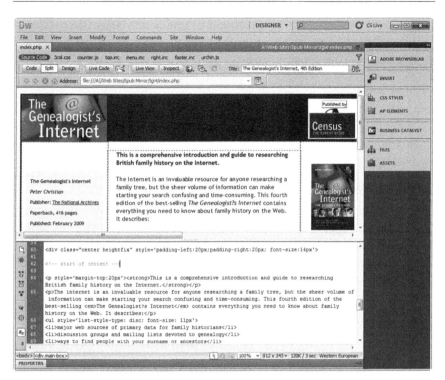

Figure 20-5 Editing the website for the fourth edition of this book in Dreamweaver CS5

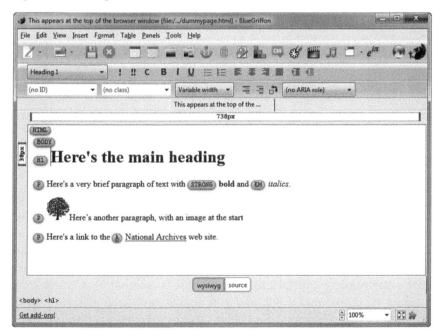

Figure 20-6 Editing with BlueGriffon

the 'Development & Web Authoring' pages at <**www.tucows.com/windows/development---web-authoring**> (that's three hyphens) and <**www.tucows.com/macintosh/development-web-authoring**> respectively.

Online software

Some free web space providers, such as Google Sites, have online tools for creating websites directly on the site without having to upload it from your own computer. Obviously, this will not help you convert your family tree for online viewing, but it is a quick way to get a website up and running.

Adobe Acrobat

All the software mentioned so far creates pages in HTML. But, in fact, browsers can cope with files in other formats, either by starting up the relevant application or by using a 'plug-in', an add-on component to display a particular file type (see p. 65).

Adobe Acrobat is a program that can turn any page designed for printing into a document for the web. It does this not by creating a page in HTML, but by using a proprietary file format ('PDF', which stands for 'portable document format'). A free reader is available, which can be used as a plug-in by any browser, allowing PDF files to be displayed in the browser window when they are encountered. (If you have not already got it installed, the Adobe Acrobat reader can be downloaded free of charge from <**www.adobe.com**>.)

This is not a complete answer to creating a genealogy website – a site consisting solely of PDF files would be very cumbersome, since the files are much larger than plain HTML files and would download slowly. But it is a good way to make existing material that you already have in word-processor files quickly available. It is particularly good for longish documents which people will want to save to disk or print out rather than read on screen. (Web pages do not always print well.) For example, if you want to put online one of the longer reports that your genealogy database can create, turning this into a PDF file would be a good way to do it. This can also be a good solution for putting trees online.

Macintosh OS-X has built-in facilities for creating PDF files, but for Windows you need additional software. You may find that your word processor already has this facility built in – LibreOffice and OpenOffice, for example, (see p. 366) can import a wide range of documents and then save them in PDF format. Otherwise you will need special software for creating PDF files. Adobe's official program for this is Acrobat X, a commercial product costing almost £300, and you really won't need a fraction of its facilities. However, you may find older versions in online auctions for much less, and these will be perfectly adequate. But, in any case, there are a number of shareware and freeware programs available which can be used to create PDF files. Though they lack the more sophisticated document management features of Adobe Acrobat itself, they will be perfectly adequate for turning word-processor documents into web pages, or creating PDF files from your genealogy software. You can find a list and downloads at <**www.tucows.com/windows/design-tools/pdf-tools/**>. Dick Eastman 's newsletters have had a number of articles on free PDF creation tools in recent years – search the archive from the home page at <**blog.eogn.com**> for 'PDF create'.

Databases and spreadsheets

If you store some of your genealogical information in a spreadsheet or database, there are several ways of putting the data on a website.

First, database and spreadsheet software can create web pages directly (probably via a **File | Export** menu or a **File | Save As** menu option). By way of example, Figure 20-7 shows the first few entries from a database of Sussex parish register entries for the surname Christian as a web page exported from Microsoft Excel. You can see the page at <**www.spub.co.uk/tgi5/excel.html**>.

If this option is not available, there is a reliable fall-back: plain text. Your database or spreadsheet will undoubtedly have a **Save as text** function, and all browsers can display plain text files. This will not look as good as the

Year	Month	Day	Place	Event	Surname	Forenames	Kin
1561	9	28	East Grinstead	C	Christian	William	s. Robert
1577	10	6	East Grinstead	M	Christian	Margaret	widow + Thomas Lullingden
1583	12	28	Lindfield	C	Christian	Jone	d. Rowland
1584	4	26	Lindfield	B	Christian	George	s. Rowland
1586	4	18	Lindfield	C	Christian	Jane	d. Rowland
1589	9	8	East Grinstead	M	Christian	Alice	+ William Goodyer
1595	2	1	East Grinstead	M	Christian	Agnes	+ Charles Adamson
1596	2	26	Pevensey	B	Christian	Joane	wife of Martin
1602	3	6	Waldron	C	Christian	Abraham	s. Martin
1602	6	19	Lindfield	B	Christian		child of Rowland
1606	2	6	Lindfield	M	Christian	Rowland	+ Joan Chantler
1606	12	26	Catsfield	C	Christian	Sara	d. Martin
1611	4	14	Pevensey	C	Christian	Marie	d. of Martine & _
1613	9	10	Lindfield	B	Christian	Rowland	
1613	11	10	Lindfield	B	Christian	Jone	widow
1615	8	10	Pevensey	B	Christian	Martin	
1615	10	19	Hellingly	M	Christian	Elizabeth	+ Steven Bankes
1615	11	13	East Grinstead	M	Christian	Robert	+ Mary Dyvol
1616	8	26	Pevensey	M	Christian	Darothie	+Thomas Harneden
1621	6	11	Pevensey	M	Christian	John	+Jhoane Hencoate
1622	12	1	Pevensey	C	Christian	John	s. Jhon & Jhoanne
1622	12	14	Pevensey	B	Christian	John	s. Jhon & Jhoanne
1623	5	23	Pevensey	B	Christian	John	householder
1624	5	1	Lindfield	C	Christian	Easter	d. Mary
1624	6	19	East Grinstead	B	Christian	Mary	
1626	3	1	East Grinstead	B	Christian	Robert	
1626	6	12	Ashburnham	M	Christian	Stephen	+ Sarah Henley
1626	12	31	Pevensey	B	Christian	Marie	d. of Martin & Darothie
1627	2	15	Pevensey	B	Christian	Willyam	s. Steven & Sarah

Figure 20-7 A web page exported from Microsoft Excel

example above, but if someone finds an ancestor in your list, that will be the last thing they will be worried about.

You can even take this text file and embed it in a proper web page. There is a special pair of tags, `<pre>`... `</pre>` (for *pre*formatted) which, when put round formatted text like this, will preserve all the line breaks and the multiple spaces, thus maintaining the original format.

Dynamic websites

In an ideal world, all of this would be unnecessary. You would simply upload your genealogy database file to your website and people could use their browser to search it, just as you do on your desktop. But the genealogy databases discussed above all produce static web pages. If you make any changes to your family tree, you will need to recreate the web pages from scratch and upload the whole lot to your site again.

A more satisfactory approach is to have a 'dynamic' website. When a visitor clicks on a link within your site, they are not taken to a fixed page, but instead a piece of software called a 'script' looks up the relevant data in a database and extracts the appropriate records to create a web page on the fly. This technology is very widely used on the web, especially for large sites with frequent changes of material, and is referred to as a 'content management system' or CMS.

For genealogists, the database may be just a plain GEDCOM file or it may be a separate database created from a GEDCOM file, but either way you can easily update the online family tree, simply by uploading a single new file, rather than having to upload perhaps hundreds of revised pages. In a database-driven site, you typically upload all the script files to your website, and then upload the data file for them to work with. You won't need to design any pages as such, though you will be able to customize them in various ways if you wish.

The disadvantage of the CMS approach for a personal website is that while it doesn't make any special demands on the browser, which just gets a perfectly normal web page, it requires special software to have been installed on the web server to make sense of the scripts. The most likely software requirement is for a scripting language called PHP, often used in combination with MySQL databases. This is not something you can simply install in your own web space on your own initiative, but it is provided as standard in a commercial web hosting environment, and is increasingly widespread in the web space from consumer ISPs and free web space. The Free Webspace site has a 'power search' at <**www.free-webhosts.com/power-search.php**> which can be used to find hosting services with specific scripting and database facilities.

If PHP is available on the web server hosting your site, there are a number of tools you could look at, but the most successful seems to be The Next Generation of Genealogy Sitebuilding (TNG), downloadable from <**lythgoes.net/genealogy/software.php**>. I have been using this for my own genealogy site for many years and the new FamilySearch site uses it for the Community Family Trees at <**histfam.familysearch.org**>. The data is held in a MySQL database. It comes with a range of reports, along with the facility to design your own, and can link photos and documents to individuals in your tree. In fact, you can have any number of distinct trees, and you can give each registered user access to branches that may not be visible to general visitors. TNG must be purchased – it is not freeware or shareware. Figure 20-8 shows a pedigree display from my genealogy site at <**www.petex.org.uk**>.

Another application which is still downloadable, though the website does not seem to have been updated for over two years, is PhpGedView at <**phpgedview.sourceforge.net**>. It has a wide range of charts and the useful ability to create PDF versions of reports. Individual users can be given access

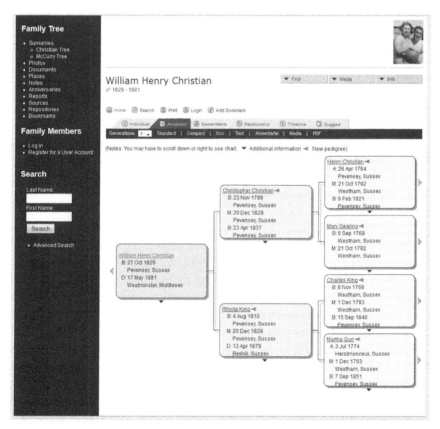

Figure 20-8 A pedigree display from TNG

to particular areas of a site. A 'portal' page allows visitors to keep track of their own particular ancestors on the site. The software is free.

While setting up a dynamic website doesn't require you to be a programmer, you will need to follow possibly detailed instructions about configuring the software for your own site, and will need to have (or develop) some understanding of how files are stored and made accessible on a website. For that reason, these are probably not appropriate tools for the reluctant or timid computer user.

Uploading your website

Once you have created a set of pages on your own computer, you need to go online and upload them to your web space. The standard way of doing this is to use a program called an FTP client. FTP stands for File Transfer Protocol, which is a long-established method for transferring files on the internet. There are many free and shareware FTP programs available. The 'Comparison of FTP client software' article on Wikipedia is a good place to start. FileZilla from <**filezilla-project.org**> is a popular free program and has all the facilities you need.

Web browsers can also be used to transfer files – see the online help in your browser for details of how to do this – and some web hosting sites provide their own browser-based uploading facility. The only problem with this is that in many cases you can only upload one file at a time.

Publicity

Once you have created and uploaded your web pages, you will need to publicize the existence of your site. One simple way to do this is to put its URL in the signature attached to your email messages. Apart from that, there are a number of possible approaches.

Search engines

Making sure your site is known to the main search engines (see Chapter 19) is probably the most effective way to publicize your website. For Google, you can submit a URL for addition to its index at <**www.google.com/ webmasters/tools/submit-url**>. You can make a submission to Bing at <**ssl.bing.com/webmaster/SubmitSitePage.aspx**>. Both Google and Bing have a range of facilities called Webmaster Tools which allow you to submit a site and receive useful information about it – incoming links, or searches which include your site, for example. These tools are at <**www.google.com/ webmasters/tools/**> and <**www.bing.com/toolbox/webmaster**> respectively. In both cases you will need to register (free) for an account.

Since search engines index pages automatically, they have no way of knowing what the most important aspects of your site and your individual pages are unless you help them by organizing the material on each page. Among the things search engines look for when estimating the relevance of a page to a search done by a user are:

- words appearing in the page title and between heading tags;
- the initial section of text;
- words which appear frequently in the page.

In addition, there is a special tag you can add to a page to provide a brief description of the page and the site. These are `<meta>` tags, which are placed in the `<head>` section of the page. They will not be visible to someone viewing your page, but the 'description' `<meta>` tag is used by search engines:

```
<meta name="description" content="The last will
and testament of Zebediah Poot, died 1687,
Wombourn, Staffordshire, England">
```

When a search engine lists this page in the results of a search, it will normally list its title (i.e. the text between the `<title>` tags) and your description. If there is no description, it will take the first couple of lines of text from the `<body>` of the page.

Don't expect submission to a search engine to produce a flood of visitors to your site within hours. It can take quite some time for the search engine to visit a new site and index it, unless of course you are using Google Sites (see above), in which case it will be indexed immediately.

Discussion and forums

A good way to draw immediate attention to a new site is to post a message to appropriate mailing lists and web forums (see Chapter 18), choosing the county lists or forums relevant to the families in your online tree. If there is a discussion group relating to some social group your ancestors belonged to it will be worth posting a message. For example, if you have information on coalmining ancestors on your site, it will be worth posting to the COALMINERS list (see Chapter 9). A message posted to a RootsWeb list will immediately be added to the list archive and you can expect search engines to index it fairly quickly.

Cyndi's List

Another useful approach is to submit details of your site to Cyndi's List using the online form at <**www.cyndislist.com/whatsnew/**>. This may or may not get your site a listing on the relevant category page on Cyndi's List, but it will still have undoubted benefits. First, all submissions to this page are included in the Cyndi's List mailing list (details of which are at <lists.rootsweb.ancestry.com/index/other/Newsletters/CyndisList.html>), which goes out to a large number of subscribers. This, in turn, will get a link to your site into the RootsWeb archive at <**archiver.rootsweb.ancestry.com/ th/index/CyndisList/**>, and your site will be permanently listed in the 'What's New' pages on Cyndi's List at <**www.cyndislist.com/whatsnew.htm**>. As mentioned above, the RootsWeb message should be discovered by search engines without much delay, and the link to your site should be followed automatically.

Requesting links

You can request other people to link to your pages, but you need to be realistic about expecting links from other personal sites. People will generally do this only if there is some connection in subject matter between your site and theirs, and if you are prepared to create a link to their site in return. Do not expect major institutions like The National Archives or the SoG to link to a site with purely personal material, just because you have made a link to theirs.

To be honest, if your site contains only personal pedigree information, it is not really worth bothering to request links from other personal sites, as this will probably not bring any significant number of visitors, certainly compared to the other options discussed so far. However, if your site has material relating to a particular subject, it will be well worth alerting the maintainers of specialist websites relating to that subject, such as those discussed in Chapters 8–11.

If you have transcriptions of original source material of broader interest than extracts for individual surnames you should contact Genuki, who aim to provide links to all UK source material online.

Preserving your family history

While the web is seen as a way of publishing your family history, in one important respect it is not like publishing it in print. A printed family history donated to a genealogy library will be preserved for ever, while your account with your web space provider is doomed to expire when you do, unless you can persuade your heirs otherwise.

But since a website is just a collection of files, there is no reason why all the information cannot be preserved, even if not online. If you copy all the files that constitute your site onto writeable CDs, these can be sent to relatives and deposited in archives just like printed material. The advantage of distributing your material in this way is that people do not need special software – a particular word processor or the same genealogy database as you – in order to view the files, and everyone with a computer has access to a web browser. HTML is a universal, non-proprietary standard which uses plain-text files, and is therefore much more future-proof than the file formats used by most current software.

Note that you won't be able to do this if your site is dynamic, as you won't be able run the relevant software from a CD.

The problem of the long-term preservation of genealogy websites is discussed in Chapter 22.

Help and advice

While you should be able to get help from your ISP or other web host for problems relating to uploading, you are unlikely to be able to get any help from them with the business of creating your website, though they may have online tutorial material. However, there are countless sources of information online about creating a website. About.com, for example, has an extensive set of articles about web design, and the 'Web Design Basics' page at <**webdesign.about.com/od/webdesignbasics/u/webdesignbasics.htm**> covers all the topics that the new web author needs to know about.

If you are looking for material specifically aimed at genealogists, there are three main places to look. Genealogy Web Creations at <**www.genealogy-web-creations.com**> has a comprehensive set of pages devoted to all aspects of website design for family historians. Dick Eastman's newsletter (see p. 382) has had many articles about creating a website for your genealogy over the last few years, and it is well worth browsing or searching the archive from the home page at <**blog.eogn.com**>. Finally, there are dedicated discussion groups. British-Genealogy has a 'Web pages design' forum at <**www.british-genealogy.com/forums/forumdisplay.php?f=226**>, which is a good place to look for recommendations and help with problems. The GENCMP mailing list is also useful for this purpose – see <**lists.rootsweb. ancestry.com/index/other/Newsgroup_Gateways/GENCMP.html**> for details.

In print

If you want a tutorial in print, a search on any online bookshop for 'HTML' or 'web publishing' will list the hundreds of general books on the subject, though it's probably best to browse in a physical bookshop to make sure you choose a book at the right technical level. As far as I know, there are only three books devoted specifically to publishing genealogical information on the web:

- Cyndi Howells, *Planting Your Family Tree Online: How to Create Your Own Family History Website* (Rutledge Hill Press, 2004).

- Peter Christian, *Web Publishing for Genealogy*, 2nd edn (David Hawgood, 1999). There is also a US edition published by the Genealogical Publishing Co. (2000). The website for the book at <**www.spub.co.uk/wpg/**> includes the complete text.
- Richard S. Wilson, *Publishing Your Family History on the Internet* (Writers Digest Books, 1999) <**www.compuology.com/book2.htm**>.

All of these, unfortunately, are now significantly out of date, though this will be much more of an issue with any specific software recommendations than with the general procedure of creating a website, which remains the same. Note that the plausible sounding *Creating Family Web Sites for Dummies* by Janine C. Warner (John Wiley and Sons, 2005) is not aimed at genealogists and does not cover putting family trees online.

21

THE WORLD OF FAMILY HISTORY

Previous chapters have looked at ways of using the internet in direct connection with your own pedigree. This chapter looks at the 'non-virtual' world of family history which exists offline, and how you can use the internet to find out about it.

▌Societies and organizations

National bodies

There are a number of national genealogical bodies, all of which have websites:

- Society of Genealogists (SoG) <**www.sog.org.uk**>
- Institute of Heraldic and Genealogical Studies (IHGS) <**www.ihgs.ac.uk**>
- Scottish Genealogy Society <**www.scotsgenealogy.com**>
- Genealogical Society of Ireland <**www.familyhistory.ie**>
- Guild of One-Name Studies (GOONS) <**www.one-name.org**>
- Federation of Family History Societies (FFHS) <**www.ffhs.org.uk**>
- Scottish Association of Family History Societies (SAFHS) <**www.safhs.org.uk**>
- Association of Family History Societies of Wales <**www.fhswales.org.uk**>
- The Council of Irish Genealogical Organisations (CIGO) <**www.cigo.ie**>

Family history societies

There are around 200 local family history societies in the UK and Ireland, the overwhelming majority of which have websites. Most of these societies are members of one or more of the four national federations/associations listed above (which are themselves umbrella organizations, not family history societies in their own right). The FFHS includes many member societies from Wales and Ireland, and most English societies are Federation members.

The definitive starting point for finding FHS websites is Genuki's 'Family History and Genealogy Societies' page at <**www.genuki.org.uk/Societies/**>. This lists the national organizations and has links to separate pages for the

Welcome to GENEVA

An online calendar of GENealogical EVents and Activities

This calendar is being run jointly on behalf of GENUKI and the Federation of Family History Societies. Event organisers are encouraged to check this calendar when picking a date to avoid clashes with other events in the same area. They are also encouraged to submit an entry for this calendar as soon as a date has been booked so that other organisers know about it and can try to avoid it.

*Please note that this calendar depends on **your** Family History Society submitting its events as well as you reading it. If your society's events are not listed, please complain to **them** rather than to me. If the calendar does not link to any further details, please **don't** ask me for further information - because I don't have any.*
At the end of this page you'll find some other groups' event lists and how to submit events to GENEVA.

The venue area codes are (mostly) the usual Chapman County Codes. The Rootsweb Helpdesk has a useful list with codes covering the rest of the world. Where it seems more helpful, London postcode prefixes and other variants may be used.

☺ – Events prefixed with ☺ have restricted access and are listed primarily for the benefit of other event organisers.

Be notified of page updates: [enter email] [OK] it's private ChangeDetection

| 2012 | 2012 | 2012 |

Skip to: Mar Apr May Jun Jul Aug Sep Oct Nov Dec 2013

February	16 London, LDN	Class: Using UK Newspapers for Jewish Genealogy
February	18 Ash, SRY	Guild of One-Name Studies Army Records Seminar
February	18 Canterbury, KEN	The Professional Approach Day Seminar
February	18 Northwich, CHS	Cheshire Family History Fair
February	18 SoG, LND	My Ancestor was an Agricultural Labourer
February	23 London, LND	Daniel Horowitz on Latin American Genealogy
February	24-26 London, SW1	Who Do You Think You Are? Live show
February	28 Walton-on-Thames, SRY	Family history using the internet at Walton Library
March	3 SoG, LND	Family Historian Software for Beginners
March	3 SoG, LND	Adding Your Family Tree to the Ancestry Website
March	4 Port Sunlight, CHS	Merseyside & Cheshire Family History Fair
March	7 SoG, LND	Getting the Most from the Society Catalogue (SOGCAT)
March	10 Harrogate, NYK	North Yorkshire County Record Office - Local and Family History Day, 2012

Figure 21-1 Geneva

constituent nations of the British Isles, where details of local societies are to be found.

The individual FHS websites vary greatly in what they offer, but all will have contact details and usually a list of publications. Most do not have their own online shops, but over 60 of them have an online 'stand' at GENfair, the FFHS online shop, at <**www.genfair.com**> – see p. 389 below.

Events

There is a wide range of genealogical meetings, lectures, conferences and fairs in the UK, from the individual meetings of family history societies to major national events such as Who Do You Think You Are? Live. One of the easiest ways to find out about such events is via the web.

The major source for the whole of the UK is the Geneva page (the Genuki Calendar of **GEN**ealogical **EV**ents and Activities) at <**geneva.weald.org.uk**>, run by Malcolm Austen on behalf of Genuki and the FFHS (Figure 21-1). This lists events from the Society of Genealogists' programme, any family history society events submitted, as well as the regional family history fairs regularly held around the country. (It does not, though, generally include society events open only to members.) The SoG offers a substantial programme of IT-related events, many of which cover the use of the internet for genealogy.

Details will be found on the Society's website at <**www.sog.org.uk/events/ calendar.shtml**>.

The National Archives' programme of events, many of which are of interest to genealogists, can be found online at <**www.nationalarchives.gov.uk/ visit/events.htm**>. All talks are subsequently made available via the Archive Media Player at <**media.nationalarchives.gov.uk**>.

The annual Who Do You Think You Are? Live show at Olympia, which includes the Society of Genealogists' Family History Show and the National History Show, has a website at <**www.whodoyouthinkyouarelive.com**>. Family History Fairs has been running local fairs around the country for almost twenty years and their website at <**www.familyhistoryfairs.org**> gives locations and details for forthcoming events. Dates of all these shows are included in Geneva.

Courses

If you are interested in getting tuition in genealogical skills, the web is an ideal place to look for courses. The SoG offers a number of half- and one-day courses, listed on their events calendar at <**www.sog.org.uk/events/ calendar.shtml**>. For more intensive study, the IHGS has a complete syllabus of genealogy courses, each leading to a formal qualification – details of the qualifications and courses are linked from <**www.ihgs.ac.uk/ courses/**>.

The website for your local authority should have details of adult education in your area. For Greater London and over 30 other counties and metropolitan areas, Floodlight provides listings of what is on offer in the region. The London Floodlight is at <**london.floodlight.co.uk**> and there are links to Floodlight sites for other local authority areas down at the foot of the home page. Family history courses are listed under 'History', then under 'Family History'. Once you are looking at the family history courses on one Floodlight site, there are links to 'Family History courses in other areas' at the bottom of the right-hand column.

It is also worth checking the website of your local universities or colleges, whose Continuing Education departments may have suitable offerings in family or local history. Birkbeck College, London offers beginners' and intermediate genealogy courses, taught at the London Metropolitan Archives, details of which are at <**www.bbk.ac.uk/study/ce2011/genealogy/ courses/**>. If you are looking for more advanced courses, both the University of Strathclyde and the University of Dundee offer postgraduate qualifications – details at <**www.strath.ac.uk/genealogy/**> at <**www.dundee.ac.uk/ admissions/distance_learning/courses/family_local_history_certificate.htm**> respectively.

Hotcourses at <**www.hotcourses.com**> provides a central listing of local authority and university external courses. Searching on [family history] as the subject rather than [genealogy] will give a larger number of results.

While there has been an explosion in online courses in the last few years, this has still to make an much of an impact on the world of family history, in the UK at least. The reason is that running online courses requires a considerable technical and administrative infrastructure, which genealogy organizations themselves are not often in a position to provide.

However, many universities are developing the possibilities of online courses, and so far there are two which include family history in their range of subjects:

- The University of Dundee offers a Certificate in Family and Local History by distance learning, the prospectus for which will be found at <**www.dundee.ac.uk/cais/certificate/FLH-Main.pdf**>.
- The University of Central Lancashire has an Institute of Local and Family History which has recently been offering online courses, details of which will be found at <**www.uclan.ac.uk/ahss/education_social_sciences/ history/online_courses.php**>. However, at the time of writing the future of these courses is uncertain.

Brigham Young University in Utah, run by the Mormon Church, has a range of free online family history courses linked from <**ce.byu.edu/is/site/ courses/free.cfm**>. Naturally, the courses are designed for North American users, so while all the courses offer good general guidance, detailed information on particular records may be positively misleading if applied to research in the British Isles. The background material in the courses on French, German, Huguenot and Scandinavian research, though, is useful to anyone with ancestors from these countries.

Pharos at <**www.pharostutors.com**> is a commercial company which runs online family history courses. There are around 40 different courses, which mostly focus on specific areas of genealogical research (e.g. the census, wills, Scottish research) rather than on general genealogical skills. All the tutors are well-known experts in their field. Pharos has partnerships with the SoG, the Guild of One-Name Studies and AGRA. Hotcourses allows you to filter the results of your initial subject search to display only 'online/distance learning' offerings.

The *Irish Times* has a commercial online course 'Tracing Your Irish Ancestors', details of which will be found at <**www.irishtimestraining.com/ tracing-your-irish-ancestors**>. *Local History Magazine* has a list of local history course providers at <**www.local-history.co.uk/Courses/**>.

Magazines and journals

Many genealogical print publications have a related website, with at least a list of contents for the current issue and in some cases material from back issues.

The most comprehensive online listing is the 'Magazines, Journals, Columns & Newsletters' page on Cyndi's List at <**www.cyndislist.com/magazines/**>. Subtitled 'Print & Electronic Publications for Genealogy', this page provides links to websites for dozens of print magazines, though many of course will be of interest only to those with North American ancestry.

The sites for the main UK genealogical monthlies available on the news-stand are:

- *Family Tree Magazine* <**www.family-tree.co.uk**>
- *Your Family History* <**www.your-familyhistory.com**>
- *Your Family Tree* <**www.yourfamilytreemag.co.uk**>
- *Who Do You Think You Are?* *Magazine* <**www.whodoyouthinkyouare magazine.com**>

ScotlandsPeople runs a bi-monthly electronic magazine, *Discover My Past Scotland*, with each issue around 40 pages long. From the main page at <**www.discovermypast.co.uk**>, you can look at a preview – the magazine opens in a special viewer – or take out a subscription.

The SoG's website has a partial subject and name index to the *Genealogists' Magazine* at <**www.sog.org.uk/genmag/genmag.shtml**> and the contents pages of the most recent issue are also available. Society members can download an electronic copy of the current magazine. This is starting to become popular with local family history societies, too, particularly the larger ones: electronic journals accessible to members and openly available subject indexes or tables of contents. For example, the Devon FHS has a public index to its magazine, *Devon Family Historian*, at <**www.devonfhs.org.uk/historian.htm**>.

One thing to watch out for is that societies often link to their journal by name, so it might not be obvious that the 'Historian' button on the Devon FHS home page or the 'Origins' link on the Buckinghamshire FHS home page at <**www.bucksfhs.org.uk**> will take you to the page for the journal.

The IHGS has a website for its magazine *Family History* at <**www.family-history.org**>, with a downloadable list of articles.

In the past, there have been a number of magazines devoted specifically to the use of computers in genealogy, but now that almost every genealogist is online, these have largely disappeared. A US magazine *Internet Genealogy* was launched in 2006 and is published bi-monthly both in print and on the web, with a website at <**internet-genealogy.com**>.

History and local history magazines are also likely to have material of interest to family historians, and the web makes it easy to check which past issues cover subjects of interest to you. The bi-monthly magazine *Local History* has a website at <**www.local-history.co.uk**> with an index to the contents of past issues back to 2003 at <**www.local-history.co.uk/acatalog/ Back_issues.html**>, as well as the usual listing for the latest issue. The site also provides links to other local history resources on the web, and a useful listing of local history societies at <**www.local-history.co.uk/Groups/**>. The *BBC History Magazine* has a main website at <**www.historyextra.com**> with details of back issues and a growing series of monthly podcasts on topics from the printed magazine.

News

Email newsletters

As well as print publications, there are of course purely online publications for genealogists. Links to these will be found on Cyndi's List at <**www.cyndislist.com/magazines/e-mail-newsletters/**>. The majority are US-based, so are not of relevance to UK genealogists where they deal with genealogical records, but they often have useful material on general genealogical topics, including the use of the internet.

Probably the best known of these US publications is Dick Eastman's Online Genealogy Newsletter, which originated on the Genealogy Forum in CompuServe, long before CompuServe was part of the internet. It is particularly strong on coverage of genealogy software and genealogical developments on the internet. Dick has many contacts in the UK, and regularly includes items of genealogy news from Britain. There are two versions of the newsletter. The Standard Edition is available free of charge and you can receive the articles by email or read them online at <**blog.eogn.com**>. The Plus Edition is only available by paying a subscription of $5.95 for three months or $19.95 for a year. It contains all the articles in the Standard Edition with the addition of one or two extra items each week. Even if you don't want to subscribe to the Plus Edition, you can purchase individual articles of interest for $2. There is also a discussion board where you can discuss individual articles and general IT topics. All issues back to the very first in January 1996 can be searched by keyword from the search box on the home page.

Many of the major organizations and data services mentioned in this book have electronic newsletters designed to keep you informed of developments. For example, you can subscribe to The National Archives' 'enewsletter' from <**www.nationalarchives.gov.uk/news/enewsletter.htm**> and details of the FFHS's 'ezine', along with links to past issues, will be found at <**www.ffhs.org.uk/ezine/intro.php**>. There will normally be a link to information about such newsletters on the home page of a site.

While most newsletters from commercial companies concentrate on their own activities, there are two that offer much more general coverage. LostCousins (see p. 236) has a fortnightly email newsletter with general family history news and good coverage of online developments in the British Isles. Non-users can see the latest newsletter at <**www.lostcousins.com/newsletters/ latest.htm**>. The newsletter of the online family tree service GeneaNet (see p. 235) is international in scope but carries many UK news items and is particularly good on latest developments in genealogy software. Details and the archive of back issues will be found at <**newsletter.geneanet.org**> with a blog version at <**genealogyblog.geneanet.org**>.

A list of particular interest to anyone who wants to keep up with new genealogy websites is the CyndisList mailing list, which sends out a daily message listing all new submissions which have been made to Cyndi's List. Details and an archive of past messages will be found at <**www.cyndislist.com/ mailinglist/**>.

Blogs

Setting up and running an email newsletter requires a certain amount of technical expertise, and there is always a problem with non-delivery to *some* subscribers. But the rise of blogging has completely transformed this situation, making it possible for anyone to set up a web-based newsletter with ease.

A blog (short for 'web log') is simply a web page where the owner(s) can use a simple interface to post messages, the most recent appearing at the top of the page. Blogging systems take care of all the issues of web page design, making it possible even for the internet novice to publish online. Blogs also have a facility for visitors to leave comments on each posting.

Although reading someone's daily ramblings about how they're getting on with their genealogical research is of limited interest, outside their immediate family at least, the blog format is ideal for publishing snippets of information or opinion, and is an ideal way to keep up with new developments in the world of family history.

The most useful listing of genealogy blogs is probably the Genealogy Blog Finder at <**blogfinder.genealogue.com**>, which tracks over 1,750 genealogy blogs, sorted into around 30 categories, with a brief description. This listing includes many personal blogs, that are only likely to be of interest to a small number people, such as the hundred or so single-surname blogs. Geneabloggers has a list of over 2,000 genealogy blogs at <**www.geneabloggers.com/genealogy-blogs/**>, but it gives only the name of each blog, making it difficult to identify those which cover a particular subject unless the blog's name is very explicit. A more concise list, concentrating on the major blogs, is the 'Blogs for Genealogy' page on Cyndi's List at <**www.cyndislist.com/blogs/**>.

Google has a dedicated Blog Search at <**blogsearch.google.com**>, but this searches the contents of blogs, not just the titles of the blogs themselves. Even so, it could be useful for identifying blogs which cover a particular genealogical topic.

A feature on many blogs is the 'blogroll', a set of links, typically in the right-hand column of the page, to other blogs the author thinks you may be interested in. This can be a good way to find other useful blogs.

Genealogical blogs of general interest include:

- British GENES (Genealogy News and Events), maintained by Chris Paton at <**britishgenes.blogspot.com**> (Figure 2-2)
- The Family Recorder at <**thefamilyrecorder.blogspot.com**>, written by Audrey Collins, Family History Specialist at The National Archives
- Irish Genealogy News at <**irish-genealogy-news.blogspot.com**>, written by Claire Santry

Figure 21-2 British GENES blog

- Kimberley Powell's blog on About.com at <**genealogy.about.com**>
- Cyndi's List at <**cyndislist.blogspot.com**>, a blog version of the newsletter mentioned above

Among the blogs from individual companies and organizations are:

- the Ancestry UK blog at <**blogs.ancestry.com/uk/**>
- the FamilySearch Labs blog at <**labs.familysearch.org/blog/**>, which reports on new developments at FamilySearch
- Findmypast at <**blog.findmypast.co.uk**>
- The Society of Genealogists at <**www.societyofgenealogists.com/posts/**>

There are also blogs devoted to very particular topics, for example:

- The Genetic Genealogist at <**www.thegeneticgenealogist.com**> covers news and issues on the genealogical use of DNA testing
- The Scottish Emigration Blog at <**scottishemigration.blogspot.com**>
- Anglo-Celtic Connections at <**anglo-celtic-connections.blogspot.com**>, covering British-Canadian issues.

For more extensive discussion of blogging for genealogists, see Dick Eastman's piece 'Blogs explained' at <**eogn.typepad.com/eastmans_ online_genealogy/2005/11/blogs_explained.html**>. Blogger.com at <**www.blogger.com**> is probably the best-known site for starting your own blog.

One problem with personal blogs is that people often start them full of enthusiasm but let them fall into neglect after a few months. It is not uncommon to come across a genealogy blog that has had no new entries for a year or more. Of course there may still be useful information in the existing entries.

News feeds

As with the web-based forums discussed in Chapter 18, it can be tedious to keep visiting a blog to see if there are any new postings, especially if it is updated irregularly or infrequently. But most blogs (and indeed many other news sites) provide a 'news feed', which means that you are alerted when a new entry is posted.

There are too many options to cover in detail, but the Wikipedia article on 'Web feed' provides a starting point for more detailed information, and the BBC News site has an article on 'News feeds from the BBC' at <**www.bbc.co.uk/ news/10628494**>, which explains how to receive the feeds from their site, and this is equally applicable to blogs. The orange-and-white icon shown in Figure

21-3 is a commonly used symbol for a news feed (and you will often see the abbreviation RSS, which, strictly, applies only to one type of feed, but is also used generically for news feeds).

Your browser may have the facility to use these news feeds – for example, Firefox's 'live bookmarks' – as does some email software, such as Microsoft Outlook. Otherwise you can download a piece of free software called a 'news reader' or 'news aggregator' to do this for you. Alternatively, if you have an account with Google or Yahoo, your Google or Yahoo home page can be set to display the titles of the latest entries from the blogs you are interested in.

Figure 21-3 RSS news feed icon

Twitter

Twitter is a so-called 'micro-blogging' service, which allows people to post brief messages called 'tweets' of not more than 140 characters. The world of genealogy is not exactly fast-moving, and the need for daily, let alone hourly updates on the activities of individual genealogists is hardly great. And there is very little useful genealogical information that can be carried in 140 characters.

Names of Twitter feeds are prefixed by the @ symbol, and to view the tweets on the web, you go to <**twitter.com/#!/***name-of-feed*> omitting the @. So the Twitter feed for the Guild of One-Name Studies is **@GuildOneName** and the web address is <**twitter.com/#!/GuildOneName**>.

If you do not already use Twitter, then there's probably no particular reason to use it just for genealogical purposes. On the other hand, if you're already a user, then there are a number of feeds worth looking at. For example, many archives have Twitter feeds, which are valuable for regular users, proving up-to-date news on new resources and any changes to the facilities, including:

- The National Archives **@UkNatArchives**, with a separate feed for their wiki (see p. 210) **@YourArchives**
- Tyne & Wear Archives **@TWArchives**
- The London Metropolitan Archives **@LdnMetArchives**
- Manchester Archives **@mcrarchives**
- The Fairground Archives **@Fairarchives**

Twitter feeds for commercial data services include:

- Findmypast **@findmypast**
- Ancestry UK **@AncestryUK**

The feeds for those professionally involved in genealogy can be useful for keeping up with what's going on in the world of family history. For example, **@SoGGenealogist** is the Twitter feed for Else Churchill of the Society of Genealogists and **@ChrisMPaton** is the feed for Chris Paton, whose British GENES blog is mentioned above.

Software

The web is an excellent source of information about genealogical software, since all the major software companies and many individual software authors have websites providing details of their products. Genealogy shareware can be downloaded from the sites, and even for normal commercial products there will often be a trial or demo version available for download.

The best starting point for genealogy software is Wikipedia, which has articles on all the main programs and comparison tables for both desktop and web-based programs. All the relevant pages are linked from the 'Genealogy software' article. Other comparison tables are provided by Family Tree Software Comparison at <**www.softwareselection.org**>, which lists the features of five popular programs and several different versions of Family Tree Maker. The best-known retailers of genealogy software in the UK are S&N Genealogy Supplies at <**www.genealogysupplies.com**> and TWR Computing at <**www.twrcomputing.co.uk**>. Both offer a wide range of products and their websites offer considerable help in choosing the right software for your budget and requirements.

For links to a wider range of programs, Cyndi's List has a 'Software & Computers' category at <**www.cyndislist.com/software/**>. This lists over 100 pedigree databases (though not all of them are for English speakers) as well as a range of other software tools for special purposes such as charting or mapping. There are links to the websites of all the major genealogy software companies.

Probably the best way to keep up with genealogy software news are two of the genealogy blogs: Dick Eastman's Genealogy Newsletter (see above) regularly includes news of major new releases and often provides fairly detailed reviews; GeneaNet's Genealogy blog at <**genealogyblog.geneanet.org**> carries announcements of new programs and software updates.

If you are just starting to use a computer for genealogy, it is probably worth downloading one of the two major freeware genealogy database programs for Windows:

- Personal Ancestral File (currently at version 5.2), often referred to as PAF, is a program developed by the LDS Church for its own members and made available for free download. It can be downloaded from the FamilySearch site at <**www.familysearch.org/products**>. There is also a link on this page to download a user guide.
- Legacy (currently version 7.5) has been made available as freeware by the Millennia Corporation, and this can be downloaded from <**www.legacyfamilytree.com**>. This is the Standard Edition, which can be upgraded online to the Deluxe Edition for $29.95.

If you subsequently decide to change to a different program, it is a straightforward matter to transfer your data from either program. These and five other free programs are briefly compared at <**www.techsupportalert.com/best-free-genealogy-family-tree-software.htm**>.

For normal commercial software, some of the online shops discussed in the next section offer a selection, while specialist suppliers have a wider range and can offer more detailed advice. If you are new to genealogy software, you are strongly recommended to use a specialist supplier who can offer advice, rather than simply selecting something off the shelf at your local computer store. Most genealogical software companies also have online ordering facilities, and if you can survive without a printed manual, you can often download the software immediately after making a credit card payment.

Mobile genealogy

With the rise of the smartphone, mobile genealogy has become much more practicable and popular, with the particular benefit that you can easily take all your family tree information with you when going to interview relatives or visit a record office. Although nothing like as numerous as the desktop genealogy programs, there are a number of smartphone apps for storing your pedigree as well as for more general tasks such as taking notes. The apps themselves can be downloaded from the relevant app store for the particular smartphone operating system.

The most comprehensive site devoted to this topic is Mobile Genealogy at <**www.mobilegenealogy.com**>, which has regular news about developments in mobile genealogy and links to software applications for the various mobile operating systems. Cyndi's List has a 'Mobile devices' page at <**www.cyndislist.com/mobile/**> with around 80 links. Mobile genealogy is a recurring topic in the Online Genealogy Newsletter of the much-travelled Dick Eastman (see p. 382).

FamilySearch has a number of articles on the subject among their TechTips at <**www.familysearch.org/techtips/**>. These can be found via two menu options: 'How To's and Tips' → 'Using Mobile devices for Genealogy' and 'Apps and Tools' → 'Phone Apps'. The articles on 'Using Your Smartphone for Genealogy' at <www.familysearch.org/techtips/2011/11/using-your-smartphone-for-genealogy> and 'Be Prepared for Genealogical Research with your Smartphone' at <www.familysearch.org/techtips/2011/11/be-prepared-for-genealogical-research-with-your-smartphone> are good places to start.

Online shops

Apart from the general online booksellers such as Amazon at <www.amazon.co.uk>, there are a number of online shops for genealogy books, data on CD-ROM, and software. Almost all use secure online ordering, though some are just online lists and orders must be sent by email or post.

The FFHS's online shop GENfair is at <www.genfair.co.uk> and sells not only the Federation's own publications, both books and data, but also books from many other publishers. As mentioned on p. 378, the site also includes many 'stands' where the publications of local family history societies can be bought (see the Supplier List at <www.genfair.co.uk/supplier_list.php>).

Parish Chest at <www.parishchest.com> offers products from around 40 different suppliers, each of whom has a separate page on the site listing their products. Also, from the index pages relating to geographically based records (e.g. census, directories) you can select a particular county to find all suppliers with products of that category for the county. A search facility lets you search for products by name.

The IHGS has an online shop at <www.ihgs.ac.uk/shop/>. In addition to buying books and software online, you can also use the site to book places on the Institute's courses.

The National Archives has an online bookshop at <www.nationalarchives.gov.uk/bookshop/>. The Society of Genealogists has an online shop at <www.sog.org.uk/acatalog/>. This offers the complete range of the Society's own publications and a selection of books from other publishers. You can also use it to book places on the Society's lectures and courses or to renew your membership.

The Internet Genealogical Bookshop run by Stuart Raymond has a website at <www.samjraymond.btinternet.co.uk/igb.htm>. However, this is not an online store – books must be ordered by email and paid for on receipt of invoice.

Many other bookshops are listed on Cyndi's List at <www.cyndislist.com/books/>.

If you are searching for second-hand books, there are also sites, such as UKBookworld at <ukbookworld.com> or Abebooks at <www.abebooks.co.uk>, that will search the catalogues of many individual booksellers. John Townsend has a large stock of second-hand genealogy books with an online catalogue but offline ordering and payment at <**www.johntownsend. demon.co.uk**>.

The online auction site eBay at <**www.ebay.co.uk**> has a wide selection of genealogy items for sale, mainly books and CD-ROMs. These can be found under 'Books, Comics & Magazines' > 'Non-Fiction Books' > 'Genealogy/ FamilyHistory', though searching on 'Genealogy' may be quicker.

Secure purchasing

Concern is often expressed about the security of online payments, and many people are wary of making online purchases by credit card, but although there are certainly some dangers, the reservations are out of all proportion to the actual risks. In fact, online transactions are much more secure than ordering over the phone. As long as your browser is using a secure connection, which means that anything you type in is encrypted before being sent across the internet to the supplier, your details will be infinitely more secure than most of the ways you already use your card.

Probably the least likely avenue of credit card fraud is someone hacking into your internet connection. The 'Fraud the Facts 2011' leaflet, downloadable from the Financial Fraud Action UK site (follow the 'Downloads' link from <**www.financialfraudaction.org.uk**>) states that the commonest type of card fraud 'involves the theft of genuine card details in the real world that are then used to make a purchase over the internet, by phone, or by mail order'. The UK Government website has some brief advice on 'Shopping safely online' at <**www.direct.gov.uk/en/HomeAndCommunity/InYourHome/Keeping SafeAtHome/DG_10038607**>.

Of course, even if you are careful, you cannot be sure that a supplier will be – there have been enough reports of account or card details being inadvertently published online. The real danger is not interception of your details in an online transaction, but that a supplier will subsequently store your card details unencrypted on a computer which is then stolen, hacked into or, of course, left on a train. But this is just as likely to happen with telephone orders.

Although individual credit card purchases are the most common way of paying for goods and services over the internet, there is an alternative method you may come across. Web-based payment systems like PayPal at <**www.paypal.com**> and WorldPay at <**www.worldpay.co.uk**> work by giving you an account from which you can then make online payments. All your financial transactions are with the payment system itself, which pays other sites on your behalf, so you are only giving your financial details to a single organization. This sort of system is particularly good for traders who may not qualify to accept credit card payments, and is much used by online auction systems such as eBay, where the participants are private individuals rather than businesses and would not be permitted to accept credit card payments.

Service online

In fact, a more significant problem with online suppliers is getting hold of them to deal with problems relating to your order or the product you have bought, particularly if the website gives no phone number or postal address. However, online traders based in the UK are bound by the same consumer protection legislation as any other trader.

Before the advent of the internet, purchasing anything abroad from the comfort of the UK was far from straightforward. Online shopping has made this much easier and, of course, those who live outside the UK can now easily order materials from British genealogy suppliers. Some practical difficulties remain: returning wrong or faulty products is not made easier by the internet, though of course it is no more difficult than with traditional catalogue-based home shopping.

Also, you are less likely to be familiar with the reputations of overseas traders, which could be a source of concern in areas where UK consumer legislation does not apply – an impressive website does not guarantee quality of service, let alone financial viability. However, one of the strengths of the internet is that it is a good word-of-mouth medium, and it is very unlikely that there could be an unreliable genealogy company whose misdeeds have escaped being reported in the discussion forums. These are therefore good places to look for reports from other customers on their experiences with companies, or to place a query yourself. For UK genealogy companies, look at the archives of the GENBRIT mailing list at <**archiver.rootsweb.ancestry.com/th/index/GENBRIT/**> for past comments on genealogy suppliers, or post a query yourself.

Professional researchers

There are many reasons, even with the internet, why you might want to employ a professional genealogist to undertake research for you: if you cannot get to the repository where original records are held, whether for reasons of time or distance; or if the records themselves are difficult for the non-specialist to use or interpret.

The SoG has a leaflet 'Employing a professional researcher: a practical guide' on its website at <**www.sog.org.uk/leaflets/researcher.pdf**>, while Cyndi's List has a page on 'Professional Researchers, Volunteers & Other Research Services' at <**www.cyndislist.com/professionals/**>. Michael John

Neill has an interesting and detailed article on his own experience with a professional researcher at <**www.rootdig.com/professional/**>.

The Association of Genealogists and Researchers in Archives (AGRA) is the professional body for genealogical researchers in the UK, with a website at <**www.agra.org.uk**>. This provides a list of members, and an index to this by specialism, whether geographical or subject-based. Most of the Association's members can be contacted by email. The Association's code of practice is also available on the site. Even if you don't employ an AGRA member to do your research, the code of practice is helpful in showing what standards to expect from *any* professional researcher.

The National Archives' website also has a database of Independent Researchers who are prepared to undertake commissions for research in records at TNA. The database is accessible from <**www.nationalarchives.gov.uk/irlist/**> and must be searched by subject heading, chosen from a drop-down list. The resulting list does not seem to be in any particular order.

For Scotland, the Association of Scottish Genealogists and Record Agents (ASGRA) is the professional association for researchers, and its site at <**www.asgra.co.uk**> has details of members and their specialisms.

The Association of Professional Genealogists in Ireland has a website at <**www.apgi.ie**> with a list of members. Individual researchers for Ireland can be found on the National Archives of Ireland website at <**www.nationalarchives.ie/ genealogy/researchers.html**>.

Membership of one of the professional organizations guarantees that a researcher has reached a high level of skill in genealogy. A similar guarantee is provided by possession of a formal qualification in genealogy, of which those of the IHGS are the best known – the Higher Certificate, Diploma and Licentiate are regarded as professional-level qualifications (see p. 379). The IHGS has a list of those who have passed its professional qualifications at <**www.ihgs.ac.uk/aboutus/graduates.php**>.

Employing a researcher beyond the British Isles is more difficult, particularly where there may be language problems, but eXpertGenealogy at <**expertgenealogy.com**> has extensive listings not only for the UK but also for Europe, the US and the rest of the world. It may well be worth posting a message in a discussion forum related to the country concerned to ask for personal recommendations.

Lookup services

If all you need is someone to check a particular reference for you, employing a professional researcher will be overkill. The internet makes it easy to find someone with access to particular printed publications, or records on CD-ROM, who will do a simple lookup for you. So-called 'lookup exchanges' give a list of publications and the email address of someone prepared to do searches in each. There is, unfortunately, no central listing of these, but most are county-based and there are links to the relevant exchanges from the individual Genuki county pages. The county forums on RootsChat at <www.rootschat.com> have places for posting lookup offers and requests.

Lookups are done entirely on a voluntary basis, so requests should be as specific as possible, and you may need to use a specific subject line in your message – see the details at the top of each page before sending a request. And, of course, be reasonable in what you expect someone to do for you in their own time.

One particular thing to bear in mind is that getting someone to do a lookup for you on one of the commercial data services is almost certainly asking them to break the terms and conditions of their subscription. Since most data services offer an inexpensive pay-per-view option, are available free of charge in a number of libraries and archives and in some cases offer a free trial, asking for lookups on these services via a mailing list may be interpreted by the uncharitable as a sign of fecklessness.

Activism

National organizations such the Federation of Family History Societies and the Society of Genealogists, as well as individual local societies, have always been involved in lobbying on behalf of the family history community. The promise of an early release for the 1926 census of the Irish Free State is largely due to the campaign of the Council of Irish Genealogical Organisations (see <**www.cigo.ie/campaigns_1926.html**>). Freedom of Information legislation has also given individuals the ability to exert pressure on government departments and agencies to release data, most notably in the case of Guy Etchells's success in getting early access to the 1911 census of England and Wales and to 1939 National Identity Card records. The web, however, has made it possible for individuals and ad hoc groups to gather support on particular issues much more easily than was ever the case before.

E-petitions

In 2006, the UK Labour government introduced an electronic petition system on the website of the Prime Minister's Office. Any online petition with 200 or more signatures was guaranteed a response from the relevant Government department. A number of petitions relating to genealogical interests were submitted, the most notable being one to reduce the census closure period to 70 years, which closed with 23,602 signatures. This petition and the official response can be seen in the Government Web Archive at <**petitions. number10.gov.uk/CensusInfoFreed/**> (3 July 2011) (Figure 21-4).

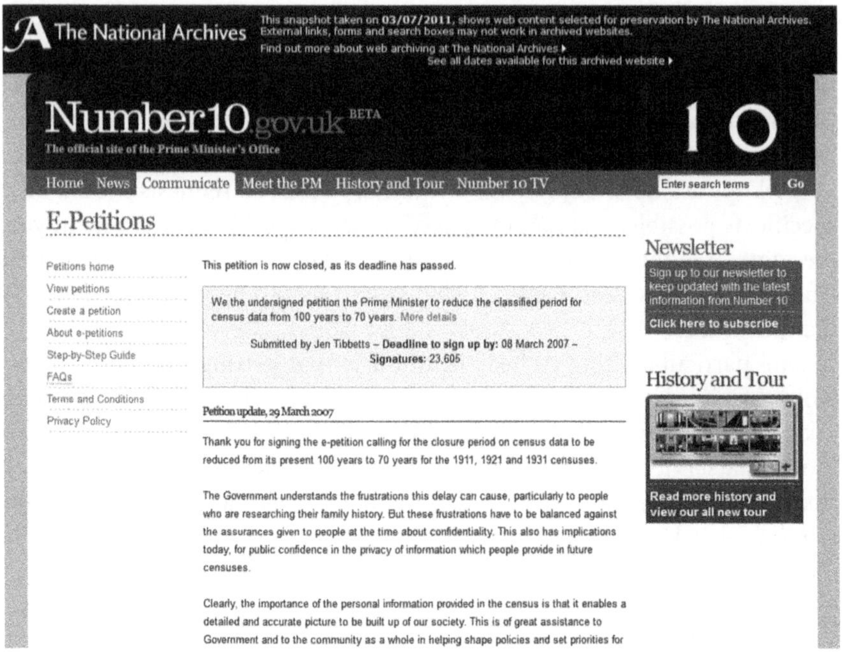

Figure 21-4 Census petition in the Government Web Archive

The Coalition government has retained the principle and a new e-petitions site was set up at <**epetitions.direct.gov.uk**>. However, while any petition with 100,000 signatures will be considered for debate in the House of Commons, no response is provided for less successful petitions, which severely reduces the value of the service for special interest groups.

At the time of writing, there are a couple of petitions relating to the issue of civil registration certificates and a few requesting earlier release of census records. None of the genealogy-related petitions has above 5,000 signatures nor looks remotely likely to reach the 100,000 threshold, and indeed the existence of several slightly different petitions on the same subject seems to reduce further the chances of success. The site only accepts petitions relating to matters directly controlled by central government, so cannot be used as a channel to raise concerns about, for example, the impact of local authority budget cuts on library and archive services, which in any case probably wouldn't reach 100,000 signatures.

So, although e-petitions are very welcome in principle, in practice it seems unlikely that any genealogy-related petition on its own, without a national publicity campaign and support from genealogy organizations, could ever be successful under the current system. And, in fact, early census release and the liberalization of access to certificates are probably the only issues ever likely to elicit a large enough body of support.

The Welsh Assembly has its own e-petition system at <**www.assembly wales.org/gethome/e-petitions.htm**> and the Scottish Parliament's e-petitions site is at <**epetitions.scottish.parliament.uk**>. In each case, all submitted petitions are considered by the appropriate committee. I haven't been able to find any genealogy-related petitions on either site.

Campaign groups

There are recently formed campaign groups devoted to two of the broad issues of concern among genealogists.

Action 4 Archives is a movement which arose in response to proposed cuts in facilities and staffing at The National Archives in 2009. While those cuts have now been implemented, the group has expanded its focus beyond this one repository to 'highlight the threat to our local archives, museums and libraries posed by budget cuts and impact on genealogy, local, social and academic history'. At the time of writing, the home page of the campaign's website at <**action4archives.com**> is merely a holding page, though using a search engine you can find sub-pages relating to the original TNA campaign. There is a Twitter feed at <**twitter.com/#!/action4archives**>, which carries news of record office developments, particularly reductions in opening hours.

The Open Genealogy Alliance was founded in March 2011, as part of the broader Open Rights movement (see <**www.openrightsgroup.org**>), to campaign for free access to genealogical records. The alliance's particular concern is that the digitization and online provision of public records has become an exclusively commercial enterprise, which conflicts with the principle that access to these records should be free (this issue is discussed in the next chapter). The alliance's aim is to support institutions and volunteer groups to develop alternative models for the digitization of archival materials so that 'all key genealogical datasets are made truly open and available under an open license that allows anyone to freely use, reuse and distribute without reservation'. The alliance's manifesto is on its home page at <**www.opengenalliance.org**>, which also has links to a blog and Twitter feed.

22

ISSUES FOR ONLINE GENEALOGISTS

While online genealogy is essentially about finding and making use of information, it is important to be aware of some general issues involved in using internet resources and in using the web as a publishing medium. Also important are the limitations in what is and is not likely to be on the internet. The aim of this chapter is to discuss some of these issues.

Good practice

Needless to say, technophobes, Luddites and other folk of a backward-looking disposition are happy to accuse the internet of dumbing down the noble art of genealogy – anything so easy surely cannot be sound research.

Loath as I am to agree with technophobes, there is actually some truth in this. Though the medium itself can hardly be blamed for its misuse, the internet does give scope to a sort of 'trainspotting' attitude to genealogy, where it is just a matter of filling out your family tree with plausible and preferably interesting ancestors, with little regard for accuracy or traditional standards of proof. Because more can (apparently) be done without consulting original records, it becomes easy to overlook the fact that a family tree constructed solely from online sources, unchecked against *any* original records, is sure to contain many inaccuracies even if it is not entirely unsound. This is far from new, of course; today's is hardly the first generation where some people want their family tree to be impressive rather than accurate. The internet just makes it easier both to construct and to disseminate pedigrees of doubtful accuracy.

But genealogy is a form of historical research, and you cannot really do it successfully without developing some understanding of the records from which a family history is constructed, and the principles for drawing reliable conclusions from them. Some of the tutorial materials mentioned in Chapter 2 address these issues – see 'Research methods' on p. 11 – but the most coherent set of principles and standards available online are those developed by the US National Genealogical Society, which can be found at <**www.ngsgenealogy.org/cs/ngs_standards_and_guidelines**>:

- Standards for Sound Genealogical Research
- Standards for Using Records, Repositories, and Libraries
- Standards for Use of Technology in Genealogical Research
- Standards for Sharing Information with Others
- Guidelines for Publishing Web Pages on the Internet

The first of these is essential reading for anyone new to genealogy, while the third has sound advice for anyone using the internet to research their family tree.

Using online information

The nature of the primary data online has an important implication for how you use information found on the internet: you need to be very cautious about inferences drawn from it. For a start, *all* transcriptions and indexes of any size contain errors – the only question is how many.

Where information comes from parish registers, for example, you need to be cautious about identifying an individual ancestor from a single record in an online database. The fact that you have found a baptism with the right name, at about the right date and in about the right place, does not mean you have found an ancestor. How do you know this child was not buried two weeks later, a fact recorded in a burial register which is not online? How do you know there is not a very similar baptism in a neighbouring parish whose records you didn't look for? How do you know there is not an error in the index/transcription? As more records are put online with images accompanying transcriptions or indexes, the last question, to be sure, will become less important, but no future internet development will allow you to ignore the other questions.

Unfortunately, the very ease of the internet can sometimes make beginners think that constructing a pedigree is easier than it is. It is not enough to find a plausible-looking baptism online. You have to be able to demonstrate that this must be (not just 'could be') the same individual who marries twenty years later or who is the parent of a particular child. The internet does not do this for you. The only thing it can do is provide *some* of the material you need for that proof, and even then you will have to be more careful with online material than you would be with original records.

In particular, negative inferences (for example, an ancestor wasn't born later than such and such a date) can be very important in constructing a family tree, but the original material on the internet will rarely allow you to make such inferences. Not even where a particular set of records has been put online in its entirety could you start to be confident in drawing a negative inference. For example, there is no simple conclusion to be drawn if you fail to find an ancestor in a particular census. He or she could have no longer been alive, or was living abroad, or is in the census but has been mistranscribed in the index, or was in the census until the relevant enumeration book went missing. Of course, such problems relate to all indexes, not just those online, but you can never be *more* confident about online records.

Also, you need to be very cautious about drawing conclusions based not on primary sources but on compiled pedigrees put online by other genealogists. Some of these represent careful genealogical work and come with detailed documentation of sources; others may just have a name and possible birth year, perhaps supplied from memory by an ageing relative – insufficient detail to be of great value, with no guarantee of accuracy, and impossible to verify. At best, you can regard such materials as helpful pointers to someone who might have useful information, or to sources you have not yet examined yourself. It would be very unwise simply to incorporate the information in your own pedigree simply because it appears to refer to an individual you have already identified as an ancestor.

Quality concerns

While the increasing amount and range of genealogical material online, both free and commercial, can only be a good thing, it does not mean that these datasets are without their problems.

In particular, there is the question of the accuracy of the indexing. Of course, anyone who indexes the 30 million records or so in a census is not going to do so without a level of error, but the question is: what is an acceptable level of error? What can digitizers reasonably be expected to do, without incurring insupportable extra costs, to minimize the level of error?

With so many massive datasets, where it's impossible to check every entry, one of the problems is that it's extremely difficult to come to firm conclusions about which site has the best quality data and which has the most (and most serious) errors. Also, because of differences in the search facilities, it's not always possible to make direct comparisons, and it is therefore not even a straightforward matter to develop diagnostic tests as a basis for some sort of independent benchmarking

But with civil registration indexes and all the censuses available at more than one site, one hopes that competition, not to mention pride in their own products, will keep the data services striving for a good reputation. On the other hand, perhaps this is an optimistic view: as there are so many reasons why one might fail to locate an ancestor in a census, only some of which can be put down to errors in transcription or indexing, it may be they can afford to be cavalier about quality. However, competition has surely led to the improvement in the quality of census images on the commercial sites, where older images have gradually been replaced by higher resolution versions.

There is an argument that the number of competing commercial data services perhaps makes the fact of errors less important. Genealogists just have to accept that the alternative to having better quality data, which would come at a significantly higher price, is that occasionally you will need to use more than one site when looking for a particular record.

Paying for records

While there are many free resources on the web, the fact is that with a few exceptions (FamilySearch, FreeBMD, the Irish census site) the major sets of digitized records are available on commercial data services. But given that these are almost entirely *public* records, is this appropriate?

Prior to the release of the 1901 census in January 2002, there was considerable debate within the genealogical community about the appropriateness of government agencies, already funded by the tax payer, seeking income by charging for online access to public records. There was a feeling that the limited offline availability of the 1901 census on microfiche, which cynics viewed simply as a move to safeguard online income, took insufficient account of the many people who had no internet access.

Ten years on, that particular argument has now lost any validity it might have had at the time. Anyone who has difficulty finding a place with internet access nowadays will surely find it even harder to get to The National Archives or a record office! For almost everyone, the costs of using a commercial data service are significantly less than the costs in time and travel of visiting a repository, not to mention the fact that the money goes to the data providers rather than to transport or oil companies. In fact, if you *can* get to The National Archives in Kew, you can indeed enjoy free access to much of the data for England and Wales.

But, in fact, now that internet access is so widely available whether in the home or from public libraries, providing a service primarily online is not the contentious issue it once was. Indeed, with the government promoting the use of the internet for the delivery of all sorts of services, it is now very hard for a public body to publish *any* records or data without being obliged to make them available on the web.

Also, it shouldn't be forgotten that traditional modes of access to records are also heavily biased against quite large groups of people: anyone who is not mobile, lives far from repositories they need to consult, or has no free time during the working day has always found it hard to make progress with their family history. One of the reasons for the growth of genealogy in recent years is that the internet has made it realistic for these people to devote time to family history research.

In purely practical terms, the fact is that progress on digitizing the nation's historical records would have been very much slower if it had to be done from existing funds, rely on Lottery funding, or just use volunteer indexers. Look at FreeBMD: even with 10,000 volunteers and highly professional infrastructure it has taken 13 years to transcribe 210 million very brief records, many of which are in printed form (see. p. 70). Since the creation of large digital resources is immensely expensive at a time when public funding for repositories is decreasing, charging seems to be the only option unless we are prepared to wait quite a long time.

And one mustn't overlook the argument of the non-genealogists: unless you're prepared to start contributing to their football season tickets or yoga classes, why should they be subsidizing your hobby?

However, while it's difficult to argue that we shouldn't pay data services for using indexes that they have created, you might still ask why we can't have access to the *images* of the records themselves, (which remain the property of the public body which holds them), without signing up with a commercial service. Why shouldn't the census and other record images be freely available in the way that Medway Council has made its parish registers available (see p. 103), or that FreeBMD has been allowed by the GRO to make the GRO index images available.

Even in less straitened times, though, this is not as straightforward as it may seem – whenever you download a free image, *someone* is paying to run and maintain the equipment on which it is held and for the bandwidth to transmit it. FreeBMD, for example, is free to the user not only because the transcription is being done by volunteers but also because the expenses of the project are being borne by others who are not demanding any money in return and the project is supported by sponsorship from RootsWeb. In any case, you would not argue that a record office should let you have free photocopies of the records in their keeping.

But this obvious truth does not tackle the broader issues of the ownership of public records, which the Open Genealogy Alliance (see p. 395) has recently raised.

I see no problem in public bodies licensing commercial developers to create digital images of public records, or granting a licence to subsequent companies to create new indexes from those digitized records. But there is a real problem where such licensing is exclusive. Regardless of any political preference for or against a free market in genealogical records, there is a fundamental practical objection to a public body granting a monopoly licence to an individual supplier, as has been the case with Scottish records for the last 14 years. For all the merits of the online Scottish records, it is inescapable that any index of a nation's entire population will have a significant level of error. And a monopoly index means that the records of some individuals, in the absence of an alternative index with *different* errors, are essentially unfindable. As it happens, the monopoly on Scottish census indexes was broken when Ancestry UK went ahead and created their own Scottish census indexes without the agreement of GROS. But GROS, in spite of public statements to the contrary, seem to be unwilling to allow their own digital images to be licensed to others or to allow alternative digitizations, so one still needs to go to ScotlandsPeople to verify the information. Now that there are several well-established data services, each with a substantial customer base and the ability to undertake new large-scale digitizations, it would seem to be problematic, in spite of competitive tendering, for government agencies to have long-term exclusive deals with one company for sets of national records.

This is not to deny that close co-operation between record providers and digitizers is undoubtedly beneficial, since those providing the records will be aware of many of the problems in the original documents, and their involvement can help to ensure a better quality of indexing.

Secondly, there is the question of restrictions on the use of the material. The data services of course have a right to protect the indexes which are the product of their very considerable investment. But should images of public records be treated the same way? Whether or not modern images of out-of-copyright historical documents are protected by UK copyright law, which is unclear,[1] record holders and data services have in fact found a way to confer on them a much more stringent form of protection: getting you to agree to their terms and conditions, effectively granting a permanent pseudo-copyright.

With copyright, the protection expires, and there are exemptions for certain types of use – and all this, even if you don't agree with it, has at least been subject to public scrutiny in Parliament. In the terms and conditions for accessing images of historical records online, the record holders and data services are effectively free to override this on the basis of a purely internal, administrative decision.

Now in purely pragmatic terms, this might be regarded as inevitable – expensive digitization projects will never be undertaken if the income can be easily undermined – and on the personal level it is rather unproblematic. Would most users of the British Newspaper Archive (p. 198) in practice be happy to give up rights which they may well not exploit, in exchange for not having to set aside a whole day to go to the British Newspaper Library in

---

1 Digital images of historical documents are regarded explicitly as copyright-free in some jurisdictions, including the US and Germany. For this reason many such images are available, quite legally, on sites like Wikipedia.

Colindale and spend hours hunting for an article? Of course they would. However, whether it is *appropriate* for a public body which is specifically funded to act as the guardian of such materials to declare unilaterally, in effect, a permanent copyright is another matter entirely.

Of course, it is not in the interest of family historians to do anything to discourage data services from creating new indexes, or to put at risk any of the already inadequate funds of the public bodies who preserve our documentary heritage, but the concerns of the Open Genealogy Alliance certainly merit wider discussion.

Copyright

The internet makes it very easy to disseminate information, but just because you *can* disseminate material it does not mean that you *should*. Both websites and email messages are treated by the law as publications. If you circulate or republish material you did not create, you may be infringing someone's copyright by doing so. Of course, genealogical facts themselves are not subject to copyright, but a modern transcription of an original record might be, and a compilation of facts in a database is also protected, though for a more limited duration.

This means you should not put on your own website, upload to a database or post to a mailing list:

- material you have extracted from online or CD-ROM databases;
- material scanned from books that are still in copyright;
- genealogical data you have received from others (unless they give their permission, of course).

There is an exemption of 'fair dealing' which allows some copying, but this is only for purposes of criticism or private study, not for republishing or passing on to others. Extracting a single record from a CD-ROM and emailing it to an individual is probably OK, but posting the same information to a mailing list, which means it will be permanently archived, is not. Note that some companies include licence conditions with CD-ROMs stating that you must not supply the information to third parties, though it is not clear that such a condition is legally enforceable – a similar ban on lookups in a reference book would seem to be ridiculous.

A number of people have been shocked to find their own genealogical databases submitted to an online pedigree database without their knowledge. Mark Howells covers this issue very thoroughly in 'Share and Beware – Sharing Genealogy in the Information Age' at <**www.oz.net/~markhow/ writing/share.htm**>. Barbara A. Brown discusses the dissemination of 'dishonest research' in 'Restoring Ethics to Genealogy' at <**www.iigs.org/ newsletter/9904news/ethics.htm.en**>. Steve's Genealogy Blog has a posting about 'Ethics in Publishing Family Histories' at <**stephendanko.com/ blog/2007/07/31/ethics-in-publishing-family-histories/**>.

The current Crown Copyright rules, however, mean that you *can* include extracts from unpublished copyright material held by The National Archives as long as the source is acknowledged. The National Archives' 'Copyright' leaflet at <**www.nationalarchives.gov.uk/legal/pdf/copyright_full.pdf**> explains which of their holdings are and are not covered by Crown Copyright, and the Government's 'Crown Copyright in the Information Age' <**www.opsi.gov.uk/advice/crown-copyright/crown-copyright-in-the-information-age.pdf**> gives general guidance about Crown Copyright. In general, you should have no qualms about the textual content of other historical material over 150 years old if you are transcribing it yourself. But a present-day transcription of a manuscript document is *prima facie* the original work of the transcriber, though it might be argued that transcribing a printed resource hardly involves the element of creativity or skill which justifies a copyright claim. The creators of recently made images of historical documents tend to claim that these images are copyright, even though, strictly, this is not addressed by UK copyright legislation.

David Hawgood's 'Copyright for Family Historians' at <**www.genuki.org.uk/ org/Copyright.html**> offers some informal guidance tailored for genealogists, while for more general and definitive information, there is the official website of the UK Intellectual Property Office at <**www.ipo.gov.uk**>.

Privacy

Another important issue is privacy. Contrary to a widespread popular belief, the UK's Data Protection legislation does not prohibit the publication of private information about an individual – if this *were* the case, then, rather obviously, certain newspapers would no longer be commercially viable. The Human Rights Act enshrines in law a right to private life, but it's difficult to see how this could be used to censor information derived from official, publicly available sources. Of course, if your online family tree says your still-living Uncle Arthur is a drunkard and he disagrees, that's another matter. The real problem with publishing information about living family members is that many people will regard it as discourteous at the very least. Your Uncle Arthur will probably not sue for libel, but he might stop talking to you or not leave you the family photographs.

In any case, even if it's just a matter of births, marriages and deaths, it's difficult to see any need to publish this information about the living in order to further genealogical research, which would be the only other justification.

Conversely, though, in the absence of any legal protection, it's not clear that you have any legal recourse if someone publishes information about your immediate family online, though if they have used a pedigree database such as those discussed in Chapter 14, you should be able to get the service to take action. Where there's a need to use the web to share information within a family, there are many sites that will allow you to restrict who can see what information.

The objection to publishing information about living family members was always that they might take umbrage. But there is nowadays a more serious objection. Many commercial services use questions about someone's past as a security check. If you can amass enough information about someone, you can impersonate them online. In principle, an online tree might put someone at risk of identity theft. But, in fact, you probably don't list the names of your cousin's first school, pet hamster, favourite book, etc., in an online tree. And any company still using the mother's maiden name as a security check should be avoided as incompetent.

Indeed, it is the information that is already available, often made so by the individual concerned, that is the real threat. In these days of blogging, Facebook and Flickr, much about people's lives is publicly available in a way which goes well beyond the 'secrets' revealed by a family tree.

On the other hand, it seems that a concern with privacy might be a threat to reasonable publication of genealogical data. In its original proposals for digitization of the civil registration service, the GRO argued that certain items of data should be withheld, including occupations, addresses, and causes of death. While no-one would argue that someone's privacy should be threatened just because genealogists 'need' access to certain types of information, there has to be a *very* good case for suppressing information on public records that are the foundations of citizenship. Given that details of marriages, for example, are published in advance specifically to permit public scrutiny, why on earth would anyone consider that the details on the eventual certificate give rise to privacy concerns? Considering how often we see reports of credit card details accidentally exposed on websites, highly confidential personal information absent-mindedly left in taxis or sent, unencrypted and unsecured, by ordinary post, it seems absurd to be worrying about 20-year-old addresses and the privacy of the dead.

In the USA, there are currently moves to restrict access to the Social Security Death Index (SSDI) as a fraud prevention measure, and US genealogists understandably see this as a misplaced and unwelcome attempt to restrict access to public records.

There is a mailing list, LEGAL-ENGWLS, for the discussion of 'legal aspects of genealogical research in England and Wales including copyright, database rights, data protection, and privacy' – details at <**lists.rootsweb. ancestry.com/index/intl/UK/LEGAL-ENGWLS.html**>.

Finding material

Information is not much use if you cannot find it, and search engines are able to capture only a fraction of the material on the web. Of course, it is impossible to foresee technological advances, but there is no sign at the moment that the coverage of search engines will improve significantly. Websites of individual genealogists, in particular, will probably become harder to find. In addition, the increasing amount of data held in online databases is not discoverable by search engines, and it becomes more important than ever that there should be gateways and directories (or even books!) to direct people to the sources of online data.

The quality of indexing provided by search engines is limited by the poor facilities currently available for marking up text in HTML with semantic information. Search engines cannot tell that Kent is a surname in 'Clark Kent' but a place-name in 'Maidstone, Kent'. This is because web authors have no way of indicating this in HTML markup. As so many British surnames are the names of places or occupations, this is a significant problem for UK genealogists.

The situation could improve when a more sophisticated markup language, XML, starts to be used widely on the web – this allows information to be tagged descriptively, and will enable the development of a special markup language for genealogical information. Such a development (and its retrospective application to material already published on the web) is very slow in coming and will require considerable work, though the LDS Church has made a start by proposing an XML successor to GEDCOM (see the GEDCOM FAQ at <**www.familysearch.org/Eng/Home/FAQ/faq_gedcom.asp**>). But the benefits of such an approach are already apparent in a project like the Old Bailey Proceedings (see p. 124), which can distinguish between the names of the accused, the victim, and witnesses.

Another problem is the increasing number of sites with surname resources, making it impossible to check *everywhere* for others who share your interests. Mercifully, the number of pedigree databases (see Chapter 14) remains manageable for the present, but the number of sites, particularly message boards, with surname-related material makes exhaustive searching impossible.

However, on a more positive note, it's clear that, with so much work being done on making archival catalogues available, it will become easier than ever to track down original documents in record offices and other repositories, and genealogists in general will start to make much more use of records that in the past only the expert might have been able to take advantage of.

Longevity

To anyone who has not grown up with the web, there is one deeply troubling aspect of internet resources: their tendency to disappear. We are used to the idea that once information is published in book form, it may become hard to find, but it doesn't generally disappear, particularly if it is important or useful, in less than a century or two. But the fact is that important internet resources are constantly at risk.

Large digitized datasets are not really threatened, because they have a commercial value which protects them from oblivion, but there are two types of valuable resource which are particularly vulnerable: publicly funded and volunteer projects.

In the first of these cases, even if the initial funding does envisage some provision for long-term hosting and maintenance, it will not be open-ended. Also, there can be no guarantee that some new broom will not cancel funding already promised, deciding that the money can be better used for some new project. Unfortunately, there is often more kudos in getting a new project off the ground than in maintaining an old one, particularly if new management is keen to make its mark.

A salutary example is Familia, a very useful, indeed award-winning site which listed genealogical holdings in UK and Irish public libraries. Its initial funding was pulled in 2001. It limped on for another nine years hosted by organizations which showed little interest in maintaining the site (by updating dead links), let alone carrying on with its remit, since after all they had limited funds, which understandably were prioritized for their own projects. Finally it was abandoned. Mercifully much of the data has in fact been rescued (by Cornucopia, see p. 207) though it is far from easy to find, but the full site is preserved only on the Wayback Machine (<**www.familia.org.uk**>, 5 July 2009). I would be very surprised if any reader of this book didn't think the site ought to have been kept going.

You can get a good idea of the problems faced by even the most successful projects from the following message posted on A Vision of Britain in December 2008 by the project's director, Humphrey Southall:

> *A Vision of Britain through Time* launched in October 2004, and for the first three years running costs were paid by the British Library. We managed to save up a little money in that period and we earned a bit more by licensing data, so we were able to keep it going for a fourth year, until September 2008.

The site is still running in December 2008 through a new grant from the Joint Information Systems Committee, the IT arm of the Higher Education Funding Councils. This grant is to build an extended version of the site to launch in the spring of 2009, but we are also using it to pay Edinburgh University, who host the site for us.

That will keep us going only until the end of March 2009, and from then on we have to pay our way. This means the site is going to look a little different, but it is still far from commercial: the only use to which money generated from the site will be put is keeping it going. The JISC grant will be funding a new web server for us, but we really need to start saving for the next new server which will be needed around 2012/13. However, the immediate problem is simply covering a five-figure annual hosting bill.

...

It is very frustrating that there seems to be no route at all by which a resource created by individual initiative can apply for public money to keep it running, no matter how uncommercial the original motive, how useful the content, how popular the end result.[2]

In 2012, it is good to see that A Vision of Britain's funding is in fact secure for another couple of years, but the problem is not going to go away, and there are many other projects in the same situation.

Some of the most valuable genealogical resources on the web are the results of a single individual or a small group devoting massive amounts of time to them. Of course, these don't have the large-scale funding issues of A Vision of Britain, but they too are at risk: inevitably, the individuals concerned will at some point be forced by circumstances to give up their efforts, even if it is only the ultimate circumstance of their death. Unless arrangements for succession have already been put in place, all the material and any domain name for the project will become the responsibility of the next of kin, who, apart from having more pressing concerns, may not know what to do or who to contact to secure its future, or have the technical skills to manage a transition.

It's true that the Wayback Machine at <**www.archive.org**> can often provide a partial back-stop, but that is not a satisfactory basis for preserving valuable resources. The British Library has a digital archiving project (see p. xv), but at present that is solely for resources of their choosing, though, logically (if not practically), it is a small step for the BL's remit for the preservation of the printed word to be extended to online publication. Of course, any archiving is better than none, but just copying files is quite

---

2   <www.visionofbritain.org.uk/footer/doc_text_for_title.jsp?topic=news&seq=12>

inadequate for many modern sites, which use a variety of techniques to generate pages dynamically, rather than delivering static pages, and which may require the web server to be appropriately configured.

As far as I can see, this set of problems has received scant attention from the genealogical world, which is otherwise so concerned and so careful about the preservation of materials and information.

Outlook

The changes in the practice of family history that have been brought about by the internet are extraordinary and on the whole very positive. However, it's important to keep a sense of perspective, and to recognize that none of this has made any difference to the fundamentals of family history research: consulting records and sharing information. Nor is there any prospect of basing a family tree solely on digitized records – just consider how long it's taking to get civil registration records online!

The internet has not 'automated' family history or modified its principles and methods. Nor does it need to – there is nothing wrong with the traditional methods of genealogy. The fact that many historical records are easier than ever to access doesn't actually make them any easier to interpret. Indeed, it may make them harder to interpret, if a search delivers an individual piece of information shorn of its context.

What the internet has revolutionized is not the process of genealogy, but the ease with which some of the research can be carried out. The key aspects of this are:

- the increasing amounts of data available online;
- the number of people with shared interests who have internet access.

Although microfilm and microfiche are not going to disappear in the immediate future, any more than books are, the internet is now the publishing medium of choice for all large genealogical data projects, whether official, commercial, or volunteer-run. Where public records or public funding are concerned, the web, because of its low cost and universal access, is now the default publishing medium as a matter of principle.

Both the number of internet users and the amount of data available have reached a critical mass, with the result that the genealogist without internet access is in a minority and at a significant disadvantage in terms of access to data and contact with other genealogists.

Of course you can still research your family tree without using the internet – just about – but why would you choose to?

INTERNET GLOSSARY

Adobe Acrobat	A file format, popular for documents which need to be made available online with fixed formatting. Files have the extension .pdf, and so the term 'PDF file' is often used. See p. 60.
blog	An online personal journal (short for 'web log').
CMS	'Content Management System', software for running large websites using a database to store the pages.
cookie	A piece of information stored on your hard disk by a website in order to identify you and your preferences each time you use the site.
database	1. A collection of individual items of information ('records') which can be retrieved selectively via a search facility.
	2. A software program for managing data records (short for 'database management system').
directory	A collection of links to internet resources, arranged in a hierarchy of subject headings.
DjVu	A graphics file format used by some of the commercial data services, pronounced as *déjà vu* (see p. 62).
domain name	The part of an internet address which is formally registered and owned, and which forms the latter part of a server or host name, e.g. *nationalarchives.gov.uk* is the domain name, while <**www.nationalarchives.gov.uk**> and <**yourarchives. nationalarchives.gov.uk**> are individual servers within that domain.
download	To transfer a file from another computer to your own computer.
FAQ	Frequently Asked Questions, a document listing common questions in a particular area, along with their answers.
flame	A rude or abusive message.
FTP	File Transfer Protocol, a method of transferring files across the internet (see p. 372).
gateway	A subject-specific *directory*.
GIF	A graphics file format, mainly used on the web for graphic design elements, less suitable for colour photographs.

hit	A matching item retrieved in response to a search.
host	A computer connected to the internet which allows other internet users access to material stored on its hard disk.
hosting	Providing space on a *host* for someone's web pages.
HTML	HyperText Markup Language, in which web pages are written.
ISP	Internet Service Provider.
JPEG	A graphics file format, mainly used for photographs.
lurking	Reading the messages in a discussion forum, but not contributing yourself.
mailing list	A discussion group which uses email to disseminate messages.
message board	A web page which allows users to read and post messages, often also called a 'forum'.
netiquette	The informal, consensual rules of online communication.
news feed	A method of getting current updates from a website (particularly a blog) delivered to you automatically.
plug-in	A piece of software used by a web browser to display files it cannot handle on its own.
podcast	An audio recording made accessible via the web (sometimes also used for video).
portal	A collection of internet resources for a particular audience – see the discussion on p. 17.
robot	A piece of software which trawls the internet looking for new resources, used by search engines to create their indexes.
RSS	A type of news feed, often used for news feeds generically.
search engine	Commonly, a website which has a searchable index of web pages, though more accurately *any* piece of software which searches an index.
server	A computer, usually with a permanent internet connection, which responds to requests for data from other computers on the internet. There are different types of server according to the service offered, e.g. mail server, web server, list server.
streaming	Making an audio or video recording play in real time via a web browser rather than requiring a separate download.
subscribe	To join a mailing list.
URL	Uniform Resource Locator, a standard way of referring to internet resources so that each resource has a unique name. In the case of a web page, the URL is the same as the web address.
validation	A method of identifying gross data-entry errors in a database, checking that an item of data falls within an acceptable range of values.
webcast	An online video.

| wiki | A site in which pages can be edited collaboratively. |
| XML | eXtensible Markup Language, a more sophisticated and flexible markup language than *HTML*, likely to be increasingly used for websites. |

All these terms are defined and explained on Wikipedia at <**en.wikipedia.org**>. There are many internet glossaries online, including:

- the Internet Language Dictionary at <**www.netlingo.com/inframes.cfm**>
- Foldoc (the Free On-Line Dictionary of Computing) at <**foldoc.org**>

For glossaries of genealogy terms see p. 15.

BIBLIOGRAPHY

Barrett, Nick. *Who Do You Think You Are? Encyclopedia of Genealogy*. London: Harper, 2008.

Bevan, Amanda. *Tracing Your Ancestors in the National Archives: the Website and Beyond*. 7th edn. London: The National Archives, 2006.

Christian, Peter. *Web Publishing for Genealogy*. 2nd edn. David Hawgood, 1999. Full text online at <**www.spub.co.uk/wpg/**>

Christian, Peter and David Annal. *Census: The Expert Guide*. London: The National Archives, 2008.

Cock Randolph and N. A. M. Rodger (eds), *Guide to the Naval Records in The National Archives of the UK*. London: Institute of Historical Research, 2006.

Fowler, Simon. *Tracing Your Ancestors*. Barnsley: Pen and Sword, 2011.

Grenham, John. *Tracing your Irish Ancestors*, 4th edn. Dublin: Gill & Macmillan, 2012.

Herber, Mark. *Ancestral Trails*. 2nd edn. Stroud: The History Press, 2004.

Howells, Cyndi. *Planting Your Family Tree Online*. Nashville: Thomas Nelson, 2004.

Lynch, Daniel M. *Google Your Family Tree*. FamilyLink.com, 2008.

Sharpe, Michael. *Family Matters: A History of Genealogy*. Barnsley: Pen & Sword, 2011.

Shea, Virginia. *Netiquette*. San Rafael: Albion Books, 1996. Full text online at <**www.albion.com/netiquette/book/**>

Wilson, Richard S. *Publishing Your Family History on the Internet*. Betterway Books, 1999.

INDEX